Solomon Islands

a travel

Dav

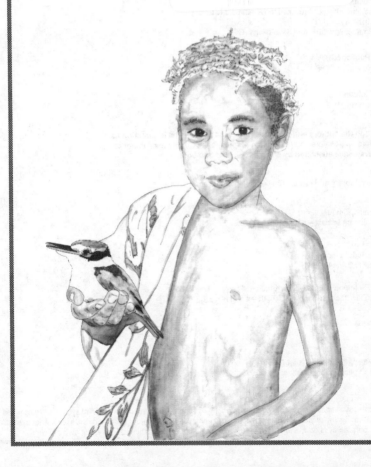

Solomon Islands – a travel survival kit

2nd edition

Published by
Lonely Planet Publications
Head Office: PO Box 617, Hawthorn, Vic 3122, Australia
Branches: PO Box 2001A, Berkeley, CA 94702, USA
              12 Barley Mow Passage, Chiswick, W4 4PH, UK

Printed by
Colorcraft Ltd, Hong Kong

Photographs by
Dr Greg Coates (GC)
David Harcombe (DH)
Michael McCoy (MMcC)
Solomon Islands Information Department (SIID)
Griff Taylor (GT)
Front cover: Girl from Savo Island (GC)

First Published
November 1988

This Edition
January 1993

Although the authors and publisher have tried to make the information as accurate as possible, they accept no responsibility for any loss, injury or inconvenience sustained by any person using this book.

National Library of Australia Cataloguing in Publication Data

Harcombe, David
Solomon Islands – a travel survival kit.

2nd ed.
Includes index.
ISBN 0 86442 168 0.

1. Solomon Islands – Description and travel – Guidebooks.
I. Title. (Series: Lonely Planet travel survival kit).

919.59304

text & maps © Lonely Planet 1993
photos © photographers as indicated 1993

David Harcombe

Born in England, David spent much of his early days reading about faraway countries and peoples. Following an Oxford economics degree he worked as a fund raiser for a large British overseas aid charity before being lured eastwards through Asia to Australia. Incurably sold on freedom and travel, he returned to Australia after a spell in Latin America and southern Africa to live in its remote north-western bush, working there among Aboriginal Australians. He also became a sparetime gold prospector, and amateur disc jockey on a community radio station.

David is also the author of Lonely Planet's *Vanuatu - a travel survival kit*. When he's not writing, interests include scuba diving and the underwater world, soccer, squash, jogging, amateur dramatics, exotic food, reading comic strips, laughing, lazing around on sandy beaches and just going places. He's a firm believer that life was meant to be easy. As he often says, 'You can only be certain of getting one go in this life, so it better be good'.

From the Author

This book grew out of a gloriously carefree Pacific odyssey I had in 1984. I particularly liked the Solomons, so after returning there two years later it was time to start writing the first edition of this book. I was there again in 1991: result – this new, updated version reflecting all that's changed in the intervening period. Helpful advice or information came from many quarters.

The Honiara people I would like to thank include:

Ben Devi, Ken Cross, Ellen Pau, John Starey, Wilson Maelaua, Floyd Smith, William Haemae, Dorothy Prince, Jay and Dellin Makana, Ron and Roxanne Gebauer, Jenny Kaitu'u, Roy Saunders, Henry Teho, Albert Wilson, Pye Robert Kuve, Leroy Kelm, Greg Fitzpatrick, Phillip Wanga, Penny Karatzovalis, Colin and Carol Brown, Tom Roberts, Patrick Murphy, Glen Krahenbuhl, John Toelke and Solomon Love. Deserving special thanks are the staff at the Honiara Hotel - Lila, Margaret, Rose, Dianne, Pioni, Carol and Karen and Tommy Chan.

Gizo and Liapari people were similarly helpful. Among these were Wendy and Rob Scheeres, Kerri and Danny Kennedy, Griff Taylor, Barbara Riley, Jody Solow, Grace Maloi and Willis Eschenbach. Others around the country who helped me just when I needed it were:

Leddie Kona (Guadalcanal), Lino Ruava (Savo), Millie and Jennie Tautua, and Morsley Tengemoana (Bellona), Eric Tema and Martin Tauniu (Rennell), Faleteau Leve, Dave Cooke and Don Croft (Munda), Joseph Tora (Lata), and Romulus Paoni (Vangunu).

Several people from outside the Solomons wrote voluminous and informative letters about the country, or gave me valuable details verbally. These were:

John and Beverley Taylor, Vikki and Miranda Kalgovas, James Saville, Greg Coates, Peter Philip, Adrian Jowett and Russell Parker (all Australia) and Edward Mayer and Susan Brown (USA). Daphne Amos (Aus), Richard Cormier (USA) Scott Damon (USA), Sister Frances (Aus), John & Jean Glenister (NZ), Penny Karatzovalis, Edward Mayer (USA), Michael McGrath (Aus), John Seach, Alison Woodwood, Gerard Zawadski (F)

My thanks go to them all, both those within the Solomons and outside it.

Lastly, I wish to thank Suzanne Ell of Minehead, south-western England, for the excellent secretarial help she gave me in updating this Solomons guide.

From the Publisher

This second edition of *Solomon Islands – a travel survival kit* was edited by Lyn McGaurr and proofed by Alan Tiller. Simone Calderwood and Tom Smallman took it through production.

Margaret Jung was responsible for the design, illustrations, cover, colourwraps and additional mapping.Tamsin Wilson and Vicki Beale drew and corrected the maps. Our thanks to Sharon Wertheim for compiling the index.

Warning & Request

Things change – prices go up, schedules change, good places go bad and bad places go bankrupt – nothing stays the same. So if you find things better or worse, recently opened or long since closed, please write and tell us and help make the next edition better.

Your letters will be used to help update future editions and, where possible, important changes will also be included in a Stop Press section in reprints.

We greatly appreciate all information that is sent to us by travellers. Back at Lonely Planet we employ a hard-working readers' letters team to sort through the many letters we receive. The best ones will be rewarded with a free copy of the next edition or another Lonely Planet guide if you prefer. We give away lots of books, but, unfortunately, not every letter/postcard receives one.

Contents

GLOSSARY **289**

INDEX **293**

Map Legend

BOUNDARIES

▬ · ▬ · ▬ · ▬	.... International Boundary
▬ · · ▬ · · ▬	.... Internal Boundary
┼┼┼┼┼┼┼┼┼┼	.... National Park or Reserve
▬ ▬ ▬ ▬ ▬ ▬	.... The Equator
· · · · · · · · · · · ·	.... The Tropics

SYMBOLS

◉	NEW DELHI	.... National Capital
●	BOMBAY	.... Provincial or State Capital
●	Pune	.... Major Town
●	Borsi	.... Minor Town
■		.... Places to Stay
▼		.... Places to Eat
☎		.... Post Office
✈		.... Airport
i		.... Tourist Information
⊖		.... Bus Station or Terminal
66		.... Highway Route Number
⛪ ✝ ⛪		...... Mosque, Church, Cathedral
∴		.... Temple or Ruin
✚		.... Hospital
☀		.... Lookout
⚑		.... Camping Area
⊓		.... Picnic Area
⌂		.... Hut or Chalet
▲		.... Mountain or Hill
		.... Railway Station
		.... Road Bridge
		.... Railway Bridge
		.... Road Tunnel
		.... Railway Tunnel
		.... Escarpment or Cliff
		.... Pass
		.... Ancient or Historic Wall

ROUTES

▬▬▬▬▬	.... Major Road or Highway
▬ ▬ ▬ ▬ ▬	.... Unsealed Major Road
▬▬▬▬▬	.... Sealed Road
▬ ▬ ▬ ▬ ▬	..... Unsealed Road or Track
══════	.... City Street
┼┼┼┼┼┼	....Railway
▬◉▬	.... Subway
· · · · · · · ·	.... Walking Track
▬ ▬ ▬ ▬	.... Ferry Route
┼╫┼╫┼╫┼	.... Cable Car or Chair Lift

HYDROGRAPHIC FEATURES

	.... River or Creek
	.... Intermittent Stream
	.... Lake, Intermittent Lake
	.... Coast Line
	.... Spring
	.... Waterfall
	.... Swamp
	.... Salt Lake or Reef
	.... Glacier

OTHER FEATURES

	Park, Garden or National Park
	.... Built Up Area
	... Market or Pedestrian Mall
	.... Plaza or Town Square
	.... Cemetery

Note: not all symbols displayed above appear in this book

Introduction

The Solomons is the third-largest archipelago in the South Pacific and covers about 1.35 million sq km of sea. It is made up of a scattered double chain of 922 islands, atolls and cays, which vary from large, rugged, heavily wooded and mountainous islands to tiny, low-lying coral atolls.

Getting around is easy enough by air or in small inter-island ships or motor canoes. However, if you choose to go by water, you need to allow yourself plenty of time to cope with inevitably changing timetables and sea conditions. Touring by car is less easy, as the longest stretch of road is less than 160 km. There is, however, plenty of room for adventure, as well as the opportunity to travel as islanders themselves do.

You'll often have to make your own travel and accommodation arrangements, but if you don't mind that, you can get to a long list of ultra-remote places. You really will have beaches all to yourself, and need guides and maybe even bearers to climb rainforest-covered volcanoes. You'll take long motor-canoe journeys between islands, explore natural coastlines by foot, and stay at small shoreside resorts or villages in traditional leaf houses.

Everywhere people smile and are friendly in the country its people call the Happy Isles. Services are improving all around, and a stay in the Solomons should be a memorable and pleasant one in all but the most humid weather.

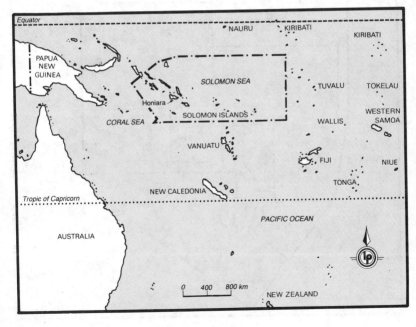

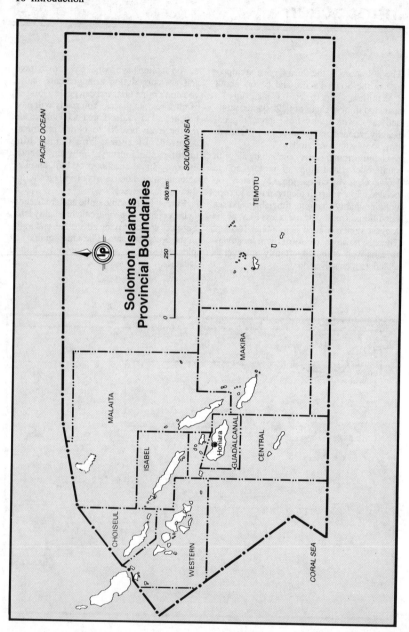

Solomon Islands Provincial Boundaries

PACIFIC OCEAN

SOLOMON SEA

TEMOTU

MAKIRA

MALAITA

ISABEL

CHOISEUL

WESTERN

GUADALCANAL

Honiara

CENTRAL

CORAL SEA

500 km

250

0

Facts about the Country

HISTORY

About 25 million years ago, the first islands of the present-day Solomons began emerging from the ocean depths. Once this seismic activity ceased, coral growth began accumulating around these newly emerged volcanic shores.

Most historians believe human settlement in the Pacific originated in South-East Asia. At least 60,000 years ago, and perhaps much earlier, island people began to migrate through Indonesia and New Guinea towards Australia and the South Pacific. This movement was facilitated by the lower sea level of the Pleistocene period, or Great Ice Age.

By about 30,000 BC, Papuan-speaking hunter-gatherers in New Guinea were settling on the nearby islands to the south and east of what is now modern Papua New Guinea, possibly reaching as far as the eastern Solomons before the sea level began to rise with the end of the Ice Age in 10,000 BC.

Agriculture developed in South-East Asia from around 7000 to 5000 BC, and Austronesian-speaking proto-Melanesian migrants from there began to arrive in the archipelago around 4000 BC, bringing with them new techniques in crop husbandry, pig breeding, and canoe building and sailing. The global warming and rising sea level which accompanied the end of the Ice Age restricted the Papuan speakers to the few islands they had already reached in the Solomons. Meanwhile, the Austronesians, who were much more skilled with canoes, settled throughout the remainder of the country, except for a few marginally fertile atolls.

Between 2000 and 1600 BC, people of the Lapita culture appeared. (They are named after an archaeological site at Lapita in New Caledonia.) In a remarkable millennium of long-range canoe voyages, they left their distinctive pottery at a string of sites from the Bismarck Archipelago in eastern Papua New Guinea all the way to Samoa. Some have suggested that the Lapita people were ancestors of modern-day Polynesians. However, it's more likely that they were absorbed by pre-existing peoples, as remains of their ceramics show clear signs of cultural change from the 2nd century AD onwards.

Meanwhile, most Melanesians in the Solomons lived in small villages on well-established tribal lands. They practised shifting agriculture and engaged in fishing, hunting, carving, weaving and canoe building. Feasting and dancing were regular activities.

Each settlement was composed of related family groups and captives from other places, and inhabitants kept to themselves except when they raided their neighbours' settlements. Rule was by custom or tradition as recalled by clan elders. Ancestors were worshipped and blood feuds, head-hunting and cannibalism were frequent.

Polynesian Settlers

Between 1200 and 1600 AD, random westward migrations of small groups of Polynesians reached the outer edges of the Solomons, only to find the main mass of the country already settled by Melanesians. Voyaging in small canoes from Polynesian islands anything from 800 to 3000 km east of the Solomons, they found only small, isolated landmasses and atolls available. The legends of their first arrivals tell of small pre-existing populations which they usually eliminated or absorbed shortly after settlement.

Once established, Polynesian settlements in the Solomons suffered intermittent raids from Tonga and Tokelau during the period from the 14th to the 18th century, as eastern Polynesian rulers tried unsuccessfully to exact tribute from their western counterparts. Long-range Polynesian canoe journeys in search of new land became a rarity in the 19th century, as the fear of Tongan violence led to a growing suspicion of all foreigners.

11

This in turn produced the widespread habit of attacking strangers on sight, further discouraging such voyages.

Spanish Discovery

Meanwhile, in the early 1560s, rumours swept Spanish-occupied Peru of the existence of a group of islands, or even a great continent, far to the west in the Pacific. Inca legends told of a sea journey made in the mid-15th century to these legendary islands by one of their kings, Tupac Yupanqui.

Legends claimed he found two islands – Nina Chumbi, or Fire Island, and Ava Chumbi, or Outer Island – and brought back with him gold, dark-skinned slaves and the head of a horse-like animal. Some also believed that a larger southern continent must exist just to balance the northern hemisphere's huge mass.

Don Alvaro de Mendaña y Neyra, the 25-year-old nephew of Peru's Spanish viceroy, was chosen to find the legendary islands or continent. He left Peru with two ships in November 1567, sighting land twice – first in Tuvalu, and later what probably was the Roncador Reef near Ontong Java in the north-eastern Solomons. Then, on 7 February 1568, his expedition saw a large island, naming it Santa Isabel.

Mendaña and his men sailed around the neighbouring landforms, giving them Spanish names, some of which have survived to this day. Much of the explorers' time

Don Alvaro de Mendaña y Neyra

was spent searching for gold or fighting with islanders over food. Finally, on 11 August 1568, after six months of constant conflict, the expedition set sail for Peru, where Mendaña described the islands in glowing terms. Initially, he and his crew simply called the archipelago the Western Islands, but by 1570 the name Yslas de Salomon – the Solomon Islands – was in common use.

Mendaña was keen to return, but wasn't able to raise enough money for another fleet until 1595. This time he sailed with four ships and 450 would-be colonists, but his second expedition was ill-fated.

At first Mendaña, by now an admiral, couldn't find the way, losing a ship in the process. Finally, he discovered Nendo, which he called Santa Cruz, and settled there. Sickness, internal squabbles and islander resistance disrupted the project, and Mendaña himself died of malaria. After only two months, the expedition abandoned its small settlement, limping back to Peru via the Philippines.

By the beginning of the 17th century, Spain was in decline, with no money left for unproductive ventures. However, Pedro Fernandez de Quiros, a Portuguese in the employ of the Spanish Crown – and Mendaña's chief pilot in 1595 – had a similar zeal to discover and colonise the fabled great southern continent.

It took Quiros 10 years of pleading to raise the cash for a third and final expedition. He left Peru with three small ships on 21 December 1605, with a crew scoured from Spanish America.

Quiros missed Nendo and instead found the Duff Islands early in 1606. He was certain the fabled southern continent, or Terra Australis, as it was also called, was just beyond. Islanders told him of 72 other islands they knew of, including a great country less than 700 km away which Quiros fervently believed would be the legendary southern continent. Instead, he found Espiritu Santo Island in northern Vanuatu.

His ill-assorted fellow expedition members soon made the colonisation of Santo a similar disaster to the two previous

Spanish ventures in the area. Quiros returned in disgrace, thereby signalling the end of Spanish interest in the western Pacific.

Rediscovery & Early Trading

The first map-makers who charted the Solomons placed it far to the east of its correct position. Consequently, except for two Dutch expeditions which are believed to have glimpsed Ontong Java twice during the following 40 years, there was no further recorded contact until the late 18th century. By then, several European governments were financing official expeditions to discover new lands in the name of scientific research.

Captain Cartaret, a Briton, blundered into Nendo in 1767 and then passed on to Malaita, at first refusing to believe that he had rediscovered the Solomons. A stream of British, French and American explorers followed, including Jean de Surville, who sighted the large islands of Makira, Malaita, Santa Isabel and Choiseul and called them La Terre des Arcasides, meaning 'the land of natural, or rustic-living, people'.

Many whalers visited the archipelago from 1798 onwards. Sandalwood traders followed between the 1840s and late 1860s, buying pigs, turtle shell and pearl shell in the Solomons to sell to islanders in Vanuatu (at the time called the New Hebrides) in exchange for sandalwood logs. Their ships would then sail to China, where the wood was highly prized for the incense it gave off when burnt in temples.

Another island product favoured by the Chinese was bêche-de-mer. Orientals paid high prices for it, even though it was fairly plentiful on reefs.

Prior to the large-scale trading contacts of the 19th century, relationships between neighbouring islands in the Solomons had been reasonably peaceful. This period, known to islanders as the Great Peace, had prevailed for several generations at least. However, the conduct of the traders quickly changed this. Some of them persuaded villagers to collect huge loads of sandalwood but then refused to pay for it, shooting the villagers if they objected.

Shortly after a ship visit, islands' populations were often decimated by illnesses. Lack of immunity to common European sicknesses, like influenza, measles, chickenpox and scarlet fever, caused islanders to die in their hundreds.

Soon the sandalwooders came to be hated by many of the local people, who would kill any White person they saw. Although the trade was worked out by the late 1860s, resentment towards European treachery and diseases was the reason for the murder of a number of missionaries at the time.

The Solomons quickly gained the reputation of being the most dangerous place in the Pacific: an island group inhabited by an often fierce, warlike and cannibalistic population. While there were many peaceful contacts, there were a number of unpredictable attacks on foreigners, and savage massacres. Churches moved cautiously in the Solomons even though this was a period of intense mission activity elsewhere in the Pacific.

Despite this violent situation, by the 1860s there were many places in the archipelago where sailors knew they would be welcome. Iron and steel tools were in great demand, as were calico, tobacco, beads, fish-hooks and, later, guns. The newly acquired firearms soon produced an explosive growth in head-hunting and slave raids.

As head-hunting by islanders increased, so also did labour recruiting (blackbirding) by Europeans. During the last 35 years of the 19th century, nearly 19,000 Solomon Islanders left for Queensland, Australia, and 10,000 for Fiji, to work on sugar-cane plantations.

Some islanders were keen to go, but many were not and were taken by force, especially in the early days of blackbirding. Islanders would be invited aboard to trade and then seized as the ship sailed away with them. Some blackbirders even dressed in priestly white, held a shoreside service and then kidnapped everyone. However, official controls over blackbirding and improved conditions in the Australian and Fijian canefields eliminated most of the trade's abuses by the mid-1880s.

The Protectorate

During the 1890s, about 50 British traders and missionaries (none of whom were female) were resident in the Solomons. At the same time, Germany was active in much of what is now Papua New Guinea, as well as in the Shortlands, Choiseul, Santa Isabel and Ontong Java.

On 6 October 1893, Britain proclaimed a protectorate over the southern part of the group. This claim was extended in 1897 and again in 1898. In 1899, Britain relinquished all claims to Western Samoa, and in return Germany ceded the Shortlands, Choiseul, Ontong Java and Santa Isabel to Britain. The new territory was named the British Solomon Islands Protectorate, or BSIP.

Britain's objectives for the Solomons were limited to keeping order, stopping head-hunting and cannibalism, and ensuring that the islanders and their lands were not exploited. In 1896, Charles Morris Woodford was appointed the first resident commissioner. He proved to be a remarkable man. Born in England in 1853, Woodford was the son of a London publican. He rejected this environment at an early age and made for the South Seas.

Woodford had to control close to 100,000 Solomon Islanders, many of them head-hunters, with only a few Europeans and a small force of local police. His worst problem was the people of New Georgia's Roviana Lagoon, who were intent on dominating all the western Solomons and were universally feared.

Woodford never carried a gun. His policy was to convince islanders of the futility of head-hunting and tribal warfare. He retired in 1915, having laid the foundations for organised government in the Solomons.

Education and health were left to the missions, as money was scarce and the Solomons had to be self-supporting. Although economical, this system produced new and deep divisions among villagers, as each missionary claimed his version of Christianity was right and the rest wrong.

Island traditions were gradually eroded as missionaries declared many customs and ceremonies to be evil. Although sorcery and head-hunting rapidly diminished, population figures also declined drastically following regular epidemics of European-introduced diseases.

Further alienation was caused by the islanders being subject to foreign ways. An insurrection in 1927 by a group of Malaitans was a clear rejection of European values. All but one of a government tax-gathering team were killed by spear-carrying highlanders who objected to paying for a foreign government they did not want. Punitive measures afterwards cowed further resistance but left an enduring legacy of mistrust in the area.

WW II

The 1930s was generally a period of calm in the Solomons. However, the by now peaceful pattern of life was completely shattered in 1942. In early April, the Japanese seized the Shortland Islands in the country's northwest. Three weeks later, Tulagi, the capital at the time, was taken.

From the beginning, the Japanese alienated local people. They defiled and robbed churches, demanded food at gunpoint, forced all healthy adult males to work for them without wages, and stole clothes and property. Their worst offence was to loot villagers' gardens, thereby at one stroke destroying a year's hard work by seizing the crops, pigs and chickens needed to feed a family for the next 12 months.

Only in the very early stages did a few local people support the Japanese, but such behaviour by the invaders soon disgusted the islanders. The Japanese, for their part, could not understand why villagers seemed to avoid them like the plague.

US planes had noticed Korean labourers building an airfield (later known as Henderson Field) on Guadalcanal. If the Japanese completed it, the way would be open for further advances against Allied territory in Vanuatu, New Caledonia, Fiji – even Australia and New Zealand. It had to be retaken, whatever the cost.

Large-scale US landings in Guadalcanal occurred in August 1942. The US forces gradually gained the upper hand, but at tremendous cost to life and limb on both sides. After six months of relentless bloodletting, the Japanese secretly withdrew. The fighting had cost them dearly in men and equipment, and had damaged their earlier aura of invincibility.

As 1943 progressed, more and more islands were recovered – though usually after fierce resistance. By the end of the year, only Choiseul and the Shortlands were still in enemy hands; these were bypassed ignominiously. The Allies recovered them after the Japanese surrender in 1945.

The islanders' loyalty was admirable. Although initially considering themselves to be under British orders to fight an opponent they knew little about, Japanese misconduct in occupied areas quickly persuaded local people of the need for direct action. They conducted their own scouting and guerrilla operations against Japanese patrols in the north-western Solomons, and rescued Allied aircrew who had been shot down. They operated behind enemy lines as 'coastwatchers', led by government officials, soldiers, traders, planters and priests who had stayed behind when the Japanese invaded. A number were decorated for their bravery.

Several thousand other islanders, mainly Malaitans, went to Guadalcanal once it was secured. They served as labourers and orderlies at the huge US supply base at Honiara. The Americans treated them as equals, shared food with them and gave them presents – something their colonial masters had never done. Not surprisingly, islanders noticed the difference. Malaitans were particularly determined that their status should permanently improve.

Postwar

Recovery was slow after 1945. As Tulagi was gutted, the Quonset-hut township of Honiara replaced it as the capital. The economy was in ruins, with many private planters not bothering to return. At the same time, a huge amount of abandoned war material littered the country, with some still to be removed even now.

A nationalist movement sprang up in Malaita and soon spread. Called Marching Rule, it was a self-reliant movement opposed to any cooperation with the restored British authorities – government or church. Its members were regimented into strictly ruled coastal villages dependent on community-based agriculture.

A cargo-cultist feature of the movement was the hope that huge quantities of US goods would be delivered to islanders by those US forces remaining behind in the Solomons after WW II. They also hoped the wealthy and generous USA would replace Britain as the country's ruler.

Though sympathetic, the USA could not accept this request. Mass arrests in 1947 and 1948 caused the movement to wane. It died out soon after the last of the US forces withdrew from the country in 1950.

The early 1960s were years of political awakening in the Solomons, leading to the creation of an elected governing council in 1970. The British Solomon Islands Protectorate was renamed the Solomon Islands five years later and independence granted on 7 July 1978.

Independence

Politics in the Solomons since Independence has mainly been about devolution. There has been secessionist talk in Western and Temotu provinces, partly as a result of fears of domination by the more heavily populated provinces of the country.

These problems have been bypassed by bringing into successive Cabinets representatives from the outer areas. The absence of large, disciplined parties has made this easier, with loyalty usually being shown to fellow provincials or to particular leading individuals. However, the position of prime minister has changed five times since Independence.

Meanwhile, in the countryside 'subsistence affluence' prevails. As long as each family has sufficient garden plots, fruit trees, pigs and chickens, the pleasant life of independent means will continue. Although the population is increasing and there is pressure for land, particularly in Honiara and Malaita, this ideal situation should exist for some years yet.

GEOGRAPHY

The Solomons is a scattered double chain of islands which extends 1667 km in a south-easterly direction from Bougainville Island in Papua New Guinea. Some of the islands are rugged, heavily wooded and mountainous; others are tiny, low-lying coral atolls.

The third-largest archipelago in the South Pacific, the Solomons covers over 1.35 million sq km of sea. Its total land area is 27,556 sq km. Within it are six large islands and over 40 other smaller but significant ones. Counting all the tiny atolls and cays within the country's borders, the total number of islands is 922, of which 347 are populated. The six major islands are Guadalcanal, Malaita, New Georgia, Santa Isabel, Makira and Choiseul. These vary in length between 92 and 181 km, and are between 24 and 56 km in width.

The country's highest peak, Mt Makarakombu (2447 metres) on Guadalcanal, is typical of most of the group's mountains. These are mostly rugged igneous formations cleft by narrow valleys.

Much of the Solomons is covered with dense rainforest, with mangrove swamps occurring along parts of the coast. Most islands have coral reefs and lagoons around them. Many have formed around an initial volcanic cone which has since been overlaid with colourful, level-topped terraces of coral rock.

Other islands are former reefs lifted high out of the water by volcanic activity. In Rennell's case, this has happened five times, creating the most striking example of an uplifted coral atoll in the Pacific.

Volcanoes & Earthquakes

The Solomons is part of the Pacific Ring of Fire. This highly volcanic area is at the inter-section of the huge Oceanic and Indo-Australasian tectonic plates. Pressing vigorously together, they cause constant seismic activity, including earthquakes and volcanoes – though less frequently here than in nearby Papua New Guinea and Vanuatu.

The Solomons has experienced up to 1900 earthquakes in some years, often with more than 40 measuring five or more on the Richter scale. The strongest one was in 1977, measuring 7.2 and causing landslides and damage to villages in Guadalcanal. Most occur in Temotu Province, Choiseul Island or the Shortland Islands. Despite this, earthquake damage and tidal waves are rare.

There are three land volcanoes and at least two submarine volcanoes in the Solomons, plus a large thermal area. The most active volcano in the last 40 years has been Tinakula, 42 km north of Nendo. Its last violent eruption, in 1971, forced all the island's small population to evacuate, though a few people have since returned.

Savo Island, north-west of Guadalcanal, has a number of bubbling and boiling springs. Its crater has not blown its top since 1840; nonetheless, seismologists constantly watch it.

In the New Georgia Islands, Simbo Island's Ove Crater emits sulphurous fumes but has not erupted within oral or recorded history. Further north there's a large area of hot springs and seething mud in north-eastern Vella Lavella.

The two main submarine volcanoes are both in Western Province. Cook is south-west of Vonavona, and Kavachi, the more active of the two, is south-west of Nggatokae. From time to time, the seas above them boil in brief but feverish activity. As the eruptions are in different spots each time, sometimes several km apart, each volcano may be made up of several cones lying close together on the ocean bed.

CLIMATE

The Solomon Islands' tropical climate is tempered by the surrounding sea. From late May to early December, during the country's winter, the south-easterly trade winds produce pleasantly mild weather. Rainfall is usually light and several days apart.

Although winter is the Solomons' calmest season, strong winds can occasionally blow up to force four, or 50 km an hour. They can last 10 days at a time, bringing heavy rain – particularly in July along Guadalcanal's and Makira's southern, or Weather, coasts. Once a storm is over, it's usually followed by days of fresh, light breezes and balmy weather.

In the summer months, from mid-December to mid-May, monsoonal winds come mostly from the west or north-west. This is the country's wet season and a time of higher temperatures, humidity and rainfall, particularly from January onwards. Short, sharp, torrential cloudbursts deluge the countryside, to be followed by bright sunshine.

In most parts of the Solomons, rain is heaviest from December to April. Choiseul is the exception. Its lowest precipitation is in December, when 207 mm of rain falls, while July, usually one of the drier months elsewhere, is Choiseul's wettest.

Sunshine Hours

The Solomons' average daily duration of sunshine is around seven hours. Sunrise is usually about 6.20 am, while sunset is usually between 6.30 and 7 pm. Throughout the year, dusk lasts only 10 minutes.

Temperature & Humidity

Daytime coastal temperatures vary through the year between 21°C and 32°C, with an occasional maximum of 33°C. At night the temperature sometimes falls to 19°C as the air is cooled by land breezes off nearby mountains and hills. Inland temperatures at sea level can be rather higher, sometimes reaching 35°C, yet mountain air remains pleasantly cooler, averaging closer to 22°C.

Humidity is highest in the morning, regularly reaching 90%, but it falls off in the afternoon. Kirakira is the country's muggiest place, with 95% humidity in February! However, humidity falls to a pleasant 69% in Honiara in August.

Even in the summer's hottest months, cool sea breezes along the shore keep the climate fresh.

But once you go more than a few hundred metres inland, you really feel the heat.

The following table gives average temperatures around the country, expressed in °C.

Average Temperatures

Place	Annual	Jan	July
Honiara	26.5	26.9	26.2
Henderson Airport	26.5	26.9	25.9
Choiseul Bay	27.2	27.6	26.5
Auki	26.6	27.1	25.8
Munda	27.0	27.3	26.4
Kirakira	26.2	26.6	25.6
Lata	27.0	27.4	26.4

Rainfall

There's an average 3500 mm (138 inches) of rain a year, although rainfall varies considerably from place to place. Gizo, though rather humid, averages only 2900 mm (115 inches) a year, while Lata in Temotu Province occasionally gets twice that.

Honiara and Henderson Airport are in a rain shadow and have a lower than average annual rainfall. However, on Guadalcanal's southern coast over 12,500 mm (492 inches) has been known to fall in a year – a colossal 12.5 metres (41 feet) of rain. Falls of 8000 mm (312 inches) annually are quite common there. The south-eastern coast of Makira is almost as wet.

The windward side of an island always gets the most rain, as do the higher parts, with some mountains almost permanently shrouded in cloud. Steep water courses in highland catchment areas cause many rivers to flash flood after storms.

Following are some of the average rainfalls from around the country, measured in mm.

Average Rainfalls

Place	Annual	Jan	July
Honiara	2154	278	99
Henderson Airport	1982	291	103
Choiseul Bay	3558	234	386
Auki	3271	406	212
Munda	3552	404	340
Kirakira	3601	362	326
Lata	4325	457	351

These high rainfall levels, together with the tall, rugged terrain, usually produce good-quality water. It's clean and unpolluted except where villages have grown up alongside riverbanks. In contrast, on the tiny outer islands and atolls there is often no surface water at all, and rainwater catchment tanks have to meet human needs.

Cyclones

On average there's at least one cyclone a year in the Solomons. Called hurricanes in the Caribbean, and typhoons in the South China Sea, cyclones are destructive tropical storms which rotate around a central low-pressure zone. They usually occur between January and April. However, they can arrive as early as November and as late as May, like Cyclone Namu in 1986, which took the lives of 140 villagers.

Most cyclones build up over the Coral Sea or the Solomon Sea. Usually they move south-west towards Vanuatu or Australia, gathering speed and strength as they go. When they strike the Solomons, they cause considerable damage to leaf-house villages, crops, water supplies and rainforests.

FLORA & FAUNA

The Solomons' indigenous land mammals are few and mainly nocturnal, such as bats, rats, possums and bush mice. Wild pigs, which live deep in the forests, are ferocious when angry and have at times gored people. Insect life flourishes, and there are small numbers of leeches in the rainforest and freshwater creeks.

Reptile life is plentiful, with several species of lizard, snake and turtle, and two types of crocodile. The seas teem with fish, including sharks, and dugong and whales are occasionally seen.

Nearly 90% of the country is covered by tropical rainforest. Most of the larger islands have a thick layer of tall trees, while the smaller ones are usually carpeted inland by a mass of scrub, which is surrounded by a thin coastal belt of coconut trees.

Nature Reserves

Both Rennell Island and New Georgia's Marovo Lagoon have been proposed for World Heritage listing. In the meantime, all Rennell is now a nature reserve.

Oema Atoll and Oema Island are treated as bird sanctuaries by Shortlands people, and Tetepare has been proposed as a nature reserve. However, nothing official has been decided on these yet.

Flora

The Solomons has over 4500 plant species, including 230 varieties of orchid. Many plants and trees are valued by islanders as sources of traditional building materials, food, medicine or clothing; tapa, for example, comes from the paper mulberry tree.

A common evergreen is the *sumai* tree, which blossoms at night. Its flowers fade and die as the daylight falls on them. Sumais usually grow close to the shore, and are recognisable by the large number of dark-green, box-shaped fallen fruits littering the adjacent ground. These contain unopened flowers.

The American vine was introduced from the southern states of the USA for use as a fast-growing natural camouflage around the WW II US installations east of Honiara. Since then, it has spread unrestrainedly in north-eastern Guadalcanal over the top of indigenous vegetation.

Flowers The hibiscus is the flower of the Pacific. Honiara is a good place to see its many single or double varieties, including whites, yellows, oranges, pinks and reds. You'll also find white and pink-flowered frangipanis, red ginger plants, colourful bougainvilleas and many other varieties around the country.

Hazardous Plants The large, purple-veined *nalato* leaf raises an unpleasant nettle-like rash on anyone who accidentally brushes against it. Your skin goes red where it has been stung, and can itch for a week. Islanders use the sap from the plant's roots or from beneath the bark as an antidote.

Another toxic plant is the *hailasi*. Its bark and sap can produce large blisters or swellings in some people, but not all. Some are affected just by coming close to it.

The *loya*, or lawyer, cane has hooks on the end of its leaves, and some of its five varieties also have barbs on their stems. Take care what you grab hold of when going up or down a hill.

Birds

The Solomons has a very varied selection of birds, with over 170 species in the country – more than 300 if all subspecies are included. There are nine kinds of hawk and eagle, 20 species of pigeon, 11 species of parrot, eight kinds of kingfisher and seven types of starling just for starters! Some have distinctive names, such as the dollar bird, the marbled frogmouth, the buff-headed coucal, the midget flowerpecker and the spangled drongo!

There are up to 40 species found only in the Solomons. The most plentiful is the cardinal lory – a familiar sight around Honiara. Some species live only on one island, such as the Rennell fantail or the slaty flycatcher of Vanikolo.

Nearly every major island group in the Solomons has its own quota of subspecies. There is probably nowhere else in the world where so many kinds of bird take such diverse forms across such short distances. For example, there are 10 different types of white-collared kingfisher.

Subspecies have often evolved whenever any of their number have been separated by the country's wide seas. There are three species found only in Temotu Province, and additional species may still await discovery. Rennell Island and Makira/Ulawa Province are similar.

Blackish male, and white-breasted female, frigate birds are the principal birds of island folklore. Their large size, deeply forked tail, long canted wings, skill in the air and habit of forcing other birds to disgorge their food have made them a favourite design in Melanesian art. Although their wings are not waterproof, so they can't enter water, they can often be seen along the shore, either hunting for skipjack or circling in their hundreds over their shoreside nests just before dark, gradually descending as the daylight disappears.

The other two birds appearing in traditional tales are the completely brown-plumaged Sanford's eagle and the megapode,

Reef heron

or incubator, bird. Local people often call Sanford's eagle the Malaita eagle, after the island where it is most plentiful.

Megapode birds can best be seen on Savo and Simbo, where they lay their eggs in hatcheries specially prepared for them, and farmed, by islanders. However, the birds are also found along some of the Solomons' sandy seashores and occasionally living inland, but seldom beyond 200 metres above sea level.

Insects

Most of the huge variety of insects in the Solomons live in the upper reaches of the rainforest. Among those found lower down are butterflies, moths, wasps, beetles, mosquitoes, centipedes, scorpions and caterpillars – some with stinging hairs.

Butterflies Of the more than 130 butterfly species found locally, 35 are endemic. The two largest forms, the Queen Victoria birdwing and the blue mountain birdwing, have spans of over 250 mm. These large butterflies are present in small numbers all around the country, though they are seldom seen in towns. However, very large moths are common at night, even in Honiara.

Wasps The orange-winged, black and orange-striped, 12-mm-long Solomons fruit wasp is very common in Bellona, and is also present in Rennell and some other islands in small numbers. It's not nearly as ill-tempered as the European wasp, but can give a mild sting if disturbed. It often lives in the wooden framework of leaf houses and usually feeds on pawpaws.

Centipedes & Scorpions Smaller centipedes may live in the roofs of leaf houses or be accidentally carried into a house in firewood. The large, dark-green centipede causes an excruciating pain for about a day if it stings you. A mosquito net is useful if you're sleeping in the bush or a leaf house, as it will stop centipedes falling on you in the night. There are also a few scorpions, particularly in drier woodland areas. Despite this, many people spend years in the Solomons and never once get stung by either creature.

Mammals

The Solomons has several bush rats, as well as the marsupial phalanger, or cuscus. Though two rat species may now be extinct, four of the surviving types are larger than domestic cats. Three live in trees, with two species in Guadalcanal and one in Santa Isabel, while the largest one nests underground, mainly in Choiseul and Guadalcanal, eating nuts, fruit and insects. There's also the Polynesian rat, and the common brown rat, which has become a pest, especially around coastal settlements.

The cuscus is in all the country's larger islands except for those of Temotu Province. Ranging in colour from pure white through fawn and grey to nearly black, it's considered a delicacy. Its teeth are sometimes used as traditional currency.

The flying fox, or fruit bat, makes a popular village meal, while its teeth are collected for bride price in some islands. In the daytime, when they aren't fighting or barking at each other, fruit bats sleep in huge colonies at the top of tall trees.

Reptiles

Snakes There are eight species of sea snake in Solomons waters, mostly 60 cm to one metre long, and all venomous, with rudder-like tails. At the same time, they are usually extremely inoffensive. One of these, the black-banded sea krait (also called the coral snake), is common along most island shores, and comes ashore occasionally, mainly to lay its eggs. It's not averse to fresh water, and has become quite plentiful in Lake Te'Nggano on Rennell. Fortunately, this snake is only hostile when treated roughly.

There are also seven land species, and one freshwater snake – the *tugihono*, which is only found in Lake Te'Nggano on Rennell. Although extremely poisonous, it's very placid, and islanders consider it harmless.

Of the other seven types, three are nonvenomous. Two of these are Pacific boas – one ground and one tree variety – while the third is the burrowing snake, or *typhlina*, a small, nocturnal brownish-red serpent, occurring in several subspecies varying in length from 12 to 35 cm.

The tree boa is only found in Temotu Province in the Solomons, but is plentiful there, especially in the Reef Islands. This arboreal snake is two metres long and silvery coloured, with dark patches along its back. The ground boa is a similar length and greyish-brown, with a continuous serrated black line down its back. It usually hides under leaves waiting for its normal prey of rats or mice to come by. Both boas are called sleeping snakes, from their habit of lying absolutely still as if asleep when disturbed by creatures larger than themselves, especially humans. However, they can bite repeatedly if annoyed.

Guppy's snake is the most aggressive of the four venomous land snakes, though the brown tree snake has occasionally bitten sleeping human babies (especially in Guam, where it has become a pest). In contrast, both the Solomons banded snake and Woodford's snake are generally docile, as long as they're not provoked. You are unlikely to see any of these snakes unless you accidentally disturb one while bushwalking.

Guppy's snake is short, with a creamy belly. It has a distinctive head and thin reddish-brown back, often with transverse bands. It lives in forests and near creeks, and is active during the day. This snake has a dangerous-sounding hiss as its call sign. However, it seldom bites.

The brown tree snake has rear-facing fangs and noticeably big eyes. Its narrow body is two metres long, light-brown to khaki in colour and crossed with darker wavy lines. It lives in trees or empty houses in bush villages and is mainly active at night.

The strikingly coloured Solomons banded snake has distinctive yellow and black bands on its body and a whitish head. This snake grows to a metre long, is very docile and lives under rotting debris on the forest floor.

The small Woodford's snake is just 30 cm long and is only occasionally found, usually living under rotting fallen timber and leaves.

Its dark-brown back gets lighter along its sides towards the belly, which can vary in colour between light brown and yellow.

Lizards Of the many lizard species, two are large enough to be eaten by villagers. They taste like chicken. The largest – the 1.5-metre monitor lizard, or goanna – is plentiful around Lake Te'Nggano on Rennell and in the Three Sisters Islands off Makira, but uncommon elsewhere. The other one – about 75 cm long – is the giant prehensile-tailed skink. It has a tail as long as its body and lives mainly in trees. Nocturnal, normally docile and slow moving, this skink can scratch and bite if severely provoked.

Crocodiles Although islanders all along knew otherwise, the scientific world until recently believed there were only saltwater, or estuarine, crocodiles in the Solomons. However, islanders have always distinguished between short and long-mouthed crocs. The short-mouthed version is the dangerous, human-eating saltwater variety which is wide-bodied and often four or more metres long. The long-mouthed one is a slim, freshwater variant which is usually between one and two metres long. Although it eats mainly fish, at this size it is strong enough to take dogs, pigs and even small children. However, it occasionally grows to three metres in length, and when it reaches this size it can even manage small cattle and adult humans.

Islanders often call the saltwater ones alligators and the long-mouthed ones crocodiles, though local terminology sometimes reverses this. The two species prefer different types of water, and are generally true to their names. Freshwater crocodiles favour clear or reedy, fresh, sparkling rivers, though ones with a sulphurous taste are also acceptable. They are definitely known to be in north Malaita's waterways and also the Ulo River area of eastern Vella Lavella, and may be in several other islands also.

Small numbers of saltwater crocodiles live in many of the country's mangrove swamps and tidal estuaries, though they're capable of travelling far inland up muddy, low-lying rivers.

Being very territorial, there are seldom more than a few in one place at a time. However, they are reasonably plentiful in the Three Sisters Islands and southern and eastern Guadalcanal – particularly in the Lauvi Lagoon – while some have been found close to Honiara, near the Betikama Seventh Day Adventist (SDA) Mission. Other places where they are known to be present are the marshy and mangrove-ridden parts of the Nggelas, New Georgia, Vangunu, Nggatokae, Tetepare, Choiseul, San Jorge, Vanikolo, Makira, southern Nendo, western Vella Lavella, eastern Kolombangara, southern Malaita and north-western Maramasike.

A few villagers are taken by crocs every year. If you are bushwalking and plan to cross muddy coastal rivers, marshes, estuaries or tidal flats, or go near mangrove swamps, always ask if there are crocodiles about and whether they are long or short-mouthed ones. If there's any chance at all, don't go there. Children are always at risk.

Frogs & Toads The Solomons has several species of frog and toad, including a number of tree varieties, one horned frog and a giant edible form which grows to 45 cm long and carries its young on its back. Accidentally introduced in WW II and now a pest, the cane toad has poison glands on its back which are able to squirt venom a metre, possibly on to a victim's broken skin, which it may then penetrate. Any animal eating a cane toad can expect to die within an hour from the toxins in it.

Tree frog

Marine Creatures
Whales used to be plentiful but worldwide depredation by whaling fleets has made them uncommon visitors to the Solomons. Dolphins and porpoises, however, frequently play around inter-island boats. People in Malaita and Makira/Ulawa sometimes organise hunting parties to drive them into confined waters. Their flesh is eaten and their teeth are used for bride price.

Occasionally dugong can be seen in the shallows eating seaweed, the female suckling her one pup on the surface. At a distance the female dugong can look like a human female – the probable source of the mermaid legend.

On most voyages through the Solomons you will see flying fish skimming along the sea's surface, their tiny, wing-like fins beating so hard that they look like fast-revolving wheels.

Two of the four turtle species frequenting the Solomons are quite common. The green and hawksbill turtles nest on most islands from November to February. The female digs her nest at night on a sandy shore, laying about 100 eggs a clutch nightly at the same spot over several weeks. The baby turtles hatch at night after two to 2.5 months.

Sharks Human-eating sharks are very common in the Solomons. It's always wise to check with local people before bathing, and take their advice.

Although some people have an almost familial relationship with sharks, particularly in the Makira/Ulawa and Malaita provinces, where there are occasional shark-calling ceremonies, most will avoid the sea if there is any danger at all from these predatory creatures.

Islanders usually consider themselves adequately protected from sharks when they are inside a reef or swimming from a white-sand, or coral-debris, beach. Black sand, however, is usually volcanic in origin, and therefore has formed too recently to have allowed a protective reef to have grown up around it. Consequently, there is no barrier

Since stonefish are very hard to see when you're walking through coral shallows, always wear reef shoes. Also avoid putting your hand down hard on any small, odd-shaped rock. It could instead be the always well-camouflaged stonefish. Scorpion fish, however, are easy to spot, due to their attractive pink colours and silvery, but venomous, spines.

Not every type of cone shell is venomous, but several are, so don't touch any of them unless you have an islander with you to tell which ones are safe. Some cone-shaped shellfish have an extremely venomous proboscis, which is a rapidly extendible, dart-like stinging device. This can reach any part of the shell's outer surface, poisoning you as you handle the creature. Cone-shell venom can be fatal.

Moray eels and clams shouldn't be a problem unless you accidentally put your finger in a coral hole or a clam's open jaws. Always carry a knife while snorkelling or diving to deal with such an emergency. Finally, don't swim with anything shiny on, or a barracuda may take a bite out of it – and you too!

GOVERNMENT

The Solomon Islands became an independent country on 7 July 1978. It's a parliamentary democracy with a single legislative assembly. The British Crown, as leader of the Commonwealth, is head of state, with the governor general, chosen by Parliament, acting as the monarch's representative.

Parliament sits in Honiara, has 38 members including the prime minister and his 15 Cabinet colleagues, and is presided over by an unelected speaker or chairperson. Elections are held within every four-year period. All citizens over 18 may vote.

Devolution

Honiara is administered by the Honiara Municipal Authority, while each of the eight provinces has its own regional assembly of elected representatives. These choose a

to exclude large and potentially predatory fish from coming close inshore.

The same applies to river mouths and estuaries. Indeed, the majority of shark strikes worldwide have occurred either at beaches in only one metre of water, or in tidal rivers.

If you're approached by a shark, try to stay as calm as possible, swimming steadily away. Shark victims must be moved from the water as fast as possible to allow any bleeding to be immediately staunched by applying pressure to the wounds.

Dangerous Reef Dwellers The extremely poisonous stonefish and scorpion, or lion, fish are both present in the archipelago. So are nonvenomous, but steel-jawed, clams and moray eels.

premier from among themselves, and a speaker to chair their meetings.

The premier has a four-year term of office and is in charge of the provincial government. Its areas of responsibility include communications, transport, health and education. While enjoying a degree of autonomy, the provinces rely heavily on the central government for finance.

Justice
The judicial system is based on British law, with a high court, a court of appeal and magistrates. In addition, there are local courts conducted by village elders and a customary land appeal court that hears appeals over land-ownership matters – a major aspect of court business. There's also an ombudsman to investigate public complaints against national and provincial government bodies.

Politics
The four main political parties are the ruling National United Party, the National Democratic Party, the People's Alliance and the United Party. There are three other smaller parties, and the independents also form a group. In addition to the National United Party – which currently holds government – the United Party and the People's Alliance, supported by various allies, have both held office since Independence.

The Solomons has generally taken a quiet position in international affairs. However, the country is a member of the United Nations and most of its special intergovernmental agencies, the World Bank, two of the European Community (EC) subgroups, the Commonwealth, the South Pacific Forum and the South Pacific Commission.

National Symbols
The national flag was first flown on Independence Day, and is blue and green, divided diagonally by a thin yellow stripe. This stands for the narrow strand of sand separating the surrounding blue seas from the country's green forests. There are five white stars clustered at the top left corner. These

National coat of arms

represent the Solomons' five main groups of islands.

The national anthem is *God Save Our Solomon Islands*. The coat of arms includes a shark, a crocodile, an eagle, two turtles and frigate birds, spears and a shield. The country's motto is 'To Lead is to Serve'.

ECONOMY
The Solomon Islands' economy is basically a rural and subsistence one. About 84% of the people live in country areas and are comfortably self-sufficient in the traditional food crops of root vegetables and fruit, as well as fishing and livestock husbandry (mainly pigs and chickens). About 30% of land is cultivable in small parcels. The only large expanse of good agricultural soil is in the Guadalcanal Plains.

The country's main natural resources are its huge number of commercially useful fruit trees (especially coconuts), forests, fisheries and some minerals. In recent years, there has been a considerable diversification from the copra-based, one-product rural economy of the colonial era. New interests include beef cattle, oil palms, cocoa and spices. Small quantities of gold, silver, copper, manganese and nickel are known to exist, as well as large deposits of bauxite and phosphates.

The seas are likely to become the country's principal resource. Fish – mainly tuna – have recently become the largest export earner. Timber is second, while copra, cocoa and palm oil come jointly third. Both tourism and manufacturing are still in their infancy.

Noncitizens, particularly Australians and Japanese, dominate commerce and industry, while many small stores in town areas are Chinese owned. About 26,000 people work for salaries and wages, and a further 12,000 either work part time or are in casual employment.

The gross domestic product (GDP) was estimated to have risen in 1990 to S$350 million, or US$126 million, producing an annual standard of living of S$1012, or US$364, a head. However, inflation has also climbed; it reached a yearly average of 13.1% between 1982 and 1988, though it has since fallen to 10%.

Agriculture

Villagers in the Solomons are often described as living in a state of subsistence affluence. Their gardens supply sufficient kumara, yams, pana, taro, cassava, bananas, pawpaws, Chinese and slippery cabbage, edible ferns, and betel and ngali nuts for their personal needs, while coconut trees, pigs and poultry produce cash income.

Before WW II, plantations used to dominate the copra trade. Since then, villagers have become the major force in it, owning 80% of the country's trees. Although plantations are still significant in cocoa production, smallholders now produce 50%.

Palm-oil output, mainly from large projects in north-eastern Guadalcanal, continues to expand, though world prices have recently been at an all-time low. Spices, including ginger, turmeric, vanilla, chillies and cardamom, are produced in small quantities by villagers.

In the 1980s, many smallholders acquired a few cattle each. However, some villagers since then have found efficient livestock management requires larger herds than they can handle. Consequently, stock levels have declined, and future cattle herds are likely to be confined to plantations.

Land Use & Ownership

Around 88% of land in the Solomons is owned under customary tenure. Neither the government nor expatriates may own it. Of the other 12% – known as registered land – over half belongs to the government. People other than Solomon Islanders may only hold leases on the latter – obtained from the custom owners or the government – for a maximum of 75 years, the average life of a coconut tree.

Traditionally, land belongs to people, not institutions. An individual's right to use land comes from his membership of a Melanesian clan or Polynesian family claiming descent from the first people to settle it. Other people may only use this land with the consent of those who have inherited rights to it.

Land transfers beyond members of the same family require payment of compensation. In some areas even now, this involves the exchange of shell money and the holding of a feast to signify publicly that this transaction has occurred.

Legal wrangles over land – particularly that desired by mining and timber interests – are common. This can make investment unpredictable – even unrewarding. However, litigation between individual islanders is also frequent, usually between the current occupant and the descendants of a family that may have last used it some two or more generations ago.

Forestry

Although nearly 90% of the country is tree-covered, under 10% of these forests are commercially useful. The main forestry islands are Kolombangara, New Georgia, Shortland, Santa Isabel, Makira, Choiseul, Malaita, Guadalcanal and Nendo. Most of the logs go to Japan, with the remainder going to South Korea or Taiwan. However, some timber is sawn locally, at the country's 17 small mills.

Despite its importance to the Solomons economy, the industry's future depends on solving differences between loggers and custom land owners. Many quite rightly say the land has often been seriously damaged by timber felling. Certainly, thousands of hectares of the country have been denuded of trees and very few effective reafforestation schemes have been introduced to replace them. Sites of traditional importance have often been thoughtlessly bulldozed. For their part, loggers say that, while no-one seems to worry before the felling actually begins, once the operation is underway there are often new demands for financial compensation over and above that already agreed upon.

Mining

Although there's a great diversity of minerals nationally, few exist in sufficient quantities and purity to justify development. Problems over compensation and customary land ownership, in addition to islanders' understandable concerns over inevitable destruction of their gardens and traditional ways of life, have often proved insurmountable. So far, mining for bauxite in Wagina, Nendo and Rennell, and phosphate on Bellona, is on indefinite hold for these reasons.

Gold prospects in the Shortland Islands and the islands of Santa Isabel, Choiseul, Vella Lavella, Mbava and Marovo (beside Vangunu) remain unexploited, usually because of customary land access and ownership difficulties. However, a mine is planned for Gold Ridge in Guadalcanal, with the nearby alluvial gold deposits also likely to be extracted.

A small manganese operation on Hanesavo Island off Nggela Sule Island proved to be unprofitable. However, nickel laterite in Santa Isabel and San Jorge is widespread, and development may go ahead if the ore can be mined economically. Offshore oil exploration is also likely to begin in the next few years.

Fishing

Since the early 1970s, fishing has become the country's largest export earner. Shore bases have been established at Tulagi in the Nggela Islands and Noro in the New Georgia Islands, and the Solomons has proclaimed a 200-nautical-mile (376-km) exclusive fishing zone.

The bulk of the catch is frozen and exported, though the amounts canned locally increases annually. Fish are mainly caught by the pole-and-line method, the majority of the catch being skipjack, yellowfin tuna and albacore.

Surveys say that three purse-seiners and 60 pole-and-liners can operate in Solomons waters. Yet, although the number of pole-and-liners actually operating is down by as many as 20, the average size of fish caught is declining. In addition, large-scale netting of baitfish in shallow waters is depleting some traditional fishing areas.

Manufacturing

The Solomons' manufacturing sector is still very small, though boat building is a major activity in Tulagi. Most other industries are in Honiara and the Guadalcanal Plains.

Palm-oil milling and timber and fish processing are new activities, as is the making of paint, furniture, fibreglass canoes, water tanks, shell costume jewellery, buttons, biscuits, soft drinks, clothing, soap, nails and coarse tobacco, and the baking of bread. However, most business ownership, along with banking and commerce, is still in expatriate hands.

Tourism

Tourism is still only a minor part of the economy. The government's target is for 72,000 nonworking visitors to be entering the country annually by the year 2000, with about 2000 tourists in the country at any one time. However, as there were only 10,000 visitors annually in the early 1990s, this aim may prove overly ambitious.

Of the 1990 visitors, only about half came to the Solomons for a holiday, with the remainder doing business of one sort or another. Most came from Australia, Papua New Guinea, New Zealand, the USA or Japan and stayed an average 11 days each.

The Solomons' deteriorating foreign-exchange position was the stimulus behind the government's ambitious new policy and the official designation of 1992 as the Year of Tourism. Some of the increased number of arrivals are likely to be cruise-ship visitors. However, the vast proportion are expected to arrive by air once facilities for wide-bodied jets are completed at Henderson Airport in the mid-1990s, just as many more accommodation spots hopefully open up around the country.

Foreign Trade

Japan is the Solomons' major trading partner, accounting for 37% of its exports and 15% of its imports. Australia supplies 38% of the country's imports, but only takes 4% of its exports. This type of imbalance has produced long-term trade deficits, representing as much as 18% of GDP in 1990. Official external reserves had been falling since 1988, leaving sufficient money in 1990 to finance only about six weeks worth of imports, while external debts rose 36% to S$373 million – slightly higher than the annual monetary GDP figure. Although overseas aid continues to run at about 8% of GDP (mainly from Britain, Australia, Japan and New Zealand), the Solomons dollar's value in 1991 continued to depreciate against the currencies of its main trading partners, varying between 6% against the Australian dollar and 23% against the British pound.

POPULATION

The nation's population was estimated to be 346,000 in late 1992. The vast proportion – 94.2%, or 326,000 – are Melanesian, while Polynesians number about 13,000, or 3.8%. There are also about 4000 Micronesian settlers from Kiribati – often called Gilbertese – and around 2000 Europeans. The remaining 1000 are Asians – mainly Chinese storekeepers and restaurateurs, and Japanese fisherfolk.

The term Melanesia comes from the Greek words *melas* and *nesos*, meaning 'black' and 'island' respectively. Therefore, Melanesians are the black island people (of western Oceania). Polynesians are the people of the *polys* (many) islands in the eastern Pacific, while Micronesians come from the *mikros* (tiny) islands to the north. Of the indigenous population, the Melanesians tend to prefer the group's larger, mountainous islands, while the Polynesians live mainly on the isolated outer reefs and atolls.

The Solomons' population density of less than 12.6 people per sq km is one of the lowest in the Pacific. However, some islands have considerably more than this, especially the isolated but overcrowded outliers of Anuta and Tikopia at the southern tip of Temotu Province, while Honiara has 1681 people in each of its 22 sq km.

A feature of the Solomons group is the large number of small villages. Of the 4000 settlements in the country, 50% have less than 41 people living in them, while the average population of each one is 87 people. Only 19% of the population live in places with more than 300 people.

Most villages are coastal, inland settlements being plentiful only in Malaita and Guadalcanal. Most islands' interiors are too rugged and mountainous to support any people.

With 107 indigenous languages and dialects, traditions and cultures vary from island to island – even village to village on the same island in some cases. A majority of people follow a traditional way of life, modified by modern education and 90 or so years of Christianity. Most villagers are subsistence farmers, growing food in their own gardens and building their own homes.

Should you ask Solomon Islanders where they come from, they will usually reply with the name of the island of their birth. Differences between islanders are also reflected in religious factionalism. However, tolerance towards people of different origins and religions has spread widely in recent years.

Until recently, there was a distinct rivalry between *man blong solwata* (coastal dwellers) and *man blong bus* (from the interior). Now that bush people regularly come down to the coast for shopping, medical attention or schooling, this distinction has much less significance.

However, a developing difference is between the lifestyle and sophistication of those who live in major towns like Honiara, and that of the other 84% of the people, who live mainly along the coastal strips of the nation's many islands. For instance, in the country you'll see lots of naked children running around, and sometimes barebreasted elderly women, whereas in the towns everyone goes fully clothed.

Population Growth

Until the mid-1980s, the most heavily populated island was Malaita. However, with Honiara's growth and the emigration there of many Malaitans, Guadalcanal now has the highest population. The number of people in Honiara has grown from 2600 in 1964 to 37,000 in 1992.

The nation's population expanded by 3.4% a year from the early 1970s to the mid-1980s, and by 3.5% a year after that. This is one of the world's highest figures, and will produce around 476,000 people by 2001 – more than trebling in 30 years. The present rapid growth rate is due to high fertility levels and a falling death rate. Infant mortality has been much reduced by improved health care and the malaria control programmes of the 1970s.

Currently 52% of the Solomons' people are male and 48% female. Of these, about 58% are under 21 years old. Life expectancy is 59.9 years for men and 61.4 years for women.

PEOPLE
Melanesians

Although Melanesians are all of the same race, their physical appearance and customs vary considerably. They range in colour from coal black to light brown. The people with the darkest skins live in the western areas and

Choiseul, and are ethnically related to Bougainville Islanders in Papua New Guinea. People in the rest of the country are lighter.

Thick, black, curly or bushy hair is usual, though fair or ginger hair with brown skin is common in some parts. Certain islanders have long, wavy, black hair, while some young people have blond or light-brown, straightish locks which usually grow curly and gingerish once they reach their teens or 20s. Melanesian people are generally short in stature, and have distinctive facial bone structures with prominent jaws.

Melanesian life is more democratic than the aristocratic and oligarchic system prevailing in Polynesian islands. Although there's plenty of intermarriage between the two races, there are occasional tensions too, particularly between Malaitans and Bellonese.

Polynesians

Typically, Polynesians have yellow-brown to very fair skin, and straight or curly, black hair, although some have gingerish or brown hair. Others may be more swarthy (particularly Rennellese) and physically bulky, tall and imposing looking – like Samoans.

Some Polynesians, particularly those from Sikaiana, have slim, Asiatic features, due to a Micronesian mixing in the 19th century. Others have the more typical rounded Polynesian face.

Many Polynesian women have intermarried with Melanesian men in the Reef Islands. Consequently, a large number of lighter-skinned people with tight, dark, curly hair now live there.

Gilbertese

Between 1955 and 1971, Micronesian settlers came from the Gilbert Islands (now Kiribati) under a British government resettlement scheme. Their own seriously overcrowded islands had been exhausted by a long period of drought. New land was offered on Ghizo, Shortland and Wagina.

Some have moved to White River Village in Honiara, or to Red Beach, just east of

Henderson Airport. Their dance, the Batere, is a regular part of the capital's tourist scene. Yandina and Tulagi also have sizeable Micronesian communities now.

The Gilbertese, or I-Kiribati, as they sometimes call themselves, are well built, have long, straight, black hair and lightish-brown skin. Though physically larger, many resemble Filipinos, to whom Micronesians are related.

Europeans

Most Europeans, or expats, as islanders usually call them, live in Honiara. A few missionaries, doctors, volunteers, hoteliers and planters live elsewhere around the country, though fewer now than before Honiara began to expand 20 years ago.

Foreigners still hold many specialist and technical government posts, most of which are based in the capital. In contrast, most overseas volunteers work outside Honiara.

The majority of expatriate jobs are held by Britons, Australians, New Zealanders, Americans and Canadians. Most have jobs in medicine, teaching, technical trades or water supply.

Islanders don't expect a European to do anything wrong, and are sometimes quite amazed if one does. In the past, most expats were missionaries, doctors or government staff (or, occasionally, planters or traders). Consequently, local people sometimes have an overly idealised opinion of Whites.

Islanders always assume all Europeans who speak English are *wantoks* – ie relatives or close friends. This can cause problems, as US Peace Corps staff report. Occasionally a foreign traveller ends up at some isolated spot bumming off villagers who are too embarrassed to confront the person. So they ask the local volunteer teachers either to persuade the visitor to leave or to start looking after the freeloader themselves.

Polynesian girl weaving a basket

Asians

The small Chinese community lives mainly in Honiara's Chinatown. There are a few Chinese stores elsewhere in the country – at Gizo, Auki and Kirakira – though Tulagi's large prewar Chinatown has now gone.

The Japanese, and a few Koreans with them, work for the Noro-based Solomon Taiyo fishing fleet. Many veterans come to see the battlefields or to find the remains of war-dead compatriots still needing cremation according to traditional Shinto rites.

Until the early 1980s, Japanese ambassadors flew from time to time over the thick bush – particularly that of Guadalcanal, New Georgia and Vella Lavella – calling on any of their nationals who might still be there to give themselves up. Very occasionally, Japanese WW II stragglers would be found. As recently as 1965, one was discovered on Vella Lavella.

Albinos

Some islanders have thick, curly hair and Melanesian features, but white, unpigmented skin. This is a result of defects in the gene which controls the human body's manufacture of melanin, the pigment which colours the skin, hair and eyes.

Albinism is quite common in the Reef Islands, the Duff Islands and Nendo, where intermarriage between different island groups has been a long-standing tradition. Although islanders are seldom aware that albinism is caused by a recessive gene, they often consider it to be hereditary.

Albinos have great difficulty with the strong light and heat of the tropics. They often screw their eyes up as protection from the sun, and despite the heat, they prefer to be heavily clothed as a protection against sunburn.

An albino's life expectancy is short. Islanders report that there are fewer female than male albinos. The maximum age males live to is about 40, while females apparently seldom live beyond 30.

Though sympathetically treated by their companions, albinos are considered to be clumsy – probably because of sight deficiencies. They seldom marry – mainly because of the general belief in the inherited aspects of albinism.

Women

Although these are the days of equal opportunity, a woman's role in the Solomons is still to be a good wife and mother. Agriculture and domestic duties are treated as women's work, though heavier tasks are done by men. While girls have to learn adult ways earlier than boys, they are expected to respect their brothers – even the younger ones.

In the past, political power and control over customary land descended through females in certain parts of the country. As clan heads, women exercised considerable power and still do so in Guadalcanal, Savo and Vella Lavella.

Women usually marry at 19, whereas men do so on average at 25. As a woman is paid for in marriage with some form of bride price, her children belong to her husband's clan, not hers.

Despite legislation providing for equal employment and political participation, women still occupy mainly junior positions in the country. Only one in six employees is female – almost the same figure as in 1976. About 50% of working women are nurses, teachers, government officials or clerical staff. The Solomons has had a few female members of parliament, though there's only one currently.

EDUCATION

Preprimary and primary education in the Solomons is not yet compulsory. It covers ages five to nine, while secondary schooling goes on up to 14. There are about 500 primary or preprimary schools, plus 20 schools for the country's 5500 secondary pupils, who represent 10% of their age group.

Of the 20 secondary schools, eight are national secondary schools, while 12 are provincial ones. The national secondary schools are more academic, and four of them have sixth forms in preparation for tertiary studies. About 300 students a year go on to tertiary level. Many of them attend the Solomon Islands College of Higher Education in Kukum to study technical subjects, while the remainder go to overseas universities, mainly in Fiji and Papua New Guinea.

The majority of primary school children are girls. However, less than half the secondary school pupils, and only one in seven of the students attending tertiary studies overseas, are female.

The large numbers of educated or partly educated school-leavers represent an increasing social problem for the Solomons. About 6400 children from all levels finish school every year, yet the steadily growing economy has only been able so far to generate between 500 and 1000 new jobs a year.

There are two six-week school holidays annually: in December and January, and in June and July. Despite such long terms, literacy is reckoned to be only 45%.

Expatriate Schooling

There are five private primary schools in Honiara, of which the Woodford School (☎ 30186) is the one most favoured by expat families. There are also three small private kindergartens for those under five. Most foreign children return to their home country for secondary schooling at 10 or 11 years of age.

ARTS

In the past, many of the Solomons' artefacts were made out of materials which rapidly decomposed in the hot, humid climate. Others used for ceremonial purposes were destroyed with the onset of the new religion of Christianity.

At the same time, certain crafts lost their market with the arrival of modern trade goods. Pottery, formerly made in the Shortlands, and possibly also in Simbo, Wagina and Kolombangara, is now only produced in north-western Choiseul.

Carving

Carving and weaving were skills basic to everyday living. Because of endemic warfare, every family had to fashion its own weapons. Weaving was required for domestic items such as bags, baskets and mats.

Ancient Designs Craftspeople paid great attention in their woodwork to human or shark-like forms, with their labours representing a form of worship. Only the best reproductions of a god's image could ensure success in war, fishing, gardening and healing. To achieve the required quality, some carvings were inlaid with small pieces of chambered nautilus shell, chosen because it had a smooth, shiny surface and was a convenient material to work in.

Traditionally, human, bird and fish motifs were favoured. The most common designs were of *nguzunguzus* (pronounced 'noozoo-noozoos'). These were figureheads used to adorn the prows of war canoes, particularly on inter-island raids.

Deities and spirits were often carved in human form, combining human-like features with those of birds, fish or other animals. Stone mortars, canoe ornaments, fishing floats, shields and ritual staffs were all made with human faces and figures.

Often frigate birds appeared on shell pendants, canoes, shields, breast ornaments, food bowls, fishing floats, dance sticks and face tattoos. Shark, tuna and dolphin designs were also used for these, and for houseposts, canoe paddles and bamboo lime containers. Turtles, snakes, crocodiles, dogs, pigs, hornbills, crabs and insects were also portrayed.

Modern Designs Motifs which once had a considerable religious significance are now reproduced to decorate a wide range of goods, including coins and postage stamps. The principal demand is from tourists.

Carvings of nguzunguzus, reef fish, dolphins, sharks, turtles, birds, crocodiles, snakes and frogs are skilfully fashioned by Western Province craftspeople to modern flowing designs, using mainly light-brown kerosene wood. A recent development is to carve human figures engaged in nontraditional activities. Although purists may decry this, they are well-finished, lifelike and popular with tourists.

Bowls Santa Ana and Santa Catalina produce small, ornately decorated ritual bowls. As these islands are well away from the tourist mainstream, their products have a much more traditional look, and are much sought after by collectors.

Canoes In everyday use in most islands, canoes play the same role as bicycles in more affluent, landlocked countries. Miniature versions are made in Western Province, Malaita, Ulawa, Santa Ana and Nggela. Polynesians make small replica outriggers from hibiscus wood in Tikopia and Bellona, while model sailing canoes are occasionally crafted in the Reef Islands and the Duff Islands.

Fish-Hooks & Floats Shark-hooks are made from branches and roots which are appropriately curved. Miniature ones are produced from bone and shell.

Floats are widely used for fishing in Makira. Along with handmade fish-hooks, they are still in everyday use and sometimes sold as tourist souvenirs.

Houseposts Makira has a tradition of large housepost carvings, often of naked human figures. Other, similar versions 1.5 metres high come from the same area, including nearby Santa Ana and Santa Catalina.

Lime Containers Some lime boxes, used by betel-nut chewers throughout the Solomons, are made from gourds or coconuts. The best ones are from Guadalcanal.

Masks Although nontraditional in design, lifelike masks are carved from kerosene wood in Western Province, Rennell and Bellona. Their designs, complete with sombre, stylised faces and lengthened ears, have been adapted from Africa and Papua New Guinea.

Weapons
Clubs, spears, bows and arrows were all part of the armoury of a 19th-century Solomons warrior. Many well-made modern replicas of these are now produced.

Clothing
Most people wear Western clothes these days, although so-called grass skirts are worn in the remoter areas of the larger islands, and at traditional dances and ceremonies. The actual material they are made from is betel leaf or hibiscus bark soaked in salt water for a week.

Tapa, decorated or otherwise, is less frequently worn in the Solomons than further east in the Pacific. However, elderly men sometimes wear it in the Polynesian outliers. Rennellese men often dance in tapa, dyed yellow with turmeric, at festivals. It's also made on Simbo and Santa Isabel.

Ornaments
Pendants are still worn on many islands. Shell-money necklaces are used as personal decoration in both Malaita and Western Province, while oyster-shell pendants can be seen in Choiseul, Malaita and Guadalcanal. Forehead discs, made from turtle shell and clam shell, are called *kapkaps* and come from Nggela, Malaita and the New Georgia group.

Belts of red, black and white shell money are worn as armbands in Malaita. Other items made from the teeth of porpoises, dogs, possums and flying foxes are used as necklaces, as forehead decorations, and as currency on several islands.

Some Malaitans wear ear ornaments complete with porpoises' teeth and beads, while earrings of brown shell are preferred in Nendo. In other places small, white cowrie shells are used as forehead or leg decorations.

Often combs are worn as hair ornaments. Some Malaitan ones have plumes of coloured fibres, with red and yellow designs woven over long spokes.

Currency
Several forms of *kastom mani* have evolved to pay bride price. Shell money is still used for certain transactions in Malaita, as occa-

sionally are red-feather coils in Temotu Province. Large clamshell rings were similarly employed until recently in the New Georgia Islands, while thin clamshell cylinders played the same role in Choiseul, as did forehead apparel made from porpoises' and dogs' teeth in Malaita and parts of Makira.

Shell money is made in several places on Malaita and costs up to S$300 for each 10-strand length. Islanders sometimes buy coils of red-feather money in Temotu Province, where S$300 is again the going rate.

Musical Instruments
Bamboo panpipes are common on most of the larger islands – especially Malaita and Guadalcanal – and are made in sets, or singly like flutes. Bamboo tubes are used as stamping drums in Ontong Java and Malaita, while Vanikolo has hollow wooden ones. Dance sticks are made in Malaita and Santa Ana.

Tattoos
In the Solomons, tattooing is common among both Melanesians and Polynesians. Many patterns have a traditional significance depending on the age and social position of the wearer.

Facial engraving is practised on Malaita, where a grooved, unpigmented design is made using a bone to scrape the skin's surface. In some other parts of the Solomons, pigment is then applied, leaving a permanent design, usually in blue and black.

Polynesians were traditionally heavily tattooed and some from Ontong Java and Anuta still are. Rennell and Bellona used to be major centres of the art until about 50 years ago, before their mass conversion to Christianity.

There are several local variations on the positioning of tattoos. Northern Malaitan men wear them below the eye, while women there decorate their breasts. Ontong Java's people prefer their tattoos to be on their foreheads, while the back of a woman's thigh is the usual spot in the Reef Islands. The chest can be tattooed in Tikopia, just as it used to be in pre-Christian Rennell and Bellona.

Weaving
Most weaving is done without looms, using split bamboo, vines, cane and dried coconut and pandanus leaves. *Bukaware* baskets, trays, table mats and coasters are made in several parts of the Solomons, especially Guadalcanal. Bukaware gets its name from its resemblance to similar items from Buka Island in south-eastern Papua New Guinea. It's made from the *asa* vine and is very tough but slow to make. Other baskets are fashioned in Gilbertese settlements, especially Wagina.

Mats are made throughout the archipelago, including on Rennell and Bellona, where they are often of checked design. In addition, Gilbertese people make sturdy, brown sleeping mats out of pandanus leaf. Finely woven shoulder bags are produced on Rennell and Bellona from vine, while those made in the Reef Islands are decorated with tufts and tassels.

CULTURE
The immense variety of the Solomons' culture and customs reflects the existence of 107 indigenous languages and dialects among a population of only 346,000. Dances, ceremonies, funerals, weddings, initiations, status and authority often differ from island to island, and sometimes from one district to another within the larger islands. Yet there are common themes, particularly the acceptance of the obligation to pay for all services rendered. This is the same throughout the country.

Custom
You will hear the word 'kastom' (custom) used constantly when villagers refer to traditional beliefs and land ownership. If something is done in a certain way because of custom, this means it has always been done this way, and people consider it right to continue doing it this way. Breaches of custom are always deplored.

Dances, songs and stories depicting the past are still common. These usually celebrate either war, hunting, the natural world or the harvesting of certain crops. Cultural displays are usually colourful and varied, with many islands having several dances unique to themselves.

Most islanders still believe in magic. Some coastal dwellers say the spirits of a dead man can live for a time in sharks, birds and reptiles. Where this is so, the creature becomes tabu to eat. Instead, it's offered gifts. Ancestors, it seems, are particularly fond of returning as sharks in Malaita and Makira.

Village Life

About 84% of Solomon Islanders live in villages. Most settlements are coastal and close to freshwater springs. Each family has a small coconut plantation for copra production and cash income, and a few scattered vegetable plots.

The nearby bush or rainforest provides traditional crops, wild nuts, ferns and fruits, as well as material for leaf-house and canoe construction, rope and basket making, and firewood. The majority of villages are laid out with houses facing each other in two lines down the middle, though larger villages may have several similarly arranged streets. There's always a church in the more important places, often a primary school and a store, and sometimes a clinic and/or police post.

Avoiding Offence

Solomon Islanders are usually very indulgent towards outsiders' unintentional errors, but they do expect their rules to be observed. If you accidentally breach some minor rule, courtesy and friendly apologies are usually sufficient. However, private property is just that, and trespassing is not appreciated. Consequently, make sure you stick to the road when passing through a village. If you leave the highway to walk on a bush path, always ask the first person you meet for permission to use it. Either approval will be given straight away or you will be introduced to the chief for his ruling.

Land ownership and food growing are extremely delicate matters, so you should resist the temptation to pick fruit and flowers growing by the wayside. They may look untended, but they still belong to someone. The same applies to reefs.

Legendary People

Whether the Mongoes of Santa Isabel, the Afukere of Anuta, the Fiti-kai-kere of Tikopia, the Hiti of Rennell and Bellona, the Mumutambu of the Nggelas, the Voromangas and Sinipi of Choiseul, or the more widespread Masi and Kakamoras have ever lived, or still do so, can only be guessed at. Little is known of the fierce Mumutambu (who are believed to have died out a long time ago), of the monkey-like Sinipi, or of the Mongoes, who were seemingly too stupid to survive. The Masi apparently were similar – the kind of people every nation likes to have as the butt of its jokes.

People from Rennell and Bellona talk about the Hiti as if they really existed, and archaeological evidence supports this claim, even if it cannot confirm or deny the modern islanders' description of them as short and hairy. Archaeological evidence also suggests that the Afukere of Anuta might once have existed.

Kakamoras are the most widely reported of such people. Islanders tell of a pygmy race, or dwarf-sized aboriginal pre-Melanesian people, who hide in caves in the mountains of the larger islands such as Makira, Santa Isabel, Choiseul and Guadalcanal, as well as a few smaller ones like Vanikolo and Nendo.

Kakamoras are said to be like humans, but are only about one to 1.5 metres tall and chatter in an unintelligible language. Allegedly, they are caught on rare occasions. Some say a male Kakamora was found on Guadalcanal in 1969 but got away. Others tell of seeing them, describing them as 'wild people' – naked with very long, straight hair hanging to below their waists, short, sturdy legs and very strong, short, pointed teeth.

Kakamoras are apparently able to run very fast through the bush and to hop speedily across rocks and boulders. Despite their small size, they are believed to be as strong as three men. Kakamoras seldom attack people and are usually harmless – just shy. However, stories abound of local females being carried off by them. No expat or tourist women have been taken – yet! ∎

Melanesians always assess a foreigner's reaction to them by seeing whether the newcomer will share food with them. They will often offer food, usually a coconut or banana, on your arrival. They won't expect you to respond with any more than thanks if you're only with them a short time. But if you stay longer, they will expect you to pay them back. In the Melanesian world, nothing comes for free. At the same time, generosity with food is considered a great virtue.

Although islanders – particularly young children – may wear few or no clothes in some traditional areas, visitors to such regions should always be fully dressed. This applies even in those places where middle-aged men and elderly women are bare-chested, or young women naked or only wearing a grass skirt or a small T-piece over their genitalia.

Foreigners dressed in scant swimwear can cause a very negative reaction in a town. In remote areas, this applies even on the beach. Indeed, many islanders often swim fully dressed. Consequently, nude bathing is always to be avoided, regardless of whether you're male or female.

It is most unwise to collect geological specimens or pan for gold without the village chief's permission. If you do, you will be considered to be stealing from the landowners – both those of this generation and those as yet unborn.

Custom Fees

At certain historic and geologically interesting places, the villagers who are the traditional owners of the site charge a landing, or custom, fee. This may be to see a collection of ancestral skulls, a cavern or a thermal area, or to visit a war site, beach or tourist-oriented island village where ancient dances or ceremonies are regularly performed.

As the site or island belongs to someone, you have to pay the custom owner a fee. Unfortunately, prices as high as S$50 are occasionally asked, although figures between S$1 and S$5 are more common. To avoid the more extortionate amounts, plead poverty, telling them how much you'd like to see the site but that you can only spare S$2 or S$3, say. Some villagers will accept this, but others may seem to be totally indifferent as to whether you see the place or not. If this is so, don't expect to get away with anything less than the price they first asked.

Tabus

You'll hear the word '*tabu*' (pronounced 'tambu') frequently. (On Polynesian islands, it may instead be pronounced 'tapu'.)

From tabu comes the English word 'taboo'. In Pacific Island terms, this expression means 'sacred' or 'holy' as well as 'forbidden'. In its simplest form, it can even mean 'no entry' when written across a doorway or gate.

Traditionally, certain places were tabu, and some still are. These can only be approached with permission from the owners. Visiting them without permission will cause much local ill feeling, and you may be required to pay compensation.

Village and island life is beset with tabus, although rules can vary from place to place. Rural women's lives are particularly fraught with them. They may not stand higher than a male, nor can they step over a fire, as its smoke may rise higher than a man.

At the same time, men may not deliberately place themselves below women. So walking under a woman's clothesline or swimming under her canoe is forbidden. If a male visitor does this in some areas, everything involved will have to be destroyed and he'll have to pay compensation.

Menstruation and birth are surrounded by all sorts of tabus. In more traditional areas – especially in certain parts of Malaita – each village has an area set aside both for childbirth and for women to go during menstruation. The area is very tabu for men to visit. Women have to remain secluded in the menstrual huts until their time is passed, though they can usually be visited by a young girl with food and firewood if need be.

It would be a serious breach of custom if a woman were to refuse to go into confinement, continued to go to her garden, fished, or cooked publicly while pregnant. She would have to pay compensation to the chief if she did so, or leave. In the past it would have meant death. Women are also barred from going near certain men's tabu places, such as skull shrines, though small boys may do so once they're initiated.

Islanders say foreigners who breach certain tabus or go to a tabu place can catch custom sicknesses. Several expats have been suddenly struck down by strange illnesses after they have gone to places which they were told not to visit. Some have suffered even though they had no warning. One foreign woman, after falling sick, lost her straight blond hair. When it grew again, apparently it was black and curly! So always ask an adult islander whether it's all right to go to a particular place or not.

Ablutions are the same. Each sex has its own area. If you're staying in a village, check which is your section as soon as possible after arrival.

The Chief or Bigman
Although inheritance is a major factor in leadership among Polynesians, it's of no significance among Melanesians. Instead, the bigman cult prevails, though not to the same intense degree as in Papua New Guinea or Vanuatu. When you ask for the chief in a Melanesian village, you're really meeting the bigman. He is the one who is either the richest or the most successful at settling disputes and is therefore the most influential villager.

Anyone may ask the chief for assistance. However, in return, his – or, in Vella Lavella, possibly her – word must be obeyed. The chief or bigman won't decide on an issue immediately but will consult other influential villagers first, to decide whether or not, for example, a foreigner or group of foreigners can stay overnight in the village.

Wantoks
You will hear the expression 'wantok' repeatedly. In its simplest sense a wantok is someone who talks the same dialect, and

therefore has the same 'one-talk', or language. This is why many islanders tend to assume all English-speaking Europeans of the same religion are wantoks.

In Melanesian terms, all people from the same settlement are wantoks because of the communal nature of village land ownership, and the ethic of sharing goods and property between relations. However, true wantoks are only those of an extended family – relatives, close friends and their immediate family.

Custom requires you always to help your wantoks. This includes helping them build their house and providing them with shelter and food. To refuse help, however justifiably, is to bring shame on yourself, your family and your clan.

This is fine when you are surrounded by well-stocked gardens in island villages, but not if you live in the urban environment. An enterprising or well-educated islander comes to Honiara, gets a good job and rents a house. Soon the wantoks, who have neither money nor jobs, arrive expecting shelter and food. Whatever the urban islander has saved is squandered on them. The worst recent example was of 30 wantoks sharing a Honiara couple's two-bedroom flat, though one working adult with up to 20 dependent mouths to feed is not uncommon in the capital.

Improved education has encouraged resistance to such situations. However, the rewards of new-found affluence are not always sufficient inducement for enterprising islanders to brave the anger of their disappointed relatives.

This is why so many shops are Chinese-owned and so few are owned by islanders. As soon as an islander opens a trade store, relatives come by and demand free food.

Polynesian Ocean Voyaging
Although regular shipping services have replaced long-distance outrigger journeys, a few intrepid Polynesians still occasionally build sailing canoes. However, any expeditions they make are short compared with the great voyages of the past. If you ask how it's

done, islanders will tell you the secret lies in the use of *kavenga*, or star paths.

Certain stars are known to indicate the presence of an island. For example, Rigel (Manu in Polynesian) can indicate the position of Tikopia and Anuta. When a south-easterly wind is blowing, a large canoe's sail leans northward, whichever way the boat is tacking. Rigel is above the line of the masthead once the canoe is in either island's latitude.

Like Micronesians, Polynesians feel the pressure from the waves reflected back from land formations while far out at sea. The best method is for a man to lower himself into the water and feel the varied wave movements on his bare testicles.

When night skies are overcast, ocean-going canoeists navigate by means of *te lapa* – 'underwater lightning'. Small flashes of light appear two metres below the waterline, indicating the direction of an island. However, this natural feature, best observed 150 to 180 km out, disappears once land is close. It's quite distinct from the normal luminescence that accompanies the wakes of most craft, even ones as small as canoes.

Birds are an island navigator's best friend – especially species that roost ashore and fly out each day to coastal fishing grounds. Terns and gulls fly up to 30 or 40 km from home, while boobies venture as far as 60 km. The sight of any of these birds is therefore a sure sign that land is nearby.

RELIGION

About 96% of the Solomons' people are Christians. Around 34% are members of the Anglican-affiliated Church of Melanesia (COM) and about 19% are Roman Catholics. Both have resident archbishops, while the COM has assistant bishops in Isabel, Temotu and Makira/Ulawa provinces.

A further 18% of islanders belong to the South Seas Evangelical Church, 11% are United (the former Methodists), and 10% follow the Seventh Day Adventist (SDA) faith.

Of the remaining 4%, half are Bahais, Jehovah's Witnesses, or members of the Christian Fellowship Church, an indigenous breakaway movement from the Methodists which is active mainly in northern New Georgia and Vonavona. The remainder are followers of pre-Christian religions and are numerous in only a very few remote areas – mainly the mountains of eastern Malaita.

Most islanders are extremely devout in their belief, with practically every village having a church. Many country people attend an early morning service daily. In some areas aspects of the old religion, such as the ancient ancestor cults of inland Malaita, are followed alongside Christianity.

During the early years of the Protectorate, medicine and education were in the hands of the churches. When the financial burden became too great for them after WW II, the government took over most health services and teaching, though some hospitals and schools are still run by churches.

During the Protectorate period, some missions introduced divisions between differing church denominations by telling their members that followers of all other churches were unbelievers. In addition, certain missionaries were extremely strait-laced, banning traditional dances and art forms. However, most of the larger churches have recently shown a great deal of tolerance towards their rivals, and religious exclusiveness has declined considerably.

All the main denominations are represented in Honiara, with worship often in Pijin. You should be able to get the address of the nearest appropriate church and information about service times by telephoning one of the following numbers:

Church of Melanesia	☎ 21892/22297
Roman Catholics	☎ 21943/22795
South Seas Evangelical Church	☎ 22388
United Church	☎ 22488
Seventh Day Adventist	☎ 21191
Assembly of God	☎ 22847
Bahais	☎ 22475
Jehovah's Witnesses	☎ 22241

Warning

If you stay in remote villages or islands, you are sure to be asked what church, or 'mission', you belong to. However, you would be most unwise to be dismissive of religion, particularly Christianity, if you are a nonbeliever. Islanders are likely to dislike you strongly if you are hostile to Christianity. The message will get around very quickly and the nonviolent disdain shown towards you may be quite obvious.

LANGUAGE

Officially, there are 63 indigenous languages and a further 44 dialects. In addition, there are the three new arrivals – Solomon Islands Pijin, English and Gilbertese. Of the indigenous number, all but 13 languages and two dialects belong to the Austronesian or Malayo-Polynesian language group. Despite distinct physical differences between individual Melanesians and Polynesians, their languages have many similarities.

It's quite common for Melanesians from villages only a few km apart to speak mutually incomprehensible languages and to use Pijin to converse with each other. Consequently, there are now 11 languages with under 200 speakers each, including three with only one family surviving. At least one language and two dialects have become extinct within the last 30 years.

The 15 Papuan languages and dialects, thought to be considerably older than their Austronesian counterparts, are spread at random through the archipelago. Many people from Rendova, the Russell Islands, Savo and Vella Lavella, and all non-Polynesians in Temotu Province, speak Papuan tongues. Although it's generally thought they preceded the Austronesian speakers, they are restricted, like the Polynesians, to the country's fringes. This suggests they may have been driven out of the central chain of islands by southward-moving Melanesians.

Pronunciation

There are a number of differences between the pronunciation of indigenous words and that of English words. In the Solomons context, this is called prenasalisation, but it's not uniform throughout the country. Conse-

quently, problems with names and words can easily occur.

Here are some examples of indigenous pronunciation using English words. A number of the examples are described more fully in the paragraph following the list.

b	as in ramble
d	as in hundred
g	as in gate
gn	as in onion
kw	as in quickly
ng	as in singer
ngg	as in finger
nj	as in range
r	as in terrace
s	as in seal

B and **d** are pronounced by islanders as **mb** and **nd** respectively, while **ng** and **ngg** stand for the **g** sound. The English **ch** is spelt **s**, while **qu** is spelt **kw** and **j** appears as **nj**. **R** is usually rolled, while **gn** is pronounced **ny**, as in the Spanish **ñ**.

Pijin Blong Solomon

The national language of the Solomons is Solomon Islands Pijin, or Pijin for short. It's the English-based lingua franca throughout the country. This enables a speaker from one area to talk to people from totally different areas, even though they all speak different traditional languages.

Where does Pijin get its name? Some have suggested it comes from the Chinese for 'business', as the China coast was a frequent destination for early 19th-century sandalwood traders. Others note the word 'jargon' was used for Pijin in the 1870s, meaning 'broken' English.

Early 19th-century sailors stimulated the evolution of Pijin, while the recruitment of labour (including Solomon Islanders) from the 1860s to 1900s to work in Oceanic canefields, plantations and mines spread the language all over the Pacific. Islanders found their indigenous languages of little use because of the varied origins of their fellow workers. Their only means of communication was through whatever broken English they might have picked up aboard their recruiting ship. When they finally returned home, they often continued speaking Pijin, seldom bothering to use their home area's vernacular again.

By the 1930s, Pijin was being spoken by missionaries in many areas, helping to spread it further. Nowadays, although English is the official language of the administration, many government staff use Pijin in everyday conversation.

Solomon Islands Pijin – like similar languages in Papua New Guinea, Vanuatu, West Africa and along the old China coast – has been condemned by all and sundry, including the UN. They've said it's 'baby talk', a 'bastard language' or a 'mongrel lingo'. This is because many Pijin speakers use two versions. One is a simplified form used by islanders to their English-speaking employers. The second is the true Pijin, which they use among their fellow countryfolk. Since the 1970s, linguists have been treating this second one with respect.

In case you don't manage to learn it, don't despair. English is common in all the main centres and among people educated to secondary school level. Some young expat children – particularly girls between four and six – are remarkably good at learning Solomons languages, including Pijin. They will speak to their parents in English, to islander children from the area where they reside in the local language, and to other children in Pijin. This is a common phenomenon.

Grammar

Pijin is a blend of English words and Melanesian grammar. Unlike English, nouns and pronouns have no gender, and verb endings do not show time. If a gender isn't clear but needs to be identified, a word can be added to clarify it – eg *man pusikat*, meaning 'tom cat'.

Most of English's irregularities are absent. For example, although English plurals generally end in an 's', there are exceptions, such as 'women'. In Pijin, this would be *olketa mere*. The word 'olketa' is used here before the noun 'mere' to signify the plural.

Pijin has two grammatical features that English lacks. The first distinguishes between the first-person plural (we) when it includes the listeners *(iumi)* and when it excludes the listeners *(mifala)*. Secondly, Pijin distinguishes between both two and three, and the plural. Thus:

iutufala
the two of you
iutrifala
the three of you
iufala
you (more than three)
iumitufala
the two of us (including you)

There are a couple of other differences between the two languages. When two vowels are placed beside each other in Pijin, both vowels are always pronounced separately, unlike in English. An example is *ia*, meaning 'here'. Pijin also has no specific words for third-person pronouns (he, she, it), as does English. In Pijin the third person is *hem*, followed by *i* and the word – eg *hem i wanfala rabis man* meaning 'he is a useless person'.

Colourful Expressions

While English has about 60,000 words in common use, Pijin has around 3000. It takes quite a bit of ingenuity to fill this gap, with some very colourful expressions resulting. For example, there are no individual words for 'bull' or 'cow', only *bulumakao*. To identify which is the male, you must say *man bulumakao*. Again, should you want to speak about Prince Charles in Pijin, you would say *nambawan boe pikinini blong kuin* – 'first male child of the Queen'.

A number of words are perfectly correct and polite in Pijin, but not so in English. In English, for example, you would say 'break' or 'broken', in Pijin *bagarap*. An angry woman at an island medical clinic was heard to chastise a man who was bothering her: '*mi kam fo meresin long klinik ia, mi no kam fo faki*'. This translates as 'I came to this clinic for medicine, not sex'. Similarly, *haos blong mi, hem i bagarap long bigfala win* is 'my house was damaged in the cyclone'.

Take care also with expressions like *mektrabol, hambag, puspus* and *basta*. 'To commit adultery' is *mektrabol long hasban/ mere*; *hambag olobaot* means 'to sleep around'; while *puspus* is 'to have sex' and *basta* means 'illegitimate'.

Textbooks

Pijin Blong Yumi (A Guide to Solomon Islands Pijin) (Solomon Islands Christian Association, Honiara, 1978) by Linda Simons and Hugh Young is the best general guide to the language, though at present it only seems to be available in Honiara library's Pacific section. Another useful publication is *Buk blong Wei fo Raetem Olketa Wod long Pijin: How to spell words in Pijin* (SICA Pijin Literacy Project, Honiara, 1982), though it's almost entirely in Pijin.

Any time you spend learning this interesting new language will be time well spent. You're sure to find plenty to say, once you get the hang of Pijin.

Greetings & Civilities

yes
 ya
no
 no or *nating*
thank you
 tanggio
please
 plis
good morning
 gud moning
good afternoon
 gud aftanun
good night
 gud naet
see you later
 okei or *lukim iu*
no worries
 no seksek

Pronouns

I
 mi

you
 iu
he/she/it
 hem
we
 iumi
 (if more than three)
you (plural)
 iufala
 (if more than three)
they, all
 olketa

Other Useful Words

and
 an
if
 sapos
of
 blong
with
 wetim
more
 moa
better
 moabetta
now
 destaem noa
the best
 nambawan
the worst
 nambaten, nogud, rabis, bulsit
no, never, no chance
 nomoa
White man, European
 araikwao, waetimani
 tie vaka (in western areas)
White woman
 misis, waetman mere
Gilbertese
 sagabo
all
 olketa
small, slightly
 lelebit
plenty
 staka, plante
child
 pikinini

woman
mere, woman

good looking
naes bola

unemployed, aimless, wanderer
liu

chief
sif, bigman

diarrhoea
beleran

bathe, swim, shower
waswas

shop
stoa

credit
kaon

government
gavman

custom money
kastom mani

traditional clothes
kastom kaliko

the past
bifoa

to do
duim

to have
garem

to want
laekem

to hit
kilim

to kill
kilim finis

to die
dae finis

bedroom
rum blong bed

bathroom
rum blong waswas

kitchen
kisin

toilet
smol haos

to, for, at, on, about, by
long

far
longwe

nearby
kolsap

this side
saedkam

that side
saedgo

baggage
basket

the interior, bush
bus

to be, stay, remain
stap

post office
pos ofis

clinic
klinik

airfield
eapot

aircraft
plen

ship
sip

canoe
kanu

road
rod

car
ka

Accommodation

Where is the rest house?
Haos blong res hem I wea?

How much does it cost?
Haomas nao?

When can I eat here?
Wataem nao baebae mifala kaikaim ia?

Getting Around

How far is it?
Haomas longwe nao?

Where is the...?
Hem i wea...?

Where are you going?
Iu go-go wea?

Where have you been?
Iu stap long wea?

We must go now.
Iumi mas go-go nao.

I'm just walking around.
Mi wokabaot nomoa.

Go away!
Go-go baek!

Emergencies

Come at once!
Kam fastaem!
Where is the police station?
Stesin blong pulis hem i wea?
Where is the hospital?
Hospitol hem i wea?
Please may I use this telephone?
Plis kan mifala iusim telefon ia?
Please may I use this radio?
Plis kan mifala iusim redio ia?
How strong is this cyclone?
Haomas strong disfela big win nao?

Time & Dates

What is the time?
Waswe taem nao?
What day of the week is it?
Watkaen dei blong wik hem i nao tude?
It's one o'clock.
Taem hem save wan klok.

Other Useful Expressions

I would like to buy...
Mifala laek fo peim...
This is yours.
Desfala blong iufala.
It looks like...
Hem i lukim olsem...
We are living together.
Iumitufala i marit long bus.
I don't understand.
Mi no save (pronounced 'savvy').
She loves you.
Hem i gel daedae long iu.
There's no more meat/food.
No moa eni mit/kaikai i stap.
Who is he/she?
Hu nao hem?
What do you want?
Warem nao?
What's your name?
Watkaen nem blong iufala nao?
How old are you?
Haomas yia blong iu?
Do you speak our language?
Iufala save toktok languis blong Solomon?
How are you?
Hao iu stap?

I'm fine, thank you very much.
Mi orait, tanggio tumas.

Numbers

1	*wan, wanfala*
2	*tu, tufala*
3	*tri, trifala*
4	*foa, fofala*
5	*faev, faefala*
6	*siks, sikfala*
7	*seven, sevenfala*
8	*eit, eitfala*
9	*naen, naenfala*
10	*ten, tenfala*
11	*eleven, elevenfala*
12	*tuel,tuelfala*
13	*totin*
14	*fotin*
15	*fiftin*
16	*sikstin*
17	*seventin*
18	*eitin*
19	*naentin*
20	*tuenti*
21	*tuentiwan*
30	*toti*
40	*foti*
50	*fifti*
60	*siksti*
70	*seventi*
80	*eiti*
90	*naenti*
100	*handred*
1000	*taosin*

Polynesian Words

A few local words will come in handy if you spend some time on a Polynesian outlier.

European, White man
papalangi
White woman
waet woman, misis
Melanesian
tongahiti
good, good day
ngaoi
good morning
ngaoi te mahoata

good evening
ngaoi te ahiahi
good night
ngoi te po
good bye
ma'avai
hello
laoi te po
please
si'arei

thank you
auw'e
yes
o or *oo*
no
si'ai or *siei*
I like you.
Kuou efifia kiake.

Facts for the Visitor

VISAS & EMBASSIES

Entry visas are not required by British citizens or British protected persons, nor by nationals of almost all Commonwealth and most European countries. Nor are they needed by holders of passports from Fiji, Tunisia, Turkey, Uruguay or the USA. A visitor's permit is issued on arrival to citizens of all these countries.

Citizens of Belize, Brunei, Namibia and Vanuatu are the only Commonwealth nationals requiring visas to stay more than one week. Western European nations similarly affected include France, Ireland, Germany, Portugal, Austria, Andorra and Monaco. The same applies to all non-Commonwealth Asian, African and Pacific nations, and most Latin American and Arab countries.

Visas are required in all circumstances by citizens of former or continuing communist countries and Lebanon. Other travellers continuing their journey to another country within seven days, and holding reserved airline seats and tickets, are excused the need for a visa.

The Immigration staff at the airport usually give you a visitor's permit for between two weeks and one month. You can then extend it without much difficulty up to a total of three months in any period of 12 at the Immigration Office (☎ 22585) in Honiara itself, although you will be required to book your flight out. A second extension of a further three months is possible, but the officials will want to be sure you're not secretly working. Once this is all done, but not before, Immigration staff will extend your permit up to your departure date.

If you want to stay longer than six months, you'll have to apply in writing and see the chief immigration officer. Good manners, tidiness and polite behaviour all help on such occasions. You will need a very good reason to get his approval.

There are only three permanently operated Immigration offices in the country. These are at Honiara's Henderson Airport, in the capital itself and at Munda. Immigration officers regularly go to Gizo and Noro and occasionally visit Lata. Officially police and Customs staff no longer process tourists' documents, though in practice local police will do so as a temporary measure if you're stuck in an isolated spot.

Solomon Islands Consulates

The Solomon Islands has no overseas embassies, but two roving ambassadors cover Europe, Asia and the United Nations. The country has one consulate general, three honorary consulates and a permanent mission to the UN. The address of the UN mission (☎ (212) 599 6195) is Suite 800B, 820 2nd Ave, New York, USA. The consulate general (☎ (07) 221 7899) is at GPO Box 850, 6th Level, NAB Building, 255 Adelaide St, Brisbane 4000, Australia. The honorary consulate in Australia (☎ (02) 281 7955) is at Level 2, 72 Campbell St, Surrey Hills 2010, while the honorary consulate in Britain (☎ (081) 946 5552/1744) is at 17 Springfield Rd, London SW19 7AL, and the one in Japan (☎ 562 2331) can be reached c/- Kitano Construction Corp, 9-2 Ginza 1-Chome, Chuo-ku, Tokyo.

Foreign Embassies in the Solomons

Seven nations are represented in Honiara at ambassadorial level. It also has a consulate and a European Community (EC) representative.

The British High Commission (☎ 21705) is adjacent to the capital's post office. Nearby are the US Embassy (☎ 23890) and Australian High Commission (☎ 21561) in Mud Alley St. Also in Honiara's town centre are four other diplomatic offices. These are the Papua New Guinea High Commission (☎ 20561) in the Anthony Saru Building, the European Community Delegation (☎ 22765) and the New Zealand High Commission (☎ 21502) in the Y Sato Building, and the Japanese Embassy (☎ 22953) in the NPF Building. Only the Taiwanese Embassy (☎ 22187) is outside the capital's downtown area. It's two km away at Lenggakiki. There's also the Honorary German Consulate (☎ 22588) in the Y Sato Building. No other nations are represented in the Solomons.

DOCUMENTS
Naturally every visitor other than a working sailor must have a valid passport. (Sailors travelling on duty may use a sailor's book instead.) Every tourist has to have onward tickets and adequate funds. The officials will usually ask to see your tickets, although they are unlikely to want to check your money.

Vaccination certificates against yellow fever are required of anyone arriving by air within six days of leaving or transitting an infected area. Yellow-fever areas are in central Africa and northern South America.

International driving permits are accepted, as are most current national driving licences.

CUSTOMS
Customs officials meet every flight at Henderson Airport. There's also a branch at Honiara for all shipping using the capital's main wharf. Customs staff based at Munda also serve Noro, and there are officials at Tulagi, Yandina, Viru Harbour and Ringgi as well to deal with any international shipping calling there.

Regulations
As long as you're over 18, you may bring into the Solomons the usual 200 cigarettes, 250 grams of tobacco or cigars, or a combination of these. Also you can have two litres of spirits or the equivalent, and other dutiable goods up to S$40 in value.

All fruit and vegetables need an import permit from the Ministry of Agriculture & Lands (☎ 21430) in Honiara unless they come from New Zealand. Without it, they'll be destroyed, even if they're in packets with unbroken seals. Cats and dogs may only come in from Australia, New Zealand and Britain.

Police permits are required for guns and ammunition and any other weapons. Pornographic books, pictures, movies and videos are all banned, as is the importation and use of drugs.

MONEY
The local currency is the decimalised Solomon Islands dollar (S$). Banks still call it 'SBD' – a relic from the days before Independence, when it was the British Solomons dollar.

There are S$2, S$5, S$10, S$20 and S$50 notes, S$1 coins and 1, 2, 5, 10 and 20c coins. The copper 1 and 2c pieces, however, are now only seen when banks issue them, as they often do when converting foreign exchange. The Queen's portrait appears on older coins and bank notes, although this is changing as new notes are produced.

Up to S$250 may be taken out of the country in local currency. However, there are no restrictions on bank transfers abroad by expatriates of Solomons-derived earnings.

Exchange Rates
The current rate for the Solomon Islands dollar in relation to selected major international currencies as well as several neighbouring ones is:

A$1	=	S$2.11
C$1	=	S$2.35
US$1	=	S$2.78
UK£1	=	S$4.45
NZ$1	=	S$1.50
DM1	=	S$1.76
Y100	=	S$2.27
PNG K1	=	S$2.90
F$1 (Fiji)	=	S$2.22
100VT (Vanuatu)	=	S$2.56

Banks
Three commercial banks are represented in the country. These are the National Bank of the Solomon Islands (NBSI), the Australia & New Zealand Bank (ANZ) and the Westpac Banking Corporation.

Banks in Honiara should have no difficulty with travellers' cheques in most major international currencies. However, hotels and banks in the provinces may only be willing to accept travellers' cheques denominated in Australian, New Zealand or US dollars or UK pounds.

There are only three towns outside Honiara with banks. These are Gizo, Auki and Kirakira.

If you do travel around, you'll need to carry a lot of cash or open a savings account with the NBSI to use at their 48 local agencies (mainly post offices and stores) around the country. Changing foreign currency where there are no banks is hard, and the exchange rate may be poor even at post offices. Frequently only cash is acceptable.

You may notice a few branches of the Development Bank of the Solomon Islands (DBSI) in the provinces. Their business is solely to offer small loans to Solomon Islanders (especially in rural areas) to finance local business schemes.

Credit Cards

Major credit cards are accepted in Honiara by the hotels, car-rental agencies, airlines and some of the tour operators and restaurants, and by a few organisations in Gizo. Both the ANZ and Westpac banks in the capital acknowledge their own credit cards – Visa and MasterCard respectively – for cash withdrawals. Outside Honiara and Gizo, plastic money is very seldom used.

Costs

It's easy to spend S$70 a day in Honiara without doing very much. It'll be S$120 plus if you stay at a moderate hotel rather than at a budget hostel, even if you only take a few minibus rides and eat at cheap places. If you're eating well, scuba diving, renting cars and buying souvenirs, then up it goes.

Much of the food consumed by visitors in the capital is imported and therefore expensive. However, fish, fruit and vegetables are all cheap in the markets.

Supermarket prices vary considerably,

though they are usually dearer than those in Chinese stores. Sugar and rice are S$1.40 and S$2.40 a kg respectively, while eggs are S$6.80 a dozen and 500-gram packs of butter are about S$1.60.

Money goes much further once you've left Honiara. While you should be able to have a pleasant, but quiet, day in Gizo for around S$70, the other provincial capitals, where most accommodation is self-catering, should cost you less than S$50.

If you are staying in a village, S$10 to S$20 should be quite sufficient, depending on how much you are charged for food and accommodation. A good idea is to offer the chief a gift of betel nut or tobacco sticks, or give your hosts some goods from the local trade store in lieu of board and lodging.

Tipping

Neither tipping nor begging is acceptable in the Solomons, and visitors are asked to respect this. Melanesians consider tipping, or giving money to beggars, creates an obligation which the receiver has to return. Naturally, a person can't do so if you pass on immediately, before he or she can pay you back. Consequently, a friendly smile and 'thank you' are sufficient.

Bargaining

There is no bargaining, bribery or black market in the Solomons. Occasionally people in isolated areas will quote you grossly inflated prices for handicrafts, custom fees or accommodation, mainly because they have no idea what the current price would be in Honiara. While trying to bargain won't be accepted or understood, you can instead say that you just can't afford that much. Then tell them what you can afford, and see if they will agree to it. With luck they will accept your offer. Otherwise, the only alternatives you have are to pay the first price they ask, or to decline politely to buy.

WHEN TO GO

The coolest months in which to visit the Solomons are from June to September. However, humidity levels are usually lowest from October to December, though December can be hot – especially in Honiara. Cyclones have occasionally occurred near the middle or end of the year, but with nothing like the frequency with which they occur during the period from January to April. Consequently, seas are calmer – both for boat rides and for underwater visibility for scuba diving and snorkelling – during the later months of the year.

June to August is a time of public holidays and festivities. Six of the country's eight provinces have their annual holiday at this time, and the Queen's Birthday and Independence Day – the best times to see traditional dancing displays during the year – are in June and July respectively. Local schools are also on holiday at this time, so if you have children of your own, this is a good time for them to meet their local counterparts.

WHAT TO BRING

People wear light, cotton summer clothes all year round. The style is always casual. Most men wear short-sleeved, open-necked shirts and shorts to work, with a singlet (ie vest) underneath to absorb perspiration. Ties and jackets are seldom seen. Women are similarly casual, but it's always worth packing something dressy but cool for the odd special occasion. For the less-affluent male islanders, T-shirts, shorts and rubber thong- type sandals are standard gear.

It's too hot to wear raincoats during showers, so a small collapsible umbrella is always useful. Villagers use disposable banana leaves or old copra sacks instead.

Sea travel can be quite cool, especially after scuba diving at night. A light pullover can be useful at such times.

You will need to wear special shoes for reef walking. Razor-sharp coral tears through sneakers in a few weeks. Diving boots give the best protection, though they tend to be rather expensive and only available at dive shops. Plastic sandals are ideal for canoe travel, though it's unwise to wear them around muddy villages because of possible hookworm infestation.

Sleeping bags or sleeping sheets are always useful for bushwalking, especially if you are camping out in villages. You'll also need strong, but light, footwear – canvas baseball boots are the best – if you plan to climb volcanoes or make your way through the undergrowth of a tropical rainforest. Jeans or long trousers are always necessary when walking through scrub to protect you against scratches, the stinging nalato plant and the blister-raising hailasi tree.

A small pack of fishing tackle allows you to catch your own food if it's running short on board ship, and plastic bags are useful for wrapping your clothes and camera gear in when travelling by motor canoe. Soft sports or sausage bags (preferably water resistant) are much better for canoe travel (as they fit easily aboard such craft) than backpacks and suitcases, which tend to be bulky and cumbersome. Other useful items include candles, matches, a flashlight (ie torch), a water bottle, a corkscrew and a can-opener. If you're going camping, or want to reduce the cost of eating out, a light, plastic picnic set can be a great money-saver. It can make all the difference between skimping on your meals in restaurants and eating in reasonable style in private.

TOURIST OFFICES
Local Tourist Offices

The Solomon Islands Tourist Authority (SITA) (☎ 22442), beside the Solomon Kitano Mendana Hotel in Honiara, has several handouts about the nation's hotels, restaurants, clubs and scuba sites. They can also advise you how to get around the country, including some of its more isolated places. Airline staff can help you with lodgings, while hotels and guesthouses can often provide you with illuminating background data about local customs and traditions.

Overseas Reps

There are two agencies in Australia that can advise on Pacific destinations, including the Solomons. These are the Pacific Island Travel Centre (☎ (02) 262 6011), 7th Floor, 39/41 York St, Sydney 2000, and General Travel Marketing Services (☎ (02) 436 0566/438 4555), Suite 20, 37 Alexander St, Crows Nest, Sydney 2065.

USEFUL ORGANISATIONS

Two private holiday booking agencies – one in Honiara, the other in Gizo – act as information centres, particularly about Western Province. These are Island Chain Holidays (☎ 20385) in Honiara, and the Western Province Tourist Information Office in Gizo, which is closely associated with the Paradise Lodge there. If you can't find out booking details for some remote accommodation place you want to stay at, ask either of these two, or SITA.

BUSINESS HOURS & HOLIDAYS
Business Hours

Banks Banking hours in Honiara are from 8.30 am to 3 pm Monday to Friday, though some branches outside the capital close for lunch between noon and 1 pm.

Offices Government offices are open from 8 am to noon and 1 to 4 pm Monday to Friday. Private businesses close half an hour later, and also operate on Saturday mornings till noon.

Shops Most shops are open from 8.30 am to 5 pm Monday to Friday and till noon on Saturdays. Chinatown is the only part of Honiara open on Saturday afternoons. Some of its shops also trade on Sunday mornings, as do a few other Chinese shops in the town centre. The Honiara branch of the Solomon Islands Consumers Supermarket stays open to 5.45 pm Monday to Friday and also operates on Saturday and Sunday mornings.

Trade Stores Village trade stores open whenever there are customers willing to buy. This includes Sundays if the shopkeeper's around and is not too strict about religion. However, it's very hard to persuade SDA members to open their stores on Saturday, which is their worship day.

National Holidays

The nine annual holidays in the Solomons are:

1 January
: *New Year's Day*

March/April
: *Easter* – Good Friday, Holy Saturday and Easter Monday

May
: *Whit Monday* – eighth Monday after Easter

June
: *Queen's Birthday* – usually second Friday in month

7 July
: *Independence Day*

August
: *Saturday Preceding Liberation Day*
: *Liberation Day* – last Monday in month

25 December
: *Christmas Day*

26 December
: *National Thanksgiving Day*

When a national holiday falls on a weekend, the accompanying public holiday is usually taken on the preceding Friday or following Monday, except in the cases of Holy Saturday and the Saturday Preceding Liberation Day.

Provincial Holidays

Each province has its own holiday, although Choiseul has yet to chose a day.

8 June
: Temotu

29 June
: Central

8 July
: Isabel

1 August
: Guadalcanal

3 August
: Makira/Ulawa

15 August
: Malaita

7 December
: Western

Provincial holidays are transferred to a weekday in the same way as national ones are when they fall on a weekend. Isabel's holiday on the day following Independence Day is sometimes merged with the national holiday.

CULTURAL EVENTS

Independence Day celebrations in early July are the Solomons' most important annual festival. Although there are festivities in every provincial centre, the largest ones are in Honiara. These include sporting events, a military parade and custom dances by performers from different islands.

There are also parades in Honiara on Whit Monday, when war veterans march to the war memorial opposite the central bank, and on the Queen's Birthday, when police march through the capital. This is followed by sporting events and custom dancing.

Liberation Day celebrates the events in August 1942 which led to the WW II Allied victory in the Solomons. Other annual events include:

March
: Annual yam-increase ceremonies in Santa Catalina

May/June
: *Wogasia* – week-long marriage ceremonies and mock clan wars in Santa Catalina

POST & TELECOMMUNICATIONS
Post

There's no postal delivery, so if you're writing to someone in the Solomons, write to a post office box or to a work address. Otherwise, the country's nine post offices in the eight provincial capitals and Munda, and most of the 98 postal agencies, offer a poste restante service. Air mail takes slightly less than a week from Australia and New Zealand, though surface deliveries take two months.

Internal postal deliveries are frequent to the main islands. However, outlying areas are serviced solely by ships, and may receive their mail only once every four to six weeks.

Philatelic Bureau

Solomon Islands stamp issues and first-day covers number between five and six new sets annually, varying from 24 to 37 stamps a

Telephone

There are 12 automatic telephone exchanges serving the country's 3800 telephone subscribers, 80% of whom live in Honiara.

In addition, there's a teleradio (ie radio telephone) network connecting isolated communities. However, the only telephone boxes in the country are the ones in Honiara's Solomon Telekom Building (☎ 21164), and these are reserved for overseas calls.

Service Messages If you want to send a telegram to one of the many villages or islands where there is no telephone or teleradio yet, you do this by contacting them with a service message: villagers regularly listen in to daily broadcasts by the Solomon Islands Broadcasting Corporation (SIBC) between 6 and 8 pm in case there are any contacts of this type.

If you want to send a service message or use the teleradio system, dial 106 or 107 respectively, or call into any Solomon Telekom office during normal working hours. There's one in every provincial centre except Choiseul Bay, and also at Munda, Noro and Yandina. If you're in an isolated part of the country and want to send a radio message, try the local clinic; it may cost you up to S$5 a time, however.

International Calls The new Domsat (ie domestic satellite) system allows international calls to be made from all parts of the country. If you want to make one, dial 102. To call the Solomons instead, the international dialling code is the ISD access code of the country you're phoning from, followed by 677 and the subscriber's number.

Fax, Telex & Telegraph

The Solomons has an international communications service for telex, facsimile and data links in addition to telegrams and telephone calls. The service operates 24 hours a day, seven days a week. If you want to send a telex, there's a public telex facility at Solomon Telekom in Honiara, which is open Monday to Friday between 7.30 am and 10

year. Recent designs have included crop pests, cowrie shells, Solomon Islands dancers, birds and reptiles. Prices vary between S$2.35 and S$5.75 for each new issue, depending on the number and value of the individual stamps. Inquiries can be made to the Solomon Islands Philatelic Bureau (☎ 22108), c/- GPO Box G31, Honiara. It's beside Solomon Telekom in Mendana Ave.

pm, and from 8 am to noon on Saturdays, Sundays and public holidays.

You can also send a faxlet (ie a personalised faxed message) through local Telekom offices for S$5. Your communications will be read out over the SIBC before 7 pm, and your correspondents will be advised where to collect them. For S$6 each you can have the faxlets delivered if they're addressed to a town where there's a Telekom office.

TIME
Solomons time is GMT plus 11 hours. It's one hour ahead of Australia's Eastern Standard Time. Noon in Honiara is 1 am in London, 7 pm in New York and Toronto, 5 pm in San Francisco, and 11 am in Sydney and Port Moresby. Local time is the same as in Vanuatu, but one hour behind Fiji and New Zealand. Time is fluid in the tropics. Don't be too surprised if things happen a bit later than planned. However, businesses, airlines and tourist activities operate on time.

ELECTRICITY & GAS
Power and lighting is provided in only 10 centres. These are Honiara, Gizo, Auki, Tulagi, Kirakira, Buala, Lata, Munda, Noro and Yandina. The current is 230/240 V, 50 cycles AC, and uses flat three-pin plugs and bayonet sockets of the Australian type. There's no piped gas supply, but bottled gas is available in most large stores.

LAUNDRY
Honiara's hotels have a 24-hour clothes cleaning service six days a week through the local laundry, Solclean (☎ 22055), in White River Village. Similar services are available elsewhere around the country at the more expensive lodgings. However, you'll have to pay one of the staff or owner's family members personally to do it for you in cheaper places, or wash your clothes yourself. While a hotel might charge you S$1.70 for a shirt, a family member at a village rest house would probably be happy with 75c.

WEIGHTS & MEASURES
The old imperial system of miles, yards, feet, inches, pounds and ounces dies hard in the islands. Although the metric system has taken over in Honiara's shops and garages, market people still talk in terms of pounds, even when their scales are denominated in kg. Many people outside the capital continue to talk of miles (both statute and nautical), while fuel for motor canoes is still almost invariably measured in gallons. There's a metric/imperial conversion table at the back of this book.

BOOKS & MAPS
General
Some of the books mentioned below are now out of print. However, you may be able to obtain copies through your library. Otherwise, the Pacific section of the National Library in Honiara should have one, though you will have to read it there.

Ann Stevensons' *Solomon Islands* (Solomon Islands Tourist Authority, Honiara, 1988) is a useful, well-illustrated background to the country in booklet form. Another good general book is Charles E Fox's *The Story of the Solomons* (Pacific Publications, Sydney, 1975). Fox, a New Zealand missionary who spent the majority of his working life in the Solomons, writes as if he were himself a Solomon Islander. Its only competitor is Janet Kent's *The Solomon Islands* (Wren Publishing, Sydney, 1972), which covers the same subject. Both books were written at the twilight of the colonial period.

A charming tale of the prewar colonial era, suddenly brought short by the Japanese invasion in 1942, is Gwen Cross' autobiography *Aloha Solomons* (USP, Suva, 1978). An entertaining travelogue which ends up in the Solomons is Justin Wintle's *Heat Treatment: The Oriental Travels of an Amorous Hypochondriac* (Penguin, London, 1990). He finds Melanesia to be just as intriguing as Asia, where his journey began.

Yours in His Service (USP, Honiara, 1990) by George G Carter is the biography of

Belshazzar Gina of New Georgia who was ordained a Methodist (now United) Church priest in the late 1930s, and recounts his subsequent life, including war service.

History

The Search for the Islands of Solomon, 1567-1838 (Clarendon Press, Oxford, UK, 1969) by Colin Jack-Hinton records the efforts of explorers first to locate, then to relocate, the Solomons, and finally to fill the geographical gaps in the outside world's knowledge of the group. Judith Bennett's *Wealth of the Solomons* (University of Hawaii Press, Honolulu, 1987) is the third in the masterly Pacific Islands Monograph Series, and is a very informative history of the archipelago from 1800 to 1978. *Passage, Port and Plantation* (Melbourne University Press, 1973) by Peter Corris is an illuminating history of the labour recruitment of Solomon Islanders for Queensland and Fijian plantations between 1870 and 1914.

Peter Dillon of Vanikolo (Oxford University Press, Melbourne, 1975) by J W Davidson, and edited by U H K Spate, is an account of the Irish trader-explorer's discovery in 1826 of the remains of the lost French La Pérouse expedition, and also of sandalwood in Vanuatu the previous year. Hector Hothouse's *White Headhunter: the extraordinary true story of a white man's life among headhunters of the Solomon Islands* (Angus & Robertson, North Ryde, Sydney, 1988) is a reconstruction of the life and times of the Scotsman John Renton, who lived from 1868 to 1875 at Sulufou, Malaita, and whose name is remembered with affection there even now.

WW II Wartime literature relates mainly to the Guadalcanal Campaign and coastwatching activities. Eric Felot's *The Coast Watchers* (Lloyd O'Neil Pty Ltd, Melbourne, 1975) tells of their lonely and dangerous vigil far behind Japanese lines. Another one is D C Horton's *Fire Over the Islands: The Coastwatchers of the Solomons*

(A W & A H Reed, Sydney, 1970). A more recent book is W Lord's *Lonely Vigil – Coastwatchers of the Solomons* (Viking, New York, 1977).

H Macquarie's book *Vouza and the Solomon Islands* (Angus & Robertson, Sydney, 1946), written shortly after WW II, celebrates the country's national hero Jacob Vouza, his daring wartime exploits and those of other similarly courageous islanders.

A notable publication is *Savo* by Richard F Newcomb (Ure Smith, Sydney, 1961). This tells the story behind the costly errors which caused one of the US Navy's worst defeats. *Guadalcanal Diary* (Random House, 1943) by war correspondent Richard Tregaskis is an interesting eyewitness account of the fighting on Guadalcanal in August 1942. A synopsis of the events of the time is the *Guadalcanal Campaign* (The Tourist Authority, Solomon Islands, Honiara, 1982).

Among Those Present (Her Majesty's Stationery Office, London, 1946) is a fascinating chronicle of the WW II exploits of those in the British-ruled parts of the Pacific. This book pays credit to the many contributions made by islanders, especially those in the Solomons. *The Big Death: Solomon Islanders Remember WW II* (jointly published by the Institute of Pacific Studies, Suva, Fiji, and the Solomon Islands College of Higher Education & USP, Honiara, 1988) by Geoffrey M White and others is a fascinating collection of memories by various islanders who took part in WW II. It's written from their viewpoint and dispels quite a few British-inspired myths about the war.

The US Navy, Marines and Army all published accounts of their part in the Solomons campaign soon after WW II. Scuba divers find these invaluable guides when locating war wrecks or identifying cargo details. These include John N Rentz's *Marines in the Central Solomons* and *Bougainville & The North Solomons* (both reissued by Battery Press, Nashville, Tennessee, 1989). Another is *The Guadalcanal Campaign* (Battery Press, Nashville, Tennessee, 1990) by John L Zimmerman.

Anthropology

Tikopia & Anuta The small outlying islands have been preferred by anthropologists to the larger ones. Raymond Firth set the tone with his remarkable *We, The Tikopia* (Allen & Unwin, London, 1936) about his studies there between 1928 and 1929. Firth wrote several other books, including *History and Traditions of Tikopia* (The Polynesian Society, Wellington, New Zealand, 1961), in which he recorded the island's history.

Dr D E Yen & Janet Gordon's *Anuta: A Polynesian Outlier in the Solomon Islands* (Bernice P Bishop Museum, Honolulu, 1973) was based on their field trip made to the island in 1973. Richard Feinberg, who had been on the same expedition, wrote several books based on material he collected at the time, including *Anuta: Social Structure of a Polynesian Outlier* (Institute of Polynesian Studies, Honolulu, 1981).

Rennell & Bellona An American, Samuel Elbert, and two Danes, Torben Monberg and Rolf Kuschel, wrote extensively about Rennell and Bellona between 1965 and 1981. Elbert & Monberg's *From The Two Canoes* (Danish National Museum, Copenhagen, and the University of Hawaii Press, Honolulu, 1965) gives a fascinating account of the history of the two islands and the dramatic desertion of their old ways in 1938. Elbert followed this with two dictionaries, the first translating the languages of Rennell and Bellona into English and the second doing the reverse. Both were published by the Danish National Museum, Copenhagen, in 1975 and 1981 respectively. He was helped with the second one by Kuschel and a Polynesian, Toomasi Taupongi.

Other Polynesian Studies Ian Hogbin had several of his works published, including *Experiments in Civilisation* (Routledge, London, 1939), which is about his period on Ontong Java in 1927.

If you wondered how small sailing canoes could journey the 1500 km between minute dots in the ocean such as Ontong Java and Tikopia, the answer is in *The Voyaging Stars: Secrets of the Pacific Island Navigators* by David Lewis (Collins, Sydney, 1978). Its fascinating text uses islanders' own accounts to explain how immense trans-Pacific journeys were made by Micronesian and Polynesian canoeists, including Solomon Islanders, right up to the 1950s.

Malaita W G Iven's *Island Builders of the South Pacific* (Seeley Services, London, 1930) details the everyday life of the Lau people, the builders of the artificial islands of north-eastern Malaita. *'Elota's Story: The Life and Times of a Solomon Islands Big Man* (Queensland University Press, Brisbane, 1978) edited by Roger M Keesing is the fascinating life story of one of Malaita's last warrior-chiefs, who was also a very capable peacemaker.

Art & Archaeology

Grass Roots Art of the Solomons – Images and Islands edited by John and Sue Chick (Pacific Publications, Sydney, 1978) has a wealth of detail about every kind of pictorial and sculptural art form found in the Solomons, and where it's still made.

If archaeology is more your interest, there's the *Solomon Islands National Sites Survey* (National Museum, Honiara, 1979) by D Miller, listing a number of ancient sites around the country, especially in Simbo.

The Solomons & the Modern World

Both major incidents in Malaita's response to the 20th-century world are covered in well-researched books. *Lightning Meets the West Wind: The Malaita Massacre* (Oxford University Press, Melbourne, 1980) by Roger Keesing & Peter Corris is the story of William Bell, the district officer killed by Kwaio tribesmen in 1927. It reveals the tensions created by colonialism and its effect on the lives of certain individuals involved, particularly Bell himself and Basiana, the Malaitan tribal leader.

The Maasina Rule Movement edited by Hugh Laracy (USP, Suva, 1983) is about noncooperation with the return of colonial authority after Malaita's comparative freedom during WW II.

Pacific Writers

The University of the South Pacific (USP) has encouraged writers from all over the Pacific to build up a body of written material about their countries.

Ples Blong Iumi: The Solomon Islands, the Past Four Thousand Years (USP & the Solomon Islands College of Higher Education, Suva & Honiara, 1989) by Sam Alasia & others, and edited by Hugh Laracy, contains contributions by 14 Solomon Islanders about differing aspects of their country. These include culture, social change and the past. In contrast, *Hostage* (USP, Honiara, 1988) by Sam Alasia is a book of personal poems.

Several works have been written by former parliamentarians and government officials. *Zoleveke: A Man from Choiseul* (USP, Suva, 1980) by Gideon Zoleveke is mainly about a Choiseul man who became a Cabinet minister in several pre-Independence governments. *From Pig-Theft to Parliament: My Life Between Two Worlds* (USP & the Solomon Islands College of Higher Education, Honiara, 1989) by Jonathan Fifi'i, and translated and edited by Roger Keesing, tells of the author's childhood in eastern Malaita, the Marching Rule Movement, and life as a parliamentarian. *Kanaka Boy* (USP, Suva & Honiara, 1985) by Sir Frederick Osifelo is the autobiography of the first Solomon Islander to be knighted.

Novels

The most distinguished author so far to write about the Solomons is James Michener. His *Tales of the South Pacific* (Macmillan, New York, 1947) and *Rascals in Paradise* (Secker & Warburg, London, 1957) have plenty of racy tales in them. The one about Mendaña's wife and the hard time she gave Quiros in *Rascals in Paradise* is my favourite.

Bring Another Glass (Angus & Robertson, Sydney, 1944) by Georgina Seton is a period thriller set on a mythical island with a strong resemblance to the Solomons. Ann

M Kengalu's *Murder on the Mataniko Bridge* (Delaponte, Honiara, 1986) is about a fictitious murder investigation with a love element intertwined in it, and contains several informative asides as to how local people view both expats and certain other islanders. *Naismith's Dominion* (Bantam Australia, Moorebank, Sydney, 1990) by Peter Corris is an entertaining story set in a fictional British protectorate, and has close parallels to the events of 1927 in Malaita.

Illustrated Books

Reflections on Melanesia (Crawford House, Bathurst, New South Wales, Australia, 1990) by Michael McCoy contains a wealth of beautiful pictures above and below water, from both the Solomons and Papua New Guinea. Kevin Deacon's *Australia and The Pacific: Exploring the Islands and Underwater World* (Simon & Schuster, Sydney, 1989) is a very fine collection of underwater pictures taken at various dive sites throughout the Pacific, including a number in the Solomons.

Women

Pacific Women: Roles and Status of Women in Pacific Societies (USP, Suva, 1988), edited by Taiamoni Tongamoa, assesses the changing situation of Solomons women in one of its six chapters.

Cooking

Indu Baburam's *Island Cook Book* (Brian Lowndes Print Ltd, Walsall, UK, 1986) contains a range of mouthwatering local recipes, some of which had previously only been recorded orally.

Yachting

Alan Lucas' *Cruising The Solomons* (Castle Books, Sydney, 1981) is a useful guide for yachties. With details of many tiny harbours, it shows a yacht to be an ideal means of exploring the Solomons as so many of its attractions are coastal.

Bookshops

There are nine book-sales outlets in the

Solomons, of which five sell church literature only. The other four shops are all in the Honiara area. The one selling the most interesting material on the Pacific and the Solomons is USP in Kukum. The Solomon Islands Tourist Authority also has a few useful booklets. Otherwise, the Stationery Shop in the Anthony Saru Building sells paperbacks, while the Bookshop beside Solomon Airlines has magazines for sale, as well as stationery and posters.

Two of the five church bookshops are in the capital. The Hon Lit Christian Bookshop is in Honiara itself, while the Adventist Book Centre is in Kukum. Auki has two branches of the Auki Bookshop, and Gizo Stationery & Sportswear is in Gizo's central area.

Libraries & Reading Rooms

The Pacific section of the National Library, immediately behind the Honiara Town Library, is the place to go if you are interested in the country's history or culture. You can also try USP's library, which has material from all over Oceania.

There are seven other centres around the country with libraries. These are Gizo, Tulagi, Auki, Lata, Kirakira, Buala, and Falamai on Mono Island. Their selections are limited and donations of quality books are always gratefully received.

The seven embassies and high commissions in Honiara, as well as the European Community Delegation and the Peace Corps, all have reading rooms. Their literature is mainly for people who want to know about the countries concerned, and includes newspapers for their own nationals to keep up to date with. The Peace Corps in Lenggakiki has the most material on the Solomons.

Maps

Ordnance survey maps are available at Ministry of Agriculture & Lands' offices in each provincial centre. Stocks at some may be low, though the Honiara branch (☎ 21511), between Mendana and Hibiscus Aves, has a full supply of charts, tidetables and maps. The latter cost from S$12 to S$20 each.

MEDIA

If you don't expect to leave Honiara but want to hear Pijin spoken, simply tune into the radio. If you'd like to know what the real local issues are, read every paper from end to end. Although some may have Pijin names, their texts are in English.

Newspapers

The government publishes *Solomon Nius* monthly and distributes it free of charge. It's partly official gazette, partly news tabloid and comes out on Thursdays.

The *Solomons Star*, costing S$1, is a privately owned weekly published on Fridays. It has thoughtful features and 'Letters to the Editor' sections which regularly discuss the problems created by rapid development and urbanisation.

A 50c bimonthly publication called *Link* has a strong educational connection and an astute eye for issues. There's also a bimonthly journal published in Gizo called *Sunset News*. It's the journal of Western Province, costs 40c and contains features, stories and poems.

The *Solomons Voice*, costing S$1 in Honiara and S$1.20 outside the capital, comes out on Wednesdays. Its editorial style is quite forthright for the Pacific, where controversial viewpoints are often studiously avoided so as not to cause offence.

Radio

There are radio stations in Honiara, Gizo and Lata and long-term plans for two more at Auki and Kirakira. Programmes are in both English and Pijin, with local and overseas features, including news broadcasts from Britain and Australia. Overall, Honiara's airtime is 119 hours a week between 6 am and 11 pm daily. Gizo and Lata's services operate between 4 and 8 pm Monday to Friday only.

TV & Video

The only TV in the Solomons at present is satellite TV from Australia at some of the hotels. However, video has a growing following in the capital, and is available at the Mendana and Honiara hotels.

FILM & PHOTOGRAPHY
Film

Bring plenty of film with you. You'll easily race through a roll or two whenever you go to an island dance night at a hotel or see a cultural display. Don't wait till you get to the Solomons to buy your camera, as there's only a handful of 35 mm ones for sale – all in Honiara.

Film stocks are limited to Honiara and Gizo, and are mainly 64 ASA 35 mm slides and 100 ASA prints. If you prefer faster material than this, bring your own supplies. Print film can be developed quickly in the capital, though slides usually have to be sent overseas.

Film needs to be protected from heat and humidity in the Pacific. Sachets of silica crystals will protect your equipment from moisture but more important is to keep your camera and film in a cool place.

Photography

It's wise to avoid the midday sun when you are taking pictures. The best times are before 9.30 am and after 4 pm. Otherwise, you may have to underexpose your shots slightly to avoid glare.

If your camera is an automatic one, it may overadjust to the Solomons strong light, causing dark-skinned faces and rainforest views to come out shadowy. Most professional photographers recommend manual settings for such pictures.

Take a flash with you to the evening hotel cultural dances. It's also useful for house interiors or for taking close-ups in the jungle dimness. A telephoto lens is invaluable on those occasions when something interesting is going on, but you'd prefer to remain unobtrusive.

Whenever you want to photograph anyone, always ask first. Most people are very happy to be filmed, though there are a few exceptions. Children are extremely photogenic and at times seem to have no greater fun out of life than to be photographed,

expecting nothing in return other than your thanks. Even so, you should seek their permission first.

Adults will usually accept your request to take their photo, though elderly women in rural areas may be reluctant to be photographed by foreign men. Some young women may feel they have to know you first, while others will have no problem with it at all.

HEALTH

The visitor to the Solomons can expect reasonably healthy conditions in the country's urban centres. Despite this, care has to be taken against malaria everywhere, including Honiara. Water purity cannot always be relied on, and hookworm is endemic in the countryside.

Other common illnesses in the Solomons are tuberculosis, gastric troubles and childhood respiratory infections. Malnutrition, though unknown in the past, has begun to be seen in some city children who have only white rice, biscuits and soft drinks in their diet, and in some beer-consuming adults. However, the infant (first-year) mortality rate continues to fall, and at 43 per thousand is slightly better than that of the Philippines.

Health-Care Facilities

Basic medical services are free at the Solomons' 11 hospitals, regardless of whether they are owned by the government or the church. The main hospital is in Honiara, with Western Province hospitals at Gizo, Nila and Munda. In Malaita they're at Kiluufi (near Auki), Malu'u and Atoifi, while Temotu, Isabel, Choiseul and Makira/Ulawa provinces have one each at Lata, Buala, Sasamungga and Kirakira respectively. There are also another 130- odd clinics and aid posts spread around the country.

The facilities at clinics vary considerably. Some are large and have eight or more beds in them. Others have only one bed with no bedding, and only one old chair for the nurse and patients to share. Stocks of medicine can be equally variable.

The majority of doctors are based in hospitals, while a few others are spread around the capital. Dental care is available at Honiara, Kiluufi and Gizo hospitals, and there's also a private dentist in Honiara. The capital has the only two chemists in the country. However, there's no optician, so bring a spare pair of glasses, just in case.

If you go exploring some of the remoter parts of the archipelago, you may find you have to face some unexpected medical problems or emergencies in the process. However, a few basic precautions taken in advance should ensure your visit to the Solomons is free of serious illnesses.

Travel Health Information

There are a number of books on holiday health care which you may find worth taking with you. The best is *Staying Healthy in Asia, Africa & Latin America* by Volunteers in Asia. This very detailed and well-organised all-round guide is compact and easy to carry. Despite its name, it's also relevant to the Solomons. Another useful book, if you have children with you, is *Travel with Children* (Lonely Planet Publications, Melbourne, Australia, 1990) by Maureen Wheeler. It has plenty of basic advice on how to protect children's health while travelling – and maintain their interest too!

If you want personalised health advice, and are in Australia, you can get this from the Medical Advisory Service for Travellers Abroad, otherwise known as MASTA. It's in Brisbane (☎ (07) 253 5416) and Sydney (☎ (02) 905 6133). Unlike some travel agents whose information is not always reliable, MASTA has up-to-the-minute data on prevailing patterns of sickness worldwide, including in the Solomons.

It's always a good idea to see your doctor for health advice before travelling abroad anywhere, but you'll need to visit him or her especially before a Solomons trip, to get antimalarial medicines.

Predeparture Preparations

Health Insurance You'll have to pay fees for medical services if you'd prefer to be a private patient. It's certainly wiser to give yourself the choice, so you'll need to take out travel insurance before you leave home, including enough to cover medical treatment.

Some policies specifically exclude 'hazardous activities', such as scuba diving and even trekking (bushwalking in the Solomons). If you plan to do either of these, choose another company.

You may prefer a policy that pays the doctors and hospitals for you to one that requires you to pay them first and claim later. If you choose a claim-later policy, make sure you keep all your medical receipts if you get sick, including all related ones for travel and accommodation. Some policies even allow you to call collect (ie reverse charges) to an international centre so you can have an immediate assessment made of your condition.

Ensure your policy covers ambulances and an emergency flight home. If you have to stretch out, you will need two seats. Make sure it's not you who has to pay for the extra one!

Medical Kit It's essential to carry a small, basic medical kit, including some aspirin or Panadol for pains and fevers. An antihistamine, such as Benedryl, can be useful as a decongestant for colds or allergies, to ease any itching from insect bites and stings, or to help prevent motion sickness.

With the worldwide spread of AIDS, it's worth considering adding a sealed syringe and needle to your medical kit in case a local doctor has to give you an injection. As long as it's sealed so your medical kit contains nothing injectable, and you have a letter from your physician explaining the purpose of the syringe, you should have no trouble from Immigration officials. Alternatively, you can buy a syringe at one of Honiara's two chemists if need be, although you might require a prescription from a doctor first.

Females should bring a supply of tampons, especially if they are likely to be away from the capital for any length of time. Some clinics and hospitals around the country may have sufficient stocks to sell you some, others may not.

Antibiotics may be necessary if you go far off the beaten track. However, they should only be used exactly as your doctor instructs and should never be taken indiscriminately.

Stomach upsets and diarrhoea are the bane of every traveller's life, so bring some Imodium or Lomotil with you. You may need a rehydration mixture for treatment of severe cases of the runs, especially if you have children with you.

You'll find coral cuts and sandfly bites are particularly hard to heal. Consequently, bring an antiseptic such as mercurochrome, and an antibiotic powder or a similar dry spray, to deal with any cuts and grazes.

Calamine lotion is effective in reducing irritation caused by insect bites and stings. Bandages and band-aids are always useful for minor injuries.

Equally handy are accessories such as scissors, tweezers and a thermometer, though mercury ones are prohibited by airlines. You'll also need an insect repellent, mosquito coils and water purification tablets.

You will need protection against the sun's rays, so bring sunglasses, a hat, some barrier or sun block, and ordinary suntan lotion or moisturiser for mild cases of sunburn.

If you require special medicines for an ailment you regularly suffer from, make sure you bring a sufficient supply. Also carry a spare prescription bearing your medicine's generic name, rather than its brand name which may be unavailable in the Solomons.

Immunisation Officially no vaccination certificates are required for visiting the archipelago apart from the usual requirements if you've come from an infected area. But it's worthwhile to seek protection at least against hepatitis, polio (booster shot) and typhoid if you plan to go outside the major tourist centres, while malaria prophylaxis is essential.

Plan ahead by arranging any inoculations well in advance. Some require an initial shot while others shouldn't be given together.

Tetanus and diphtheria boosters are necessary every 10 years, and protection is highly recommended. Gamma globulin for infectious hepatitis is not a vaccination but a ready-made antibody, which has been successful in reducing the chances of getting hepatitis. However, it should be given as close as possible to your departure date because of its relatively short-lived protection period of, at most, six months.

Basic Rules
Many health problems can be avoided by taking simple precautions. Cuts and scratches easily become infected in the humid tropics, so wash them immediately with soap and running water. If they become infected, treat them with an antibiotic cream or powder immediately. Otherwise they may take weeks to heal.

Wash your hands frequently, as it's quite easy to contaminate your own food, giving yourself diarrhoea or worse. Constipation can be almost as common. You can easily avoid this by eating plenty of fresh fruit and vegetables.

All salads and fruit should be washed in treated water, or peeled. Thoroughly cooked food is safe, as long as it has not been left to cool or been reheated. However, take great care with shellfish, reef-caught fish and undercooked meat, particularly pork.

In general, places packed with tourists, expats or islanders should be fine. However, empty restaurants and fast-food outlets may be questionable.

Nutrition Always be sure your diet is well balanced. Eggs, beans and nuts are all good ways to get protein. Peelable fruit, such as bananas or oranges, is always safe. They, along with pawpaws and coconuts, are a good source of vitamins.

Make sure you drink enough during the Solomons' hotter seasons. Don't rely on feeling thirsty to remind you to do so. Indeed, not needing to urinate, or passing a very dark-yellow urine, should be treated as warning signs that you're not drinking nearly enough. Always carry a water or soft-drink bottle with you whenever you go on a long trip, whatever your means of transport.

You may, instead, find you're sweating excessively. This can lead to salt deficiency and consequent muscle cramping. If this occurs, extra salt with your daily food should help. Alternatively, you can add a third of a teaspoonful of salt per day to a litre of water without the taste being objectionable. Salt tablets, in contrast, cause some people to vomit.

Water Purification The simplest way of purifying water is to boil it thoroughly. Otherwise treat it chemically. Chlorine tablets, such as Puritabs and Steritabs, kill most, but not all, pathogens. Iodine is very effective and is available as a tablet, eg Potable Aqua. Follow the directions carefully, remembering that too much iodine can be harmful, as some people can be allergic to it.

Although both chemists in Honiara are likely to stock either chlorine or iodine-based water purifiers, their supplies may at times be limited. So bring whichever brand suits you from your home country, just in case.

If you're really stuck without a drink of clean water, nature provides the purest drinking fluid there is. The best is young coconut milk, followed by watermelon juice.

Show the same strictness towards water used for dental care as you would if you were drinking it. If you don't consider a particular town's water supplies are clean enough to drink, then only clean your teeth using boiled or purified water.

Islanders may say their water is safe because it comes from a rainwater catchment tank. But if the roof or guttering is dirty, so also will the water be. In addition, unless the tank is regularly cleaned with a 30% bleach and water solution, algae will grow in it, contaminating the water.

Normal Health A normal body temperature is 36.9°C, or 98.4°F. More than 2°C higher is a high fever. A normal adult pulse rate is 60 to 80 per minute (children 80 to 100, babies 100 to 140). You should know how to take a

temperature and pulse rate. As a general rule, the pulse increases about 20 beats per minute for each 1°C rise in fever.

A high respiration (ie breathing) rate is also an indication of illness. Count the number of breaths per minute – between 12 and 20 is normal for adults and older children (up to 30 for younger children, 40 for babies). People with a high fever or serious respiratory illness (like pneumonia) breathe more quickly than normal. More than 40 shallow breaths a minute in an adult usually means pneumonia.

Medical Problems & Treatment
Self-diagnosis and treatment can be risky, so wherever possible seek qualified help. Your hotel or the tourist office in Honiara will know of a good doctor.

If you're in an isolated area and you start feeling really sick, your best plan is to get aboard a plane and fly straight to the capital. This is where your medical insurance pays for itself many times over, as long as your policy includes emergency transport and medical evacuation costs.

Afflictions Caused by Environment
Sunburn You can get sunburned surprisingly quickly in the Solomons, even through cloud, especially if you sunbathe near water, which acts as a reflector. Use a high-factor sunscreen, taking care to cover those parts of the body which don't normally see the sun, eg your feet. A hat gives added protection, and zinc or some other barrier cream can be useful for your nose and lips. Calamine lotion is a common treatment for mild sunburn.

Fungal Infections Hot weather can produce a range of fungal infections in the scalp, the folds of the skin and other moist areas. Particularly prone are the gaps between the fingers and toes (athlete's foot), and the groin. Ringworm (a fungus, despite its name) spreads all over the body. It comes from animals or through walking on damp places, such as shower floors.

Fungal growths can easily make your life

a misery. To prevent these occurring, wear loose, comfortable clothes and avoid artificial fibres. Also wash frequently and dry carefully. If you do get infected, bathe the wound daily with disinfectant or medicated soap and water, rinsing and drying it well. Then apply an antifungal powder such as Tinaderm, and expose the infected area to air if possible. Wash all towels and underwear in very hot water and change them often.

Prickly Heat This is an itchy rash caused by excessive perspiration trapped under the skin. It sometimes strikes people who have just arrived in the country's hot and humid summer season and whose pores have not yet opened sufficiently to cope with a greater degree of sweating than normal. The secret is to keep cool, bathe often using a mild talcum powder, and sleep in fan-cooled or air-conditioned rooms.

Heat Exhaustion Dehydration or salt deficiency can easily cause heat exhaustion. If you arrive in the Solomons in the southern summer, you may need time to get acclimatised.

Vomiting and diarrhoea can deplete your liquid and saline levels, so make sure you get enough salt. Saline deficiency is accompanied by fatigue, lethargy, headaches, giddiness and muscle cramps.

A rare form of heat exhaustion is caused by an inability to sweat. This is only likely to afflict those who have been in the archipelago for quite a while, not new arrivals.

Heatstroke This sometimes fatal condition occurs when the body's heat-regulating mechanism breaks down, allowing your temperature to rise to a dangerous level. Long, continuous periods of hot weather can leave you vulnerable to heatstroke. Avoid excessive alcohol or strenuous activity when you first arrive in the country.

The symptoms are feeling unwell, not sweating very much if at all, and a high body temperature: around 39°C to 41°C. If there's no sweating, your skin will become flushed and red. You'll also experience severe, throbbing headaches, a lack of coordination, and a tendency to be confused or aggressive. Eventually, you'll become delirious or start convulsing. Your friends must get you out of the sun immediately, remove your outer clothing, cover you with a wet sheet or towel, and then fan you continuously until they can get you to hospital.

Motion Sickness Eating lightly before and during a journey will reduce the chances of motion sickness. If you are prone to it, try to find a seat where the disturbance is least. Near the wing in an aircraft, close to amidships on boats, and near the front in buses are the best places. Fresh air usually helps, or concentration on a fixed point of reference like the horizon, but reading or cigarette smoke make things worse.

Commercial preparations designed to prevent motion sickness can cause drowsiness. To be fully effective they should be taken before the trip commences. Ginger is a natural preventive and is available in capsule form.

Stugeron is highly regarded by the British naval and yachting people. Although it has to be taken 24 hours before your journey, it doesn't produce drowsiness. Sea-Bands worn on both wrists have no side effects, and are also useful for headaches and pregnancy-related nausea.

Diseases of Insanitation

Although villages in the Solomons are usually hygienic, individual bowl toilets in some parts of the country are a rarity, especially away from towns and resorts. Consequently gastric upsets are commonplace.

Although usually only affected mildly, a high proportion of islanders per year need treatment for some sort of intestinal complaint. These are caused by a range of illnesses, including dysentery, hepatitis, viral gastroenteritis, giardiasis and worm infestations.

The chances of getting a hygiene-related illness, other than simple diarrhoea, are pretty negligible unless you go exploring in some very remote places. However, you should seek immediate medical attention if you have any anal bleeding or fever.

Diarrhoea A change of water, food or climate can bring on the runs, but more serious is diarrhoea caused by contaminated food or water. However, a few rushed toilet trips are not a sign of any significant illness if there are no other symptoms.

Dehydration is the main danger with any persistent diarrhoeal outbreak. This is particularly the case with children, so fluid replacement is the primary treatment. However, a rehydration solution is necessary in severe cases to replace lost minerals and salts. You should stick to a bland, spice and fat-free diet while recovering.

Imodium or Lomotil can bring relief, although they don't actually cure you. Imodium is preferable for children. However, don't use these medicines if you have a high fever or are severely dehydrated: an appropriate antibiotic is necessary to treat any diarrhoea severe enough to cause nausea, vomiting, stomach cramps or fever.

Dysentery Contaminated food or water causes this illness, which gives you severe diarrhoea, often with blood or mucus in the stool. There are two kinds of dysentery. Bacillary dysentery develops rapidly and produces a high fever. Headache, vomiting and stomach pains are other symptoms. It generally doesn't last longer than a week, but it is highly contagious.

Amoebic dysentery develops more gradually, has no fever or vomiting but is more serious. It is not a self-limited disease: it will persist until treated and can recur and cause long-term damage.

A stool test is necessary to diagnose which kind of dysentery you have. Seek medical help urgently if you suspect either form.

Cholera Cholera is rare in the Solomons. Although vaccination is not very effective, cholera outbreaks anywhere in the world are generally widely reported, so you can avoid such problem areas.

Viral Gastroenteritis This viral affliction produces cramps, diarrhoea, occasionally vomiting and sometimes a slight fever. The standard treatment is rest and a large intake of fluids.

Hepatitis The most common form of this liver illness is Hepatitis A. It's spread by contaminated food or water. The first symptoms are fever, chills, headache, fatigue, weakness, and aches and pains. These are followed by a loss of appetite, nausea, vomiting, abdominal cramps, darkened urine, light clay-coloured faeces, and yellowing skin and eyes.

A doctor should check you over to assess whether or not you need hospitalisation. But in general there's not much you can do apart from rest, drink lots of fluids, eat light meals and avoid fatty foods. Lay off alcohol for six months after the illness to allow your weakened liver time to recover.

Hepatitis B, which used to be called serum hepatitis, is spread through sexual contact or skin penetration. It can be transmitted via dirty needles and blood transfusions, for instance. Avoid having your ears pierced, tattoos done, or injections where you have doubts about the sanitary conditions. The symptoms and treatment of type B are much the same as for type A, but gamma globulin as a prophylactic (advisable in the Solomons) is effective against type A only.

Typhoid Typhoid fever is another gut infection that travels the faecal-oral route – ie contaminated food and water are responsible. Vaccination against typhoid (recommended in the Solomons) is not totally effective. It is one of the most dangerous infections, so medical help must be sought.

In its early stages typhoid resembles many other illnesses. Sufferers may feel like they have a bad cold or flu coming on, as early symptoms are a headaches, a sore throat, and a fever which rises a little each day until it is around 40°C or more. The victim's pulse is often slow relative to the degree of fever present and gets slower as the fever rises –

unlike a normal fever where the pulse increases. There may also be vomiting, diarrhoea or constipation.

In the second week the high fever and slow pulse continue and a few pink spots may appear on the body. Trembling, delirium, weakness, weight loss and dehydration are other symptoms. If there are no further complications, the fever and other symptoms will slowly disappear during the third week. However, you must get medical help before this because pneumonia (acute infection of the lungs) or peritonitis (burst appendix) are common complications, and because typhoid is very infectious.

Giardiasis The giardia parasite normally lives in contaminated water but readily migrates to the human body. Once there, it causes stomach cramps, nausea, a bloated belly, frequent gas and malodorous diarrhoea. These symptoms can disappear for a few days and then return. This process will repeat itself until you get medical attention.

Worms These parasites are common in rural areas. You can pick them up by eating unwashed vegetables and undercooked meat, or through your skin by walking about in bare feet. Always wear shoes when visiting villages or gardens. Only the seashore is free of hookworms.

Any worm infestation you have may not be obvious for quite a while. However, if it's left untreated, it can cause continuing health problems. A stool test is necessary to pinpoint exactly which sort of worms you have. Once identified, medication for it is usually readily available at chemists.

Malaria

The Solomons' most serious public health problem is malaria. There are regular spraying programmes in the capital, though much greater emphasis is now being placed on improved sanitation. Despite this, the number of malaria cases per year has increased sufficiently for about 37.5 % of the population now to expect to get the disease annually. The risk of infection is distinctly higher in country areas and during the hot monsoonal summer.

Different Types There are four kinds of malaria: vivax, falciparum, ovale and malariae. These are mainly carried by the female anopheles mosquito. The plasmodium parasites enter the human bloodstream through the mosquito's saliva and then travel in the blood to the host's liver. The mainly malignant falciparum form is the most common one found in the Solomons.

Symptoms The first sign of malaria can be a continuous gentle murmur in the ears. This is then followed by headaches, fever and pains all over. When it's settled in properly, you'll feel intensely cold. Despite the hot sun, you'll shiver for between 30 minutes to around two hours. Then you'll get really hot and dry, may vomit and become delirious. Throughout this time, your vision may blur. After four to five hours of this hell, you'll start sweating profusely and your temperature should fall.

The parasites multiply in human red blood cells every 48 hours – or 72 in the case of the malariae form. These blood cells are destroyed, particularly with falciparum malaria.

The illness releases poisons which themselves produce a severe fever. The parasites then multiply rapidly. If they collect in the brain, you may end up with cerebral malaria. If instead they lodge in the kidneys, you may have renal failure and blackwater fever, where you would pass blackish urine and could die within a few days.

Fortunately, not all malaria cases are of such a lethal form. Whatever sort it is, a similar attack to your first one will almost certainly occur one to two days later. When that's over, as long as you've not been stricken too severely, you should slowly recover your strength. However, you may have periodic relapses every few weeks or months – sometimes several years – after the initial bout.

Safer Places Tiny offshore islands, bathed

by fresh sea breezes and free of any swamps or standing water, are often safe from mosquitoes, as the insect can only fly a short distant without a rest. Mountainous areas are also usually immune from the disease, as they are often too cool at night for the anopheles variety to survive. However, although local people claim some islands, such as Bellona, Anuta and the Reefs, are free of malaria, most medical authorities disagree. In their view the disease is prevalent almost everywhere in the archipelago.

Any visitor who stays exclusively in the capital would be most unlucky to contract this malady. Even so, you should take all normal precautions, including regular antimalarial tablets. Remember that mosquitoes can be attracted by perfume, aftershave, perspiration and dark coloured clothes.

Preventive Measures & Medicines You can protect yourself by keeping as much of your normally exposed skin covered, especially around the ankles. Or you can spray yourself with a powerful insect repellent containing diethyl toluamide, particularly after sundown between 6 and 7 pm when mosquitoes like to feed.

Alternatively, you can rub yourself over with Mosbar – a Solomons-produced mosquito repellent manufactured to look like a bar of soap. Its protective effect lasts more than 10 hours.

In addition, you should sleep either under a mosquito net or a fast rotating fan, behind a flyscreen-protected window, beside a slow-burning mosquito coil, in an air-conditioned room, or with an electrically powered permethrin dispenser operating.

Chloroquine tablets are the usual prophylactic nowadays. However, the disease has developed a resistance to it in certain parts of the world, the Solomons included. Consequently, it should be supplemented with a weekly dose of Maloprim or a daily helping of Proquanil. Take care not to exceed your weekly Maloprim dose, as it can have rare but serious side effects. Some doctors recommend a checkup after every six months of its continuous use.

Start you chloroquine treatment two weeks before you arrive in the Solomons and continue for a further six weeks after you leave it or any other malarial area. If you run out of tablets, chemists in Honiara will supply them without prescription. Should any fever with malaria-like symptoms occur after you've returned home, get medical attention smartly and tell your doctor where you've been.

Dengue Fever
This sickness is characterised by a sudden high fever accompanied by headaches and severe bodily pains. A rash then develops which spreads from the trunk to the face and limbs. After a few days the fever subsides and recovery begins.

Dengue fever (pronounced 'deng-ie') can be fatal. It's transmitted by infected mosquitoes. At present there is no agreed treatment or vaccine. Consequently, you should take the same strict precautions to avoid being bitten by a dengue-bearing mosquito as you would to avoid being bitten by a malarial one.

Santa Cruz Fever
This mosquito-borne sickness mainly afflicts Temotu Province. Its fever is similar to malaria's but its effects are milder and are not usually considered to be life-threatening.

Other Disease-Bearing Creatures
Leeches These pests are rare in the Solomons, and usually small. However, if you go walking through thick bush, you may find some leeches attaching themselves to your legs. Again, if you swim in some invitingly clear, freshwater creek, you may attract some.

Salt or a lighted cigarette end will shake leeches off, while insect repellent may also keep them at bay. Don't pull them off, though, as their mouthparts can remain in the wound, which may then become infected.

Ticks There are usually ticks wherever cattle have been living. In the Solomons, this mainly means northern Guadalcanal, Kolombangara, the Russell Islands, around the Auki area of Malaita, south-eastern Vella Lavella and the southern part of the Three Sisters Islands. So always check yourself carefully after walking through long grass in these islands, or anywhere else where you see cattle. A strong insect repellent can deter ticks, whilst petroleum jelly (ie Vaseline), alcohol or oil will remove them.

Ticks can spread typhus, as can mites and lice. This disease begins as a bad cold, and is followed by fever, chills, headaches, muscle pains and body rash. Frequently, there's also a large and very sore spot where you were bitten, while the nearby lymph glands swell painfully.

Bedbugs The Solomons' tourist hotels maintain a high standard of cleanliness, including most of those at the cheaper end of the price range. However, in some village leaf houses there will probably be, at best, an old bed and worn mattress. More likely, there will be nothing more than a few old woven pandanus mats on the floor. This is where you may occasionally have trouble from bedbugs and lice.

Dirty mattresses are a favourite home for bedbugs. Spots of blood on bedclothes or on the wall beside the bed are a sure sign of their presence. Bedbugs leave itchy bites in neat rows on your skin, though calamine lotion can help relieve the pain.

Lice You may get lice in your hair or clothing from being too close physically to infected people, or from sharing clothing or bedding they've used. Special powder and shampoos will get rid of the infestation. Infected clothing should be washed, using a detergent and very hot water.

Diseases Spread by People
Tuberculosis Although this is prevalent in the Solomons, it is not usually considered a serious risk to visitors, because almost all the 400 cases a year live in very isolated areas.

Young children are more susceptible than adults. Consequently, it's a sensible precaution, if you have children under 12 years old with you and you're planning to go to the country's remoter areas, to have them immunised beforehand. Tuberculosis in the archipelago is mainly spread by coughing, as most milk consumed in the country is imported and therefore pasteurised.

Diphtheria This illness is rare in the Solomons because of the general cleanliness of Melanesian homes. However, it may at times be present in dust in villagers' houses. Diphtheria is spread by contaminated dust coming in contact with the skin, or by inhaling the cough or sneeze droplets of an infected person. Frequent washing and keeping the skin dry will help prevent a skin-borne infection. A diphtheria inoculation will prevent the throat form of this ailment.

Other Diseases Spread by Animals
Tetanus This potentially fatal disease may be present in certain rural areas. It occurs when a wound becomes infected by a germ which lives in animal or human faeces. Consequently, you should clean all cuts, abrasions or animal bites. The first symptom of a tetanus infection may be discomfort while swallowing, and a stiffening of the jaw and neck, followed by painful convulsions of the body and jaw. A simple immunisation prior to departure will protect you.

Rabies Bites or scratches from infected animals, particularly dogs, can cause rabies. Any bite or scratch, or even a lick from a suspect animal, should immediately be thoroughly cleaned with soap and running water and then disinfected with alcohol. After that, seek medical attention.

Even if the animal is not rabid, all bites should be treated seriously, as they can become infected and lead to tetanus. A rabies vaccination is available. You should certainly consider having it if you're a cave explorer (against bat bites), or expect to be close to animals while you're in the archipelago. Some travellers who only plan to go briefly into remote areas favour having an antirabies inoculation simply because it reduces the effect if they are actually bitten.

Ciguatera & Fish Poisoning This is an often-serious illness which occurs when a certain toxic organism in plankton is eaten by reef fish, which are themselves consumed by large flesh-eating species, such as rock cods, trevallies, sea perches, moray eels and barracudas. Only the oldest, and usually largest, are likely to contain sufficient toxin to be fatal to humans – though there are no outward signs that a particular fish is actually infected.

Ciguatera's symptoms include vomiting, diarrhoea and cramps, alternating fevers and chills, and tingling in the skin and mouth. Outbreaks of the disease seem to coincide with major traumas to reefs such as cyclones, heavy rainfalls, earthquakes and major building or demolition works.

Some reef species, such as puffer fish, box fish and the prickly, ball-shaped porcupine fish, are toxic at all times, whatever their size and age. Eating them leads to muscular paralysis and respiratory failure.

Ask local people for advice if you catch any fish close inshore. In contrast, open ocean and deep-water species are usually considered safe to eat in all seasons.

Cuts
Skin punctures can easily become infected in hot climates and may be difficult to heal. Treat any cut with an antiseptic solution and mercurochrome. Where possible avoid bandages and band-aids, which can keep wounds wet. Coral cuts are notoriously slow to heal, as the coral injects a weak venom into the wound. Avoid such injuries by wearing shoes when walking on reefs, and clean any coral-caused abrasion thoroughly.

Sexually Transmitted Diseases
Gonorrhoea has been a serious scourge in the Pacific in the past. If you suspect you have an infection in your genital or urinary area, get to a hospital quickly, preferably the one in Honiara. Delays in treatment can sometimes produce long-term side effects. Condoms give the best protection against infection.

As AIDS has begun to appear, always insist on a new needle if you require an injection.

Women's Health
Gynaecological Problems Poor diet, lowered resistance due to using antibiotics for stomach ailments, and even contraceptive pills can lead to vaginal infections when travelling in tropical areas. Doctors advise keeping the genital area clean, and wearing cotton underwear and skirts or loose-fitting trousers. These all help to prevent yeast infections taking hold. Their characteristic rashes, itches and discharges can be treated with a vinegar or lemon juice douche. Alternatively, Nystatin suppositories can be prescribed.

Pregnancy Most miscarriages occur during the first three months of pregnancy, so this is the most risky time to travel. The last three months should also be spent within a reasonable distance of good medical care, as quite serious problems can develop at this time. Pregnant women should avoid all unnecessary medication, though vaccination and antimalarial courses should still continue where possible. You should take particular care at this time to remain healthy, paying particular attention to eating a well-balanced, nutritious diet.

The safest time to go on holiday while pregnant is after 16 weeks and before 24 are up. This is when you are least likely to suffer complications. Even so, you should always be near a doctor.

Airlines may refuse to fly you if you are visibly pregnant unless you can show a doctor's certificate. You'll certainly need one of these if you've gone beyond 28 weeks, and you'll be barred from flying, even with one, after 35 weeks' pregnancy.

WOMEN TRAVELLERS
The Solomons is very tolerant of the many puzzling ways of the modern world. However, islanders are sometimes more accepting of foreign male idiosyncrasies than of female ones.

Clothing

As recently as the mid-1980s, local women wearing jeans, slacks or longish shorts were rare in the capital, let alone in the rest of the Solomons. However, these are now acceptable in Honiara, and increasingly around the country, especially in Polynesian areas and the more cosmopolitan parts of Western Province, such as Gizo, Munda and the expat-managed plantations. However, as local fashions inevitably change at differing paces, it's best to ask first and take careful note of what others are wearing. At the same time, scant and revealing clothing should always be avoided, while wearing a swimsuit in the street is considered very immodest.

Women Alone

It's against custom for a young woman to be out at night by herself. If you are in Honiara and want to avoid misunderstandings, take a taxi and remain in busy areas. In the country, remain in a group. In addition, female tourists should not swim or sunbathe alone at isolated beaches.

Foreign women travelling solo around remote villages are rare at present. However, if such a person arrives without warning at a village, she should contact the local police station if there is one, or ask to see the chief, preferably offering a gift of tobacco, betel nut or food from the village store.

If the chief and his people accept her, they'll probably appoint a young local woman to supervise and see no harm befalls their guest. The chief may be loath to allow a lone foreign female to stay in his village, but quite prepared to accept a female if she has a male companion.

DANGERS & ANNOYANCES
Safety

No-one goes into the pot these days, nor are heads hunted. Although people in some islands in the past made a sport out of pig and taro theft, there were other islands where stealing from neighbours was unheard of before White people arrived. However, criminal activity has recently increased in Honiara, where it is usually associated with alcohol abuse and youth unemployment. Thieves occasionally steal money from cars parked in isolated spots or break into houses looking for alcohol or electrical equipment such as stereo systems and VCRs. There have been reports of hotel rooms and occupied bedrooms being robbed, and bags have sometimes been snatched.

A particularly bad period was in 1985 and 1986, when prisoners from Honiara's prison used to let themselves out at night, commit crimes, and return before sunrise to give themselves an alibi! Fortunately this is unlikely to recur, as the jail is now much more secure.

Despite the mid-1980s crime wave, violence towards expats or visitors is extremely rare. In fact, it's usually quite safe for foreign males to walk around at night anywhere in the country. Drunks may need to be avoided, but that applies all over the world. However, islanders in Honiara walk close to the road at night to be in the light, because even now there's the danger of inter-island feuding.

Valuables are usually safe in your hotel room. But naturally don't leave wallets or handbags visible in parked cars or lying around anywhere. It's just a matter of taking the same precautions as you would back home.

A very sensible extra precaution is to photocopy all your travel documents, such as passports, travellers' cheques and airline tickets, keeping the copies with you but separate from the originals. Replacements are much easier to get if you have these duplicates.

Discourtesies

Bad manners are exceptionally rare in Melanesia, while thoughtlessness and impatience are usually the preserve of foreigners rather than islanders. Most local people will act as if nothing has happened, silently forgiving you for not knowing that you have broken a local rule. However, Malaitans and Shortland Islanders will be quite direct with you if you breach one of their tabus or act inconsiderately.

Some of Honiara's young unemployed

regularly do the rounds of shops, claiming falsely to represent certain local charities and asking for donations from both shopkeepers and customers. If you respond, they'll ask you repeatedly, though they're unlikely to approach you on the street.

Unexploded Munitions
Although WW II finished nearly 50 years ago, unexploded shells and grenades, mortar bombs and bullets are still being found, particularly around Honiara. Children regularly unearth small arms ammunition and will offer to sell it to you. Instead, warn them of the risks they run handling such volatile material and advise them to hand in their trophies to the authorities at once!

Flora & Fauna
There are a number of plants and animals to be wary of in the Solomons. See the Flora & Fauna section in the Facts about the Country chapter and the information about shell collecting and swimming in the Activities section of this chapter for more details.

WORK
Work & Residence Permits
Anyone who is not a Solomons national must have both work and residence permits before working inside the country. Each lasts two years and includes voluntary and unpaid workers. Work permits are issued by the Labour Division, Ministry of Commerce & Primary Industries (☎ 21849), PO Box G26, Honiara.

The rules say your prospective employer can only apply for you while you're outside the Solomons unless you're waiting to extend an already existing permit. However, some applicants prefer to wait in Honiara, occasionally visiting the Labour Division, hoping to speed things up.

Despite this, it's quite easy to get permission to work as long as the job you've been offered specifically involves training a local person to take over from you in due course, and the officials have received your new employer's letter or statement about you. However, although the usual waiting period

for approval is two months, it can sometimes drag on indefinitely without explanation.

The only exceptions to these rules relate to the wives and children of expats who already have work permits, and a very few special categories, such as pilots, aircraft engineers and scuba instructors. Self-employment is possible, but again you have to wait for your clearance.

Any visitors who are not authorised to work but do so, or who overstay their visitor's permits, are likely to be deported. They may have to face unexpected tax liabilities, and have their future applications to visit the Solomons refused. These restrictions include researchers and prospectors, even if their efforts lead to nothing.

Registering a Business
Although a single-person business doesn't have to be registered, two or more people operating together do. Getting a small operation registered shouldn't be too difficult as long as you have adequate funds, but really large capital investments can take up to four years to be approved or rejected.

Tax is only liable for income which accrues in, is derived from, or is received in, the Solomons, though double-taxation relief is available on overseas earnings. Registration is with the Foreign Investment Board (☎ 23105) in the Ministry of Commerce & Primary Industries.

Expatriate & Local Incomes
Wages for gardeners, domestics and unskilled staff range between S$1000 and S$1500 per annum, while government employees earn from S$3000 to S$20,000 a year on average. However, expatriates usually require more than that.

The approximate annual expenditure to run a car, pay a reasonable rent, shop freely, enjoy a modest level of entertainment, and be able to afford emergencies would be around S$20,000 to S$25,000 for a single expatriate. A married couple with two children would probably spend S$30,000 to S$35,000 a year. Residence involves a liability for tax for any income derived in or from the Solomons, and a stay of six months is sufficient to qualify. Tax levels start at 14%, and then rise steeply before levelling off at 42%.

Citizenship

Acquiring citizenship of the Solomons requires 10 years' residence in the country and renunciation of your previous nationality. However, only two years' residence is required of foreign women who marry Solomon Islanders, though 10 years' residence is required of foreign men. Nationals who marry foreigners and go to live abroad may not become dual nationals. Instead they lose their Solomons citizenship.

ACTIVITIES

Although there's not much nightlife, sightseeing around the Solomons could keep you occupied for most of the six months the Immigration Department will allow you in any one year. In that time, you could have been bushwalking, canoeing, mountain or volcano climbing, scuba diving, snorkelling, swimming, surfing, looking at war wrecks, fishing, shelling, bird-watching, caving, lazing on beaches, examining archaeological sites, observing ancient customs and taking scenic drives near the capital.

Golf, Squash & Tennis

The Solomons' only golf course and sole squash club are both in Honiara's suburbs. The only tennis courts outside the capital are in the nearby Guadalcanal Plains.

Bushwalking

You might think the Solomons would be too hot and humid for bushwalks. But in the cooler months of the midyear, an island walking tour would provide a genuine insight into Melanesian village life. Unfortunately, that's just the time when Guadalcanal's southern coast has its heaviest rainfalls, though the Honiara area is usually dry then.

Several islands could suit a brief trip on foot, as long as you are well prepared and carry a reasonable stock of food, money and items to use as gifts. Among these islands would be Nggela, Kolombangara, Nggatokae, Rennell, Nendo, Vella Lavella and Savo. In addition to village life, there are beaches, mountains, craters, waterfalls, hot springs, caves and lakes to see – depending which island you choose. Some have tracks from one side to the other, like Choiseul, or along part of the coast, like Malaita, Santa Isabel and Makira.

When bushwalking, always watch the weather, as heavy rain in the hills can cause sudden and dangerous flash floods downstream.

Volcano & Mountain Climbing

Tinakula may be too sheer to climb, but there are other volcanic peaks on Simbo, Savo and Vella Lavella. Climbing either Rendova's or Kolombangara's peaks would require a strenuous but rewarding two-day hike, with magnificent views over Western Province from their summits. Guadalcanal has the nation's two highest peaks, but you would

---

Visiting Small Islands

If you've always felt a particular fascination for small-island life, several of the Solomons' larger landforms have diminutive neighbours with fine beaches, coral gardens and friendly people. Among these are Guadalcanal's dwarf-sized companions in Marau Sound, the many islands of the New Georgia group's Marovo, Roviana and Vonavona lagoons, the islands of Malaita's Lau and Langa Langa lagoons, Makira's small neighbours to its north and east, the Polynesian outliers such as Ontong Java, Sikaiana and Bellona, and other lesser islands like Tulaghi, Wagina and Ndai.

The archipelago also has a province and three groups which are made up entirely of small islands. These are Temotu Province, the Shortlands, and the Western and Arnarvon islands to the north-west of Santa Isabel, though the latter are unpopulated. ■

need to be very well prepared to consider these.

Bird-Watching

The Honiara area is as good a place as anywhere in the Solomons to see most of the country's tropical birds, including the unfortunately named spangled drongo. If you want to see some very rare and specialised species, you must go to Temotu Province, Lake Te'Nggano on Rennell, or the highlands of Makira and Guadalcanal. If instead you prefer sea birds, you'll find plenty of these in Ontong Java, on the smaller offshore islands in the Shortlands group, and in the coastal parts of Makira/Ulawa. Try to see megapode birds at their hatcheries if you can. Savo and Simbo are the best places for these, though they are also present on several other islands.

Wildlife Viewing

Guadalcanal has snakes, rats and crocodiles. Snakes are also plentiful in the Reefs, Rennell and Vella Lavella, while crocodiles favour Nendo, Guadalcanal, Makira/Ulawa Province, San Jorge, Vanikolo, Choiseul and several of the New Georgia Islands. Santa Isabel has wild horses and rats, wild pigs have made a home in Choiseul, Malaita, Nendo, and Ovau Island in the Shortlands, and wild cattle are plentiful on Malaupaina in the Three Sisters group.

Viewing War Relics

Without doubt, scuba divers get the most thrilling view of the country's many wrecks. Even so, there are plenty more relics ashore in Guadalcanal, Central and Western provinces to satisfy any war buffs who aren't licensed scuba divers yet.

Hundreds of US and Japanese citizens come annually to see the battlefields. They find more than enough remains, including old planes, guns and vehicles, to evoke poignant memories of the events of 50 years ago.

Visiting Archaeological Sites & Caves

There are ancient remains all over the country. The easily accessible ones are in Malaita, Simbo, Bellona, Nendo, New Georgia and Santa Ana. However, you may have to pay a custom fee to visit them, and certain natural wonders too, like caves, hot springs and waterfalls.

Some archaeological sites may still be in daily use, especially the artificial islands in Malaita. One person may claim something is all right for you to do, but the true custom owner may say otherwise. However, as long as you're tactful and polite, you should be able to see most skull and traditional-money collections.

It's illegal to remove anything from such places, especially personal objects such as skulls, without the traditional owner's agreement. It's also illegal to export them.

Rockshelters and caves are widely spread around the country. The largest concentration is in Nggela, though Bellona has several too. Other places with two or more rockshelters and caves are Santa Ana, Makira, Guadalcanal, Choiseul, Malaita, New Georgia, Kolombangara and the Reef Islands. If you want to see all Nggela's caverns, come prepared to camp, unless you're on a yacht.

Petroglyphs are much scarcer. There's a site close to Honiara, and another on Guadalcanal's southern coast. The remainder are in Simbo, Vella Lavella and Maramasike.

Shell Collecting

Anyone going beachcombing on the outer islands will find a huge range of beautiful shells; but beware of ultrapoisonous cone shells and stonefish. Go with an islander until you know what to avoid, and wear reef shoes.

You should ask permission before shell collecting. Each section of coral which can be reached on foot or by a skin diver (ie an islander diving without scuba tanks) has its own custom owner. Taking small shells will seldom be a problem. However, large or distinctive ones may have a commercial value if sold at the local market. Alternatively, a live one may represent food for the owner's family.

Seeing Ancient Customs

Seeing traditional activities like shell, clam-shell or red-feather money being used for bride price is perfectly possible. It's just a matter of luck. Shell money is still made in Malaita, and tourists can see this happening at Laulasi Island or in villages near Auki.

Ceremonial dances are put on around the country on Independence Day, and Santa Catalina has two regular festivals a year. But to see custom dances and ceremonies elsewhere could mean spending a lengthy period living in a remote tribal village. So if you do see any traditional rites performed, count yourself extremely lucky.

Water Sports

The Solomons offers a full range of water sports, including swimming (beach or poolside), sunbathing, fishing, boating, surfing and snorkelling, while scuba divers make regular pilgrimages to northern Guadalcanal and Gizo's war wrecks.

Fishing Although most tropical marine life is colourful, it's usually small. If you're after larger fish, you'll find them mainly at the reef's outer edge.

You can try your hand at game fishing, particularly off the southern New Georgia Islands. Sailfish, marlin, shark, tuna, barracuda and wahoo are regularly caught. Game fishing is only permitted in deep waters, as coastal landowners will not permit it in shallow areas for fear of depleting traditional fishing grounds.

Trolling is the best way to catch large fish if you're in a moving boat. Just hang a baited line over the side whenever you take a ship or canoe ride, and pull them in as soon as they bite.

River fishing is also worthwhile, particularly for freshwater crayfish and prawns. Most of the larger islands have fast-flowing creeks where you can land some reasonably sized catches. But avoid any muddy coastal rivers which empty into shoreside swamps, as these are more likely to conceal human-eating estuarine crocodiles than fish! And, as always in Melanesia, check whether the river and fish in it belong to anyone before casting your line.

Swimming There's a multitude of beaches around the country. Although many are white or gold, in geologically young areas they're more likely to be blackish or grey.

Islanders say sharks are more likely to be around black-sand beaches than white or golden ones, as the former are too young for reefs to have formed around them. A white beach is invariably composed of coral debris, and is usually protected by a reef. Certain sharks do cross these natural barriers, but human-eating species are less likely to do so. Nonetheless, it's best to ask local advice first as there have been occasional fatalities from

shark attack in northern Guadalcanal, and the shark deity traditions of Malaita and Makira also indicate their presence.

Swimmers should strictly avoid crossing any offshore reefs. Instead, you should always remain within a reef's calm, protected waters, close to land. Beyond the reef are strong ocean currents which can quickly sweep you out to sea. If there's no reef, stay close inshore, or out of the water altogether.

Surfing Surfies have found some good waves at Pailongge on Ghizo, Poro on Santa Isabel and Tawarogha on Makira. Surf has also been reported at Beaufort Bay in southern Guadalcanal, Malu'u, Manu and Fakanakafo Bay in northern Malaita, Byron and Carlisle Bays on Nendo, and between Nifiloli and Fenualoa islands in the Reefs group. However, some of this may be across coral rock rather than sand, and therefore dangerous.

Islanders have accommodated surfies quite readily in the past, but they expect you to respect their customs and rules. That means asking a village's permission before you surf, bathe, use their washing facilities, or stay there.

Snorkelling Snorkellers can usually join scuba trips for between S$25 and S$50 a time. Otherwise, there's a mass of coral around the country to view for free. It seems to be dead when you're walking on it, but it's dazzlingly alive at its underwater edge.

When snorkelling in the tropics, you'll find it's comparatively easy to enter the water off a coral ledge, but often fearfully hard to get back on to dry land again, especially if the sea is at all rough. Islanders always plan their exit point before they enter the water.

Avid snorkel fans won't need reminding to bring their own double-sealed mask, snorkel tube, diving boots and fins. Also useful is a knife. If you come too close to a moray eel, or are foolishly tempted to touch a clam's beguiling lips, you may need your knife to force the creature to release you. It's much wiser not to touch at all.

Scuba Diving There are registered land-based scuba operators in Honiara, Tambea, Gizo, Uepi and Munda, and sometimes on Pigeon Island in the Reefs. If you tried every dive spot they visit, you would be kept spellbound for weeks. Otherwise, touring yachts with their own compressors find plenty of places for diving throughout the country. There are good sites off northern and south-eastern Guadalcanal, in Marovo and Vonavona lagoons and north-western parts of Roviana Lagoon, and off Ghizo Island, the Shortland Islands, north-eastern Vella Lavella, western Choiseul, north-western Santa Isabel, north-eastern Malaita, Sikai-ana, Ontong Java and the Roncador Reef, the Russells, the Nggelas, south-eastern Makira, the Reef Islands, Utupua, Vanikolo, and the Indispensable Reefs to the south of Rennell.

Scuba divers score over snorkellers and shell collectors as far as customary law is concerned. As traditional ownership of reefs is limited to as deep as an islander can free-dive, there's no need to worry about possible breaches of customary law as long as you're more than 10 metres down. However, taking souvenirs from wrecks is treated as looting, so don't be tempted.

Live-Aboard Dive Craft Bilikiki Cruises Ltd (☎ 22103, PO Box 414) of Honiara has two well-equipped vessels which regularly take divers on one or two-week luxury scuba trips around the country, particularly through the clear, blue waters of the Russell Islands. The charge is US$375/245 a day each for single/twin occupancy on the MV *Bilikiki*, and A$145 on the MV *Kirio*. The company also runs occasional two-day dive excursions from the capital for S$400 each.

Water Temperatures It's quite warm enough to scuba without a wet suit during the day, though there's always the possibility of getting hard-to-heal coral grazes. However, night diving can be rather chilly in the archipelago's cooler months. Lycra suits are usually quite warm enough, though most operators have standard-type wet suits for hire also.

Visibility The Solomons' underwater visibility is usually around 30 metres. It seldom falls below 20 metres, unless you're diving in a busy harbour, inside the hold of a wrecked ship, or more than 30 metres down.

Equipment Rental Many divers bring their own gear, though renting is possible at all Solomons dive shops, and also on live-aboard dive boats.

Learning to Dive As long as you're over 15 and healthy, you can learn to dive. There are instructors in Honiara, Gizo, Tambea, Munda and Uepi. Expect to pay between S$450 and S$800 for a brief seven to 10-day training course to bring you up to PADI open-water certification standard.

Decompression Facilities There's no decompression chamber in the Solomons, despite the large number of scuba-diving tourists visiting the country. The nearest one is at Townsville on Australia's northern coast.

Dive Holidays Three Sydney dive companies organise dive tours to the Solomons. These are Dive Adventures (Australia) (☎ (02) 299 4689/(008) 22 2234), 9th Level, 32 York St, Sydney 2000; Sea Life International Pty Ltd (trading as Pro Dive Travel) (☎ (02) 665 6335), 27 Alfreda St, Coogee, Sydney 2034; and Dive Travel Australia (☎ (02) 879 7160), Shop 3, 50 Kalang Rd, Elanora Heights 2101. All three offer divers and nondivers packages. Both Pro Dive Travel and Dive Adventures (Australia) offer divers six nights aboard the MV *Kirio* for A$1725, including return airfares from Sydney.

HIGHLIGHTS

Any list of a country's highlights is bound to be highly personal and selective. Mine is no exception.

Honiara

Your likely place of arrival, Honiara has scuba sites, battlefields, restaurants, handi-craft shops, banks and comfortable accommodation.

Guadalcanal Coastal Resorts

Drive through the countryside to Tambea or Vulelua. Both are on a beach and provide meals and accommodation. At Tambea you can also go scuba diving.

Savo & Simbo

Both these destinations have megapode birds, hot springs and a volcano. Simbo also has archaeological sites, but Savo is the more accessible.

Marovo Lagoon

Visit some of the many small sand-fringed islands and resorts here, such as Uepi, and enjoy the scuba diving.

Munda & Lumbaria

Both of these, or an island resort in nearby Vonavona Lagoon, give access to Roviana and Vonavona lagoons.

Gizo

This attractive town is near the Gilbertese villages. Visit the beaches or go scuba diving.

North Malaita

Take the coastal route from Auki to the Lau-populated artificial islands. See shell money being made near Auki and at Laulasi.

Polynesian Outliers

Of particular interest are Bellona with its culture and history, Rennell with Lake Te'Nggano, and the Reef Islands.

Sea Trips

Travel by boat around Temotu Province or Western and Choiseul Provinces. Or take a sea trip around Malaita Province, including visits to Sikaiana and Ontong Java.

Waterfall Viewing

Guadalcanal has nine cascades and falls, with four of them quite close to Honiara. Seven other islands have one or more waterfalls; Choiseul, Malaita and Nendo have two each.

Mountain Climbing

Climb Kolombangara's central peak, either with a tour group or employing your own guide.

ACCOMMODATION

The Solomons has none of the typical budget-priced lodgings you can find so easily in Asia and Latin America. At the bottom end of the scale are village leaf houses, which are spartan but cheap.

If you prefer something a bit more comfortable but can only manage S$30 a night, there may be a few towns or villages that you will not be able to stay in overnight. If, however, you can afford as much as S$70 a night, you should be able to stay almost anywhere other than in any of the country's few high-cost international resorts.

Once you've decided where you want to go, as far as possible always book at least one night's accommodation prior to departure. This way, you can ensure there's a vehicle or canoe to meet you at the airport or landing place when you arrive.

Camping & Staying Overnight in a Village

Camping is rare in populated areas but quite acceptable in the bush, so if you want to use a tent, first ask the landowner for permission. However, if you have arrived at a village, the chief will usually find an empty house for you to sleep in, or offer you the visitors' house if there is one, as long as your stay is only for a night or two. Alternatively, one of the villagers may invite you into their house. Otherwise, you could try the local school while it's empty at night, or the grounds of the village police station if there is one. Unfortunately, rats are the curse of village life, so hang your food up overnight or else they will eat it.

Money has little value in the bush, so if you offer cash for your accommodation, amounts requested of you may be unrealistically and alarmingly high. In addition, don't show all your supplies at once, as villagers will assume you're giving them a present to be enjoyed there and then.

If you want to repay your hosts' kindness later with a gift, present them with some tinned meat, matches, candles, tea, coffee, fresh bread or sugar. Tobacco sticks are almost always appreciated, particularly when presented with a few pages from a school exercise book that can be used as cigarette paper. Alternative gifts are betel nut, betel leaves and lime, or fishing gear if you're visiting a small island. However, no SDA and few SSEC members touch tobacco, alcohol or betel nut, so try to find something else suitable for them.

Leaf Houses

Leaf houses can be pleasantly cool and clean, or they can be very basic indeed. However, prices are seldom more than S$15 and are usually less. You'll probably eat with the family and have a paraffin lamp to see by at night.

Washing will be outside, often behind a partition of corrugated iron. Usually there will be a hole-in-the-ground toilet, unless there is no running water, in which case there may only be a 'thunder box', or bush toilet.

Rest Houses & Hostels

Places in the S$15 to S$25 range include church hostels, provincial government rest houses and some private rest houses. Most have portable fans, shared washing facilities and a communal kitchen. Although the rooms are sometimes dormitory style, they are usually friendly and quiet places. Good value for money in this price range are the Mothers Union Rest House at Buala and the Suani Rest House in Bellona.

Provincial and district council rest houses are designed for visiting government staff but can be used by visitors as long as there's room. Sometimes you have to evacuate if a government official wants a bed.

There are a few places with large dorms costing around S$5, which may sound your price, but they tend to be 'blood-houses' –

noisy, overcrowded, far from clean and not recommended.

Resorts & Hotels

S$40 may not really sound like a budget or backpacker price, but by Solomons standards anything up to that is a good deal. Some small resorts, like Lumbaria Island Resort in Rendova, fall into this category, as does Paradise Lodge at Gizo.

The more moderately priced hotels often have some cheaper rooms without air-conditioning, but with ceiling fans and personal showers. Some offer boat trips, scuba facilities and regular performances by island dancers, or have restaurants and bars. Although these hotels are mainly for tourists, they also suit islanders and visiting government staff.

If you want a bit of luxury now and again, it will cost you between S$50 and S$75 a head. A good place in this price range is the Maqarea Resort at Munda.

The few international-style hotels and resorts provide plenty to do day and night, and usually have rooms with air-conditioning. These hotels have either a beach or swimming pool, a bar, a restaurant and often a dive shop. Singles are priced from around S$80.

Finding Accommodation

If you want to get around where there's no recognised accommodation, ask in the provincial capital. People will know which villages have a visitors' house, local transport details, who to contact and whether there are any special tabus to be aware of. Once you've got all this information, send a service message well in advance of your planned arrival warning the villagers of your intended visit. Give them adequate time to consider your request, and to refuse it if they want to.

Government Tax

There's a 10% government tax on all hotel and restaurant charges, but not on provincial government rest houses, church hostels, village visitors' houses and snackbars.

FOOD
Restaurants & Snackbars

Although the Solomons isn't noted for *haute cuisine*, you can eat quite well in Honiara. All the hotels have restaurants, but their prices can be rather high at times. You can usually keep the price down by asking for sandwiches instead of a hot meal.

Honiara has a number of reasonably priced Chinese restaurants and snackbars. Although some of the latter are a bit greasy, if you look around you'll soon find one you'll like.

In the country, restaurants are scarce and usually attached to the local hotel or resort. Provincial government rest houses are usually self-catering. If you stay at one of these, bring some of your own food, as the local trade store may have very little to choose from.

Markets

There's no bargaining at markets, as prices are fair and cheap. Coconuts, bananas, pawpaws, betel nut and kumara are always on sale, and taro, yams, pana and manioc are usually available also. In some parts of the country you'll find breadfruit, slippery cabbage, edible ferns, mangou and ngali nuts, as well as bush limes, oranges, starfruit, pineapples, mangoes and sugar cane.

The principal food market in the Solomons is the Central Market. See the Honiara section of the Guadalcanal Province chapter for more information.

Trade Stores

Don't expect too much of village trade stores. They mainly sell tinned meat and fish, rice, noodles, soap, dry biscuits, tea and sugar. In larger places the selection may extend to cigarettes, cotton cloth, canned beer and soft drinks.

Coconuts

The primary food of the Pacific, the Solomons included, is the coconut. In addition to being the staple diet, it has other valuable uses. Bearing fruit for about 70 of its 75 years of life, the coconut provides leaves for roofing and weaving, sennit for rope, fibre for making fire, shells for containers, and trunks for house, bridge and canoe building. The plant tolerates sandy soils and is the only large tree which grows on atolls and sandbars without needing human help.

Each of the coconut's five growth stages provides a different form of food or drink. In the first it's ideal for drinking because as yet there's no flesh inside. The next stage is when tasty jellied flesh appears inside.

The best eating stage is the third one, when the flesh inside is firm, but thin and succulent. After this, the flesh becomes thick, hard and ideal for drying into copra. At its fifth stage, the nut begins to shoot while the milk inside goes crispy, making what is known throughout the Pacific as coconut ice cream.

Betel Nut

Bia Blong Solomon is what islanders lightheartedly call the nut of the areca palm. The betel nut is chewed along with the leaves of the betel plant and lime made from burnt crushed coral. It has a mildly intoxicating and tonic effect. Betel-nut chewers usually have a lime box and a few betel leaves with them.

The nut is best eaten when the fruit is hard, ripe and has turned yellow or orange. First bite off the top of the nut, then hold it sideways between your teeth and bite it open. After this, roll up the betel leaf and chew it. Finally, use a spatula or finger to put the lime into your mouth.

Although some members of the Provincial Assembly chew betel nut during debates, very few expats have taken to it, despite its effects. Its acidity is a major drawback. And the lime that is used to make it more palatable is almost certainly carcinogenic. After prolonged use, the juice stains your mouth crimson and makes your teeth go black. The lime eventually eats away your gums and induces mouth cancer, especially among people who chew 10 or more betel nuts a day. About 17% of all local cancer cases – about 30 people per year – are associated with chewing betel nut.

DRINKS
Alcohol

There are no pubs in the Solomons, although a number of hotels and private clubs have bars, and a brewery is under construction in Ranadi. However, any trade store with a fridge usually has some 'Blue can' (Foster's Lager) or a similar brew.

Hotel hours when alcohol may be sold are from 10 am to 10.30 pm weekdays. On Sundays bars open from noon to 10 pm; however, only hotel residents may buy liquor between 2 and 7 pm.

Islanders make their own beverage in Ontong Java and Sikaiana – a fermented coconut juice or palm toddy, sometimes called white beer. A popular, but illegal, drink is known as home brew. The most common form, widely drunk on Bellona, is a coconut toddy fermented with yeast and sugar. Some people can become quite pugnacious and argumentative if they drink too much of it.

Water

Fresh water is usually abundant throughout the main islands but can be scarce on the smaller coral atolls, where local populations often depend on water catchment for their survival. There is also piped water at Munda, Malu'u and Noro and all provincial capitals except Choiseul Bay. Although only a third of the rural population presently has drinkable water, the proportion increases yearly.

Town water is filtered and usually chlorinated. Even so, it's not always safe to drink. Only Buala's is clean and plentiful, while Auki has supply problems. Gizo people always boil their water, of which supplies are limited. Honiara's water is plentiful but variable in quality and so should be boiled or treated. Most hotels will provide boiled water on request.

ENTERTAINMENT
Film

The only regular film screenings are in Honiara, Auki and Gizo. Elsewhere there'll be one on in a school or public hall whenever a plane or a ship brings a film. There's usually a public notice board near the post office or police station with details. Otherwise, just ask around locally.

Dancing

There are several regular dance places in Honiara, though outside the capital modern dances can be hard to find. If you're looking for one, check out any public notice boards and ask around for *sisi*, the Pijin word for parties or dances.

Dancing outside the capital is mainly traditional, though you can also see this in Honiara. There are regular performances each week on hotel premises, and around the town at other times, particularly on Independence Day.

Villagers will probably invite you to any custom dance they have planned, as long as they feel you will obey their rules and do nothing tabu. They will expect you to watch and not to participate, unless specifically invited to do so.

Spectator Sports

Although every provincial capital is also the local sports centre, the best place to watch is in Honiara. Many of the country's best soccer, rugby and cricket leagues are there. Boxing, athletics, basketball, netball and volleyball are also popular.

THINGS TO BUY

There are no duty-free shops currently in the Solomons, though there are plans to open one at Henderson Airport once the new terminal has been completed.

Handicrafts

The only handicraft shops are in Honiara. Elsewhere purchasing is by direct contact with villagers themselves, particularly in the New Georgia Islands and Makira/Ulawa Province.

The Solomons' most distinctive products are nguzunguzus from Western Province, including some which are heavily inlaid with pearl shell. Other items unique to the country are shell money (which is made into headbands, armbands, belts and necklaces) Malaitan *ramos'* (assassins') wands, kapkaps (forehead discs) and ceremonial bowls, fishing floats, dance sticks and housepost figures from Makira/Ulawa.

Other interesting buys are model sailing and outrigger canoes from Temotu Province, shell fish-hooks, bangles, bracelets, carved model dolphins and bat fish, woven bags, mats, fans, stone bowls and figures, and crude clay pots, all from Western Province. In addition, the recently arrived Gilbertese make place mats, trays, laundry baskets, fans, shark-teeth swords and daggers.

Restrictions on Artefact Exports

Many countries, including the USA, Australia and New Zealand, restrict the importation of the bodily parts of sea and land animals. Although there are many beautiful and rare shells for sale in the Solomons, they may be restricted in your country. Turtle shell, while available in the Solomons, is particularly severely embargoed overseas.

Traditional currencies and ornaments incorporating the teeth of porpoises, bats and dogs are frequently subject to foreign Customs controls. Red-feather money from Temotu Province is similarly regulated.

The Solomons government prohibits the export of original artefacts. A great deal of early material was destroyed in the early days of Christianity, or was eagerly scooped up by foreigners and museums at paltry prices. Consequently, there isn't much left.

While there's no problems for replicas, restrictions apply to all original carvings as well as to most clam-shell money and products, as these haven't been made for many years now. Skulls from head-hunting collections are similarly embargoed.

Wrecks on a reef are treated as the property of the local custom owners. Wrecks in the depths are national treasure. Looting results in heavy penalties, confiscation of what's been recovered and deportation. ■

Guadalcanal also makes lime containers, baskets, place mats and tableware, while Rennell and Bellona produce replica spears, clubs, wooden shark-hooks, masks, inlaid bowls, pandanus bags, mats, and model crocodiles, turtles, fish and frogs.

If you're not sure how much a particular handicraft should be, Temotu people suggest you value the item in your own mind in Blue cans (Foster's Lager) – a great favourite there. If it's only worth five Blue cans to you then S$15 is the price you should pay – no more, no less. That's all the islanders pay, so why shouldn't you also?

Getting There & Away

AIR

The Solomons' only international airport is at Honiara (air code HIR) – the old wartime Henderson Field. Until recently, international flights to Kieta in Papua New Guinea also operated through Munda, though these have been suspended.

Honiara's Henderson Airport is 11 km from town and has friendly staff but spartan arrival and departure sections. It has neither duty-free shops nor an information desk, but it does have a foreign-exchange counter that opens for some, but not all, incoming and departing international flights. There are also two car-rental desks, and a handicraft and soft-drinks counter.

The Solomons is serviced internationally by Solomon Airlines, Air Pacific, Air Niugini and Air Nauru.

Round-The-World

Round-The-World (RTW) airline tickets have become very popular in the last few years and are often real bargains. Since the Solomons is on the other side of the world from Europe and the east coast of North America, it will probably be cheaper, if you are setting off from either of these regions, to keep travelling in the same direction than to make a return trip.

The official airline RTW tickets are usually put together by two airlines and permit you to fly anywhere you want on the routes of either airline as long as you don't backtrack. You must usually book the first sector in advance, and cancellation penalties then apply. There may also be a limit to how many stopovers you can make.

Usually the tickets are valid for from 90 days up to a year. Typical prices for these South Pacific RTW tickets are from UK£825 to UK£1130, or US$2100.

An alternative type of RTW ticket is one put together by a travel agent using a combination of discounted tickets. A British agent

like Trailfinders can design some really worthwhile London-to-London RTW combinations. Your local travel agent should be able to advise.

Circle Pacific Tickets

Circle Pacific tickets are similar to RTW tickets and use a combination of airlines to circle the Pacific. Like RTW tickets, they have advance-purchase restrictions and limits on how many stopovers you can make. Typically, fares range between US$1200 and US$1600.

Solomon Airlines has designed its Discover Pacific Pass to add on to any other fares, including RTW and Circle Pacific ones. It permits an unlimited number of stopovers in the Solomons for up to 30 days at a time at a cost of US$399/499/599 for two/three/four stopovers at Pacific destinations not counting Honiara. However, there's an extra US$100 charge if the journey commences in, terminates at, or is via, Auckland in New Zealand, or Brisbane or Cairns in Australia. Furthermore, these tickets may only be purchased in Asia, Europe and North America.

Following is a list of some Solomon Airlines branches and representatives overseas.

Australia
    Brisbane (☎ (07) 229 6441)
    Sydney (☎ (02) 957 0158)
    Melbourne (☎ (02) 602 6758)
Fiji
    Nadi (☎ 72 521)
Germany
    Frankfurt (☎ (69) 172260)
New Zealand
    Auckland (☎ (09) 308 9098)
Papua New Guinea
    Port Moresby (☎ 25 5724)
USA
    c/- Air Promotion Systems, Los Angeles (☎ (213) 670 7302)
Vanuatu
    Port Vila (☎ 2643)

To/From Australia

Solomon Airlines flies once weekly between Honiara and the cities of Brisbane and Cairns in north-eastern Australia, and again once weekly between Honiara and the cities of Sydney and Brisbane.

Solomon Airlines' cheapest one-way fare between Australia and Honiara is from Cairns and costs A$511, or S$1047 if purchased in the Solomons. Prices for the Brisbane and Sydney routes are A$619/S$1264 and A$774/S$1588. Thirty-day excursion returns to or from Cairns cost from A$672 to A$740 (depending on the season), or S$1517, while prices for the Brisbane route are A$897/S$1839. Excursion fares for the Sydney route are from A$977 to A$1076, or S$2206 from Honiara.

Australian Visas

All visitors to Australia except New Zealanders and Norfolk Island residents require a visa. These are issued by Australian high commissions and consulates, including the one in Honiara. Proof of return or onward passage out of Australia must be shown when applying for a visa.

To/From the Pacific

Fiji Air Pacific and Solomon Airlines share a twice-weekly schedule between Nadi (pronounced 'Nandi') in western Fiji, and Honiara. Fares are F$766/S$1334. Both airlines' excursion returns require that you stay a minimum of 10 days and a maximum of 28 days, and cost F$1015/S$1766.

A number of airlines have Central Pacific travel passes: Air Pacific's return triangle fare from Nadi to Tonga and Apia (Western Samoa) is US$448 or F$747, and there's a similarly priced one connecting Vila in Vanuatu and Noumea in New Caledonia.

The Fijian visa position is very easy. Citizens of almost every Commonwealth, European or Asian nation other than Portugal, India, Hong Kong or former or continuing communist countries are admitted without visas. The remainder must first apply to a British consulate or a Fijian high commission – the nearest ones being in Canberra, Australia, and Wellington, New Zealand.

Nauru Air Nauru has schedule fares only, but these are by far the cheapest in the Pacific. It has the lowest one-way fares to Honiara from Auckland (NZ$755), Melbourne (A$529), Sydney (A$475), and Suva in Fiji (F$334). Air Nauru's return fares are a straight doubling of its one-way prices. The only inconvenience is that all its flights are via Nauru, with an unavoidable stopover of one or two nights.

Surprisingly, Air Nauru flights are seldom fully booked. However, they are often delayed, and occasionally postponed at very short notice for up to two days at a time.

The Nauru government allows you to enter its country without a visa as long as you have a ticket with a confirmed onward booking on the next available flight to your immediate destination after Nauru, provided this means that you will be departing Nauru within three days of arrival. Otherwise, you'll need a visa.

Visas are issued by Nauruan consulates in Melbourne, Tokyo, Guam, Honolulu, San Francisco and London. The nearest one to Honiara is at Nauru House (☎ (03) 653 5709), 80 Collins St, Melbourne, Australia.

New Zealand Solomon Airlines has two return flights a week between Honiara and Auckland for NZ$957/S$1482. Its 60-day excursion return costs NZ$1336/S$2075.

Visas are not needed by Australians, Americans, Britons, Canadians, Japanese and most European nationals visiting New Zealand.

Papua New Guinea Both Air Niugini and Solomon Airlines have a once-weekly service between Honiara and Port Moresby. Tickets purchased in Papua New Guinea are priced in kina (K), the currency of that country. One-way fares between Port Moresby and Honiara are K318/S$855, while 30-day excursion returns cost K412/S$1106 and require that you stay a minimum of 10 days.

You can get a 30-day visa on arrival at Port Moresby for K5. This is available to most Western European citizens, North Americans, Australians, New Zealanders and Pacific Islanders. All other nationalities must have a visa prior to arrival. These are issued at Australian consulates or Papua New Guinea government commissions, the nearest ones being in Brisbane, Sydney and Canberra in Australia, Wellington in New Zealand, and Suva in Fiji.

Vanuatu Solomon Airlines flies three times a week between Honiara and Vila for 32,100VT (the airline uses the symbol VUV instead of VT for vatu, Vanuatu's currency), or S$720. It also has a 30-day excursion return fare of 45,000VT/S$1007.

Vanuatu gives 30-day entry permits on arrival to most nationalities, and these permits can be extended for up to four months in any 12. Visas, should you need one, are only issued by the principal immigration officer in Port Vila (☎ 2354).

To/From Asia

If you're going from the Solomons to South-East Asia, the easiest way is to go via Australia, travelling the Honiara-to-Sydney sector with Air Nauru. Once in Australia, Garuda has an apex fare from Brisbane and Sydney to Denpasar and Jakarta in Indonesia. Its one-way low and high-season fares are A$757 and A$898 respectively. It also has a return fare allowing a maximum stay of 45 days for A$1090.

One-way low and high-season prices from Indonesia to eastern Australia are US$592 and US$702 respectively. The same route return is US$852. Alternatively, Qantas can get you from eastern Australia to Singapore during its low season for around A$840 one way or A$1211 excursion return. If you buy the ticket in Singapore, it's SI$1067 one way or SI$1534 excursion return.

While you are in Australia, you can check out a range of onward connections through STA Travel. Its head office (☎ (03) 47 4711) in Australia is at 224 Faraday St, Carlton,

Melbourne. It has offices all over Australia, as well as in the USA, Britain and Asia.

If instead you plan to go to North-East Asia, Solomon Airlines' fares work out the cheapest if you can buy them in Honiara. Its one-way flights are all in concert with other airlines, but cost S$2706/US$998 to Manila, S$2857/US$1054 to Seoul, and S$3167/US$1168 to four Japanese airports, including Tokyo.

To/From Europe

London is the best place in Europe to find cheap fares. If you look around the big agencies and the bucket shops, you may be able to get to Australia for between UK£300 and UK£400 one way or UK£540 and UK£700 return. These tickets can be written on normal IATA airlines such as British Airways, Qantas etc, but are considerably cheaper than the normal one-way fare to Australia. When dealing with bucket shops, make sure you understand the sort of ticket you are buying, and don't hand over your money until you have both your ticket and a confirmed seat aboard the flight of your choice! Don't pay if you're only waitlisted. In addition, when paying a deposit, get the details of the flight you've requested, including any restrictions on it, and a receipt. Also check whether all your money will be refunded if the flight is cancelled or changed to an inconvenient date. Finally, watch out for any unexpected extra charges.

Once in Australia, you can take the Solomon Airlines' A$511 flight from Cairns to Honiara, or Air Nauru's A$475 service from Sydney. Otherwise, there are several airlines connecting Australia to Europe for around A$1300 one way or A$1800 return.

To/From North America

USA Your best route between the Solomons and the USA is via Fiji. Air Pacific flies from Nadi to Los Angeles in the low season for F$955 one way or F$1400 return. If you come from the USA, the fare is US$947 one way or US$1104. This round-trip fare is an apex one requiring a return within three months. Air Pacific's flights stop at Los

Angeles, but you can get to New York with local carriers, such as United Airlines, which has a fare of US$361 one way or US$503 return. Alternatively, you can buy multiple one-way air passes outside the USA for around US$300.

Canada Canadian Airlines International's one-way fare from Vancouver to Sydney is C$1180/A$1337; from Toronto to Sydney it's C$1509/A$1709. The same airline's low-season nonrefundable return fare, which requires a minimum stay of seven days and a maximum stay of two months, costs C$1191/A$1349 from Vancouver to Sydney or C$1367/A$1549 from Toronto to Sydney.

SEA
Cruise Ship
Honiara has not been visited regularly by cruise ships since the mid-1980s, though there are plans to reintroduce such services. When this happens, it's likely that getting to or from the country this way on a one-way ticket will be more expensive than flying, although food, accommodation and entertainment would be included in the cruise price. Guadalcanal Travel Services may be able to help you find a berth on a cruise ship from the Solomons to Australia if one's available. P&O Lines and Sitmar Cruises used to service the Solomons and may do so again. Their Australian addresses are P&O Booking Centre (☎ (02) 23 70333), World Travel HQ Pty Ltd, 33 Bligh St, Sydney; and Sitmar Cruises (☎ (008) 42 2277/22 2277), 39 Martin Place, Sydney.

Cargo Boat
Gone are the days when tramp steamers plied the world's oceans, picking up stray travellers with little or no fuss. Yet it's still possible to book a passage on a freighter with the help of an experienced travel agent in a major port. Otherwise, although few of the cargo lines take passengers at all readily, you may be able to get aboard if you ask the captain. However, the usual answer is that there's no room for passengers – the only accommodation is for the crew.

Despite this discouraging news, two organisations in the USA can sometimes help you get aboard the occasional cargo boat. These are the Freighter Travel Club, PO Box 12693, Salem, Massachusetts 97309, USA; and Freighter World Cruises, Suite 335, 180 Salt Lake Ave, Pasadena CA 91101, USA.

Yacht
Entry & Departure Procedures Yachts should check in on arrival at Gizo or Lata to go through Customs. Otherwise, you can call in at one of the country's international shipping ports where there's a Customs branch or a local police station. Staff will radio your arrival to officials in Honiara, who will allow you seven to 14 days grace to get to Honiara or Munda, where you can formally clear Immigration. They'll also want to know your planned port of departure.

There's a rather discouraging light fee for yachts sailing in Solomons waters. This is for the use of lighthouses and buoys. The cost is a flat S$100 fee plus 5c a tonne. Immigration staff collect the fee at Honiara and Munda.

Hitching a Ride It is much easier to get to the Solomons by yacht than by cargo boat. The best way is to hang around yachting marinas. There are plenty of good places on the US west coast and along Australia's north-eastern seaboard. Auckland, Tahiti, Noumea and Vila all have sizeable yachting communities where you might find a boat.

Conversely, if you're in Honiara and want a ride onwards, try the Point Cruz Yacht Club, where yacht owners sometimes leave notices up saying 'crew wanted'. Yacht skippers, if they accept you, will charge an average of US$15 or US$20 a day, though you may be lucky and find one who will charge less. They will expect you to have an onward or return air ticket if you're planning to travel on to another country with them. Otherwise, the skipper will have to drop you off when he leaves the Solomons.

Before going on a long trip, spend a few days sailing on the yacht to get your sea legs. That way you'll also be able to see how prone you are to seasickness – especially if you've been put to work in the galley. If you're sensitive to seasickness, every moment will be torture, and you will only be a burden to your skipper.

Canoe

There is a very rarely used route between the Solomons and Papua New Guinea via Ontong Java in Malaita Province, and Nukumanu in Papua New Guinea. It's only really feasible if you've a definite reason to go to either place, as they're both pretty out of the way to start with. The Ontong Java section of this book tells you how to visit Nukumanu.

TOURS
Package Tours

Although unlikely to suit budget travellers with time to spare, package tours are ideal for those full-time employees who only have two to three weeks annual holiday.

Surprisingly, a well-selected package holiday can turn out much cheaper than a budget trip, and with high-class facilities thrown in. This is because package deals take into account so-called reverse discounts. These can include free car hire, subsidised hotel prices, vouchers to dine out around the capital, and free sporting activities, including some on or under the water.

The Pacific Island Travel Centre in Sydney (☎ (02) 262 6011) has several excellent eight, 10, 12 and 14-day packages from Brisbane and Sydney to Guadalcanal and/or Western Province. Eight-day trips cost from A$1156/1005 each for singles/doubles, while 14-day ones are A$1809/1430. Alternatively, seven, nine or 12-day combined Solomons and Vanuatu or Fiji packages cost from A$1320/1160 to A$1480/1425 each for singles/doubles.

If these don't suit you, try some other travel agents. You are sure to find at least one package holiday that fits your bill.

Environmental Tours

Scobie's Walkabout Tours (☎ (049) 57 0458), PO Box 43, Newcastle 2300, Australia, takes groups of between six and 15 on mixed culture and nature trips around some of the New Georgia Islands, and occasionally also to Rennell. Its 10-day trip costs A$1523 for the Solomons part (international fares are extra). The Solomons part of its 15-day trip costs A$2285.

LEAVING THE SOLOMONS

There's a S$20 airport tax charged against all international passengers leaving the country. The only exemptions are transit passengers who don't leave the Customs and Immigration area at the airport, and children under two years old.

To avoid your airline cancelling your booking, you should confirm your onward flight either on arrival in Honiara or, at the latest, 72 hours before your departure. At the same time, find out your check-in time, and be sure to be at the airport by then.

WARNING

This chapter is particularly vulnerable to change: prices for international travel are volatile, routes are introduced and cancelled, schedules change, special deals come and go, and rules and visa requirements are amended. Airlines and governments seem to take a perverse pleasure in making price structures and regulations as complicated as possible. You should check directly with the airline or a travel agent to make sure you understand how a fare (and ticket you may buy) works. In addition, the travel industry is highly competitive and there are many lurks and perks. The upshot of this is that you should get opinions, quotes and advice from as many airlines and travel agents as possible before you part with your hard-earned cash. The details given in this chapter should be regarded as pointers and are not a substitute for your own careful, up-to-date research.

Getting Around

The Solomons' initial entry permit is for two to four weeks, which is not sufficient time in which to see the whole country. However, you can now get this permit extended to a total of six months, which is ample time in which to go to even the remotest places.

AIR

Domestic services are operated by Solomon Airlines (☎ 20031), PO Box 23, and Western Pacific Air Services (☎ 30533), PO Box 411. Solomon Airlines provides regular services to 20 airfields around the country. Western Pacific also services six of these, as well as nine other smaller ones. Another airfield, at Tagibangara in Choiseul, is temporarily closed but will reopen when repairs are completed. Construction is proceeding on the East Rennell Airfield. Western Pacific is SDA-owned and doesn't fly on Saturdays.

Solomon Airlines flies about 150 sectors a week, while Western Pacific does about 75. Both airlines operate charter services if required, and restrict the free baggage allowance to 16 kg. You are more likely to be charged excess baggage at Henderson Airport than elsewhere if you're slightly over the limit.

BOAT

The country's division into numerous islands, with many small settlements and a low population density, has made inter-island shipping the country's main means of transport. While air transport carries 50,000 internal passengers a year, ships move this number every seven weeks. Even so, shipping services to remote areas are irregular, and wharves infrequent. Vessels visiting the outer islands often use their dinghy to ferry people to and from the shore, while new passengers often come aboard by canoe.

Ships occasionally sail several days earlier or later than scheduled. Details of shipping movements are posted up in company offices at main ports, but the

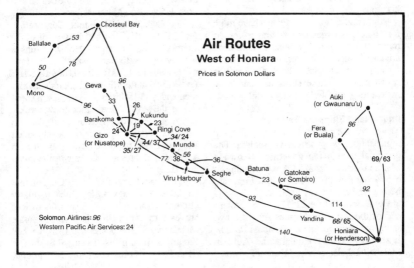

Air Routes
West of Honiara

Prices in Solomon Dollars

Choiseul Bay
Ballalae — 53
50
78
Mono
96
Geva
96 — 33
26
Barakoma — Kukundu
19 — 23
24 — Ringi Cove
Gizo — 34/24
(or Nusatope) — 44/32 — Munda
35/27 — 77 — 38 — 56
36
Viru Harbour — Seghe — Batuna
23 — Gatokae (or Sombiro)
93 — 68
114
Yandina
140 — 66/65
Honiara (or Henderson)
Auki (or Gwaunaru'u)
86
Fera (or Buala)
69/63
92

Solomon Airlines: *96*
Western Pacific Air Services: *24*

83

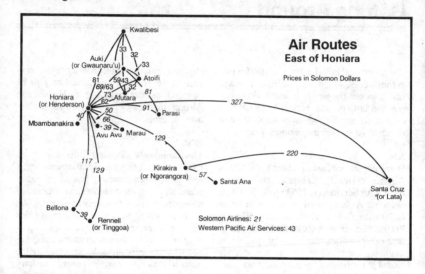

Air Routes
East of Honiara

Prices in Solomon Dollars

Kwalibesi
Auki (or Gwaunaru'u)
33
32
33
81
59
43
69/63
73
32
62
Atoifi
81
Afutara
Honiara (or Henderson)
327
50
91
Parasi
40
66
Mbambanakira
39
Avu Avu
Marau
129
117
129
220
Kirakira (or Ngorangora)
57
Santa Ana
Santa Cruz (or Lata)
Bellona
39
Rennell (or Tinggoa)

Solomon Airlines: 21
Western Pacific Air Services: 43

captain's decision to leave is final. So keep your eye on the vessel. Once the cargo is loaded, the skipper may not wait.

When your ship is travelling from island to island, there's usually ample time to go ashore at each stop. Ask the captain when he's leaving each anchorage. He'll stick to his word.

Copra and cargo boats always have room for some passengers. Most bigger vessels have one or more cabins. The Marine Division's six B and L-class boats have room for 70 passengers each, plus 14 more in their seven cabins. These ships are under 40 metres long, so they're pretty snug!

Inter-Island Shipping Services

There are nine passenger-carrying shipping organisations with offices in Honiara. The principal one is the government- owned Marine Division (☎ 21535), whose ships go everywhere in the country. Its offices are beside Honiara's main wharf.

Coral Seas Ltd (☎ 22811), at the eastern end of the capital's Hibiscus Ave, has two ships, the *Iuminao* and the *Compass Rose II*. Both ply between Honiara and Auki in Malaita, and also service Western Province,

while the *Compass Rose II* does monthly services to Maramasike and Makira/Ulawa as well.

Solomon Islands Navigation Services (☎ 22404), in Honiara's NPF Plaza, operates a weekly schedule with its vessel the *Solomon Princess II* between the capital and both Malaita and Maramasike.

The Isabel Development Corporation (☎ 23337), or IDC, with offices on top of the Lena Cinema in central Honiara, runs a weekly service to Santa Isabel, and a fortnightly one to Makira/Ulawa. KHY (☎ 30134), with offices in Kukum's factory area and also facilities at Gizo, has a small vessel, the MV *Hiliboe*, which does a weekly return trip between Honiara and Western Province. National Fisheries Development Ltd (☎ 21507), opposite Coral Seas Ltd, has a service six days a week between Honiara and Tulagi.

The Guadalcanal Provincial Government (☎ 20041) owns vessels which regularly circle the country's main island. Its offices are east of the main wharf in Honiara's Mendana Ave. Opposite them, in the MP Kwan Building, is Tavuilo Shipping (☎ 22831), whose vessel, the MV *Faalia*, has two cabins and plies between Honiara and Auki. Finally, there's Olifasia Shipping (☎ 21032), with an office in a warehouse beside Honiara's main wharf. It operates the *Olifasia II*, which connects Honiara with the New Georgia Islands between Marovo Lagoon and Gizo.

Life Aboard Ship Deck travel is all right for a short journey. So also is 1st class on the *Iuminao*. But if you're going any distance, hire a cabin. They are only double the deck price.

Fares are pretty cheap considering some of the trips are nearly two weeks long, such as those to the far end of Temotu Province or the full circuit of Western Province. The dearest single cabin fare in a Marine Division vessel is only S$126 from Honiara to the Shortland Islands.

In addition to having somewhere to spread your baggage, your cabin is a place to go when the sea gets rough. While everyone else is seasick, you can be happily sleeping on your bunk until the weather improves. The below-deck cabins get pretty hot and stuffy, but the cabins on the upper deck are usually kept cool by sea breezes on otherwise steaming hot nights.

No-one will go into your cabin unless you invite them to, but an open door at night on board ship means it's all right for deck passengers to sleep there too. So shut your door, or else the next morning you'll find a number of sleeping bodies curled up on your floor!

There's a good chance you'll be the only foreigner aboard. Many of the other passengers will tell you about their home islands, and show you around them when the ship gets there.

What to Take Mattresses are provided in the cabins, but you'll need a sleeping sheet or bag, and a sleeping mat if you prefer to go deck class. A pillow is also a good idea and definitely preferable to using your very hard life jacket as one.

There's usually plenty of drinking water aboard, and hot water on the boil in the kitchen. But food can be pretty sparse, unless you've brought your own.

You'll also need your own cutlery, plastic cups and plates, and small pots and pans, as – other than the ever-steaming kettles – there's no cooking gear provided.

If you bring too much food, so what? If you give some away, your new friends are sure to repay your generosity with unexpected kindnesses throughout the trip.

Although you might expect villagers to sell you bananas, coconuts and pawpaws at every stop, surprisingly they seldom do. Instead, crew members will often trail a line from the stern. When a large fish is caught, everyone gets a helping. If you want to do some fishing of your own, colourful squid lures are particularly good for catching kingfish and tuna.

Canoe
Fibreglass-hulled outboard-motor boats, commonly known as motor canoes, or just simply canoes, connect anchorages and island wharves with nearby shoreside settlements. Although motor canoes sometimes cover considerable distances – up to 80 km each way in often choppy seas – they are much better suited to protected lagoons, such as those around New Georgia and northern Malaita.

Always dress for wet weather when you take a motor-canoe ride. Although there's usually an enclosed area in the bow where your baggage should remain dry, everywhere else aboard gets wet!

If you look around a motor canoe for safety equipment, you won't find much, except perhaps spare fuel, paddles and a bailer. Flares, life belts and fire extinguishers will be conspicuous by their absence. Every year some motor canoes are lost in bad weather, so think twice before taking a long journey in one.

Motor-canoe prices can be alarmingly high, as fuel in some parts of the country costs S$2 to S$2.25 a litre, despite being S$1.05 a litre in Honiara. In addition, a new fibreglass boat, plus a 25 to 30-horsepower engine, costs up to S$5000.

Shared motor-canoe fares are mostly based on a one-way journey for the driver plus two passengers. One-way or return charters usually cost the same – ie six times the shared price. This takes into account the need for the boat driver and the canoe to return to their starting point even if you don't. Motor-canoe charter fees are currently based on a price of S$25 a half day, or S$50 a full day, plus fuel.

Paddle canoes are still commonly used in sheltered waters, especially by children. Although you may see some using a palm leaf for a sail if the wind is right, sail-driven craft which used to venture far offshore for fishing and trading have now been almost entirely replaced by motorised ones.

CAR & MOTORBIKE

There are 1300 km of motorable roads in the Solomons, mainly in Guadalcanal, Malaita and Western Province. Only 84 km of these are bitumen sealed – mostly in and around Honiara. The remainder are coral or gravel surfaced. There are also about 1500 km of secondary plantation and Forestry roads varying from all-weather quality to tracks suitable only for tractors and trailers. You drive on the left-hand side.

Rental

Hire cars and 4WD vehicles are only available in Honiara.

HITCHING

If you want a ride through the countryside, just flag down a passing vehicle and ask the driver the cost of a lift. Many will give you a free ride, but others will charge between 10 and 15c a km. However, if you charter someone, or get them to go far out of their way, you will have to pay up to 50c a km.

WALKING

Footpaths vary from clearly defined trails over a metre wide to some which are very indistinct and less than the width of an adult. Some islanders, particularly in Santa Isabel and Choiseul, talk lightly of roads through the bush, when they only mean footpaths.

Always ask how wide the road is if you suspect your informant really means a path.

If you need to use footpaths in the bush or over mountains, you should hire a guide. If you only need directions through a village, often young children will be detailed to show you the way, as there are sometimes dozens of paths – all unsignposted – leading in many different directions.

However, you will need an adult guide if you're bushwalking through unpopulated areas. Fees for their services vary from island to island, but they are usually around S$6 to S$8 a day, or S$8 to S$10 if the guide also acts as your bearer. In addition, you should pay for any nights your guide is away from home, and whatever meals and accommodation they need during the journey.

If you're going through really dense undergrowth or rugged mountains, it's wise to have a companion as well as a guide. If one of you is seriously hurt, the guide will know where to find help, while one other remains to comfort the injured person.

Avoid leaving the path in a rainforest, as it's quite possible to get completely lost within 30 metres of your route. Crossing fast-flowing rivers can also be very hazardous.

LOCAL TRANSPORT
To/From the Airport

International flights are usually met by the Red Buses (minibuses) owned by Zankos Express (☎ 21291), which will give you door-to-door service for S$6 to wherever you want to stay in Honiara. Otherwise, taxis cost about S$20, while public minibuses are S$1.50. For the latter, wait under the trees by the main road going west (left) into Honiara. You will be expected to pay in Solomons, not foreign, currency.

Bus

Minibus services are only plentiful in Honiara. Public transport elsewhere is only available in the Guadalcanal Plains. Preferably, tender the correct fare. Smoking is banned on most buses.

Taxi

Taxis are plentiful in Honiara. It's best to agree beforehand on the price, which may be slightly higher at night. However, the vast majority of taxi drivers charge the right price. Currently this is around S$1 a km, which is also the minimum fare. Most drivers have some small change, though very few will have anything bigger than a S$10 note. Taxi drivers don't expect a tip.

TOURS

Tour operators from Honiara specialise in taking tourist groups to WW II battlefield sites along the north-western Guadalcanal coastline. Other tours from the capital are to Tulagi and Nggela's war sites, and Savo's megapode birds and hot springs. Trips further afield from Honiara include western Malaita's Langa Langa Lagoon, Santa Ana Island in eastern Makira, and Lake Te'Nggano on Rennell.

Western Province tours mainly originate in Gizo or Munda, though local operators in New Georgia's Marovo Lagoon can also show you around their area. From Gizo, tours go mountain climbing on Kolombangara, visit Simbo's volcano and megapode birds, and view war sites in northern Kohinggo, the Shortlands and Choiseul. Some of these are combined with scuba trips around Ghizo Island and the northern part of Vonavona Lagoon. There are also trips from Munda around north-western New Georgia and across to northern Rendova.

See the relevant chapters for more information.

Warning

You should think carefully about visiting the more remote and traditional parts of the country, as there's a rather ambivalent attitude to tourism in such places. The Moro area of south-eastern Guadalcanal has strict rules for both its members and visitors, while the Kwaio people of east-central Malaita don't appreciate fellow islanders, let alone outsiders.

Many outlying areas are very isolated, being visited by only one vessel every four to six weeks – less frequently if the seas are rough. Exploring the smaller islands for a few hours while your ship is anchored offshore is never a problem, but staying any length of time may well be. You should give the chief ample warning by radio if you want to stay – and be prepared to accept the answer no. ■

Guadalcanal Province

Guadalcanal is the largest island in the Solomons group, and a province in its own right. Originally called Wadi-al-Canar by its Spanish discoverer, the island's name was anglicised to Guadalcanar, becoming Guadalcanal in the 19th century. It is known in Pijin as Galekana, or just simply as Solomon.

Today, Guadalcanal's northern coast is the hub of the new nation's life. Government, commerce and tourism are all centred in the capital, Honiara, and access is relatively easy to anywhere along its adjacent coast. Consequently, development in this part of the island has proceeded apace.

In contrast, the southern coast, or Weather Coast, as it is known, is much less accessible. Here life moves slowly, always dependent on the weather, as the area's name suggests. While transport around the north is normally on four wheels, any visit to the southern coast is likely to involve at least some travel on foot or across water.

HISTORY

A cave on the Poha River, north of Honiara, is believed to have first been occupied about 6000 years ago, and then again around 1000 BC. However, European discovery was not until 9 April 1568, when the crew of the 30-tonne Spanish skiff *Santiago* first sighted Guadalcanal.

Gallego, the vessel's commander and one of the leaders of the Mendaña expedition, named the island after his home village of Wadi-al-Canar in southern Spain. A month later, Mendaña himself formally claimed Guadalcanal for the Spanish king.

The Spaniards are believed to have searched for gold in several rivers along the island's northern coast. Despite local legends to the contrary, they probably failed to find any and sailed away two months later.

No other Europeans visited Guadalcanal for over 200 years. Then two Britons, Shortland in 1788 and Ball in 1790, sailed by.

They were followed three years later by the French explorer D'Entrecasteaux.

By the 1890s, a few traders and missionaries were living on Guadalcanal. On 6 October 1893, the British government proclaimed a protectorate over most of what is now the Solomon Islands, including Guadalcanal. The islanders' lives in the following years remained basically unchanged. Fighting and killing diminished, however, as the influence of missionaries and the Protectorate government steadily spread.

WW II & After

The events of 1942 changed all that. First there was the panic-stricken departure of colonial Europeans, followed by the arrival of the Japanese forces on 8 June. Then an immense US fleet appeared, followed by the landing of US marines at Red Beach between 7 and 8 August. Six months of desperate fighting ensued until the secret Japanese withdrawal from Cape Esperance in early February 1943.

Prior to the US arrival, the sole Allied force on the island consisted of 12 islander volunteers and one Australian-born officer.

One of the islanders was Sergeant-Major Jacob (later Sir Jacob) Vouza, who, when found by the Japanese with a US flag on him, was tortured in the hope that he would reveal the marines' position. The Japanese tied Vouza to a tree and bayoneted him in both his cheeks, his chest and his neck. Left for dead, he managed to free himself, swim a creek with his hands still bound, and crawl three km back to the US lines. Although exhausted, he refused medical treatment until he had told his friends the enemy's positions.

While recovering, Vouza told his incredulous admirers, 'When I was a police-boy before the war, I often was naughty and caused plenty trouble for the government. So I told myself to do something good for King George to pay him back for all that trouble I gave'. Enter one instant hero!

Meanwhile the USA quickly established daytime air supremacy, which meant that enemy ships had to move at night. Japanese

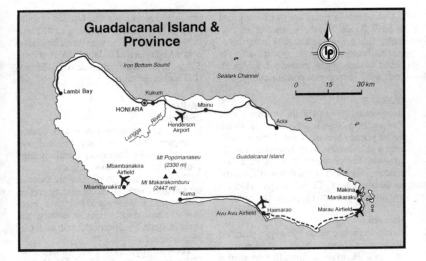

Guadalcanal Island & Province

destroyer transports ran close inshore under cover of darkness to deliver their cargoes of men and supplies. This occurred with such regularity they were called the Tokyo Express.

Once their loads were delivered, the Japanese warships would shell US positions on their way back to base. At the same time, routine nightly nuisance raids by two Japanese seaplanes, nicknamed Louie the Louse and Washing Machine Charlie, kept the marines awake.

During the Guadalcanal campaign, six naval battles were fought, and 67 warships and transports sunk on both sides. Although US casualties were heavy, with over 7,000 Americans killed, Japan's casualties were crippling. Of more than 24,000 soldiers lost, over a third died from disease, starvation or war wounds. Another 15,000 perished in sea actions. More than 800 Japanese aircraft were destroyed and over 2400 irreplaceable pilots and aircrew lost. Admiral Tanaka, one of Japan's most successful fleet commanders, said of his country's defeat on the island the Japanese called Guadakanaruku, 'On that insignificant shore, inhabited only by islanders, Japan's doom was sealed'.

Once WW II was over, Honiara replaced Tulagi as the national capital, and Guadalcanal became readily accepted as the most important island in the group. Large agricultural projects were begun in 1976 along the northern coastal plains. Following Independence, government, commerce, transport and tourist services were concentrated in the Honiara area – a process begun in the closing days of British colonial rule.

GEOGRAPHY

Guadalcanal is 160 km long by 48 km wide and has an area of 5336 sq km. The island has a north-western to south-eastern mountainous spine lying close to its southern coast.

Guadalcanal's interior is forbidding, with many sheer and ragged mountains. Mt Makarakomburu (2447 metres) and Mt Popomanaseu (2330 metres) are the nation's tallest peaks.

Guadalcanal's north-western corner is composed of quiescent volcanic cones rising to 700 metres, while on the north-eastern coast these mountains descend into wide alluvial plains, thickly planted with coconuts palms, cacao trees and oil palms.

Guadalcanal's rivers are short and prone to flash floods. Similarly, treacherous currents, fierce seas and strong undertows, especially along the southern coast, make the island's anchorages hazardous for small craft, even in moderate conditions.

CLIMATE

Guadalcanal has two main weather zones. The southern coast is exposed to the south-easterly trade winds, which blow straight across it, releasing very heavy rainfall. In contrast, the northern coast is in a rain shadow, sheltered by the island's central mountain chain. Consequently, Honiara usually enjoys calm and pleasant weather.

Honiara

It rains in the capital on 196 days a year, and the average annual rainfall is 2154 mm (85 inches). Honiara's morning humidity reaches 89% in March, but averages 85% through the year. Afternoons are always much less humid, with the reading falling to 69% in August. Annual maximum and minimum temperatures are 31°C and 21°C respectively.

Guadalcanal's weather diversity is such that Henderson Airport, only 11 km east of Honiara, has 19 fewer days of rain a year than the capital and an annual average of only 1982 mm (78 inches). Honiara's period of heaviest rain is from December to April, when as much as 363 mm (14 inches) may fall a month, while Henderson gets most of its rain from November to March.

The Weather Coast

Although Guadalcanal's southern coast is commonly called the Weather Coast, a better name would be the Bad-Weather Coast or the Wild-Weather Coast. Heavy rain on this side of the island frequently causes floods, with food gardens, and even houses, occasionally washed away. Heavy seas accompanying the wild weather often prevent ships anchoring.

The Weather Coast averages 5000 mm (197 inches) of rain a year, with its heaviest falls coming from July to September. Choghiri, halfway along this coast, holds the

province's record for the heaviest annual rainfall. In 1972 an astonishing 13,452 mm (529 inches) fell in the year there. Similarly, over a 13-day period in July 1965, Avu Avu, 23 km further to the east, received 3125 mm (123 inches) of rain.

FAUNA
Crocodiles

Most large estuarine rivers and coastal swamps in Guadalcanal have resident salt-water crocodiles. There's a particularly large concentration in the Lauvi Lagoon.

The closest crocs to Honiara are those in the Lungga River and its connecting creeks. Small numbers are likely to be in every sizeable northern coastal river or estuary, and even in quite small creeks, east as far as Marau Sound.

The same applies along the southern coast. Villagers warn of crocodiles in the Hoilava River and most other large or muddy waterways east of it.

Birds

Bird-watchers need only go up to the ridges just behind Honiara to see a great range of birds. However, to see species endemic to Guadalcanal you must search highland areas. A Guadalcanal subspecies of the thicket warbler only lives in places above 500 metres, while the Guadalcanal mountain owl has only been seen around the island's tallest peaks.

ECONOMY

The island's economy centres around Honiara and the Guadalcanal Plains area. While Honiara is the nation's business centre, the plains are the only large flat and fertile expanse of land in the country.

Since 1976, successful large-scale copra, palm-oil and cattle-raising projects have come to the plains. However rice farming, another large-scale venture, failed in 1986 when cyclone Namu destroyed fields and equipment.

There is an experimental clam farm at Aruligo, and commercial piggeries and poultry farms have been set up elsewhere along the northern coast.

Many creeks in the island's central mountains have grey shale beds and may be gold-bearing. Several of the wide alluvial rivers along the northern coast have similar features.

Even so, mining only occurs in a very small way. A few villagers in the highlands of central Guadalcanal regularly pan for gold, especially along the Matepono River and at Gold Ridge, and a small open-cut mine is planned for the latter area.

PEOPLE
Guadalcanal has about 96,500 people, of whom 37,000 live in the Honiara area. Of the remaining 59,500, most are coastal dwellers,

with about 7500 living in small, isolated hamlets in the highland interior. Although there is a continuous line of settlements along the southern coast, only about 14,000 people at present make their home there.

Many people from the Marau Sound area are descended from Malaitan settlers who migrated there between the 17th and late 19th centuries. These people still follow their original island's customs, buying shell money from Malaita to pay bride price. This tradition has now spread to other parts of the southern coast and into the isolated highlands.

ARTS
Guadalcanal's main products are bukaware baskets, trays, coasters and table mats. Bamboo panpipes and decorated lime containers, used by the omnipresent betel-nut chewers, are also produced. Turtle-shell pendants, which incorporate a frigate-bird design fixed to a crescent-shaped piece of gold-lipped oyster shell, are made on the southern coast, while pendants, earrings and bracelets are made in Marau Sound.

ACCOMMODATION

If you're planning to travel around the southern part of the island, call into subprovincial headquarters and the Guadalcanal provincial government offices in Honiara's town centre. Staff members will know where you can camp, or which villages have an empty hut for visitors to use and who you should see once you're there.

FOOD

Most villages have a basic shop. However, it's wise to carry some food of your own when travelling outside Honiara in case the local trade stores have run short of their standard stocks of curried meat, rice, etc. Fresh fruit is only available in season and can be hard to find, especially in isolated mountain villages.

WATER

Honiara's water quality has been rather varied at times. Many expats regularly boil or treat theirs.

Honiara

The word Honiara is derived from the islanders' name for a piece of land about 400 metres to the west of Point Cruz – Na-ho-ni-ara, meaning 'facing the north-east winds'. Because of its size and importance, the capital is administered separately from Guadalcanal Province, by the Honiara Municipal Authority.

Several Honiara companies offer sightseeing tours on either side of the town, while others do scuba and snorkel trips to view the many underwater sites in the area. There are also plenty of restaurants, cafés, bars and handicraft shops to while away your time in.

Although many reminders of the wartime Guadalcanal campaign have now been removed, occasional ones still turn up. Frequently when a major building project is underway, human bones or unexploded munitions are found. If you hear a series of short, sharp booms, you can be sure old shells are being detonated and the sound is being carried all the way from the bomb-disposal centre beside the Alligator Creek 12.5 km away.

HISTORY

Honiara owes its life to the huge military-supply depot the USA built between Kukum and Point Cruz in 1943. To support its war effort in the north-western Solomons, the USA constructed wharves, roads and storage sheds and completed the airfield at Henderson. With the Americans' departure at the end of WW II, the British moved their capital from the devastated Tulagi to Honiara to make use of these brand-new facilities.

Originally built along a narrow coastal strip, the capital has spread inland on to several nearby ridges, many of which were battlefields in WW II.

POPULATION & PEOPLE

Honiara is the Solomons' melting pot. People from all over the country come here for work, holidays, or just to shop. Consequently you will see an immense range of human features in the town, including the full diversity of Melanesian physiques, and also Polynesian, Gilbertese, European and Chinese faces.

Honiara's population has grown from 2600 in 1959 to its present figure of 37,000. This is just under 11% of the new nation's population and 38% of Guadalcanal's.

INFORMATION

Tourist Office

The Solomon Islands Tourist Authority (☎ 22442) office is beside the Mendana Hotel in Honiara's town centre. Its friendly staff can advise you about tours and what to see, both in Honiara and throughout the country.

Money

Foreign exchange is handled by all three banks. The National Bank of the Solomon Islands (NBSI), the Australia & New Zealand Banking Group Ltd (ANZ) and Westpac Banking Corporation all have branches in Mendana Ave. The NBSI and Westpac also have Chinatown branches.

The Mendana Hotel will change foreign currency and travellers' cheques outside normal banking hours, but at a reduced exchange rate.

Post & Telecommunications

The post office, just off Mendana Ave, is open Monday to Friday from 8 am to 4.30 pm and Saturday mornings. Its postage, parcel and poste restante services are all reliable.

Close by are the Philatelic Bureau and Solomon Telekom. The latter's public telex facility is open Monday to Friday from 7 am to 6 pm, and Saturday and Sunday mornings.

Travel Agencies

Guadalcanal Travel Services (☎ 22587), commonly called GTS, is in the Y Sato Building. It is the only international travel agency in the Solomons, and also represents Air Nauru.

Film & Photography

If you come to the Solomons without a 35-mm camera, the only place you'll get one is at the Chan Wing Supermarket in Chinatown. You can also buy slide film there, and at the Honiara Dispensary in the NPF Plaza.

Print film is more plentiful. Both Solomon Fastfoto below the Lona Cinema and Kings Photo Service in the NPF Plaza stock it and can develop it in 24 hours. You can also get print film at The Pharmacy in Ashley Street and at the Technique Radios Centre in the MP Kwan Building.

Medical Services

The Central Hospital (☎ 23600) in Kukum, known colloquially as Nambanaen, provides free medical attention. For quick service and to avoid a queue, make an appointment. The Honiara Dental Clinic (☎ 22746) is in Ashley St, beside Kingsley's Fast Food Centre. There are seven public clinics in the Honiara area and four other private clinics. Ask your hotel or embassy for a recommen-

dation. There are two chemists in town: The Pharmacy (☎ 22911) in Ashley St and the Honiara Dispensary (☎ 23595) in the NPF Plaza.

Emergency

Following are telephone numbers which may be of assistance.

Hospital	☎ 23600
Ambulance	☎ 22200
Police	☎ 22999
Fire	☎ 22999
Marine emergency	☎ 21535

ORIENTATION

Although there's a constant stream of minibuses, the best way to see Honiara is on foot. The central area from the Solomon Kitano Mendana Hotel (locally known as the Mendana or the Mendana Hotel) to Chinatown can be covered in a 20-minute stroll along Mendana Ave, the town's main thoroughfare.

The nation's principal business houses are in this compact sector, including national and provincial government offices, two of the three hotels, the main shopping centre, the nation's largest port complex, transport and communications bureaus for contact with the outside world, the market, banks, the majority of the restaurants and snackbars, and several church buildings.

The capital's 12-km-long urban sprawl has within it several separate communities. To the west are the settlements of Rove and White River Village, while immediately to the east of the Mataniko River (pronounced 'Muh-tanny-koh') are Mataniko Village, populated by settlers from Ontong Java, and Chinatown. Beyond them are Kukum and Ranadi.

Behind the main town and larger suburbs are many recently built housing areas, some of which started life as squatters' camps. New settlements have occupied the ridge overlooking Honiara and Iron Bottom Sound, many of them with breathtaking views. Amongst these are Lenggakiki, Vavaea and Mbokonavera to the west of the

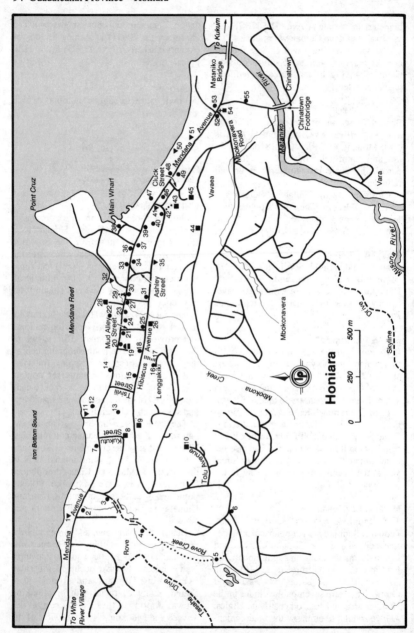

■ PLACES TO STAY

8	YWCA
9	Island Chain Holidays Guest House
10	Testimony Guest House
26	Hibiscus Hotel
28	Solomon Kitano Mendana Hotel
43	Church of Melanesia Transit House
44	SSEC Transit House
45	United Church Rest House

▼ PLACES TO EAT

1	Rove Market
8	YWCA
11	La Perouse Restaurant
32	Point Cruz Yacht Club
35	Hong Kong Palace Restaurant
41	Garden Fast Food Bar & Hot Bread Kitchen
50	Seoul Cafetaria
51	Central Market

OTHER

2	Prison
3	SIBC
4	Botanical Gardens
5	Water Pump Village
6	Taiwanese Embassy
7	Minana Handicrafts
12	G Club & Dive Solomons
13	Honiara Tama Sports Ground
14	National Government Offices
15	Parliament
16	US Peace Corps
17	Steps Between Hibiscus Avenue & Lenggakiki
18	Immigration/Map Sales Division of Agriculture & Lands Dept
19	Post Office
20	Solomon Telekom & British High Commission
21	NBSI
22	War Memorial & Canoe Shed
23	Police Station
24	Central Bank
25	Australian High Commission & US Embassy
27	Museum & Cultural Centre
29	Tourist Authority & Budget Rent A Car
30	NPF Plaza & Western Pacific Air Services
31	Anthony Saru Building
33	Solomon Airlines
34	Y Sato Building
36	ANZ Bank
37	Lena Cinema
38	Marine Division
39	Westpac Bank & Avis
40	NPF Building
42	Coral Seas Ltd
46	Air Niugini
47	Shell Fuel Depot
48	Guadalcanal Provincial Government Offices
49	MP Kwan Building
52	Honiara Municipal Authority
53	Quonset Huts
54	Holy Cross RC Cathedral
55	Library

Mataniko River, and Kolaa Ridge, Vura, Naha and Panatina to its east.

THINGS TO SEE

All distances are from the Mataniko Bridge.

Quonset Huts (0.3 km)

A short distance west of the Mataniko River are six US-built WW II Quonset huts, now used by the Guadalcanal Province. On the hill opposite is the Roman Catholic **Holy Cross Cathedral**.

Nearby, on the Mataniko River's western bank, are the remains of two very rusty **wartime pontoons**. Several of the coconut trees close by show clear evidence of wartime damage.

Central Market (0.6 km)

Although small by Asian standards, the Central Market is the Solomons' principal food market. In addition to fruit, vegetables, fresh fish and elegant shells for household decorations, Malaitan shell money is sometimes for sale.

Produce comes here from outlying villages along Guadalcanal's northern coast and across the water from Savo. Business is brisk every day, and best before 10.30 am. Produce sells quickly, although coconuts and bananas should be available until the afternoon. Saturday is usually the busiest day, Wednesday the cheapest.

Point Cruz (1.4 km)

On 12 May 1568, Mendaña and his men erected a cross at a spot traditionally called Kua by islanders, renaming it Point Cruz. They then said their prayers and claimed the whole island, and all those they had visited previously in the group, for Spain.

Island legends claim the site of this historic event is where a medium-sized tree now stands. It's beside Point Cruz's public toilets and just south of the Marine Division.

Since the 1950s, this generally low-lying spur of land has been greatly extended with wharves and copra sheds. Boat services reach out from Point Cruz to the remotest destinations in the island group. There's always a busy scene here as copra boats and inter-island passenger vessels load and unload.

National Museum & Cultural Centre (1.6 km)

The National Museum and Cultural Centre (☎ 22309) are immediately opposite the Mendana Hotel. The museum is open Monday to Friday from 9 am to 4.30 pm, and entry is free, though donations are welcomed. Photographs may only be taken with the director's permission.

The museum's exhibits covers many traditional Solomons subjects, including dance, body ornamentation, currency, weaponry and archaeology. Behind it is the new Cultural Centre. This has seven traditionally constructed houses – one for each province. The Makiran building is particularly striking, with boldly carved black statuettes adorning its front.

To the west of the museum is a green **Japanese howitzer**, believed to be one of the guns which were collectively known as Pistol Pete. If this is so, this gun helped destroy many parked US aircraft and huge stocks of fuel at Henderson in late 1942.

A large **canoe shed** beside the Mendana Hotel is an annexe to the museum. Although

it is not open to the public, if you ask you may be able to peek at the six huge war canoes inside, stored here for the occasional pan-Pacific cultural event staged in Honiara.

Central Bank (1.8 km)

This large, modern building beside the police station has a number of interesting displays. Inside are some very fine wooden carvings from Rennell and Makira.

For those not journeying beyond Honiara, the compact display of traditional local currencies is well worth seeing. Its showcases contain examples of Santa Cruz red-feather money, Malaitan dolphin-teeth and shell money, mbaravas from New Georgia, and clamshell currency from Choiseul.

Opposite the Central Bank is a park with a **war memorial** to the US casualties of the Guadalcanal campaign. Beside it is the **governor general's residence**, complete with a uniformed guard.

The Botanical Gardens (2.4 km & a 400-metre side-track)

Beside the jail is a road leading past the SIBC Building and over a bridge to the Botanical Gardens. There are a herbarium, an orchid garden, a cascading creek, and a selection of bush plants and trees, most of them typical of any rainforest area in the country. The herbarium and orchid gardens are only open on weekdays.

The path by the cascading creek reaches up to **Water Pump Village**, so called because it's by a pump house which feeds water up to Lenggakiki, a housing area behind Honiara. Water Pump Village is similar to many others in the Solomons and gives a good idea of rural life if your only stop is the capital.

Rove (2.6 km)

The small Rove (pronounced 'Rove-y') Market, opposite the jail, operates daily, including Sundays.

A wartime jeep track called Tasahe Drive follows several nearby ridges from Rove and is a back way to White River Village.

Top Left: Young girl, Bloody Ridge, Guadalcanal Island (DH)
Top Right: Young boy, Tikopia Island (SIID)
Bottom Left: Father and son, Reef Islands (SIID)
Bottom Right: Malaitan boy (SIID)

Top: Main Wharf, Honiara (DH)
Bottom: Children at Bloody Ridge, Guadalcanal Island (DH)

White River Village (5 km)

This friendly Gilbertese settlement is where the Sendai Trail started. The Japanese Sendai Force cut this track in October 1942 so that they could outflank the US position at Bloody Ridge. After dragging several heavy guns along the trail, they were repulsed by the Americans once they finally emerged. Villagers will point out where the route starts.

Chinatown (0.1 km)

The first place eastwards across the Mataniko River is Chinatown. Beside the Chinatown Footbridge is **Friendship Park**, with Independence Arch at its centre. This monument was presented to the town of Honiara in 1978 by the town's Chinese community to celebrate the Solomon Islands' independence.

Chinatown's main street, **Chung Wah Rd**, is 400 metres of colourful Oriental stores. Most of them have verandahs and high porches while some are raised on stilts. A sample of some of the shop names completes the picture: Yee Bing Store, Sie Tu Cheung, Win Win Store and Yip Yuk Store!

To the west of Chung Wah Rd is a recently built area called New Chinatown. Another 100 metres further on is Gina Crescent, where you'll find a house in a tree.

Kukum (0.5 km)

The district to the east of the Mataniko River is known as Kukum. This whole area lines the southern side of the Kukum Highway, with several roads leading off to the hillside housing estates of Koloale and Kolaa Ridge.

Honiara's Central Hospital is known colloquially as Nambanaen. Built in Kukum by US forces, it was given the wartime name of 9th Station, thus its Pijin name. Opposite the hospital is the large, open-sided Church of Melanesia Cathedral of St Barnabas, where there's a small memorial to Bishop Patterson, killed at Nukapu in the Reefs in 1871.

Despite the large number of people living in Kukum, it has only a very small centre. You'll find what little there is beside the Kukum Market, which operates daily and has cheaper prices than Honiara's market. There's also the Salo Fresh Fish Market, opposite Kukum's SDA church.

Ranadi (4 km)

To the east of Kukum is the Ranadi (pronounced 'Ranandi') trading estate. It's named after the Marine Division's old training ship of the same name which was formerly moored here, and is the country's principal light-industrial zone.

The Honiara Golf Course is built beside the remains of Fighter Two, a US wartime airstrip. Modern buildings now cover the WW II tarmac. Beyond the golf course and facing the sea is Ranadi Beach. The black-sand shore which begins here extends all the way to Poposa, near the eastern tip of Guadalcanal.

ACTIVITIES
Sport

If you want a game of tennis, courts open to visitors are at the G Club, the Honiara Hotel (free for residents) and beside the Kukum Indoor Sports Centre. For the third of these, contact the Honiara Municipal Authority (☎ 21133). There are also tennis courts at the Tenavatu Country Club 19 km east of the capital.

The Honiara Golf Club's (☎ 31174) nine-hole course at Ranadi is the only golf course in the Solomons. Its bar is open to visitors from 10 am to 6 pm. Green and caddy fees are S$5 each for every nine-hole round you play.

The Honiara Squash Club welcomes visitors to its courts on Chinatown Ave, Kukum. The charge is S$8 an hour a head.

Scuba Diving & Snorkelling

Two internationally recognised dive companies offer comprehensive scuba trips, including dives among brightly coloured tropical fish and through sunken WW II

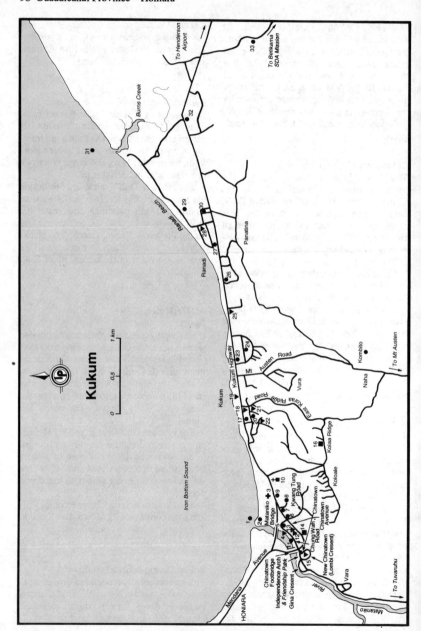

Kukum

wrecks. They also train novice divers up to full scuba certification over an intensive period of around seven days and provide briefer 'resort courses' for those who wish to have the thrill of diving without full training. In addition, snorkellers can accompany divers to the many reef sites and sunken WW II wrecks near Honiara for S$12 to S$15.

These two Honiara scuba companies are Island Dive Services (☎ 22103) at the Mendana Hotel and Dive Solomons (☎ 20520) at the G Club. The temperature of the water at Honiara's dive sites is between 27°C and 28°C, while visibility is 30 metres. Most of the sites are within easy reach of the capital.

Both dive companies accept both Solomon and Australian dollars, but usually quote in Australian dollars. Dive Solomons charges A$45 a dive, or A$30 if you bring your own kit.

Island Dive Services charges A$55 a dive, or A$35 if you bring your own equipment. It is also the agent for the two live-aboard dive boats active in Solomons waters.

The two companies' resort courses cost between A$50 and A$75 each, while certification prices range between A$300 and A$375. The final fee depends on how many other trainees there are.

Scuba & Snorkel Sites There are several interesting scuba and snorkel sites around Honiara. Mendana Reef is only 250 metres from the Mendana Hotel and is a good place to learn scuba diving. There's a sunken Japanese tank lying in the shallows just to the north of Mataniko Village. And the *Gyoshu Maru* is a Japanese tuna boat 21 metres down off Ranadi Beach.

Swimming
Honiara's sea swimming is rather a disappointment. There's a small stretch of sand in front of the Mendana Hotel and Point Cruz Yacht Club, but the water's murky and not used by islanders.

The nearest beaches are at Ranadi and Kakambona, four and 6.5 km away respectively. Ranadi has a narrow black-sand beach, while Kakambona's is grey coloured. Both are around 1.5 km long.

Local villagers are seldom seen in the water. They've been somewhat discouraged since 13 islanders were taken by sharks when a small coaster foundered nearby in the 1960s. Safer bets are the swimming pools at the G Club and the Mendana and Honiara hotels (though the latter pair are reserved for hotel guests only).

Organised Tours

Honiara's two land-based operators are GTS (☎ 22586) in the Y Sato Building, and Tour Solomons (☎ 21630) opposite the Shell fuel depot. In addition, there's Heli Solomons (☎ 30033) out at Henderson Airport. Tour Solomons quotes for single tourists but gives discounts for groups of two or more, while Heli Solomons needs four passengers aboard each helicopter to charge its basic fees.

Prices for land trips vary between S$45 and S$60 a head, depending on which one you choose. All of GTS' tours are outside the capital.

Heli Solomons does a seven-minute flight around Honiara and out to Bloody Ridge for S$70 a passenger.

PLACES TO STAY

Honiara has three hotels and two small guesthouses. However, a number of religious bodies have transit hostels which are open to all. These have dormitories and also cooking facilities.

If you're choosy about what sort of room you have, get your travel agent to book you into a hotel prior to your arrival. Otherwise, once you're there, let your taxi or Red Bus drive you around until you've found somewhere to stay.

Places to Stay – bottom end

Close to the town centre is the *Church of Melanesia Transit House* (☎ 21892). Its seven rooms cost S$15/30 for singles/doubles, but are frequently booked out by visiting islanders. Better is the *United Church Rest House* (☎ 20028), which is just up the hillside at the southern end of Cluck St. Its 10 rooms are popular with budget travellers. It provides mainly dormitory accommodation at S$20 a person a night.

The *SSEC Transit House* (☎ 22800) in

Vavaea has four rooms and charges S$20/30 for singles/doubles a night. Smoking and drinking are strictly forbidden. The *YWCA* in Kukutu St is mainly for island women, but has two guest rooms which foreign females can use, if the rooms are spare. These cost members S$10 a night and nonmembers S$15. If you prefer to stay in Kukum, there's *Pakoe Accommodation* (☎ 21336) up on Kolaa Ridge. Its nine private rooms with shared washing facilities are also popular with islanders and cost S$20 a night a head.

Places to Stay – middle

The *Testimony Guest House* (☎ 21530, PO Box 122), also known as the Testimony Motel, is in Lenggakiki at the end of Tolu Ave. It has nine rooms, all with fans. Two of them are self-contained and cost S$60 a night, whilst the other seven share washing facilities and cost S$35/50 for singles/doubles. Both the kitchen and living room are communal.

Island Chain Holidays Guest House (☎ 20385, PO Box 913), at the western end of Hibiscus Ave, has one room for singles/doubles at S$60/80 a night and a four-bed dormitory for S$35 a person.

The *Hibiscus Hotel* (☎ 21205, PO Box 268) in Hibiscus Ave has 10 rooms with fan, shower and fridge costing S$71.50/88 including breakfast for singles/doubles. Another four rooms are air-conditioned and cost S$82.50/104.50. It also has a restaurant and bar.

Places to Stay – top end

The *Honiara Hotel* (☎ 21737, PO Box 4), just behind Chinatown, has 66 rooms. Cheapest rates for singles/doubles for rooms with fans and communal washing facilities are S$65/80. Prices for air-conditioned, fully serviced rooms range from S$90 to S$150 for singles and S$110 to S$175 for doubles. It has a swimming pool, restaurant and bar. The hotel has nightly videos for guests accommodated in the new wing, tennis courts and a pool table.

The *Solomon Kitano Mendana Hotel* (☎ 20071, PO Box 384) is the nation's principal international-style hotel. It has around 100 air-conditioned rooms, conference facilities, two restaurants, a bar, a scuba-diving shop and a swimming pool. Singles/doubles range from S$100/120 to S$160/180 a night. Carving salespeople have a small shed in the car park and cultural groups perform frequently.

The Mendana Hotel is a good place to meet other expats or visitors. Its terrace bar is a popular lunchtime watering hole.

PLACES TO EAT

Eating places are cheap and plentiful in Honiara in the daytime. These include cafés, takeaways, supermarkets, Chinese stores and several colourful markets, all offering sustenance at reasonable prices. But at nighttime, prices rise once the cheap places have closed.

Places to Eat – bottom end

Most of the budget places I've mentioned don't charge the 10% tourist tax. Where they do, the price range I've indicated includes it.

Cheap Eats True rock-bottom prices can only be found at Honiara's markets. Coconuts are 20 to 30c each, pawpaws range from 10 to 50c, while bananas vary between 40 and 80c a bunch.

The *Hot Bread Kitchen* is open seven days a week, with buns costing 20c and upwards. There's another branch in Kukum.

Supermarkets & Chinese Stores Chinatown gets its name from its many Chinese stores, but there are several others in Honiara's town centre also. Many of these stay open on Saturday afternoons, with a few even operating on Sunday mornings. The *Chan Wing Supermarket* in Chinatown has a very broad range of groceries for sale, including bread and beers from Europe.

Y Sato, the supermarket in the building of the same name in central Honiara, has very good prices. Sometimes these are a third the price of those in other stores. The *Joy Supermarket*, opposite the large Shell fuel depot,

also has competitive prices, and is popular with islanders.

The *Solomon Islands Consumers Supermarket* has two branches, both selling a broad range of groceries. Its bigger shop, the largest store in the country, is immediately behind the NPF Plaza, while its smaller branch is in the Chinatown Plaza. The Honiara one stays open to 5.45 pm on weekdays, and opens on Saturday and Sunday mornings.

If you're hungry late at night, you can call into the two small 24-hour stores on either side of the Hong Kong Palace Restaurant in Hibiscus Ave. However, their range is restricted mainly to canned meats, rice, flour, etc.

Fast Food & Takeaways Walking west to east, you'll find the *Lokol Store*, facing Mendana Ave in the NPF Plaza, is a good place for tasty lunchtime roti, as well as refreshing coconuts.

The *B Kool Dairy*, with outlets in both the Central Market and beside the NBSI branch in Chinatown (facing Kukum Highway), offers tasty ice creams at low prices. Beside the B Kool Dairy's Chinatown branch is the *Chinatown Fast Food Bar*, which serves fish and chips and egg buns. Just behind them, in the Chinatown part of Kwang Tung Rd, is the *C W Cake Shop*, whose fare ranges from 80c doughnuts to S$5 chicken pieces.

There are two more places out in Kukum. Closest to the town centre is the *East Ocean Fast Food Bar*, beside the Salo Fresh Fish Market. The *Shell Fast Food Bar* is about 800 metres further east along the same road.

Snackbars & Cafés Most westerly of the cheap snackbars is the *YWCA Café*, in the YWCA grounds. Although it's on premises misleadingly marked 'Rove Infant School', you'll find a clean, friendly lunchtime service here, with helpings of curry, roti or pizza for S$3 to S$5.

The *Fountain Corner* in the Anthony Saru Building serves drinking coconuts, and snacks in the S$3 to S$8 range. *Family Favourites* in the NPF Plaza and opposite the

Solomon Islands Consumers Supermarket, offers somewhat similar meals.

Most central of the cheaper places is *Kingsley's Fast Food Centre* in Ashley St. It's open from 7.15 am to 8 pm every day except Sunday, when it opens from 9 am to 7 pm. Noodles and curried rice are the specialities, with simple but wholesome meals costing between S$5 and S$9. Kingsley's closes early if there are no customers.

The *Kai Bar*, opposite the Solomon Islands Ports Authority and just to the west of the main wharf, serves curry and rice for around S$6. Opposite the Shell fuel depot and beside the Downtown Mini Cinema is the friendly *Refa Café*, where a coffee and a cake costs about S$5.

The Honiara branch of the *Garden Fast Food Bar*, beside the Hot Bread Kitchen, has hamburgers for between S$2 and S$3. The Chinatown branch, on the western side of Chung Wah Rd, operates as a takeaway with the same price range.

Beside the South Seas Restaurant in Cluck St is the spartan but clean *South Sea Kai Shop* where noodles cost from S$2 to S$3.50. Similar prices apply at the *Happy Snack Bar* on the south-western side of the Central Market.

In Chinatown Plaza, the *LUC Kitchen* serves an islander clientele curry and rice, roti, and taro and pork. Its prices range from S$1.80 to S$6.

Just before you get to Ranadi Beach, there's the *Café Ranandi*. It's only open during the working week though.

Places to Eat – middle

The three hotels offer convenience and moderate prices for breakfast and lunch, and elegance and comfort at dinnertime. The *Honiara Hotel* is usually the cheapest of the three in the evening.

Honiara has six Chinese restaurants and one Korean one. However, two of them are only open for dinner, whilst the *Seoul Cafeteria*, just west of the Central Market, is open from 8 am to 6 pm only. Its Korean meals, served with ginseng tea, cost between S$8 and S$20.

The *Mandarin Restaurant* (☎ 22832) is in Chinatown's Chung Wah Rd and overlooks the Mataniko River. It's only open at night, from 7.00 to 9.30 pm, and serves quality Chinese food. Dinner prices range from S$18 to S$30.

The *Super Club Restaurant* (☎ 22168), on the western side of Chinatown Ave, serves very good Chinese dinners for S$30 to S$60. If you have a meal there, entry that night to the gambling upstairs is free.

The *Sea King Chinese Restaurant* (☎ 23621) in Ashley St serves authentic Taiwanese fare. Business lunches are moderately priced, while dinners range between S$15 and S$50. Cooking is Mongolian hot-pot style.

The *South Seas Restaurant* (☎ 22363) is on the western side of Cluck St in Honiara. Some of its helpings of noodle soup are large enough to be a full meal in themselves. Meal prices vary between S$10 and S$50.

The *Hong Kong Palace Restaurant* (☎ 23338), behind the town centre in Hibiscus Ave, is open daily for lunch and dinner. As at the *Kumho Court Restaurant* (☎ 21687) in New Chinatown, Saturday and Sunday lunches here are dimsim, with multiple dishes at S$3 each. Get there early before all the tastiest dishes go. Prices at the Hong Kong Palace range between S$20 and S$60 except on dimsim days, when they're more like S$12 to S$18.

The Kumho Court's weekend dimsim lunches are equally popular, while its dinner prices vary between S$30 and S$50. On Thursdays and Saturday nights, there's karaoke as well as Chinese food!

Places to Eat – top end

Honiara's best restaurant is the *La Perouse Restaurant* (☎ 23720). Built in a very attractive island style, it's beside the sea and just to the west of the G Club. An excellent evening meal will cost upwards of S$50, though lunch may be about half that.

Similarly priced at dinnertime is the restaurant at the *Hibiscus Hotel*. The meals here are of a similar quality to those served at the La Perouse.

ENTERTAINMENT

There's plenty to do in Honiara day and night. This includes relaxing by shoreside or poolside bars, gambling, dancing, singing to karaoke, and watching movies, custom dances or amateur dramatics.

Casinos

The Super Club and Club 88, in adjacent buildings on Chinatown Ave, are Honiara's only gambling spots. Both open at 6 pm and operate till midnight on weekdays, and till 2 am the next morning at weekends. The atmosphere tends to liven up once hotel bars start closing around 10 pm.

The gambling at both clubs is roulette, blackjack and baccarat, with minimum bets of S$1 for the roulette and S$5 for the blackjack. There's also plenty of 20c video and poker machines to play if you prefer.

Both clubs allow temporary holiday memberships. There's normally a S$10 entry for nonmembers, but the Super Club will let you enter for free if you've had your dinner in its restaurant that night.

Private Clubs

The Point Cruz Yacht Club (☎ 22500) is the capital's best place at which to meet expats, yachties, volunteers and divers; and cheap holiday memberships are available. Tuesday and Saturday nights are film nights. You can also check out the notice board if you are looking for a yacht to be crew on, or you need crew for your own vessel.

The G Club (☎ 22212) (the G is for Guadalcanal) offers temporary memberships for S$10, and there are reciprocal arrangements for members of the Gizo and Yandina clubs. Inside the club building there's a bar with a pool table and darts board, while outside are a swimming pool, tennis courts, a dive shop and a large Japanese WW II howitzer.

Cinemas

Honiara is well-stocked with movie halls. It has one cinema and seven mini cinemas. Five of them are to the west of the Mataniko River, while two are in Chinatown and another is in Kukum. Prices at the mini cinemas (basically public video halls) are usually S$1.50 for adults and S$1 for children, while cinema prices are around S$2 a person.

Honiara's movie halls are open seven days a week. Screenings start between 10 am and noon, with repeat showings every two hours until closing time, which varies between 7 and 10 pm. Programme changes are frequent, with fast, action-packed movies the favourites of the young unemployed of Honiara, the mini cinemas' principal clientele.

You'll find the Lena Cinema in the town centre, opposite the ANZ Bank. Nearby, and facing the Shell fuel depot, is the Downtown Mini Cinema. The Hapai Mini Cinema is also central. It's close to the Hong Kong Palace Restaurant.

The Chinatown Mini Cinema is just to the south of the Chinatown Plaza, on the eastern side of Chung Wah Rd. Kukum's East Ocean Mini Cinema is beside the Salo Fresh Fish Market.

There are also three Super Mini Cinemas. The most central is just west of the Hot Bread Kitchen, on the same side of Mendana Ave, and there's another on the western side of the Central Market. The third one is in Chinatown, four doors to the south of the Westpac branch there.

Discos & Dances

The G Club has rock dances on Tuesday nights and frequently at the weekend also. The Super Club in Chinatown provides a disco on Wednesdays, while the Hibiscus Hotel is another regular venue, this time with a dinner-dance ambience, on Friday or Saturday nights. The Point Cruz Yacht Club and the Honiara Golf Club at Ranadi occasionally have functions also. Dance announcements are usually made over the radio the same or preceding day.

Custom Dancing

You can see a group called the Gilbertese Dancers at the Honiara Hotel on Wednesday and Friday nights between 8 and 10 pm for free, as long as you're resident at the hotel or you've had the barbecue meal there for S$27.50 that night. Otherwise the entry fee is S$5. The Mendana Hotel also has regular performances.

Karaoke
The Kumho Court Restaurant has very friendly karaoke on both Thursday and Saturday nights. You're free to sing along to rock videos with English and Chinese subtitles as long as you eat there.

Amateur Dramatics
The Honiara Hams are a group of friendly, mainly British, expats who get together fortnightly to monthly beside the Honiara Squash Club courts in the evening for plays, pantomimes, folk-club meetings and film shows.

Events are advertised around the town by posters in shop windows. There's a bar, and the entry fee, which varies according to what's on, is usually around S$2.

Spectator Sports
The weekend is the time for spectator sports in Honiara. You can see soccer, rugby and athletics on Saturday afternoons at the Lawson Tama Sports Ground in Kukum, and volleyball and softball at the Honiara Tama Sports Ground. In summer, there's cricket at either place, while boxing has an ardent year-round following at the Kukum Indoor Sports Centre.

THINGS TO BUY
There are several places in Honiara where you can buy handicrafts. Mostly these are either excellently crafted wooden carvings from Western Province, traditional items from Makira/Ulawa or personal weaponry and masks from Rennell and Bellona. There are also basketware and lime containers from Guadalcanal for sale, if you are looking for this island's products only.

The largest handicraft shop, specialising in Western Province products and stylish modern copperware, is Betikama Carvings at the Betikama SDA Mission. Other places include Minana Handicrafts, opposite where

Kukutu St meets Mendana Ave; Solomon Islands Art Gallery in the NPF Plaza, which specialises in traditional Makiran/Ulawan carvings; Melanesian Handicrafts, with branches in both the NPF Plaza and opposite the Shell fuel depot; King Solomon Arts & Crafts Centre in the Y Sato Building; Island Souvenirs which is 50 metres west of Solomon Airlines; the National Museum; the handicraft counter at Henderson Airport; the Mendana Hotel car park's carvers stall; and the Central Market, particularly for Malaitan shell money and for lime containers.

Seashells
Western Pacific Shells in Chinatown is both a shell shop and a crustacean museum, with displays including trocchus, green snail (ie conch) and bêche-de-mer.

GETTING THERE & AWAY
Air
All international flights arrive at Henderson Airport, where passengers clear Customs and Immigration. See the introductory Getting There & Away chapter for details on international flights to and from the Solomons.

Within the country most of the larger islands have at least two flights a week to and from Honiara. Gizo, Auki, Munda, and Seghe in New Georgia all have daily air services to and from the capital. Even the smallest islands are connected at least weekly to Honiara as long as they have an airfield.

Airline Offices Air Nauru is represented by Guadalcanal Travel Services (GTS) (☎ 22587) in the Y Sato Building. The four other airlines flying into or around the Solomons also have offices in Mendana Ave. These are Air Niugini (☎ 22895); Solomon Airlines (☎ 20031); Air Pacific (☎ 23791), which is next door to GTS and also represents Qantas; and Western Pacific Air Services (☎ 30533), which is opposite Budget Rent A Car.

Boat

Most cruising yachts arrive at Honiara's Main Wharf, where Customs and Immigration can be cleared. See the introductory Getting There & Away chapter for details.

There are boats between Honiara and Tulagi six days a week, and between Honiara and both Western Province and Auki at least once a week. More distant destinations are serviced between fortnightly and six weekly, weather conditions permitting.

Motor canoes ply regularly between Savo Island and Honiara. The best places to find them are at the small beach beside the Point Cruz Yacht Club, or at the Central Market. In addition, Dive Solomons offers a once-weekly day trip to Savo for S$120, while Island Chain Holidays, Tour Solomons and Tour Savo also do trips. The details are in the Savo section.

Car

Honiara has two car-hire companies. Both offer unlimited km rates and reductions for week-long rentals, or hourly and half- day rates if you prefer. Even so, car rentals are costly, though they are ideal for a one or two-day trip around the battlefields, or along the island's northern coast.

Avis (☎ 21113), with branches beside Westpac in the town centre and also across the road from Henderson Airport, offers 24 hours worth of collision damage waiver and personal accident insurance for an extra S$33 and S$13 respectively. Avis' cheapest vehicles are a small utility for S$88 a day and a 4WD vehicle for S$106 a day.

Budget Rent A Car (☎ 23205) offers slightly cheaper insurance. Its cheapest cars cost S$90 a day, while its cheapest 4WD vehicles cost S$105 a day.

GETTING AROUND
To/From the Airport

Airport buses cost S$6 a head, or S$8 on Sundays, to and from Honiara. Zankos Express (☎ 21291), which has an office in the NPF Plaza, operates the Red Bus service, as it is commonly known, which meets every international flight, and many internal ones

also. Its door-to-door service allows you to book it as you would a taxi, and then be conveyed between your hotel and the airport – all for the same S$6 fare.

Even cheaper are minibuses, which can get you to and from Henderson Airport for S$1.50. You can pick them up outside the ANZ Bank in Honiara, or beside the main road outside the airport terminal. If you're going to the airport, make sure your bus has Henderson or CDC 1, 2 or 3 on it.

Should you prefer a taxi, the fare between Honiara and the airport will be S$20. As there's no booking system for cabs, you'll have to hail one in the street.

Minibus

The cheapest way around Honiara is by minibus. The standard fare within the main town area is 60c, however long or short your journey. Just flag one down. It will almost always stop unless it is already full.

An almost continuous stream of minibuses travels between Kukum and Rove during daylight hours. Though they are noticeably less frequent after dark, you can still catch them, particularly from the town centre, up to 9 or 10 pm.

Taxi

There are plenty of cabs around, even up to midnight, though many are now rather decrepit. None have meters, so inquire as to the price before getting aboard.

The taxi fare between Point Cruz and Chinatown is S$3, or S$4 after dark. Decline anything higher, as there will always be another one at the right price during the daytime only one or two minutes later.

There are no taxi stands in Honiara, just lots of taxis during daylight hours plying for hire. There are fewer after dark, but you can still find them quite easily right up to midnight. The best place to catch them at any hour is outside Solomon Airlines, in Ashley St, or outside the Mendana Hotel.

Car

For information about renting a car, see the previous Getting There & Away section.

You need to be quite pushy when driving in Honiara. You can wait for ages at an intersection before someone will let you into the traffic stream. The only solution is to push in.

Walking

Most places in Honiara's central area are less than 10 minutes apart on foot. If your destination is farther than that, you might as well go by minibus.

Pedestrians should take particular care crossing Honiara's roads, especially in Ashley St and in Mendana Ave between the Y Sato Building and Solomon Airlines. In Kukum, the worst place to cross is from the northern side of Kukum Highway over to Chinatown. Few motorists slow down for pedestrians crossing the road.

Around Honiara

Close to Honiara are a number of places which can be approached easily enough by road, but require some walking. A morning or afternoon is all that would be needed. The distances given are west to east from Mataniko Bridge.

KAKAMBONA (6.5 km)

This village has a 1.5-km-long grey-sand beach and a Sunday market. It's the furthest point westwards to which town buses (marked 'White River') go.

The Sunday market spreads along the highway for over one km, using between five and seven sites, mostly on the southern side. Prices can be slightly higher than those at Honiara's Central Market.

Some local people may regard Kakambona's beach as village property, so ask first before you swim there.

SKYLINE DRIVE (0.6 km)

You can still follow this wartime jeep track the five km between Honiara and Valeatu. As it leaves Honiara, Skyline Drive overlooks the Mataniko River, providing a magnificent view of village life below it in Vara. About one km further on, the track reaches a ridge above the Musona River and its several small cascades. It then continues on to Valeatu, passing one km to the north of Galloping Horse Ridge – a WW II Japanese strong point – as it approaches the village.

This whole area is good bird-watching country. Cardinal lories, pigeons, parrots, dollar birds, Sanford's eagles, and the brown and white-plumaged Brahminy kites can often be seen.

Once you've reached Valeatu, ask local people to show you the footpaths from there back to Tasahe Drive or Honiara.

MATANIKO FALLS (6 km)

This double-sided waterfall thunders down a cliff into a cave that swarms with swallows and bats and is full of stalagmites. During WW II this cavern, and others nearby, were hideouts for Japanese soldiers trying to evade capture by the Americans.

The 2.5-km road through Chinatown and Vara ends at Tuvaruhu. A track from there leads into the bush, and then follows the Mataniko River, often crossing it. It's about three km up the river to a gorge. You'll then have to wade and swim a further 500 metres to reach the falls and the cave.

You should watch out for storm clouds all along the river. Flash floods do occur, and there have been fatalities.

Tour Solomons does a four-hour trek to the Mataniko Falls for S$60 a person, or S$50 a head for two or more.

BETIKAMA (8 km)

On the way to Henderson Airport, and about 600 metres beyond the King George VI School, the road is spanned by a charmingly worded sign saying 'Welcome' and 'Farewell' in English and Pijin. Just beyond, at a point about 6.5 km from Honiara, is the turnoff southwards to Betikama.

Within the grounds of the Betikama SDA Mission are a large handicraft shop, a carving shed, an indoor and outdoor WW II museum, and a pen containing saltwater crocodiles. Much of the carving is done by schoolboys who've come to Betikama from SDA villages in the New Georgia Islands.

The small wartime museum's outdoor section has a collection of salvaged material (mostly US aircraft), two small Japanese antitank guns and a well-preserved British Bren gun carrier. The indoor part of the museum, at the rear of the handicraft shop, has a collection of WW II photographs and memorabilia. Just behind the nearby hedge is a sturdy-looking wartime US military bulldozer.

There are two saltwater crocodiles in the small pen between the museum and the carvings shop. Both were taken from the nearby Lungga River.

Fine carvings are on display, and may be bought at reasonable prices. The shop's weekday opening hours are 8 am to noon and 1 to 5 pm. It's also open on Sundays, but shut on Saturdays. A small donation is expected if you don't buy.

If you ask them, the carvers will point out the tita tree growing nearby. Its nuts produce a resin which is used by canoe builders to make their craft waterproof.

MT AUSTEN ROAD
Solomons Peace Memorial Park (4.5 km)
The road to Mt Austen begins in Kukum, and passes through Vura before climbing up to the historical sites beyond.

This large, white memorial was built by Japanese war veterans in 1981 to commemorate all who died in the WW II Guadalcanal campaign. There's a magnificent view from it over Honiara and towards Savo and the Nggelas.

The ridge 1.5 km south-west of this memorial is Sea Horse Ridge, a Japanese strong point in 1942. It was given this name by US aviators because it looked like a sea horse from the air.

'The Gifu' (7.5 km)
The thick bush on either side of the route opens on its western side to reveal an elevated clearing about 200 metres from the

road. This is the site of 'the Gifu', named by its wartime Japanese defenders after a district in Japan most of them came from. Very fiercely defended, it was the Japanese' forward command post, directing their efforts to capture Henderson. It finally fell to the Americans in mid-January 1943 after its starving defenders were wiped out making a final banzai charge.

Mt Austen (8.5 km)
There's a clearing by the roadside with a marvellous view north-eastwards over Henderson at the 410-metre-high summit. WW II Americans dubbed this spot Grassy Knoll. At the northern end of the hilltop are the remains of a small dugout, which acted as an observation post for the Japanese artillery bombarding Henderson.

Around Guadalcanal

Arts
Visitors to the southern coast's villages and the central mountains still find armbands and belts woven from red and yellow-dyed fibres. Plain black wooden bowls, now made with metal tools instead of stone, are still in common use. In addition, well-finished sea and turtle-shell jewellery is fashioned on Marapa Island in Marau Sound.

Information
Medical Services In addition to Honiara's Central Hospital and its 11 public and private clinics, there are 13 rural health centres around Guadalcanal. Visale, Mbinu, Ruavatu, Aola and Totongo serve the northern coast, while Tangarere, Chocho, Kuma, Avu Avu and Manikaraku cover the south. The only inland clinics are at Nuhu, Kolochulu and Mbumbunuhu in eastern Guadalcanal.

Activities
Organised Tours The three tour operators – GTS, Tour Solomons and Heli Solomons –

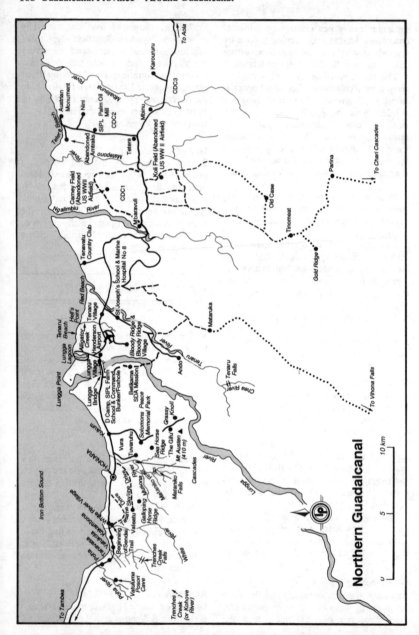

Northern Guadalcanal

have made visiting the battlefield sites on either side of Honiara, the road to Tambea, and the nearby Tenaru Falls their bread and butter. However, tour routes differ widely from company to company, so if there's a place you're especially interested in check first to see which organisations actually visit it. See the Honiara Getting Around section for the locations and telephone numbers of these companies.

GTS does an eastern battlefields trip for S$45 a head, while Tour Solomons' one costs S$70 but also visits Tenaru and Tetere Beaches. GTS' western battlefields and Tambea tour is S$80, while Tour Solomons' one is S$20 more but includes the clam farm at Aruligo. Both GTS and Tour Solomons do a Tenaru Falls trip for S$70 a person, with GTS offering children half-price fares.

Heli Solomons' trips range from a 15-minute flight around the battlefields between Red Beach, Honiara and Mt Austen plus Tenaru Falls if there's time, to a half-hour one covering the whole battlefields area, both local waterfalls and the two sunken Japanese transports at Bonegi Beach. Prices range between S$400 and S$800 a passenger, depending on how many air minutes you have.

Accommodation
Accommodation is available in Vulelua, Tambea, Tavanipupu, Komuniboli, Haimarao and Manikaraku. See the relevant sections for details.

Getting There & Away
The central point for arrivals and departures in Guadalcanal is the capital, Honiara. See the Honiara Getting There & Away section for air and shipping details.

Air Guadalcanal has three minor airfields in addition to Henderson Airport, all of which serve the southern coastal area. These are at Mbambanakira, Avu Avu and Marau. Solomon Airlines flights connect Honiara with Mbambanakira and Avu Avu three times a week, and Marau twice a week. Fares from Honiara are S$40, S$50 and S$66

respectively, while a flight from Avu Avu to Marau costs S$39.

Boat Because of the lack of roads, Marine Division vessels travel around the island on a weekly basis. Fares are cheap and vary between S$5 to Ndoma and S$17 to Marau Sound.

Taxi A taxi ride will be rather costly. A trip along the northern coast from Honiara to Lambi Bay and back will cost about S$140. A return trip eastwards to Aola will cost about S$150. The advantage of taking a taxi is that any accident will be the taxi driver's problem, not yours.

Getting Around
The island has approximately 450 km of roads and tracks. There's a main trunk route from Lambi Bay in the north-western part of the island through Honiara eastwards to Aola. There's also a road from Kuma to Avu Avu, and a tractor trail from there to Makina, in the south-east. A number of other feeder roads extend out from the northern highway, particularly across the Guadalcanal Plains and towards the central foothills. Footpaths join Lambi Bay with Kuma, while a combined footpath and canoe route links Makina with Aola, thereby completing the island circuit.

There are two or three ill-defined tracks across the mountains that some villagers know and use occasionally. However, they are exceedingly strenuous, always hard to follow, and are therefore not recommended.

Boat Guadalcanal's all-weather anchorages are at Rere Point and Makina on the northern coast, and Ghoverighi Harbour, Kopau Harbour, Tiaro Bay, Lambi Bay and Wanderer Bay in the south. Talise is used in calm weather. In addition, ships often call in at Inakona.

Kopiu Bay, Mbalo and Savuna are only suitable when north-westerly winds blow, from mid-November to mid-April, while Aola and Haimarao are only feasible from late April to early November, when it's the season for south-easterlies.

Most yachts make straight for Honiara and the Point Cruz Yacht Club, or dally at Tavanipupu or Vulelua islands. However, some of the Guadalcanal's ship anchorages may also be suitable for yachts during calmer weather.

Minibus & Truck There are regular services between Kakambona and White River Village to the west of Honiara, and Henderson, CDC 1, 2 and 3 (Mbaravuli, Nini and Karoururu respectively) to the east. Beyond these places, people depend on flagging down trucks for transport.

Car The best way to get around, and at the same time have the day to yourself, is by car. (See the Honiara Getting There & Away section for information about car rental.) If you stop to see everything in each direction along the northern coast, and have the occasional swim, you'll need two days in which to see it all comfortably.

Petrol and puncture repair facilities are only readily available in Honiara, so fill your car up before you set out. Also watch out for villagers and animals on these usually very quiet roads.

Tractor Hopping aboard the Guadalcanal provincial government's tractor along the southern coast will only cost you 50c, payable to the driver, or, if it's being chartered, to the charterer, whatever distance you travel. If you charter it yourself, it'll cost around S$2 a km.

Hitching Villagers will give you a ride in their car if you offer them around 10 to 15c a km, but ask the fare first.

Walking There's an excellent booklet called *Walks On Guadalcanal* for those who are thinking of doing some bushwalking on or around the island. Written by J L O Tedder and A Clayton some years ago, copies are now hard to find. Inquire at the Solomon Islands Tourist Authority to see if there's been a reprint. Otherwise you'll need to

study one of the National Library's copies before you venture forth.

HONIARA TO RED BEACH – THE BATTLEFIELDS

Today the WW II battlefields are hallowed ground to US war veterans. Pilgrims also come from Japan, some of them searching for the bones of relatives to give them a proper cremation according to traditional Shinto rites.

All distances in this section are measured from Honiara's Mataniko Bridge.

Lungga Village (8 km)
About 50 metres across Lungga Bridge, on the eastern side of the main road, beside a tree, is the original foxhole. It was named after Colonel Fox, a US marine stationed here in 1942. This small, concrete-lined hole in a bank was the colonel's command bunker.

You'll see a track going up a bank on the southern side of the road by the bridge. A small opening in the ground leads to the old US underground command post, known as D Camp, where radios, field telephone systems, maps and plotting rooms once were. Now it's empty except for a few bats. You'll need a torch to see around. About 30 metres up the track at the top of the same bank, and on the south-eastern side of an intersection, you'll find a Japanese anti-aircraft gun, placed here as a trophy.

Just beyond Colonel Fox's command bunker, or foxhole, is a track through the grounds of the Solomon Islands Plantations Ltd (SIPL) Farm School. About 50 metres along on the southern side of the track is a very rusty and wrecked Quonset hut. This was General Vandergrift's first command post in the Guadalcanal campaign. The route then circles the 300 metres or so round to the Japanese gun above D Camp. If you meet any SIPL staff, ask them to point out these sites, and get their permission to see them.

Lungga Lagoon
(8.4 km & 4-km side-track)
There's a four-km track from Lungga Village

out to the lagoon. Turn north (left) after 2.6 km and continue 1.4 km to the end of the track. At the end of a long, sandy beach are the ocean-battered remains of a wartime US Navy jetty. Fifty metres away is a small landing craft. Beached for repairs, it's now immobilised forever by a large tree which has grown up right through its centre.

In the sea off Lungga Lagoon are six sunken US pontoons in about eight metres of water. They are from about 50 to around 200 metres offshore, and can easily be seen from the air.

Henderson Airport (11 km)

A small memorial honours US forces and their Pacific Islander allies outside the airport entrance. In front of it is a Japanese anti-aircraft gun. Inside the airport terminal are plaques explaining how Henderson Field – as the Americans called it in WW II – was named after a US flier of the time. About 100 metres to the west of the buildings is the now disused scaffold-style WW II control tower. It hasn't been used since the early 1950s.

There's an ambitious long-term plan to create a Solomon Islands WW II museum at the airport. This will display both US and Japanese war remains, including several working WW II aircraft from both sides. These planes will be aircraft which actually served in the Guadalcanal campaign, restored sufficiently to be able to offer joy-rides and perform air displays at Henderson.

Bloody Ridge

(12 km & 3.5-km side- track)
Immediately after you pass the eastern end of Henderson's runway, you'll see a track running westwards along its southern perimeter. Follow the most well-used route for 3.5

km, first over two cattle grids and then up past two small leaf-house settlements. The second one, called Bloody Ridge Village, is just below the actual Bloody Ridge. In it is a small house on top of a tall pole, reserved for young men and teenage boys.

A small, white monument commemorates the 50 or so US defenders who died, while at the northern end of the escarpment immediately opposite Bloody Ridge two wooden posts honour the 2000 or more Japanese killed at this spot.

Hell's Point (14.5 km)

There's a white wooden monument at Hell's Point in the bush 50 metres back from Alligator Creek's exit to the sea and surrounded by long grass. This is a poignant site for Japanese visitors. According to the inscription, the Japanese Colonel Kiyono Ichiki and his 800 men 'died honourably' there on 20 August 1942. In Western terms, it was a futile and wasteful operation; the Japanese made a suicidal banzai charge from the eastern side of the creek against US machine guns and artillery mounted on its western bank.

A sunken pontoon 30 metres from the shore at Hell's Point in 10 metres of water is clearly visible from the air.

To get to Hell's Point, first cross the bridge on the main road beyond the eastern end of Henderson Airport. Then take the first track northwards through the SIPL cocoa plantation beside Alligator Creek to Tenaru Beach, having initially asked permission and directions from any of the workers you might see. They are usually very amenable. Once you reach the sea, walk 200 metres westwards until you reach a creek exiting to the sea. That's Hell's Point.

Bloody Ridge & Edson's Raiders

Bloody Ridge – also called Edson's Ridge – was named after Edson's Raiders, commanded by Colonel Merritt Edson. They were rushed here after their gory battle against the Japanese on Tulaghi in early August 1942. In two bloody night actions, on 13 and 14 September and 23 and 24 October 1942, Japanese forces tried to burst past Edson's men to seize the airfield. On both occasions the Raiders threw them back, with hideous losses to the Japanese. ∎

Tenaru Village (14.5 km)
This tiny settlement is close to the main road and has a house in a tree in it.

The large US troopship *John Penn* was bombed and sank about four km offshore from the part of Lungga Beach parallel to. Tenaru Village. This sunken vessel is complete with gun turrets and swarms with open-ocean fish, but is on the deep side for scuba, as it's 36 to 50 metres down.

Red Beach (15 km & 1.5-km side-track)
One lonely, very rusted Japanese gun, placed there by US veterans, points forlornly out to sea. This is the only reminder on this long, sandy beach of the US landings here in 1942.

GUADALCANAL PLAINS TO AOLA
The Guadalcanal Plains extend from the Lungga River just short of Honiara in the west to Kaoka Bay 77 km to the east. At the Matepono River, the plains widest point, they reach 12 km inland. The distances given in this section are taken from Honiara's Mataniko Bridge and follow the northeastern coastal road.

Marine Hospital No 8
(14.8 km & 1.5-km side-road)
The remains of the USA's first wartime hospital in Guadalcanal are in the grounds of St Joseph's School, Tenaru. This operated until the Americans built Honiara's Central Hospital. Many of the old WW II buildings and the concrete base remain.

Tenaru Falls
(14.8 km & a 7-km side-track)
This 63-metre-high waterfall tumbles on two sides into a deep swimming hole and the cascades beyond. Here, as at all mountain creeks, watch out for signs of rain because there is an ever-present danger of flash flooding. You may also need insect repellent and sunscreen.

Getting There & Away The road to the falls first passes St Joseph's School, Tenaru. It then keeps to the west of the Tenaru River

for about three km, disregarding two junctions – the first to the east, the second to the west – until it reaches Ando. You should ask permission there to proceed, and pay any custom fee the villagers require.

The track then follows an old logging route down to the Tenaru River. Beyond this point there are many footpaths. The correct one cuts across the river's many bends, crossing and recrossing it up to 20 times over a seven-km stretch, until the Tenaru reaches the Chea River. The falls are 300 metres up the Chea.

Both GTS and Tour Solomons do regular trips to the falls. GTS charges S$35/70 for children/adults, while Tour Solomons' fee is S$70 a head or S$60 a head for two or more.

Vihona Falls
(14.8 km, 9-km side-track & 21-km walk)
These waterfalls are approximately 900 metres above sea level in central Guadalcanal. There are two higher ones, and a lower one with a pool at its base, surrounded by undisturbed rainforest and abundant bird life.

Getting There & Away The best route passes St Joseph's School, Tenaru, bears east across the Tenaru River four km later, then continues south-east to Mataruka. (See the Northern and Western Guadalcanal maps.) There's a 17-km footpath via Tulambirua to Malukuna. The last four km is through bush. You will certainly need a guide.

Tenavatu (18 km & 1-km side-road)
The *Tenavatu Country Club* (☎ 31174), with tennis courts and fully licensed bar, is open from 4 to 10.30 pm on weekdays and from noon to 10 pm at weekends.

Carney Field (2.5 km & 4-km side-track)
This abandoned US wartime bomber field is hidden at ground level by plantations, though it's plainly visible from the air. Three km to the south is another derelict former US bomber base called Koli Field.

Top: Central market, Honiara (DH)
Bottom: Gilbertese child with canoe, Vulelua Island, Guadalcanal Island (DH)

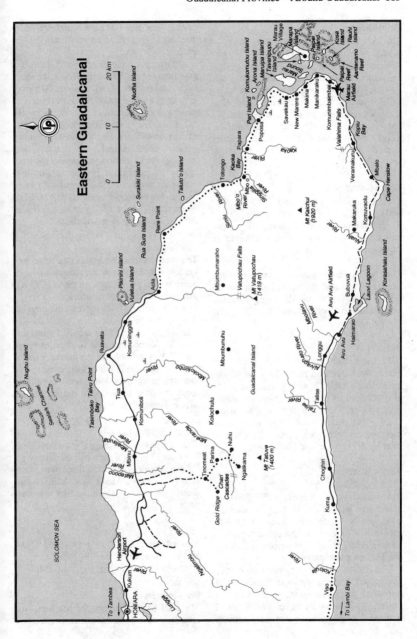

Eastern Guadalcanal

Gold Ridge

(26.5 km, 12.5-km side-track & 4-km
walk)

Alluvial gold was found here in payable
quantities in 1931, on the western edge of Mt
Tatuve. There was a brief gold rush. Local
village names such as Tinomeat and Old
Case are reminders of the time. Nowadays,
the only outsider allowed to remove the
yellow metal is the local mine, as villagers
consider the gold to be under their custom
ownership.

Chari Cascades

(26.5 km, 12.5-km side-track & 13-km
walk)

There's a long line of attractive shallow cascades on the Chari River about one km from
Ngalikama.

Getting There & Away The route continues
on from Tinomeat via Parina to Ngalikama,
where you should ask the local villagers
permission to visit the cascades. You will
need a guide.

Tetere (33.5 km)

SIPL has a large mill here. On both sides of
Tetere thick palm-oil plantations, popularly
known as CDC1, 2 and 3, line the road.
Beginning in 1976, the British-owned Commonwealth Development Corporation
(CDC) initiated several large agricultural
programmes in the area. These were all taken
over by SIPL in the late 1980s.

Tetere Beach

(33.5 km & 3-km side-track)

The road to the beach runs past SIPL and an
abandoned amtrak. Just before the shore, a
track leads westwards (left) about 300
metres to 30 or more of these elderly amphibious vehicles. Many of these rusty relics are
shielded by prickly thorns.

The access to the amtraks is now very
overgrown. It's beside a small cemetery and
opposite a group of three small shoreside leaf
houses. There's a custom fee of S$2.50. If
you go looking for the amtraks without

paying, you may be charged up to S$20 by
the custom owners as an unofficial fine for
trespassing!

Returning to the beach road, there's a
monument about 300 metres along the shore
to the east (right). Standing about 50 metres
in front of a white house is a cross commemorating four Austrian explorers from the
Albatross. They were killed in 1896 (and two
of them eaten) for trying to climb Mt Tatuve.

Local tribes believed the mountain was
tabu, yet the 25-person party under the leadership of geologist H R von Foullon-
Norbeeck persisted in the ascent with tragic
results. Local people believed that if White
people climbed the 1400-metre-high mountain, all the villagers would die.

Mbinu (36 km)

The road crosses the Mbalisuna River one
km beyond Mbinu, a subprovincial headquarters, and passes through the large CDC3
palm-oil plantation at Karoururu.

You'll notice a thick, green vine growing
over the natural bush once you leave the
plantations behind. This is called American
vine, introduced from the southern states of
the USA as a fast-growing natural camouflage during WW II. Since then, it has spread
unrestrainedly over indigenous vegetation
along the road between Karoururu and the
Mbokokimbo River.

Komuniboli (44 km)

The *Komuniboli Training Centre* (☎ 23160,
PO Box 536) has a nine-bed dormitory for
S$10 a person a night, and three twin rooms
at S$15 a head. Meals cost S$30 a day,
though toilets are basic. Rainforest walks are
priced at S$5 an hour.

Tiua (51 km)

Most villages east of Tiua (pronounced 'Djew-
ah') have houses built on stilts, raised variously
from a half to two metres above ground.

Ruavatu (58 km)

The road finally reaches the sea here, and
then follows the coast south-eastwards.

Taivu Point (58 km & 6-km walk)
The black-sand beach at Taivu Point extends two km inland. Many of the riverbanks around here and Tasimboko Bay have populations of megapode birds that hatch their eggs in the sandy alluvial soil. Take great care crossing rivers in this area, as there have been occasional shark and crocodile incidents locally.

Vulelua Island (66 km & 3 km by boat)
This two-hectare, almost-circular island is about 250 metres long and surrounded by sand. Also known as Neal Island, Vulelua has a tiny neighbour 600 metres to its north-east called Pikinini (ie baby) Island, which in fact is no more than a raised sandbar and reef.

Things to See & Do There's excellent snorkelling almost all around the island, especially on its western and north-western sides. There's also a small aviary at the resort.

Places to Stay & Eat The *Vulelua Island Resort* (☎ 23684, PO Box 96) is the island's only occupant. Its four units cost S$80 to S$95 a person. Meals, based on island-type foods, are delicious, with succulent seafood lunches costing S$30 a head.

Getting There & Away Tour Solomons does a full-day tour for a minimum of two people for S$100 a person. This includes visits to various WW II sites on the way to the island. Zankos Express' Red Bus service takes an hour to Vulelua's landing point at Komuninggita for S$25 a head each way, or S$30 on Sundays. You will need to organise your return trip with them prior to leaving Honiara.

The return speedboat ride between Komuninggita and Vulelua is free as long as you have a meal at the resort. Ask your bus or tour company to arrange with Vulelua for its motor boat to meet you. The waves can be quite strong at Komuninggita, so be prepared to get wet when getting in and out of the boat.

Aola (76 km)
The prewar capital of Guadalcanal, now a subprovincial headquarters, is where the road ends. There are only footpaths and a short stretch of logging track beyond.

Getting There & Away Trucks leave Honiara's market most afternoons except Sundays at around 3 pm for Aola and charge about S$10 a person.

One or two trucks a day make the return trip towards Honiara or the plains, usually early in the morning. Ask around in Aola, as people will know who's going.

Rua Sura Island
(76 km & 13 km by canoe)
There's an extensive coral reef on the northern side of this island and a narrow white-sand beach. To its east is tiny, sand-surrounded Surakiki Island.

A chartered motor-canoe ride from Aola takes an hour each way, so a full-day visit to Rua Sura will cost up to S$120.

Vatupochau Falls
(76 km & 17-km walk)
The falls are in very dense bush three km due north of Mt Vatupochau. If you want to see them, hire a guide in Aola to take you first to the awkwardly named village of Mbumbumaraho to get directions for the remaining five km to the falls.

AOLA TO MARAU SOUND
All distances are from Aola along a coastal path.

Rere Point (15.5 km)
Rere Point and its sandy beach are connected to Aola by a clearly marked shoreside footpath. There's a custom site near the village where skulls were stored – some of which can still be seen. Villagers will show you, if you ask them.

Taluto'o Island (20 km)
The coastal footpath passes within half a km

of this tiny, yet very attractive, sand-sur-rounded islet.

Simiu River (25 km)
This is one of Guadalcanal's largest water courses and care is needed crossing it. There's another custom site 7.5 km inland along the river.

Mbo'o (32.5 km)
This settlement is at the mouth of two very deep waterways – the Mbo'o and Singgilia rivers. Ask the villagers to canoe you across.

Papara (36.5 km)
You'll need a canoe to cross the Kaoka River to Papara, which is on the eastern bank. Once you're across, take the footpath along the coast to Poposa.

There's a custom site 4.5 km inland from the village.

Poposa (45.5 km)
Opposite this village are three small, coconut-covered, sand-fringed islands: Pari, Komukomutou (or Symons) and Arona. They form a line extending from two to four km offshore, and are all about 1.5 km apart.

You can get from Poposa to Manikaraku in Marau Sound on foot, but the path is beside swamps for the next 11 km to Savekau. The next seven km are better, though there's more swamp at New Marere. The route finishes with a 2.5-km tractor trail between Makina and Manikaraku.

It's much easier to charter a motor canoe the 20.5 km from Poposa to Manikaraku. However, canoes can be scarce in Poposa, and you may have to wait several hours. A charter will cost around S$60.

Manikaraku (66 km)
This village is a subprovincial headquarters. There's a *provincial government rest house* here that has three rooms with shared facilities for S$20 a person. Marau Airfield is 1.5 km beyond.

Tavanipupu Island
(66 km & 4 km by canoe)
A 20-minute ride through the lagoon, this 16-hectare island lies only about 200 metres from its much larger neighbour, Marapa Island.

Places to Stay The *Tavanipupu Island Resort* (☎ 22672, PO Box 236) has two self-catering, island-style cottages, each large enough for four people. Activities include snorkelling, fishing, shelling and canoeing. Cost for one or two persons in a cottage is S$40 each a night, but you should bring your own food.

Marapa Island (66 km & 4.2 km by canoe)
Marau Sound's largest island is high and wooded, with a white beach to the north. On its north-eastern side are extensive reefs and several sand-fringed islands.

At its south-western tip is Marau Village, where highly polished seashell and turtle-cara-pace jewellery is made, including pendants, earrings, bracelets and napkin rings.

Marau Sound
The lagoon has Guadalcanal's largest expanse of fringing reef, and best sea fishing. It also has several clusters of islands, reefs, shoals and coral gardens.

Particularly dazzling are the Paipai and Aaritenamo reefs which enclose the tiny, sand-girthed Paipai, Kosa and Rauhi islands. This whole area is a favourite of scuba divers.

HONIARA TO LAMBI BAY
All distances are from Honiara's Mataniko Bridge westwards along the coastal road.

Iron Bottom Sound
The seas between Guadalcanal's north-western coast and Savo Island were the site of constant naval actions between August 1942 and February 1943. By the time the Japanese finally withdrew, so many ships had been sunk, it became known as Iron Bottom Sound.

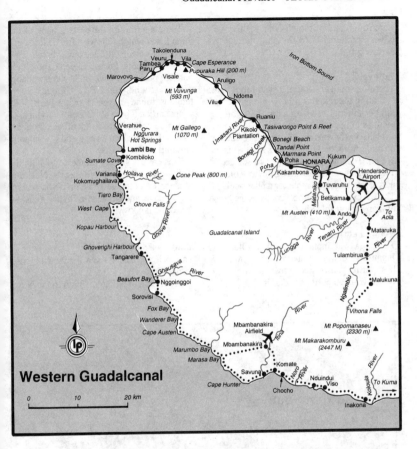

Western Guadalcanal

Some of the wartime wrecks have become encrusted with coral, and are turning into reefs. Fish swim in and out of the holds and decks, while steel hulls have become carpeted with marine growth. A few of the wreck sites are accessible to snorkellers, while others are well beyond sports-diving levels. Even so, you'll find plenty of safe scuba sites.

Trenches Creek Falls
(7 km & 5-km walk)
These small falls tumble 40 metres into a

narrow gorge. There are several cool swimming pools before you reach it.

If you want to see them, ask the people of Vatukola for permission to do so. They'll direct you up the Trenches Creek (or Kohove River, as it's also called). The creek splits about half a km south of the village, and you follow the eastern branch. Around 1.5 km further on it splits, and again you take the more easterly course. Half a km later you take the western stream, followed by an eastern one a short while afterwards. Some of the route is along dry creek beds or requires scrambling over rocks. Always watch out for storm clouds here, as this creek is very prone to flash flooding through its narrow gorges.

Tanavasa (7.5 km)

There's a small collection of war relics here, including the remains of a twin-engined US light bomber. The villagers will let you see them as long as you ask first.

Half a km beyond the village and 700 metres offshore from the Poha River's sea exit is the *Solsea*. This inter-island schooner, scuttled in 1980 and now sitting on a ledge 18 to 30 metres down, is an underwater photographer's delight. The wreck, covered in soft corals, is the home of many colourful fish.

Poha (9 km)

There's a war memorial in this village. A Japanese floating crane, wrecked in 1957, lies partly submerged, close to the shore where you can easily snorkel it.

There's a trail on the eastern bank of the Poha River which follows it for 1.5 km, until it reaches a steep cliff and cave shelter. This is the Vatuluma Posori Cave. Lapita-style petroglyphs on the cave walls were probably carved around 1000 BC, although some remains found on the floor go back 3000 years earlier. There are 26 wall carvings, of which some are hard to identify; others are clearly fish, snakes, a skull and a woman in childbirth.

This cave is strictly protected by both the Poha villagers and Honiara's National Museum. Ask the latter's help if you want to see the cave, and be prepared to pay a custom fee to the landowners as well.

Mamara Point (10.5 km)

This is a good scuba site for viewing coral formations.

From here to Ndoma, 13 km to the north-

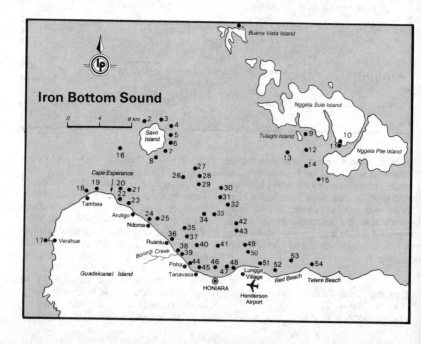

west, many of the coconut trees are scarred with WW II bullet holes.

Tandai Point (11.5 km)
There are plenty of sea fans, colourful fish and coral growth here. It's also a good spot for night divers to see turtles sleeping.

Bonegi Creek & Beach (14.5 km)
Two large Japanese freighters sank here, with appalling loss of life, on the night of 13 November 1942. Scuba divers call them simply *Bonegi I* and *Bonegi II*, as their true names were not known until recently.

Bonegi I, a 6800-tonne transport, believed to be the *Hirokawa Maru*, is in three metres

of water descending to 55 metres. As this 172-metre-long ship is only 20 to 30 metres offshore, snorkellers can easily reach her bows.

You can swim through *Bonegi I's* engine room and her bridge amidst hundreds of colourful fish. Growing on the wrecks are fan corals, sponges, coral polyps and gorgonia sea fans. There's a display of brass ammunition in open cases 12 metres down, and a 75 mm gun pointing to the sea bed at 35 metres.

As the upper works of *Bonegi II* break the surface, it can be snorkelled, though its stern reaches down to 24 metres. This ship was the 132-metre *Kinugawa Maru*. It's 300 metres

USA		NEW ZEALAND	
1	B24 Bomber	9	Minesweeper *Moa*
2	Heavy Cruiser *Vincennes*		JAPAN
5	Destroyer *Duncan*		
7	Heavy Cruiser *Astoria*	3	Submarine *I-3*
8	Heavy Cruiser *Quincy*	6	Destroyer *Fubuki*
11	Tank Landing Ship *LST 325*	10	Destroyer *Karishama*
12	Tanker *Kanawa*	14	Destroyer *Kikizuki*
13	Destroyer *Barton*	16	Heavy Cruiser *Furutaka*
15	Transport *George F Elliot*	18	Submarine *I-23*
17	B17 Flying Fortress Bomber	19	Wrecked Plane off Takolenduna
21	PT Boat *PT44*	20	Destroyer *Terutsuki*
22	PT Boat *PT112*	25	Transport
23	PT Boat *PT43*	26	Battleship *Kirishima*
24	B17 Flying Fortress Bomber	27	Destroyer *Ayanami*
28	Destroyer *Benham*	36	Transport *Ruaniu*
29	Destroyer *Walke*	37	Destroyer *Takanani*
30	Destroyer *Preston*	38	Transport *Bonegi I*
31	Destroyer *Laffey*	39	Transport *Bonegi II*
32	Destroyer *Cushing*	41	Destroyer *Yuduchi*
33	Destroyer *Blue*	49	Battleship *Hiei*
34	Light Cruiser *Juneau*	51	Destoyer *Akatsuki*
35	Destroyer *Monssen*	53	Heavy Cruiser *Kinugosa*
40	Heavy Cruiser *Northampton*		
42	Transport *Gregory*		MODERN VESSELS
43	Transport *Little*		
46	Wildcat Fighter	44	Japanese Floating Crane
47	Cruiser *Atlanta*	45	Inter-island Schooner *Solsea*
50	Transport *Calhoun*	48	Japanese Tuna Boat *Gyoshu Maru*
52	Troopship *John Penn*		
54	Tug Seminole		
	AUSTRALIA		
4	Heavy Cruiser *Canberra*		

north of the first wreck and has become a fascinating garden of coral and small fish.

There's a S$1 fee for all adult visitors using the Bonegi Beach, and a 50c fee for children. This price is usually included in your dive package if you're with a scuba group.

Tasivarongo Point & Reef (15 km)
Just past the Bonegi II site, and around 300 metres before you reach Tasivarongo Point, there's a bush track off to the south. It runs about a quarter of a km to a well-preserved US Sherman tank called *Jezebel* which was used for wartime target practice once the Guadalcanal campaign was over.

There are plentiful soft corals and colourful tropical fish at Tasivarongo Reef in depths of five to 35 metres. A site 400 metres beyond is very good for night scuba dives, with numerous small coral heads, drop offs and shells.

Ruaniu (19.5 km)
Three km short of Ruaniu village is a 6500-tonne Japanese transport, tentatively identified as either the *Yamaura Maru* or *Yamazuki Maru*. This 140-metre vessel was lost on the same day as *Bonegi I* and *Bonegi II*. The vessel is upright, lying from six to 45 metres down. Because its stern is fairly intact, it's a favourite among experienced divers, who have called it *Ruaniu* because of the uncertainty over its name. The colourful tropical fish here are very tame and enjoy being hand fed. Access to the wreck is through the Kikolo Plantation.

Ndoma (24 km)
Straight out from a creek and 100 metres from the shore is a US B17 Flying Fortress bomber. Encrusted in soft corals, it's in 15 metres of water, with its engines and 0.50-calibre machine guns still intact.

There's an attractive 400-metre beach of dark-grey sand just before Ndoma where a large new resort is likely to be built.

Vilu (25.5 km & 1-km side-track)
A turn to the south (left) from the coastal road leads to the Vilu War Museum. The collection has in it four large Japanese field guns and the remains of several US aircraft, including a Wildcat fighter whose wings can still be folded as they were for naval carrier-borne operations. There are also US and Japanese memorials. Entry costs S$3.

Aruligo (29.5 km)
The Iclarm (International Centre for Living Aquatic Resources Management) Farm (☎ 22130) operates a giant-clam project. These clams have been heavily overfished in the Solomons recently because of the high value to Chinese cooking (S$200 a kg) of the creature's adductor muscle. The farm grows giant clams until they are large enough to be safe from predators when placed on a reef. Once in their natural habitat they reproduce and create small clam colonies of their own. When they're really full size, they're sold as food.

You should telephone the farm before you visit it.

Cape Espérance (39.5 km)
Named by D'Entrecasteaux in 1793 after one of his ships, the *Espérance*, it was from here that the Japanese successfully evacuated most of their 13,000 starving men at the end of the Guadalcanal campaign in January and February 1943. Many of them were also sick or wounded.

The Japanese assembled on the 200-metre-high Pupuraka Hill just behind the cape to wait for evacuation. Once there, they were given one hour to get off the hill and into the Japanese ships. Some were killed as they made their way down the steep and slippery hillside in total darkness. Those on stretchers were particularly vulnerable.

The narrow, sandy beach here is continuous for 2.5 km in each direction.

Vila (40 km)
Canoes travel regularly from here to Savo. Shared rides to Reko in Savo's south and Mbalola in its north-west cost S$7 and S$12 respectively each way.

Visale (41 km)

The large Roman Catholic mission has the interred remains of Bishop Epalle, who was murdered on Santa Isabel in 1845.

Takolenduna (42.5 km)

There's a wrecked Japanese plane on the reef. Local villagers will know where it is.

Veeru (43 km)

The Japanese I-class submarine *I-23* is 350 metres from the shore on a nearby reef. Local villagers here are custom owners of the site and will canoe you out to a point above the wreck. They charge both a waiting and a custom fee.

The submarine is lying from three to 30 metres down, and parts can be snorkelled. It was blown open by salvagers, so you can dive through much of it, exiting close to the stern. To add to the fun there are said to be two live torpedoes still aboard!

Tambea (45.5 km)

The beach here was the other main site from where Japan's exhausted troops were secretly evacuated in early 1943.

Things to See The village has an attractive beach. There's a small Japanese monument commemorating the 200 soldiers who died before they could be evacuated and so were buried here. You can also view the remains of a WW II plane.

Activities The resort can help you arrange horse riding, canoeing and scuba diving through Island Dive Services. There are several popular scuba sites, including the submarine *I-23* at Veeru, the Big Bommies at Paru, the Caves and Dreadnought Reef. The Caves provide an amazing labyrinth of coral caverns, most no deeper than 15 metres and some just one metre below the surface. Dreadnought Reef is close to the resort and features a two-metre-high dreadnought (ie battleship) anchor lying on a reef.

Organised Tours GTS and Tour Solomons

both do north-western coastal tours which stop at the Tambea Resort for lunch. They cost S$80 and S$100 respectively.

Places to Stay & Eat The *Tambea Village Resort* (☎ 23629, PO Box 506) has 24 Melanesian-style bungalows, a restaurant, a bar and a dance floor. Prices range from S$68 to S$88 a night for singles, and from S$90 to S$110 for doubles.

Getting There & Away Transfers each way from Honiara to Tambea by Zankos Express' Red Bus are S$25. From Henderson Airport it's S$31 each way.

You can arrange transport to nearby Savo for around S$120 through the resort in collaboration with Dive Solomons.

Paru (47.5 km)

The Big Bombies, two large coral heads rising to three metres below the surface, are three km offshore. Fish congregate around them in huge numbers, and underwater visibility is always good.

Verahue (60.5 km)

The Nggurara Hot Springs are five km inland. The track is hard to find, so you'll need a guide.

Lambi Bay (70 km)

This village at the end of the road is a sub-provincial headquarters. The southern coastal route continues on as a footpath from here.

Getting There & Away Trucks leave Honiara's Central Market daily for Lambi Bay, except on Sunday. The best time to wait for a ride is 3 pm; the fare is about S$9 each way. Other destinations are usually serviced more frequently. To return to the capital, ask around in Lambi Bay, as trucks leave there for Honiara most mornings.

THE WEATHER COAST

The southern shore's poor weather conditions have discouraged human settlement.

Although there's a string of villages along the southern coast, most of these have only small populations.

There's a long strip of variously grey or black-sand beach eastwards from Viso, broken only by occasional wide alluvial rivers. Fast-flowing creeks tumble down the steep sides of tall, jagged mountains, some in a continuous chain of small cascades. Ridges covered in thick, green bush fall abruptly to the shore.

Making a foot journey around the Weather Coast can be very hard indeed, often requiring a guide. Small creeks regularly swell to raging torrents in a few minutes, especially during the local wet season of July to September.

It's a four to six-day coastal ramble from Lambi Bay to Kuma, with fine scenery all the way. Although there's a shoreside path most of the time, be prepared for quite a bit of rock hopping by the water along some stretches of this route, and diversions over small hills and through bush to bypass the occasional rocky promontory.

The three to four-day walk from Kuma to Marau Sound is beside the most interesting part of the island's southern coast. Alternatively, you can catch the occasional vehicle along the road from Kuma to Avu Avu, or tractor from Avu Avu to Marau Sound. Much of the route is beside long, narrow black-sand beaches.

All distances along the southern coast are from Lambi Bay.

Kokomughailava (7 km)
The Hoilava River reaches the sea here. In its shallower parts are boulders decorated with carvings. The designs include a giant, canoes, the sun and a shield. There are also hungry crocodiles lurking near this river's crossing point and in many other adjacent creeks.

Tiaro Bay (11 km)
The coastal route from here to both Kopau Harbour and Ghoverighi Harbour passes

along some pleasant sandy beaches, particularly near West Cape.

Ghove Falls (27 km & 8-km walk)
This waterfall is at the 200-metre mark to the south-east of 800-metre-high Cone Peak.

Getting There & Away The eight-km hike is initially through lowland country along the banks of the Ghove River. Inquire at Ghoverighi Harbour for a guide.

Tangarere (30.5 km)
There's a good surf beach near the mission at the northern end of Beaufort Bay. The Ghausava River in the southern part of the inlet can be hard to cross when it's swollen after heavy rain.

Sorovisi (39.5 km)
There's a very attractive beach in a small cove here. The route on to Fox Bay and Wanderer Bay requires some walking on shoreside rocks.

Wanderer Bay (47.5 km)
Benjamin Boyd, an Australian sheep farmer, landed here in October 1851, planning to take control of Guadalcanal and import sheep on a large scale. He named the place Wanderer Bay after his ship the *Wanderer*, and went ashore alone to shoot game, but was never seen again. Several British warships searched the area for him, but without success.

The route eastwards requires more boulder hopping, both to Marumbo Bay and to Marasa Bay. After that, the path goes inland to Mbambanakira.

Mbambanakira (68.5 km)
This village, beside the wide Itina River and Mbambanakira Airfield, is a subprovincial headquarters.

Komate (73.5 km)
The path from Mbambanakira passes over a 100-metre-high hill before reaching the sea at Komate. It then follows the beach for

about six km, rises again to around 100 metres before descending to the Noro River, crossing at the shore.

Koloula River (95 km)

July and September rains frequently make this crossing impassable, as floodwater can turn the river into a channel up to 400 metres across.

Kuma (105.5 km)

There are a number of custom sites very high up in the adjacent mountains between 1500 and 2000 metres above sea level, in areas of very heavy rainfall. You will need a local guide, adequate bush clothing and supplies. If the guide says the sites are tabu, you should accept it.

Mbolavu River (131 km)

This river regularly floods to as much as 500 metres wide during the midyear wet season. However, it's often dry at other times of the year.

Avu Avu (132 km)

None of the rivers beyond Avu Avu present too much difficulty, except after especially heavy rain.

Haimarao (133 km)

The Avu Avu Airfield is at Haimarao, which is a subprovincial headquarters. There's a small *provincial government rest house* here that has two rooms with shared facilities and charges S$20 a person a day.

Lauvi Lagoon (133.5 km)

The brackish waters of this four-sq-km sea-level lake are separated from the ocean by a narrow sand spit, though it overflows into the sea following heavy rain. As well as herons, cormorants, eels, river prawns and plentiful fish, there are some crocodiles living at the lake's swampy edge, so don't swim in it. Mosquitoes also are a problem.

If you are looking for a guide to show you the best places to view the local wildlife, inquire at Bubuvua, the nearest sizeable village.

Korasahalu Island
(133.5 km & 3.5 km by canoe)

Until very recently, this 70-hectare, quarter-moon-shaped island was just a reef. Submarine earth movements have raised it in the last 15 years so that it now stands a few metres above high tide level, and is covered in dark-green foliage.

Makaruka (148.5 km & 3-km side-track)

Turn inland at the attractive Alualu River for the path to the village. Makaruka is the name for a group of four villages called the Moro Custom Company. There are more than 100 houses occupied sporadically by Moro people from different parts of south-eastern Guadalcanal. Anyone wishing to visit Makaruka should ask permission from the villagers first.

Many ancient manual arts are being preserved at Makaruka, including the making and wearing of tapa. Shell money, sacred stones and traditional tools such as stone axes and weapons are collected and stored. Two leaf houses, called the Custom House and the House of Antiquities, serve as

---

The Moro Movement

The Moro Movement began quietly in 1953 but took off in 1957 when its leader, Moro, called on local people to return to their old customs. He claimed he dreamt about a spirit who told him to lead the Marau-language speakers of south-eastern Guadalcanal. A short jail sentence made him a hero.

In 1965, the Moro people offered the government the equivalent of A$4000 for the independence of Isatambu (their name for Guadalcanal). Though this was refused, the Moro Movement has remained significant – even after Independence. ∎

depositories of these traditional objects. You can see inside the buildings if you ask first.

Komuvaolu (153 km)
This is also a Moro village, and the one where most of its influential members live.

Valahima Falls
(164.5 km & 3-km side-track)
These falls are three km inland from Vera-makuru. To get there, follow the river 1.5 km inland until it forks, then stay with the eastern channel for another 1.5 km as far as the waterfall.

Komunimbaimbai (185 km)
Marau Airfield is beside this village. The track continues on another four km, via Manikaraku, to Makina.

Central Province

Central Province is an oddity both geographically and culturally. It comprises the Melanesian islands of the Nggela (or Florida) group, Savo and the Russells in the centre of the archipelago, plus the two Polynesian outliers of Rennell and Bellona about 260 km to their south. At the very base of the province are the Indispensable Reefs, briefly called Willis' Shoals, which extend south eastwards over 123 km of sea.

The islands of this 1276-sq-km province are the most scattered in the Solomons, and among the least developed. Despite the presence of the large fishing base at the provincial capital of Tulagi, and the huge coconut plantations owned by Levers in the Russells, the province is one of the country's poorest, with most of its 22,000 people engaged in subsistence farming.

The Polynesian outliers have little in common with their Melanesian provincial counterparts. Inhabitants of Rennell and Bellona would prefer their islands to form a separate province, despite their small populations.

Central Province

0   50   100 km

The Nggela Islands

Initially called Flora, and later the Florida Islands, by the Spanish in 1568, the Nggela group consists of four largish islands and about 50 others of various sizes. Lying between Guadalcanal and Malaita, the Nggela group is 57 km across and covers an area of 391 sq km. There is a rural population of about 8500, in addition to the 2000 inhabitants of Tulaghi – a small island half a km from the south of Nggela Sule.

The two main islands are divided by a long, sinuous channel called Mboli Passage. West of the passage is Nggela Sule, or Big Gela, while Nggela Pile, or Small Gela, is to the east. At the group's western extremities are the two other sizeable, but sparsely populated, islands of Sandfly and Buena Vista.

These four larger islands have fairly rugged interiors. Long white-sand beaches flank the northern coasts of Nggela Sule and Nggela Pile and skirt the group's many small islets. There are also mangrove swamps, some with a resident crocodile population.

However, Tulaghi people insist their island is free of these cunning reptiles.

Locally, the entire group of islands is known simply as Nggela.

History

The Nggelas suffered the same fate as many other Pacific islands during the early days of blackbirding in the late 1860s. In two months in 1867 over 100 men were forcibly carried off to Queensland to become virtual slaves, and another 18 were murdered. However, by the late 19th century, islanders were departing voluntarily to work overseas, but this, combined with intervillage warfare and the introduction of new diseases, contributed to a steep population decline.

In the 1930s, the secessionist Chair and Rule Movement from Santa Isabel also became popular in the Nggelas. When they experienced US wartime generosity, Nggela people, along with Malaitans, tried to buy US rule. However, the British authorities quickly insisted that any money paid to the USA should be returned. Nonetheless, some islanders believed they had bought a new government!

Arts

Forehead discs similar to kapkaps but called *biru* in the Nggelas are produced from clam and turtle shell and are worn on ceremonial occasions. Small model canoes and dog-teeth necklaces are also made.

Culture

Legendary People The Nggela Islands' legends tell of an early race called the Mumutambu – a wild, hairy, cannibalistic race – though nothing is known of their demise.

Information

Medical Services The Church of Melanesia has a large clinic at Taroaniara. Although it's often called a hospital locally, most of its patients are referred to Honiara. There are three other clinics, at Tulagi, Salesape and Leitongo.

Activities

Organised Tours Tour Solomons of Honiara organises a one to two-day trip to Tulaghi, Tanambogo and Ghavutu Islands, and also visits Tokyo Bay, Halavo and the Mboli Passage for S$600 for one person or S$500 each for two to four people. Heli Solomons, of Henderson Airport, does a 30-minute helicopter ride via Savo Island to Tulaghi, Ghavutu and Tokyo Bay for S$800 a head.

Getting There & Away

Air There are no operational airfields in the Nggelas at present, though Anuha will reopen once the resort does. An airfield to serve Tulagi has been proposed for Makambo Island, but it's only in the planning stage.

Boat The *Tulagi Express*, owned and operated by National Fisheries Development Ltd (☎ Honiara 21507 or Tulagi 32121), does a 1½-hour trip, costing S$15 each way, between Honiara and Tulagi six days a week. The Marine Division's weekly trip from Honiara around the Central Province costs S$10 to Tulagi and S$13 to all other destinations in the Nggelas.

Yacht There are sheltered bays and anchorages throughout the Nggelas. Tulaghi has three: at Tulagi's main wharf; at Sasape; and at the Solomon Tulagi Base, though yachties may find this too busy for their liking due to trawler activity. Other anchorages are at Leitongo, Taroaniara, Ghavutu Island, Siota, Tanatau Cove, Mbike Island, and Hanesavo Harbour.

Getting Around

There's a track around Tulaghi, and a footpath along Nggela Sule's coast between Mboromole and Rara. There's another from Siota in Nggela Pile to Toa, though the going is difficult in places.

Boat The Marine Division services from one Nggela port to another cost S$9 each way, except for that from Tulagi to Sandfly Island and Hanesavo Harbour, which is S$12.

Canoe A shared canoe ride from Tulagi to Taroaniara costs about S$6, to Hakama S$9, and to Toa S$18.

NGGELA SULE ISLAND

Most of thickly wooded Big Gela's inhabitants live along its northern coast from Rara to the Mboli Passage. There are also a few villages on the southern coast, including Halavo, the island's subprovincial headquarters and former Australian WW II seaplane base.

AROUND NGGELA SULE ISLAND
Tokyo Bay
The WW II Japanese destroyer *Karishama* lies half submerged in this inlet near Mbola. Sunk beside it is its tender.

Taroaniara
The beached bow section of the US tank landing ship *LST 325* is about 1.5 km north-

east of Taroaniara, its stern submerged. Taroaniara has white, sandy beaches on both its northern and southern sides.

1	US B24 Bomber
2	Anuha Airfield (Nonoperational)
3	Anuha Wall Dive Site
4	Wrecked Fishing Vessel
5	Sunken US Destroyer *Barton*
6	Wrecked Japanese Destroyer *Karishama* & Tender
7	Beached US Tank Landing Ship *LST 325*
8	Watering Point & Watering Hole Cave
9	Talama Caves
10	Langoakama Rockshelter
11	Suku Caves
12	Tanavala Caves & Rockshelter
13	Tanarorobe Cave
14	Mbambanakaili Caves
15	Malagede Cave
16	Varavura Cave
17	Sunken US Transport *George F Elliot*

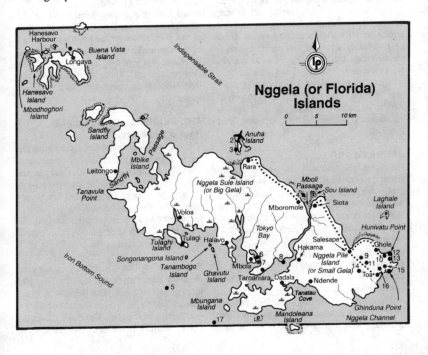

Watering Point

Villagers will direct you to the water pipe running out from the shore at the bottom of Mboli Passage. Built by US forces in 1943 and used to supply their ships with drinking water, it runs 12 km from an underground stream high inland.

You can follow the pipe up the cliff face to a small cave called Watering Hole Cave. You will need a powerful torch (flashlight). In a grotto inside are giant stalactites. Beyond a pool is another cave, followed by a larger cavern called the Cathedral, which is alive with bats, has dripping stalactites, and extends 500 metres to a natural sinkhole through which water cascades from above. In these caves is a rare spider-shaped scorpion whose sting has not yet been analysed – so beware.

Mboromole

About half a km offshore is a very picturesque, small, sand-surrounded, coral-fringed island. Around 1.5 km further out to sea, beside tiny Sou Island, is a large coral bank with a small wrecked fishing vessel at its north-western tip. You can see the sunken vessel's skeleton very clearly from the air, with its bow protruding above the surface.

There's a path along a sandy shore from here to Rara, where canoes can take you to Anuha Island. This well-populated area is extensively planted with crop and fruit gardens.

ANUHA ISLAND

Only two km offshore from Nggela Sule is Anuha, whose name in the Nggela language means 'peace' or 'sanctuary'. This lush 64-hectare island, with white-sand beaches in a deep-blue coral lagoon, was the site of the luxurious *Anuha Island Resort*. The resort burned down in 1988, but there are plans to rebuild it on stilts over the sea, with accommodation in air-conditioned thatched bungalows. Anuha's airfield will reopen once the resort does.

The island is renowned for scuba sites, and its best one is Anuha Wall. Beside this coral cliff face are huge gorgonia sea fans, sea whips, trumpet shells and black coral. Turtles and manta rays are occasionally seen.

From Anuha you can also make great dives among lobsters and large pelagic fish such as tuna, whaler sharks and barracuda. Tanavula Point in Sandfly Passage offers a wall dive plus an unexpected submarine current.

BUENA VISTA ISLAND

This island was given its name by its Spanish discoverer, Gallego, because it seemed so fertile. It's 18 km from Nggela Sule, has extremely clear waters, is ideal for snorkelling and scuba diving, especially on the reef in Hanesavo Harbour, and has a long, sandy beach on its southern shore.

About 1.5 km north of Longava is a sunken US WW II B24 bomber. Nearby Mbodhoghori Island is shaped like a pyramid.

NGGELA PILE ISLAND

Small Gela has a path from Siota to Toa which runs along golden-sand beaches much of the way. However, some inland sections of the path are hard to follow, especially near Salesape, and you may need to walk along the beach instead. Three km offshore (north) from Ghole is tiny, sand-surrounded Laghale Island.

AROUND NGGELA PILE ISLAND
Nggela Pile's Caves

The eastern tip of Small Gela is pockmarked with caves and rockshelters. If you want to see any of them, you'll need to get permission at Salesape and Ghole from the custom owners, as well as a guide; and accept any restrictions they put on you. As very few of these sites have been properly studied, the owners will want to be sure you don't touch or disturb anything!

Salesape to Toa There's a six-km-long footpath inland over the hills to Toa, past three groups of caves. The Talama Caves are first and are about two km along the path and 400 metres to the east. The Suku Caves are one km further on, close to the footpath and

Top: Canoe on Lake Te'Nggano, Rennell Island (SIID)
Left: War canoe launch, Chumbikopi, Marovo Island (GT)
Right: Making string from natural fibres, Rennell Island (SIID)

Top: Harbour view, Gizo, Ghizo Island (DH)
Bottom: Marovo girl, Mbuini Tusu Island, Marovo Lagoon (GC)

on the same side. Last are the Mbam-banakaili Caves – one km beyond and about 800 metres to the west of the path. From there it's only two km to Toa and the sea.

You'll probably find it easier taking a motor canoe from Toa back to Tulagi, rather than pressing on along the often very indistinct paths around Nggela Pile's south-eastern coast to Hakama, the island's subprovincial headquarters.

Ghole to Ghinduna Point If instead you follow the shore between Ghole and Toa, you will find 13 more caverns – six rockshelters and seven caves. The majority of these sites are around one km inland, though five are close to the shore. The most interesting caves are called Varavura, Malagede and Tan-arorobe. There is also a rockshelter at Langoakama, and two caves and a rockshel-ter at Tanavala.

Langoakama Rockshelter is 1.5 km along the shore from Ghole. The three Tanavala sites are at Hunivatu Point, while Tanarorobe Cave is about 1.25 km to its south. You'll find Malagede Cave by crossing a small creek about 150 metres south of Tanarorobe and then going inland for about three-quar-ters of a km. Varavura Cave is inland and one km north-west of Ghinduna Point.

MANDOLEANA & MBUNGANA ISLANDS

Both these small, attractive islands to the south of Nggela Pile are completely sur-rounded by sand. In 1880, several of the crew of HMS *Sandfly* were killed on Mandoleana. The US WW II transport *George F Elliott* lies in the depths about three km to the south of Mbungana.

TULAGHI ISLAND

Most of the south-eastern end of Tulaghi Island (pronounced 'Too-lar-gie') is occu-pied by the town of Tulagi (same pronunciation, different spelling). Boat building, trawler repairs and provincial gov-ernment are its main activities.

The island's largest complex is the Solomon Tulagi Base. Formerly a fish cannery, it's now a fishing-boat maintenance centre. The Marine Division slipway at Tulagi builds and repairs ships up to 300 tonnes, while the smaller Sasape Marine yard at Sasape handles lesser loads.

History

Tulagi was established as the capital of the Solomons in 1897, four years after the Pro-tectorate was proclaimed, because of its central position in the archipelago and deep-water anchorage. By 1910, Burns Philp, the large Pacific trading company, had opened a store, Chinese boat builders and carpenters were at work, and a government hospital was in operation on nearby Tanambogo.

The island's population had grown to 1000 by 1927, the year of the Kwaio Rebel-lion on Malaita. However, there were only 35 government officials for the whole Solo-mons with a population at the time of just under 100,000. Of these 35, 30 lived at Tulagi.

Shortly before he was hanged in 1928, Basiana, the Kwaio rebel leader, prophesied, 'Tulagi will be torn apart, and scattered to the winds'. Fourteen years later, his prediction came true with the Japanese invasion in May 1942, the chaotic and panic-stricken flight of Europeans the day before, and the destruc-tion of the town when US marines recaptured the island three months later.

Early on 7 August 1942, US forces landed at Blue Beach, recapturing Tulaghi the next day. However, the Japanese were dug in on the tiny nearby islands of Ghavutu and Tan-ambogo, inside deep, reinforced dugouts and caves. As in similar actions elsewhere, the Japanese refused to surrender, preferring to hide, fight and die in these deep caverns.

Once Tulaghi was secured, US forces operated a PT boat base from the wharf, and a seaplane base at Ghavutu. A number of buildings and relics remain from those times, including several rusty and ungainly pon-toons rotting on the island's shore at Sasape and Blue Beach. After the war, Tulagi was too badly damaged to be reconstructed as the national capital, so the honour passed to Honiara.

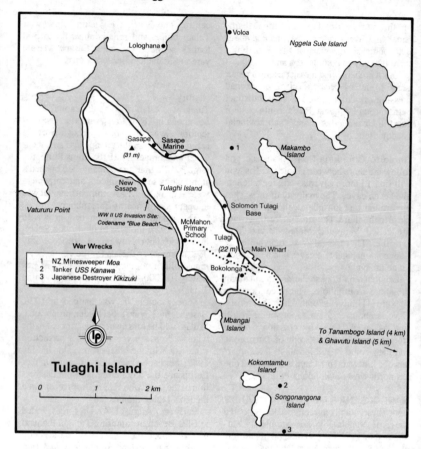

Tulaghi Island

Map legend:
- Voloa
- Lologhana
- Nggela Sule Island
- Sasape (31 m)
- Sasape Marine
- 1
- Makambo Island
- New Sasape
- Tulaghi Island
- Vatururu Point
- WW II US Invasion Site: Codename "Blue Beach"
- Solomon Tulagi Base
- McMahon Primary School
- Tulagi (22 m)
- Main Wharf
- Bokolonga

War Wrecks
1 NZ Minesweeper *Moa*
2 Tanker *USS Kanawa*
3 Japanese Destroyer *Kikizuki*

- Mbangai Island
- To Tanambogo Island (4 km) & Ghavutu Island (5 km)
- Kokomtambu Island
- 2
- Songonangona Island
- 3

0 1 2 km

Orientation

It is a leisurely 2½-hour walk following the seven-km-long gravel road around the five-sq-km island. The island's north-western end between Sasape and New Sasape is unpopulated, so consequently the track has become rather overgrown there.

AROUND TULAGHI ISLAND
Tulagi

The town of Tulagi occupies the shoreside area from the main wharf to the east of the Cutting, and north to and including the Solomon Tulagi Base. Bokolonga is to the Cutting's west.

Immediately to the west of the main wharf is the Marine Division's slipway. There's a wrecked trawler close inshore about 300 metres to the north.

The large Solomon Tulagi Base and surrounding buildings are beside where Tulagi's Chinatown used to stand, though this has now completely disappeared. Beyond the fishing base are the remains of a WW II ammunition shed.

Places to Stay & Eat There's a *provincial*

1 WW II Ammunition Shed
2 National Fisheries Development Ltd
3 Customs Office
4 Stores
5 Tulagi Market
6 Tulagi Bakery
7 Trawler Wreck
8 Tulagi Restaurant, Disco Club & Fast
   Food Bar
9 Police Station
10 Nambawan Haos
11 Marine Division Slipway
12 Marine Division Office
13 Footbridge & Cutting
14 Solomon Telekom
15 Provincial Government Offices
16 Post Office & NBSI Agency
17 Clinic
18 Library
19 Bokolonga Meeting Hall & Stores
20 Bokolonga Market
21 Central Islands Provincial Assembly
   Rest House
22 Unofficial WW II US Marine Corps
   Monument

government rest house here. Close to the police station is a small market and the *Tulagi Bakery*. The *Tulagi Restaurant*, which incorporated a disco club and a fast-food bar, was closed as this book was being researched, but it plans to reopen in late 1992. Just south of the Solomon Tulagi Base are three stores.

Bokolonga

Just 100 metres south-west of the Cutting, built by prewar jailbirds, is the village where all Central Province's administration is, as well as a post office, NBSI agency, library and clinic. Half a km to the north-west, and only 22 metres up, but dominating the whole area, is Nambawan Haos where C M Woodford set himself up as first resident commissioner. A now-rotten footbridge leads over the Cutting to the house, which is currently in private use. However, there are

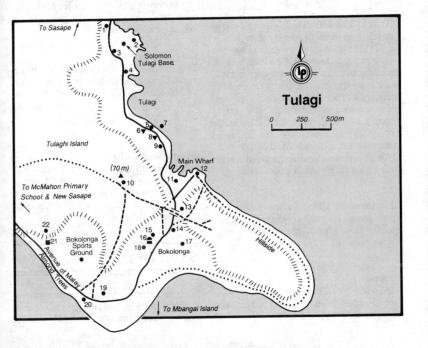

magnificent views from the steps in front of it towards Tanambogo Island.

Behind the Bokolonga sports ground is a very unofficial US marines' WW II memorial. It's the figure of a small, naked woman, fashioned in concrete on a slab of natural rock, and concealed among thick shrub. You will need local people's help to find it, as there's no obvious footpath to it.

The island lacks attractive beaches. However, there's a short stretch of white sand in a small cove about 200 metres to the south of the large McMahon Primary School, itself about 1.5 km to the north-west of Bokolonga. The shore from there on to New Sasape was the site of the US Blue Beach landings in August 1942. Now only litter-strewn sand remains.

Bokolonga has a number of Gilbertese settlers who commonly say yes by simply raising their eyebrows and smiling. Tiny, thickly wooded Mbangai Island is 100 metres offshore to the south.

Places to Stay & Eat The five-room *Central Islands Provincial Assembly Rest House* (☎ 32175) beside the sports ground has two beds a room, and costs S$20 a head a night, including shared washing and kitchen facilities. Bookings are through the provincial secretary's office in the provincial government complex in Bokolonga. It's best to phone in advance from Honiara, as the building is really for members of the Provincial Assembly and is often booked out.

There are two stores and a small market near the sports ground in Bokolonga.

Entertainment Close to the Bokolonga sports ground is the rather elderly Bokolonga meeting hall, where films are shown most Friday evenings.

Sasape

The sunken New Zealand minesweeper *Moa* lies 20 metres down on the sea bed between Sasape and Makambo Island.

TULAGHI'S SMALL NEIGHBOURS
Makambo Island

In prewar days, Makambo was Levers' headquarters. It was the Solomons' commercial centre while Tulagi was the country's shipping and administrative base. There's a very rusted vessel beached near the island's south-western end.

Ghavutu Island

The Japanese made a last-ditch stand at Ghavutu and on its tiny neighbour Tanambogo. The two islands are joined by a narrow causeway. Once the USA began using Ghavutu as a seaplane base, the Japanese bombed it repeatedly. Old and rotting parts of wrecked US warplanes litter the wharf, including rusting Catalina aircraft engines which are now used as bollards.

There's a sunken Catalina seaplane eight metres down close to the wharf. Snorkellers can also see the dim underwater shapes of two others in the same area.

The oysters growing on the jetty belong to local islanders. Don't take any without asking permission first.

Kokomtambu Island

This islet is often illuminated by fireflies at night. Close by in 25 metres of water is the 14,500 tonne armed tanker USS *Kanawa*. Sunk by Japanese bombs, and still leaking oil, its silent anti-aircraft guns point vainly to the surface.

Songonangona Island

About one km south-east of Songonangona and 18 metres down is the sunken Japanese destroyer *Kikuzuki*. About 6.5 km to its south-west and in much deeper water is the US destroyer *Barton*.

Savo Island

Savo is an active volcano with a pair of dormant, but potentially dangerous, craters – one enclosing the other. In addition, the island has a number of hot springs and thermal areas containing mud pools.

Savo is a 31-sq-km island lying 14 km north of Guadalcanal. It has a resident population of megapode birds, while its waters teem with sharks, dolphins and flying fish.

Savo has about 3000 inhabitants, who speak a Papuan tongue called Savosavo. It's similar to that of the Russells, and thought to be older than the languages of most neighbouring islands.

From a distance, particularly along the western coast, Savo looks like a woman lying on her back with one of her knees slightly raised. Much of the island is fringed by coconut groves and continuous beach. It's mostly grey in colour, with golden sand along the southern side and a light-brown shore in the island's north-western corner.

History

Mendana's expedition saw Savo erupting in April 1568, and called it Sesarga. In 1840 it erupted again, with considerable loss of life. Despite this, Savo was one of the first islands in the Solomons group to have a European trader – in 1869. Although Savo's population was about 4000 at the beginning of the 20th century, several devastating epidemics seriously reduced numbers, though these had recovered to 1300 by 1970.

In the very early hours of 9 August 1942, while the US landings on Guadalcanal were in progress, a Japanese naval force slipped out of Rabaul in Papua New Guinea. Its commander's plan was to attack and destroy the US transports at Red Beach before they unloaded their supplies. Although seen three times – by a US Flying Fortress bomber, a US submarine, and an Australian Hudson pilot – no warnings got through.

The Japanese task force took an Allied naval squadron completely by surprise. Three US heavy cruisers were sunk, each with 12 huge 203-mm (eight-inch) guns, as well as an Australian one, HMAS *Canberra*, with eight similar guns. Another US heavy cruiser, USS *Chicago*, had its bow blown off by a torpedo. Fortunately for the Allies, the Japanese failed to press home their advan-

tage against the troop transports and instead retired, satisfied with the damage they had done.

This action – now called the Battle of Savo – was one of the heaviest defeats in US naval history. To make it worse, the survivors had to cope with frenzied shark attacks as well as their wounds. In all, 1270 Allied sailors were lost.

Geography

Hot Springs & Thermal Areas Ground temperatures rise to nearly 85°C (185°F), and mud boils in several spots in Savo's centre. The largest site is at Fisher Voghala on the edge of the main crater. This one churns out hot, sulphurous water day and night. Nearby Mbiti Voghala is an area of boiling mud. About 400 metres from the crater's southern tip is a thermally active area called Voghala. This has spectacular mud pools and geysers, and extends 600 metres southwards along the Poghorovuraghala River.

At Mbokiaka the Tanginakula River has several sectors which flow alternately warm and cool, making it a favourite haunt of freshwater prawns, though you must ask the villagers first for permission to catch any. Two km from the large village of Kaonggele is Vutusuala. This large hot-spring site has boiling water and heated ground.

The three hot springs near Sesepi, called Reoka, Mbulika and Tavoka, are all small sites. The ground is hot underneath but only a limited amount of water boils up. However, the Kolika River runs warm because of its closeness to these thermal sites.

The two other hot-spring sites, at Talughau and Toakomata, are hard to reach and concealed by thick bush.

Information

Medical Services The only clinic on the island is at Panueli.

Activities

Organised Tours Dive Solomons of Honiara does a Saturday-morning round trip to Savo for S$120 a head, taking you by motor boat to Mbalola to see the megapode

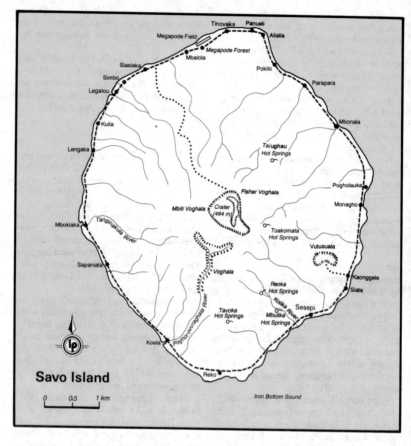

Savo Island

0   0.5   1 km

Iron Bottom Sound

birds, and then on to Kaonggele to visit the Vutusuala Hot Springs.

Island Chain Holidays of Honiara charges S$200 for its canoe and S$45 an hour for a round trip of the island of up to nine hours, so it's best to go in a group of about six. It visits Mbalola, Kaonggele and the former US gun base at Tinovaka.

Another organisation is Tour Savo, which charges S$15 a head each way for the Vila-to-Savo motor-canoe trip, though it requires a group to make it worthwhile. Bookings are made through the Solomon Islands Tourist Authority's office in Honiara. Staff will

design a tour to suit your needs, including lodgings if you wish.

Tour Solomons of Honiara does a full-day trip for S$300 a head, or S$140 each if there are four of you. Its boat goes to and from Tambea, with land connections to Honiara.

Finally, Heli Solomons does a Savo trip if required, or passes over the island's attractions en route to the Nggelas on its 30-minute Tulagi air tour for S$800 a head.

Accommodation

Accommodation is available at Pogholauka. See that section for details.

Water
Although now mainly served by piped water supplies, some drinking and washing water on Savo still comes from wells whose water is often quite warm. You should always boil or treat any well water before drinking it here.

Getting There & Away
Boat Savo is serviced by Marine Division vessels both on Central Province runs, and also by its vessels doing runs around Guadalcanal. The fare from Honiara is S$9, and it's the same price from Savo to Tulagi. It's S$12 to Yandina in the Russells.

Yacht Anchorages are at Kaonggele and Alialia, though both are exposed to easterly winds.

Canoe Canoes travel regularly between Savo and Vila in north-western Guadalcanal and also between Savo and Honiara. The cost of a shared ride between Mbalola and Vila is about S$12. It's a 20-minute trip in calm seas, but an hour if the surface is at all choppy. The fare from Honiara to Mbalola is about S$23. It's S$20 for the 1¾-hour trip between the capital and Kaonggele.

You can usually find at least one Savo-bound motor canoe a day in Honiara, either at the small beach beside the Point Cruz Yacht Club or at the Central Market.

Getting Around
There's a 23-km route around the island which varies from wide-footpath size to tractor width.

AROUND SAVO ISLAND
All distances are from Mbalola.

Mbalola
The Megapode Field is about half a km north-east of Mbalola and extends for around 400 metres along the shore. It's about 50 metres inland from the beach and around 80 metres wide.

Halfway between the Megapode Field and Mbalola is the Megapode Forest. You can usually see Megapodes throughout the day perched high up in its trees.

Places to Stay & Eat A *rest house* is being

Megapode Birds
Savo is renowned for its megapode, or incubator, birds – known in Pijin as *skrab dak* or *scrab faol*.

Even by tropical standards, this chicken-sized, usually dark-brown bird, with yellow beak and large, orange legs, is an oddity. It digs an unusually deep hole for a nest, laying one egg at a time. After a long incubation period of eight to nine weeks, the young hatches fully-feathered. Once it has pecked its way out of its shell, it scratches its way upwards through the soft sand to the surface. It is able to run immediately and fly shortly afterwards, never having experienced maternal care.

The large white or pinky-brown oval eggs contain a very high proportion of yellowish yolk to enable the young to develop fully prior to hatching. Megapodes have an attractive two-tone song which you can hear throughout the day around Mbalola.

The Megapode Field is divided into small family plots. These are separated by fences, or lines of young yellow hibiscus trees, which the megapode birds roost on prior to laying their eggs.

Villagers clear the warm, grey volcanic soil, leaving about 100 shallow depressions in each family plot. These are the megapodes' hatcheries. From about 3 am nightly throughout the year, from 300 to 500 female birds come to the Megapode Field. They dig down to about 90 cm, the depth which their ultra sensitive beaks tell them will provide the ideal temperature (ie 33°C) to incubate their eggs naturally. This subterranean heat is generated by a nearby underwater volcanic fissure.

The megapodes are still running around at 9 am but fly off once the villagers come to harvest the eggs. On average, about 20 eggs are laid for every hundred depressions, or about 400 a day. These are then cooked or sold for S$1 each. A small breeding hatchery in Mbalola ensures plenty of megapodes survive. ■

built at Legalou, six km south-west of Mbalola. Meals are likely to be available here.

Tinovaka (1.5 km)
The USA had a gun base here in WW II to close off the northern approaches to Iron Bottom Sound. There are a few remains, including a complex of concrete pads and spars where the batteries once were.

Mbonala (4 km)
The island's subprovincial headquarters is in this village.

Pogholauka (5.5 km)
The nightly rate at the leaf-style *Monagho Rest House* is S$5 a person. Meals are S$1.50.

Kaonggele (7.5 km)
The easiest access to any of the hot springs is from this village to the Vutusuala Hot Springs site. A footpath from Kaonggele follows the course of a small, warm-water creek part of the way to Vutusuala, where boiling steam billows out of the ground. Villagers heat their food in holes in the adjacent earth, taking two to three hours to cook a full meal.

Ask in Kaonggele for permission to visit Vutusuala, and for a guide. The custom fee is S$5 a head.

The Russell Islands

There are two main islands in the Russells group, called Pavuvu and Mbanika, plus 70 smaller islets, mainly to their north and east. Occasionally also known simply as Cape Marsh, this group's pre-European name was Laube. It's 210 sq km in size, with about 5000 residents, a third of whom are Tikopians or Rennellese imported to work in the local plantations or to tend cattle. There's also a sizeable number of Malaitans and Gilbertese.

Many children in the Russells have corn-blonde hair and light-brown skin. Their hair, which is sometimes curly, sometimes straight, often turns dark ginger or brown as they mature. Some remain blonde up to their 30s.

History
Captain Ball in 1790 was the first explorer to see these islands. In the late 19th century Savo warriors regularly made head-hunting forays against the Russells. So also did raiders from New Georgia's Roviana Lagoon.

The Americans made unopposed landings on both Pavuvu and Mbanika in February 1943. Despite repeated air-raids, the US soon built two large airfields on Mbanika. Huge quantities of supplies were stockpiled, most of which were dumped in the sea at the end of the war.

Much of this abandoned war matériel has become an underwater mecca for divers from live-aboard dive boat trips. However, in 1988 a stockpile of US WW II mustard gas shells was found locally. At first the US refused to acknowledge their parentage, but finally disposed of them in early 1991.

Information
Medical Services There are two clinics in the group: at Yandina on Mbanika, and at Pepesala on Pavuvu.

Activities
Organised Tours Live-aboard dive boats such as the MV *Kirio* and MV *Bilikiki* do regular week-long trips around the Russells from Honiara.

Accommodation
As much of the Russells are owned by Levers Solomons Ltd (☎ 21779), you are expected to have somewhere to stay before you arrive. This applies to Solomon Islanders as much as to foreigners. So, if you want to see these islands but have no accommodation, contact Levers first. However, if you have a personal invitation, there's no problem.

Accommodation is available in Yandina.

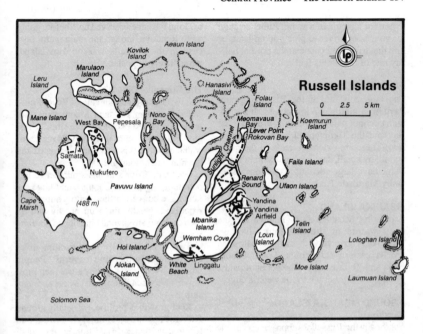

Russell Islands

0   2.5   5 km

Aeaun Island
Kovilok Island
Marulaon Island
Leru Island
Mane Island
West Bay
Pepesala
Hanasivi Island
Nono Bay
Folau Island
Meomavaua Bay
Lever Point
Rokovan Bay
Koemurun Island
Faila Island
Samata
Nukufero
Pavuvu Island
Sunlight Channel
Renard Sound
Ufaon Island
Cape Marsh
(488 m)
Yandina
Yandina Airfield
Mbanika Island
Wernham Cove
Telin Island
Loun Island
Lologhan Island
Hoi Island
White Beach
Linggatu
Moe Island
Alokan Island
Laumuan Island
Solomon Sea

See the following Mbanika Island section for details.

Food

There's good-quality fresh beef for sale in Yandina, and a market selling fish, vegetables and fruit.

Getting There & Away

Air Solomon Airlines flies into Yandina from Honiara three times a week. Its fare is S$66, while Western Pacific charges S$1 less. If you are leaving by air, arrange transport back to the airfield soon after arrival, as vehicles at Yandina are reserved mainly for plantation business.

Boat Yandina is one of the Solomons' main deep-water ports and has Customs facilities, but no Immigration.

The *Iuminao* stops at Yandina en route to Gizo every Sunday afternoon, returning the following Tuesday night. Marine Division vessels also service the group, charging S$20 to and from Honiara.

Yacht Crews need prior permission before stopping at Yandina's wharf, though it's usually granted quite readily for brief visits. There are wharves or jetties at Yandina, Nukufero and Telin Island, and other anchorages at Wernham Cove, Renard Sound, Nono Bay, West Bay, Samata and Faila Island.

Getting Around

There are 48 km in all of roads and tracks on Mbanika and Pavuvu. The longest stretch is between Lever Point and White Beach on Mbanika. Hitch a ride with any plantation vehicles going your way.

Canoe Visits to some of the two main islands' small, sandy neighbours are restricted. Once you've checked out which ones you can go to, take a motor canoe over to one for a picnic or a swim. Either arrange for your boat driver to pick you up later, or hire the driver and canoe at the normal half-day rate of S$25 plus fuel.

PAVUVU ISLAND

The largest island of the Russells group, Pavuvu is almost 17 km across. It's thick with coconut palms, especially around West Bay and the Tikopian settlement of Nuku-fero. There are extensive reefs to the north and many small, sandy islands within them. Some have large coconut plantations, especially Marulaon Island.

MBANIKA ISLAND

Separating Mbanika from Pavuvu are the deep waters of the Sunlight Channel. Mbanika is covered with coconuts palms, as are its eastern neighbours, Loun, Ufaon, Faila and Telin islands. The coconut palms often grow right down to the water's edge.

AROUND MBANIKA ISLAND
Yandina

Yandina is the Russells' subprovincial head-quarters. Its wharf and Quonset huts (now used as copra sheds), and the group's large network of roads, were all built by WW II Americans. It's also a company town managed by Levers Solomons Ltd.

The Yandina Club has reciprocal member-ship arrangements with both Honiara's G Club and the Gizo Club.

Places to Stay Levers operates the two-room, air-conditioned *Yandina Guest House*. The nightly charge is S$20 a person, though electricity and water supplies are sometimes turned off in the midevening. Levers will need plenty of warning of your intended visit because of their steady stream of business visitors.

White Beach & Wernham Cove

White Beach is the best beach in the area and where villagers often barter shells to visitors. The nearby inlet of Wernham Cove was a small, temporary PT-boat base in 1943, and there are still some large wartime guns close

by. John F Kennedy served here before going on to Rendova, though the main patrol boat base in the Russells was on Hoi Island, immediately opposite.

The Russells' Dive Sites

The two inlets on either side of Lever Point, called Rokovan Bay and Meomavaua Bay respectively, are excellent dive sites. A vast quantity of war relics lie in only 24 metres of water. Much of it is now coral encrusted and the home of colourful fish.

Wernham Cove still has a number of PT-boat mooring points. Sponges and large sea fans have converted these into a submarine woodland. Neatly lined up nearby and 36 metres down are several abandoned wartime vehicles.

Two of the Russells' most exciting dives are through submarine caverns. People who've dived them say they are at their most impressive when illuminated by the noonday sun.

Reef growth is prolific, especially around Kovilok, Aeaun, Hanasivi, Folau and Koemurun islands. In addition, several small islets are fringed with sand and have attrac-tive coral gardens, especially Lologhan and Laumuan islands.

Rennell & Bellona Islands

Traditionally known as Mu Nggava and Mu Ngiki respectively, Rennell and Bellona are Polynesian outliers with similar languages and culture. Both are uplifted coral atolls and are extremely rocky. Rennell appears to have been raised five times in the remote past, as five separate stages can be clearly seen on its cliff face. Because of its unique and specialised ecology, this island has been made a national wildlife park and nominated for World Heritage listing.

Rennell is 202 km south of Guadalcanal and by far the larger of the two. Nearly 80 km long, it is, at most, 14 km wide, and 629 sq km in area. At its south-eastern end is Lake Te'Nggano, the South Pacific's largest expanse of fresh water.

Rennell is sparsely inhabited for its size, with only 2000 inhabitants. Bellona is only 9.75 km long and 2.5 km wide, but has 1500 people living on it.

History

Lapita people briefly occupied Bellona in about 1000 BC. This was followed by settlements on both islands around 130 BC, with another major occupation in about 1000 AD. However, the present-day Polynesian inhabitants say their ancestors landed on Bellona around 26 generations ago in about 1400 AD. There were seven couples led by a chief called Kaitu'u. Each couple produced a clan, but only Kaitu'u's descendants have survived.

According to legends, they found a people called the Hiti on both islands who were small and hairy and had strange customs. Over the years the newcomers steadily eliminated them all in what the Bellonese call the Hiti Wars. Nevertheless, there are occasional reports of Hiti being seen on Bellona even now. Some Rennellese claim they've actually been taken to Hiti villages but inexplicably can't find their way back once they've escaped. Others dismiss these claims as either dreams or sheer fantasy.

The people of Rennell and Bellona say their ancestors came from 'Ubea'. They assume this to be the modern-day Uvea, or Wallis, in the French-ruled Wallis and Futuna group. Several small settlements are nostalgically named Ubea. The two islands were free of cannibalism, but had long periods of internecine war, with the eastern and western ends of both islands fighting each other until well into this century.

The two islands were officially discovered in 1793 by Captain Boyd in the merchant ship *Bellona*, after which the smaller island was named. There were only five brief visits by Europeans prior to Bishop Selwyn's brief landing in July 1856. He met about 20 people on Rennell and 13 warriors on Bellona.

The first missionaries came in 1910, and three stayed – all Melanesians. An epidemic followed, during which many people died, including a chief's mother, and the missionaries were blamed. Because the pagan priests realised the new religion represented a serious challenge to their traditional authority, the three were killed.

The Protectorate government closed both Rennell and Bellona to outsiders to avoid further casualties, and to protect the inhabitants from the scourge of foreign diseases, from which they had no immunity.

Isolation lasted until 1934, when three mission ships arrived to recruit a few villagers each for training elsewhere. The trainees came back in 1936. For two years the people of both islands worshipped their ancient gods alongside Christianity.

The inevitable climax came in September 1938. A Christian Rennellese teacher, Moa, set out for Bellona during a storm which miraculously abated once he had prayed. Arriving in Bellona in the middle of a major clan skirmish, he destroyed the two ultra-sacred statue-gods which had been brought from Ubea by the original settlers.

Bellonese priests foretold his immediate death for this exceptional blasphemy – but he survived. Moa then healed a dying non-Christian priest and others too. Because of this and the gods failure to punish him, the Bellonese stopped fighting and became Christian.

Even more dramatic events occurred the following month on Rennell in the so-called Niupani Madness. Those who were undecided between Christianity and paganism were keen to find out which religion was the strongest. They therefore called on the believers to pray daily, either to God or, in the pagans' case, to Semoana. One of the undecided advised the Christians to get ready for the Day of Judgement, claiming only married people could go to heaven. So all the Christians were married – each adult, teenager and child – including the handicapped and suckling infants. When the Judgement Day failed to materialise, non-Christians began beating Christians up and vice versa. Several people were killed.

After three days the fervour subsided and the dead were buried. Then, at a church service a few days later, a picture of Jesus was seen by some to speak. His lips seemed to move, though no sound was heard. This was widely reported around Rennell, convincing the vast majority to become Christian and so ending the madness.

The new order required old settlements on both islands to be abandoned. Fighting between Christians and non-Christians ceased, and everyone moved into larger villages with newly built churches in the centre. The ancient rituals and gods were abandoned. Sadly, centuries-old traditions were forgotten, to be replaced by fundamentalist Christianity.

Climate

Though Rennell and Bellona are much wetter than Honiara, they are several degrees cooler. Rennell, being broader, is a bit warmer, even though it's slightly to the south and generally higher above sea level than Bellona.

Rennell's annual rainfall is about 4250 mm (167 inches). January and March are the only months when it doesn't rain almost daily, though long droughts sometimes occur. Bellona is similar.

Rennell has two distinct climates. West Rennell is normally drier and less humid than East Rennell, which can be quite stormy.

People

Life on Rennell and Bellona is so different from that in the rest of the Solomons that you can easily feel you're in another country. Values are often dissimilar and life goes on regardless of events elsewhere in the nation. Many people in both islands regard the Solomons as another country, thinking wistfully of themselves as citizens of a separate nation.

Bellonese people sometimes talk as if the two islands are one. Consequently, just like the Rennellese, they speak of Lake Te'-Nggano on Rennell as 'the lake', as well as saying 'east' and 'west' to mean east and west Rennell.

Arts

The people of Rennell and Bellona are skilled and inventive woodworkers. They carve and inlay nontraditional walking sticks, as well as strikingly fierce-looking masks. They also make model outrigger canoes, replica shark-hooks from an unjointed bend of a branch or root, and, on Bellona, necklaces from flying foxes' teeth.

More than a dozen different kinds of clubs were used in the two islands' fierce tribal wars over the limited garden land available. Modern replicas have stone heads, while miniature ceremonial ones are carved with multiple barbed points.

A number of carvers from Rennell and Bellona live in White River Village, just west of Honiara, and carve extremely vivid models of island life. Dramatic examples of these are the ones on display in the capital's Central Bank.

Islanders also carve eagles, crocodiles, turtles and snakes, and weave quality shoulder bags locally. Traditionally the patterns were in black, using vine skin on Rennell and banana stems on Bellona. However, recently red, blue, purple, yellow, orange and green tints have been introduced. The bags are woven in a check design, bordered with black geometric patterns. Mats are made in similar styles.

Tattoos Since the conversion to Christianity, there has been much less tattooing done on both islands, and the practice of near-total body decoration has died out. However, there are plenty of middle-aged and elderly people, especially on Bellona, who have an ornate arrangement of tattoos, each with a particular meaning. However, only a very few young people are tattooed nowadays.

Formerly, special tattoos were reserved for priests and chiefs, symbolising the god's presence in the tattooed part of the body – a useful defence in battle. To attack a tattoo was to attack the god and so blaspheme.

Tattooing was so painful that men gained considerable prestige by being tattooed, and likewise forfeited it by refusing such bodily decorations. A heavily tattooed young man could be sure of plenty of attractive female company, and would draw attention to his tattoos in courtship.

Culture

The Danish National Museum of Copenhagen has specialised in recording and publishing the traditions of these two closely related islands. Since 1961, several of their anthropologists, especially Torben Monberg, a Dane, and Samuel Elbert, an American, have made detailed studies of the two island's oral histories, traditional religions and languages. Their first book, *From the Two Canoes*, gets its name from the inhabitants' popular name for their two neighbouring islands.

Legendary People Present-day islanders consider the Hiti to have been the aboriginals of Rennell and Bellona. They are said to have lived in caves and the depths of forests. The Hiti were seldom dangerous, but played tricks on the newly arrived Polynesians, including making off with their women.

Apparently the Hiti could disappear at will. They had beautiful gardens, could easily find water on porous Rennell, and taught the newcomers how to cook certain plants.

The Hiti's hair apparently was very long, reaching variously to the soles of their feet or their waists. They were a short, light-brownish people, with skin as hairy as a flying fox's. When islanders from Rennell or Bellona, while visiting modern zoos, have seen baby gorillas, they have immediately called them Hiti.

Cultural Change The people of Rennell and Bellona used to wear tapa and were ornately tattooed. They also used to press their noses together like Maoris do when greeting each other, though this has now almost completely disappeared.

Great changes came with both islands' conversion to fundamentalist Christianity. Clothes have replaced tapa except during cultural festivals and wrestling.

Both SDA and SSEC people on Rennell and Bellona have renounced such ancient activities as traditional dancing, tika-dart throwing, shark fishing, eel netting, bird and flying-fox snaring, harvesting shell fish and coconut crabs, and searching for fat white or brown tree worms called longicorns. While the old tabus have gone, new ones have developed, including rulings against the eating of scaleless fish, flying foxes, grubs and crustaceans.

Wrestling *Hetakai* is a traditional form of wrestling on Rennell and Bellona which involves males of all ages. With two contestants competing at a time, the victor is the one who knocks down his opponent first, becoming champion by winning all his bouts. Hetakai wrestlers wear loin cloths made from tapa.

Language

People in Rennell and Bellona speak similar Polynesian tongues, both of which are closely related to New Zealand Maori. Frequently these two languages have many words where English only has one. 'Break' has 88 Rennellese or Bellonese equivalents, 'cut' has 82, and 'carry', 31. The two Polynesian tongues have 136 words for tree varieties, 48 for yams and pana and 68 equivalents to English and Latin for fish – plus 33 more of their own expressions.

Young Love
In pre-Christian Rennell and Bellona, no connection was noticed between intercourse and childbirth. Sex was regarded as an enjoyable diversion, while illegitimate or unwanted children were treated as a sign of a god's displeasure. As a result premarital relationships among young adults and adolescents were – and still are – granted considerable licence.

Activities
Organised Tours Scobie's Walkabout Tours of Newcastle, Australia, does seven or nine-day trips around Rennell approximately twice yearly.

Getting There & Away
Air Solomon Airlines flies into Rennell Airfield from Honiara twice a week. There's a stopover at Bellona on each occasion. Fares from Rennell are S$39 to Bellona and S$129 to Honiara. Flights between Honiara and Bellona alone cost S$117 each way.

There are plans to open the East Rennell (or Lake Te'Nggano) Airfield in late 1992, which will remove all the transport horrors of getting there at present.

Boat The Marine Division services the two islands from Honiara approximately once a month. Deck class to Bellona is S$39, and to Rennell, S$43. A ship between the two islands (24 km) costs S$9.

Rennell's only anchorage is at Lavanggu, though ships also wait offshore at Tuhungganggo. However, this practice will cease once the road to Lake Te'Nggano is built in 1993.

Vessels calling at Bellona moor about 200 metres offshore at Potuhenua. Smaller boats are used to convey passengers and cargo to and from the beach through a narrow channel blasted in the coral. This anchorage is usually too rough for yachts.

RENNELL ISLAND
Rennell is almost totally surrounded by tall limestone cliffs which are up to 200 metres high, and covered by dense bush. At their base is a narrow fringing reef which completely encompasses the island.

The northern coastline is generally straight, but the southern coast undulates, and has a deep inlet in its centre at Kanggava Bay. From the island's raised and rocky rim, the land surface gradually descends to just above sea level in Rennell's central basin.

Both the east-central and far-western parts of Rennell are uninhabited wildernesses of towering trees. Between these two wastelands is the most fertile part of the island.

Scattered throughout the western end are shallow pockets of bauxite, with total deposits of about 25 million tonnes. Unfortunately, these pockets are where the majority of the island's cultivable land is. Though mining operations would leave the wild surrounding bush intact, no fertile ground would remain for the Rennellese to grow their crops on.

Flora & Fauna
Birds A number of bird species are endemic to Rennell. They have become restricted to the island because of its large size, isolated position and the existence of a considerable mass of fresh water at its eastern end and dense scrub in the west.

These birds include the very tame Rennell fantail and Rennell white-eye, the Rennell shrikebill, which likes the undergrowth, the Rennell starling, the Woodford's white eye, and the now-rare Rennell white spoonbill. Finally, there is the very common Rennellese pygmy version of the white ibis, locally called *tagoa*, which is also found on Bellona.

Bird-watchers have identified at least eight subspecies on Rennell of other common fowls. These have evolved distinctive features through confinement to this remote island. These include the pygmy parrot, which has red on its abdomen, and yellow on its wings and chest. In addition, Lake Te'Nggano has its own versions of both the little pied cormorant and the black bittern. The former is smaller on Rennell than elsewhere, while the latter is paler. Ornithologists suspect more endemic bird subspecies may yet be found.

Reptiles Living in Lake Te'Nggano's brackish waters are the black and white-banded sea krait, widespread but usually preferring the sea, and the endemic tugihono, found only in Lake Te'Nggano, is also venomous, but very docile. According to islanders it has never been known to bite anyone. Tugihonos are striped, varying in

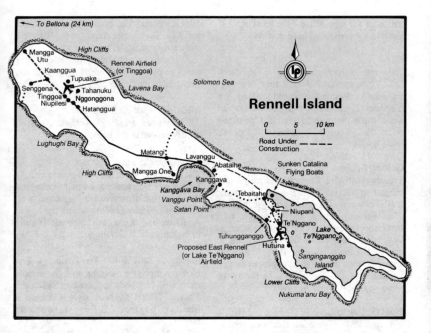

colour from yellow, red and blue to greyish-brown and black, depending on the kind of vegetation in which they live.

Flora The endemic Rennellese orchid is particularly striking. It has multiple mauve veins on a white body, with a pale-yellow undersurface.

Despite the poor soil on most of the island, Rennell's coconut palms, known as Rennell talls, give very high early yields. Seed nuts are sent to plantations all around the country, especially those in the Russell Islands.

People

Around a quarter of Rennellese men and nearly a third of Rennellese women lack the *Fibularis Tertius* muscle in their legs. This is the highest proportion worldwide for any ethnic group. Although the phenomenon has little effect on their health, studies of other Pacific Islanders who also lack the muscle

may help identify more precisely where the Rennellese originally came from.

Information

Medical Services There are clinics at Tinggoa and Te'Nggano, and a first-aid post at Lavanggu. You can send radio messages from the latter for S$5 a time.

Accommodation

There's no electricity on Rennell and modern toilets are rare. In some villages there are pit latrines with wooden boards for sitting on, but in other settlements there is simply a specific area of bush reserved for toilet use!

Accommodation is available at Lake Te'Nggano, Lavanggu and at the base of the cliff below Abataihe. See the Lake Te'Nggano and Lavanggu sections for details.

There's nowhere to stay at present at Tinggoa. If you're stuck, ask at the police station or the area office – the local equivalent of a subprovincial headquarters.

Water

There are no rivers or streams on the island. Lake Te'Nggano is brackish, though villagers use it for washing and cooking. There are rainwater catchment tanks and occasional wells throughout the island for drinking water, though only enough for most people's basic needs

Getting Around

Transport around Rennell is limited and subject to delays. There's a 25-km tractor trail between Tinggoa, west Rennell's administrative centre, and Lavanggu, plus two rather overgrown extensions to Mangga One and Mangga Utu. There are plans to extend the main road by 1993 from Lavanggu through the island's very rocky central isthmus to Lake Te'Nggano, as far as the planned East Rennell Airfield.

Boat Getting to Lake Te'Nggano is difficult. It's an S$80, 45-minute chartered motor-canoe ride each way from Lavanggu to the cliff side at Tuhungganggo. Although it's usually calm in Kanggava Bay, once you're past rocky Vanggu Point and the appropriately named Satan Point, the open sea is always rough and often stormy. Because of prevailing winds and tides, the eastward journey is usually harder than the westward one back to Lavanggu.

It's a steep and slippery climb up the 120-metre-high coral cliffs at Tuhungganggo, followed by a 3.5-km walk to Lake Te'-Nggano. It's usually possible to hire bearers for S$7 a time.

Tractor A tractor and trailer always meets the plane at Tinggoa and the ship at Lavanggu. It's a bumpy 2¼ hour ride through dense rainforest if there are few passengers, and a four-hour ride if it's heavily loaded and the weather's bad.

The tractor also does normal government cartage work and is available for charter. As with all charters, you pay for the driver and

vehicle's round trip, even if you only travel one way. The charter cost between Tinggoa and Lavanggu is S$67.

Anyone can get aboard the tractor and travel anywhere on its route by paying the charterer or the driver 50c.

AROUND RENNELL ISLAND

All distances are from Rennell Airfield, locally known as Tinggoa.

Lavanggu (25 km)

The cliffs are lower here and access is easy for ships. Lavanggu has a small white-sand beach and an attractive fringing coral reef. There are similar beaches across the bay at Abataihe and Kanggava. Rennell is only three km wide at Lavanggu.

Places to Stay & Eat The *Lavanggu Rest House* is a private dwelling with one simple room with four beds in it, costing S$10 each a night. Toilets are bush style. Cooking is free if you buy the food. There are two stores nearby.

The *Abataihe Rest House* is by a beach at the base of the cliff below Abataihe. Access from Lavanggu is by motor canoe.

Lake Te'Nggano

(25 km, 18 km by canoe & 3.5-km walk)
The eastern end of the island is essentially a shallow sea-level lake surrounded by lofty cliffs. The 130-sq-km lake's brackish waters are about 42 metres deep, and it's 27 km long and nine km at its widest point.

Lake Te'Nggano's western end is dotted with about 200 coral islets, and small swamps where taro grows in profusion. Four large villages – Te'Nggano, which is the local subprovincial headquarters, Tebaitahe, Niupani and Hutuna – hug the shore.

The lake is noted for its brilliant sunrises, with houses on stilts over the water in the foreground and coral limestone hills in the distance.

Bird life is abundant. Cormorants and teals seem to be everywhere, constantly diving into the water. The lake teems with

Top: 'War games' with real Japanese plane wreck, Shortland Islands (GC)
Left: Rainforest beside Ulo River, Vella Lavella Island (DH)
Right: Showering under a small waterfall, Mbiche, Nggatokae Island (GC)

Top: Gilbertese house, New Manra, Ghizo Island (DH)
Left: Rendovan pig-hunting party heading for uninhabited Tetepare Island (GC)
Right: Skull shrine, New Georgia Island (MMcC)

fish, especially the recently introduced tilapia, freshwater prawns and giant eels, while its reed-lined shores provide cover for plenty of monitor lizards.

Lake Te'Nggano's surface is blue like the sea. Snorkelling in it is like swimming over a dead reef, for that's exactly what it is – a raised atoll.

The US had a Catalina seaplane base at Tebaitahe in WW II. Eight of them were sunk in a surprise Japanese raid, including some at their moorings. Some of these, including one in good condition, are lying only four metres down about a km east of Tebaitahe.

Activities Full-day motor-canoe rides around the lake are S$120, while guided rainforest walks cost between S$10 and S$15 an hour. As well as fishing, you can go bird-watching and snake viewing by the lake, and lobster catching and snorkelling by the sea.

Places to Stay & Eat *Tahamatangi Rest House* has room for eight adults at S$30 a head, plus meals for S$15 each – or you can cook for yourself. There are plans for up to three more rest houses around Lake Te'Nggano.

BELLONA ISLAND

Bellona (pronounced 'Bell-oh-na' and sometimes spelt Bellon) is densely populated and has an extremely fertile interior. It's 180 km south of Guadalcanal, 15 sq km in size and surrounded by sheer, forest-covered cliffs ranging in height from a modest 30 metres to frequently as much as 70 metres.

Bellona's cliffs are often easy to climb, unlike Rennell's, which are impossible in all but a few places. The cliffs descend quite abruptly into a depression in the island's centre, reaching right down in places to sea level.

Bellona's people often call the island Te Baka, meaning 'the Canoe'. The V-shape of the island, the ubiquitous sound of the crashing surf and the cliffs visible in every part of the low-lying interior give you the impression of being aboard a ship in the middle of the ocean – or in the hull of a canoe.

A 10-million-tonne phosphate deposit has been found on the island, but the project is on indefinite hold. The villagers are aware of what has happened on other Pacific islands. Once such minerals had been extracted, only bare hollows, sharp coral pinnacles and a deep-brown moonscape would remain where once lush gardens and green forests grew.

Since the late 1970s, there has been a reaction against the dominance fundamentalist religion has over Bellonese life. Many people, especially the young, while grateful the killing and fighting has stopped, are sorry so many of the old traditions have been lost and so many artefacts destroyed. Consequently, many Bellonese people have deserted the large church-dominated villages and returned to their traditional lands in small one or two-family settlements strung along the island's central road.

Fauna
There are mosquitoes everywhere, and there is also a very common orange-coloured wasp. You'll also see plenty of swifts flying low over the ground, hunting for insects on the wing.

People
Many young Bellonese are extremely articulate. They often regard their wantoks on Rennell as rather conservative and distinctly quieter people than themselves. Many people on Bellona are much less respectful of others than Melanesians are. Indeed, young Bellonese won't hesitate to laugh at your misfortunes if they see them happening. The people of Bellona have a particularly tense relationship with Malaitans, regularly getting in strife with them in Honiara or on plantations around the country.

Information
Medical Services Bellona's only clinic is at Pauta. Local staff say there's no malaria on the island, despite the multitude of mosquitoes.

Accommodation
Accommodation is available at Tangakitonga.

See that section following for details. There are plans to open a rest house at Ou'taha.

Water

As on Rennell, drinking water here is always scarce. There are freshwater springs, but as they flow only intermittently, most islanders depend on rainwater catchment for their supplies.

Getting Around

A tractor trail runs east to west. Along it is a regular sequence of villages, gardens and coconut plantations. Transport is on foot or by the one tractor on the island, which meets every flight and ship. The fare, payable to the driver, is 50c, however long or short your ride.

The central road is the island's main meeting place. People will stop and talk to you wherever they meet you along it. Islanders claim this route was in use before the ancestors of the present-day Bellonese arrived.

The central island road begins at Potuhenua, Bellona's only anchorage, and continues to the eastern tip at Ana'otanggo.

1	Nggabengga Sacred Site
2	Hiti Pool
3	Sungaghina Battle Site
4	Tetau'aahiti
5	Ma Cave
6	Tapuna Cave
7	Saamoa Cave
8	Bellona Airfield
9	Teahaa Cave
10	Hiti Walls
11	Ana'otanggo Cave
12	Blowholes

AROUND BELLONA ISLAND

Bellona is pock-marked with caves, many of them the scene of island fables. There are also sites from the legendary Hiti Wars, though most of these, as well as ancient burial places and temples, are now overgrown. You will need the help of an informed islander to identify them.

Tika-dart throwing was a favourite pastime in pre-Christian Bellona. However, this ancient sport has been abandoned in favour of rugby and soccer. Currently, the

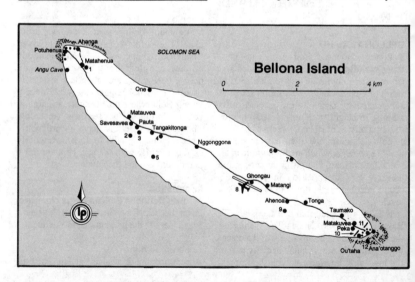

former pitches at Pauta and Ghongau are obscured by long grass, and the one at Nggongona has been replaced by a modern sports field.

All distances given in this section are from Potuhenua.

Ahanga (0.2 km)
Bellona's main beach is here. The only other beach is at One.

Matahenua (0.5 km)
Bellona's most sacred ancient rituals took place at the Nggabengga site in this village, where there were the two sacred 'godstones' – Guatupu'a and Tepoutu'uigganggi. These had been brought by Kaitu'u and his companions when they first arrived from mythical Ubea.

The gods of these stones were believed to be human-eaters. Great courage was required to invoke them, as the slightest error in the ritual meant certain death. Moa destroyed the stones in September 1938 without suffering any harm. The gods' failure to react caused the islanders to abandon their old religion.

Around here is a network of caves, where early Bellonese settlers used to live. These were occupied right up to the 1930s.

Angu Cave is about 450 metres to Matahenua's south-east. During one of ancient Bellona's long civil wars, a family – the sole survivors of an annihilated tribe, hid in this cave for many years before they were discovered. By then, peace had returned and they were allowed to survive.

Matauvea (2.8 km)
Bellona's last pagan priest was buried here in 1956.

Pauta (3 km)
This village is the island's subprovincial headquarters, locally called the area council.

Sungaghina (3.4 km)
According to island tradition, Kaitu'u fought an epic battle here against the Hiti, and killed 100 of them by a ruse. There's also a Hiti pool nearby.

Tangakitonga (4 km)
Islanders will point out a place close by the road here called Tetau'aahiti. It's where the Hiti wounded Kaitu'u. About 400 metres further south is the Ma Cave, where they hid afterwards.

Places to Stay & Eat The friendly *Suani Rest House* (☎ 23846) costs S\$23 a night and charges S\$5 for each meal.

Nggonggona (5 km)
This large village, popularly known as Nggo or No, is where Bellonese men play rugby most afternoons. Women also play volleyball here, but less frequently.

Matangi (7 km)
One km to the north are Tapuna and Saamoa caves. Tradition says the Hiti lived in stone buildings inside them. Some stone remains can still be seen in Tapuna Cave, where Kaitu'u trapped and killed most of the Hiti. One survivor escaped to Saamoa but was tracked down there by Kaitu'u.

Ahenoa (7.5 km)
About 300 metres south of the road is the Teahaa Cave, the site of another of Kaitu'u's victories over the unfortunate Hiti.

Taumako (8.8 km)
On the northern side of the road is a now-overgrown burial ground where many past chiefs of Bellona were interred.

Matakuvea (9.4 km)
Stone plates were found in a cave here, but were subsequently lost, though islanders expect other similar artefacts lie hidden in the surrounding area.

The two ancient graves at Peka are those of Kaitu'u and his successor, Mu'akitanggata. Kaitu'u's is the one to the east.

Ou'taha (9.6 km)

The Hiti Walls at Ou'taha are a line of tall, weathered coral rocks which superficially appear to be huge dressed stones, concealing a line of labyrinthine walls behind them. However, a closer look suggests they are the remains of a coral reef which by chance resembles human-made walls. Island tradition says these huge coral structures were built by the Hiti before Kaitu'u and the first Bellonese arrived. Some people make similar claims for large coral blocks at Potuhenua at the island's western end, though these look even less artificial than those at Ou'taha.

Ana'otanggo (9.7 km)

There are very fine views towards Rennell from the cliff tops here. Below is a cave with a large gallery and throne-like platform inside. At the base of the cliff are small blowholes.

Western Province

Formerly the largest administrative area in the Solomons, Western Province was reduced to 5279 sq km in size when Choiseul and Wagina departed to form a new province in late 1991. The region is often colloquially called the West, while its 57,000 people describe themselves as westerners.

Western Province's 19th-century speciality was head-hunting, so for self-protection most people lived on easily defended ridges. Evidence of abandoned inland settlements, such as standing stones, defensive walls and house foundations, can be found throughout the area. However, the interior has reverted to thick forest, with most cultivation now in shoreside villages cooled by fresh breezes.

In 1978, talk of a Western Solomons secession from the newly created Solomon

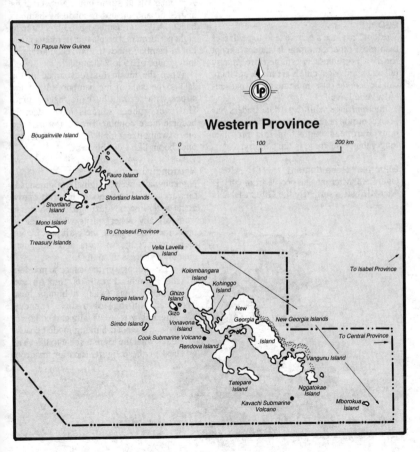

Islands led to a local boycott of the country's Independence celebrations. Since then, several westerners have taken up prominent positions in subsequent Solomons governments, believing their interests are now better protected by unity than division.

Western Province's economy in the past depended heavily on logging and plantations. With logging currently in decline, fishing and tourism have become the new growth industries. There are coral gardens and war wrecks to dive on, and a continuously expanding selection of places to stay in.

PEOPLE

Western Province's people tend to be darker than most other Solomon Islanders, except for the Choiseulese. Westerners are usually tall and slim. Most chiefs are male, but there can be female ones in some areas, particularly Vella Lavella.

Intermarriage with expatriate traders has been common here, as there has been continuous European contact in this province longer than elsewhere in the country.

Gilbertese Resettlement

Over 2500 Micronesian people from what is now Kiribati – formerly the Gilbert Islands – were resettled in the Solomons between 1955 and 1964. Their home islands had become seriously overcrowded and were frequently devastated by drought. The main Gilbertese settlements in the province are in Ghizo and Shortland.

The larger Gilbertese villages each have a *maneaba*, or village meeting house, where dances, marriages, feasts, communal singsongs and village meetings are held.

ARTS
Bamboo Bands

A popular island music in the New Georgia and Shortland groups is made by bamboo bands. A typical bamboo band has three to eight performers who play instruments made out of bamboo tubes that are each arranged into groups of 15 to 24 lengths.

When the music first developed in the 1920s, the ends of the bamboo tubes were struck with coconut husks to make a tune. However, rubber sandals have recently become more popular. The shorter bamboo tubes twang like a ukulele, while the longer ones boom like a double bass.

Nguzunguzus

Nguzunguzus were originally figureheads on war canoes. Positioned on the craft's prow at the water line, a Nguzunguzu's job was to ward off any water spirits which tried to upset the canoe, guide the craft past jagged reefs, protect the warriors aboard it, and guarantee success in combat.

Depending on the canoe's mission, the figurehead rests its chin on two clenched fists (war), a human head (head-hunting) or a dove (peace). Nguzunguzus are usually carved nowadays in the head-hunting mode because that's what the tourists seem to like. The best of these figureheads are made of real ebony, while cheaper ones are carved from brown-streaked kerosene wood, blackened with furniture polish. Pieces of pearly nautilus shell are then inlaid, making an extremely striking contrast against the smooth, highly polished, jet-black background.

Clamshell Money

A mark of status in the New Georgia group, clamshell money was often worn around the neck, although this custom is now rare. This traditional currency is made of pure-white clamshell rings between 10 and 25 cm across. The smaller pieces are the more valuable ones, while the most prized items have traces of yellow in them.

Mbaravas

An mbarava was a Western Province symbol of chiefly authority, which held such mystique that no chief could claim authority without one. Made from a solid piece of white clam shell, using stone drills and fibre saws, mbaravas were either carved with a frieze of squatting human figures and shaped like a lattice-work plaque, or as a hollowed ring with a bird or human motif above.

Mbaravas were deliberately fractured at a chief's death to signify that his life was finished, and then placed by his graveside. Consequently, few have survived intact.

ACCOMMODATION

Gizo and Munda are well equipped with accommodation spots, and there are several other well-advertised places to stay at in the Vonavona Lagoon and at Uepi, Lumbaria and Liapari. Island Chain Holidays (☎ 20385, PO Box 913) of Honiara, in cooperation with the Western Province Tourist Information Centre in Gizo, specialises in organising bookings for small-scale resorts and village rest houses around the province, and has regular radio linkups with them all.

Staying at missions is another possibility. Several churches have radio networks and may be able to help you. The United Church has its centre at Munda, while the Roman Catholics are based in Gizo. Ask them for permission if you hope to stay at one of their centres. If they accept your request, they'll send all the necessary messages.

You should always give enough time for a reply, but no answer usually means yes. Missions are often very welcoming, but contributions towards their expenses should always be made.

THINGS TO BUY
Melanesian Products

Western Province is the home of the Solomons' most prolific woodworkers. Westerners now make carvings mainly to European taste, but even so they are fashioned with exceptional skill.

Nguzunguzus vary in size and price. Tiny miniatures sell for about S$8, while larger ones up to 30 cm tall may be worth over S$150 each. They are made throughout the province.

Other carvings include masks, sharks, dolphins, turtles, canoes and paper knives made from kerosene wood or black ebony. They are often inlaid with pearly nautilus shell.

Forehead discs called kapkaps are also produced. Thin carved strips of turtle carapace are placed over a circular piece of clam shell to produce a most distinctive facial ornament.

Gilbertese Products

Domestic products such as pandanus sleeping mats are mainly made by Gilbertese women. These two-metre-long brown mats are always sturdy and long lasting, yet only cost about S$12.

GETTING THERE & AWAY
Air

The major settlements are well serviced by aircraft. Gizo – the provincial capital – has the most flights, while New Georgia, Kolombangara, Shortland, the Treasuries, Vella Lavella, Vangunu and Nggatokae all have airfields.

Boat

The Coral Seas Ltd vessel the *Iuminao*

makes a weekly return journey through the New Georgia Islands to Gizo. Ports visited include Mbili Passage near Nggatokae, Gasini and Patutiva in Vangunu, Viru Harbour, Munda and Noro in New Georgia, Ughele on Rendova and Ringgi in Kolombangara. The return journey is via the same ports.

Although disembarking is easy enough, getting aboard the *Iuminao* can sometimes be difficult, even when you have prepaid bookings, as you can be refused admission if the ship is already full. The southward journey through the Marovo Lagoon is particularly busy, as sometimes is the northward leg at Munda.

Olifasia Shipping's vessel *Olifasia II* sails regularly between Honiara, the Marovo Lagoon and Gizo to the Shortlands, while KHY's MV *Hiliboe* travels between Honiara and Gizo via New Georgia's Roviana Lagoon.

A notice board outside the Marine Division office in Gizo announces when its vessels are departing, while shops usually act for the private boats. Where there's no agent, just go aboard and pay.

Canoe Transport beyond the main settlements is on foot or by motor canoe. The provincial rate for a day's hire, including the driver, is S$50 plus fuel.

The New Georgia Islands

The majority of Western Province's population and land area is in the New Georgia group. This is a line of 12 large and well-populated islands, of which New Georgia itself is the largest, plus a considerable number of smaller neighbours. They extend diagonally from Vella Lavella and Simbo southeastwards past Nggatokae and Tetepare to isolated Mborokua.

The region's three large lagoons are often said to be among the Pacific's most beautiful spots. The Roviana and Marovo lagoons hug New Georgia's coast, while Vonavona Lagoon separates Vonavona from neighbouring Kohinggo.

Submarine volcanoes in the region have

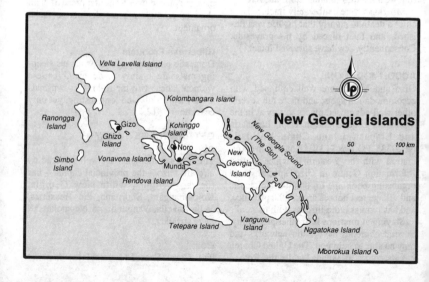

occasionally erupted from the sea's depths. While some have made regular appearances, others have rapidly sunk into permanent obscurity.

In 1942, the New Georgia Sound between the island group and Santa Isabel was a favourite corridor for the Japanese Navy. US forces called it the Slot; the nickname has stuck and is commonly used today.

The influence of the church and missions in the province is clear from the biblical names of some of the New Georgia group's villages. Bethany, Jericho, Nazareth, Nine-veh, Paradise and Sidon are just a few examples.

Customary land in the New Georgia Islands differs from place to place. Skulls and sacred objects are cited as evidence of continued occupation. Land disputes are frequent and may be over parcels of empty ground unoccupied for over 60 years.

GHIZO ISLAND

Formerly called Guizo and Injo, Ghizo is 11 km long and about five km wide. It's a low island with the 180-metre-tall Maringe Hill

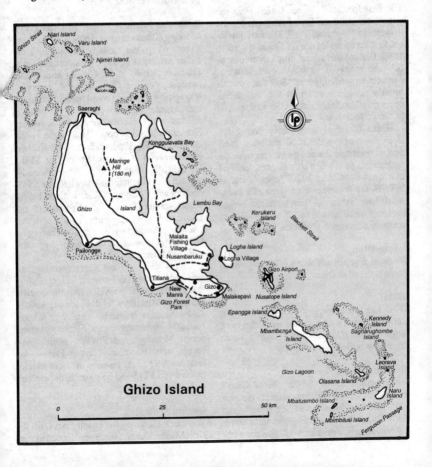

Ghizo Island

its highest point. Ghizo is often humid inland, and in certain months it seems to rain every afternoon.

Ghizo's total land area is 37 sq km, and it has a population of about 6000. Its main town, Gizo (same pronunciation, different spelling), is the second largest in the Solomons, with around 4500 people.

Scuba and snorkelling fans are well served here. Local war wrecks and coral gardens provide some of the Solomons' best dive sites.

History

The first foreigners to see Ghizo were the Americans Read and Dale from their ship the *Alliance* in November 1787. The first outsiders to take up residence on Ghizo did so in 1869, finding this island much more peaceful than many of its neighbours. Trading contacts expanded, so in 1899 the government's second station in the Solomons opened at Gizo to administer the western half of the Protectorate.

Ghizo Island suffered badly during the Depression of the 1930s. There was a great deal of resentment among villagers over the poor wages paid when copra prices declined to a quarter of their 1920s level. Then, in WW II, the Japanese used Gizo as a barge repair base. Although they withdrew before the town was liberated by US marines, it was severely damaged by wartime bombing.

Information

Medical Services There's a large government hospital at Gizo.

Water

Gizo has water supply problems causing daily restrictions despite frequent deluges of tropical rain. Consequently, Gizo's water should be boiled.

Getting There & Away

Air Nusatope Island is the site of Gizo's airfield. Solomon Airlines connects the area with Honiara, Munda and Seghe daily and with Choiseul Bay and Ballalae three times a week. Ringi Cove gets two flights per week

from Gizo, but Mono and Yandina only one each.

The Solomon Airlines fare from Nusatope Island to Honiara is S$198, and between S$96 and S$99 for Mono, Choiseul Bay and Ballalae. However, fares to Ringi Cove and Munda are cheap – S$35 and S$44 respectively.

Western Pacific Air Services flies to Munda, Ringi Cove and Yandina and charges slightly less in each case. It also flies to Barakoma for S$24 and Kukundu for S$19, and connects Gizo with Viru Harbour, Batuna and Gatokae airfields.

Boat The *Iuminao* arrives in Gizo every Monday afternoon from Honiara, leaving on its return trip later the same day. It gets back to the capital at noon on Wednesdays for a 1st-class fare of S$65. Getting aboard the *Iuminao* is easy at Gizo, so if you're travelling southwards, get aboard here. Its owners' local agent is the Gizo Hotel.

Marine Division voyages between Honiara and Gizo cost S$53, while twice each month KHY's launch the MV *Hiliboe* plies between Gizo and Honiara for S$48. Olifasia Shipping's *Olifasia II* does a weekly trip between the capital and Gizo for S$49 each way, while the *Vele*, a Gizo-based vessel, services Simbo and the Shortlands on an alternating weekly basis. In addition, the *Thomas E*, owned by Vasivapada Trading in Gizo's Middenway Rd, does eight-day round trips to Choiseul.

Gizo's daily market guarantees regular motor-canoe traffic between neighbouring islands. People from Vella Lavella usually visit on Mondays and Fridays, as do Kolombangara Islanders – many of whom come on Wednesdays also. Simbo villagers prefer Mondays and Fridays, while Ranongga Islanders mainly favour Friday. As long as it's a routine journey, the fares should be between S$15 and S$40 each, depending on the departure point.

Getting Around

You can walk along the beach from Gizo to New Manra. Beyond there you'll need to use the road. The only way you'll get to Saeraghi at Ghizo's north-western tip is on a tour or dive bus, or by hitching a ride from a passing truck.

Airport Transport Motor canoes meet both airlines' flights, charging S$5 each way between Nusatope and Gizo.

GIZO
You will see Gizo's best aspect on arrival by motor canoe from Nusatope. Small copra boats line the wharf, with a green canopy of poincianas and coconut trees as their backdrop. Gizo's waterfront covers a compact one km along Middenway Rd. This highway is named after the district officer for the western Solomons who was resident here for part of the 1920s.

The KHY jetty is at the port's western end. This Chinese-operated boat-building yard was constructed by the Japanese to build and repair their barges in WW II. Above and behind the harbour are residential areas, most of them with spectacular views of either Kolombangara or Gizo Lagoon.

People
There's a very friendly expat community in the town. You are sure to be welcomed into its activities from the word go.

A large number of Gilbertese moved to Ghizo in the mid-1950s once their home islands in Kiribati became overcrowded. Many of these newly settled Micronesians, as well as Chinese storekeepers, work in local shops and are active members of the town's business community.

Information
Tourist Office The privately operated Western Province Tourist Information Office beside Gizo Market will give you all the answers you need, both about Gizo and about how to get around the province.

Immigration There is no Immigration Office in Gizo, even though yachts often drop in here as their first port of call. Customs officers come to Gizo on a visiting basis only.

Should you require an extension of your visitor's permit, ask at the police station.

Money Gizo has branches of the ANZ Bank and NBSI.

Radio Messages Service messages can be sent by Solomon Telekom (☎ 60187) via SIBC's Radio Happy Lagoon (☎ 60207); the two are in adjacent buildings. In addition, the Roman Catholic Church's provincial headquarters maintains a regular radio schedule with several missions around the province.

Film The only place outside Honiara where you can get 35-mm slide film is Gizo, though it may be stored without air-conditioning. Try some of the shops opposite Gizo's NBSI, such as New Generation or Wing Sun Co. Make sure to check the expiry date on your film.

Library The small public library is open weekdays from 8.30 am to 4.45 pm, with a break between 1 and 2.30 pm.

Things to See
Views There are three magnificent views along the hilltop above the town. In the north-eastern foreground is Gizo's harbour and nearby Logha Island. In the distance is the mist-covered bulk of Kolombangara. The south-eastern panorama from the hilltop above the prison is equally fine, with views of tiny islets and surf breaking on the reefs of Gizo Lagoon, with Vonavona and Rendova beyond.

The third view is from just beyond the turn-off to Phoebe's Rest House, and overlooks Olasana Island.

Monuments In front of the police station are two monuments. One is to Captain Ferguson of the *Ripple*, who used to trade between New Georgia and Shortland, but was killed in 1880 on Bougainville. Ferguson was such a popular figure that the Shortlands' Chief Gorai avenged him by burning the village where Ferguson was murdered. The other monument commemorates Captain Wood-

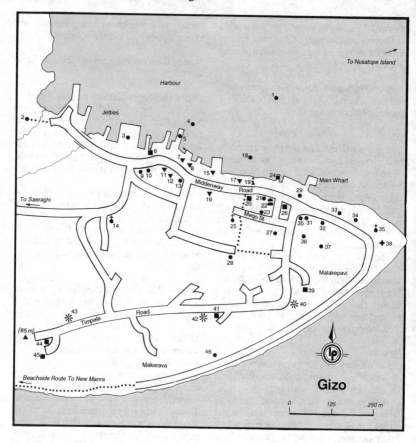

Harbour

To Nusatope Island

Jetties

To Saeraghi

Middenway Road

Mego St

Main Wharf

Malakepavi

Timpala Road

(65 m)

Makerava

Beachside Route To New Manra

To New Manra

Gizo

0   125   250 m

house, who traded in these waters between 1876 and 1892, dying in Gizo in 1906.

Malakepavi This friendly suburb stretches from the hospital to the jail. At low tide you will see many of its residents combing the onshore reef for shellfish.

New Manra is 2.5 km beyond, along the shoreline. It's a much cooler walk this way than along the humid first few km of the road across the island.

Activities
Scuba Diving & Snorkelling Gizo has two schools for prospective scuba divers, with training dives that include viewing war wrecks, colourful fish and dazzling reefs.

These are Dive Wreck & Reef Gizo (☎ 60021/60153, PO Box 120) in the Gizo Hotel, and Adventure Sports (☎ 60253, PO Box 21) at the western end of Middenway Rd. Both visit the northern tips of Vonavona and Kohinggo islands, as well as Ghizo's many dive sites.

Prices for single dives are S$110 with both companies, though snorkelling prices vary between S$25 and S$50. Resort courses and open-water certification prices also differ

■ PLACES TO STAY

6 Divers Lodge
20 Western Council Rest House
26 Gizo Hotel
39 Phoebe's Rest House
41 Western Provincial Government Rest House
44 Koburu Tavia Lodge
45 Paradise Lodge

▼ PLACES TO EAT

7 Rendova Trading
8 Zipale Blue Restaurant
11 Trescoll Island Restaurant
12 Vasivapada Trading
15 Solomon Islands Consumers Supermarket
16 Gizo Daily Bread Kitchen
17 Gizo Market

OTHER

1 Wrecked Japanese Seaplane
2 Old Copra Sheds
3 Customs Shed
4 Zero Two – Wrecked Japanese Fighter (off KHY, Jetty)
5 KHY Jetty & Slipway
9 Western Pacific Airlines
10 Adventure Sports
13 NBSI
14 Christian Fellowship Church
18 Zero One – Wrecked Japanese Fighter (off Gizo Market)
19 Western Province Tourist Information Centre
21 ANZ Bank
22 Post Office
23 SIBC & Solomon Telekom
24 Solomon Airlines Jetty
25 St. Peter's RC Church
26 Gizo Hotel/Dive Wreck & Reef Gizo
27 Primary School
28 Library
29 Provincial Government Stores
30 Woodhouse & Ferguson Monuments
31 Police Station
32 Solomon Airlines Office
33 Marine Division
34 Gizo Sports & Social Club
35 United Church
36 Government Offices
37 Sports Ground
38 Hospital
40 Lookout
42 Lookout
43 Lookout
46 Prison

between the two companies, the cheapest courses being S$110 and S$450 respectively.

Scuba Sites in Gizo There are three Japanese plane wrecks on the harbour bed. However, because of constant port activity, poor visibility and local water pollution which has caused some divers ear problems, great care should be taken when viewing these sites.

Zero One This wrecked Japanese fighter, only 10 metres beyond the market and in five metres of water, was dumped here after WW II by salvagers. This is a busy spot for canoes and is therefore a hazardous dive.

Zero Two This aircraft is just beyond the KHY jetty in seven metres of water. Its cockpit and engine are still intact, although the wings came off when it crashed. Watch out, as this spot is also busy.

Japanese Seaplane Three hundred metres offshore from the post office, this wreck is in 27 metres of water. Although the plane is upside down, one folding wing is still intact, with its hinges clearly visible.

Organised Tours The Gizo Hotel (☎ 60199), Paradise Lodge (☎ 60021) in conjunction with Dive Wreck & Reef Gizo (PO Box 120), and Adventure Sports (☎ 60253, PO Box 21) all organise trips from or around Gizo.

Sea Paradise Lodge and Gizo Hotel organise tours of Simbo for around S$150, which includes the local custom fees to see the volcano and the megapode-bird hatcheries. It also conducts hikes up Mt Veve on Kolombangara, costing around S$150 a head. This is an overnight camping trip.

Paradise Lodge and Adventure Sports will

organise two to five-day tours of the Shortland Islands, and the same for Choiseul. Other, shorter trips include visits to some of the islands in the nearby Gizo Lagoon, usually Olasana. This is all organised by Gizo Hotel for S$20 a head. It and Paradise Lodge also arrange local fishing trips.

Land The Gizo Hotel organises a S$10 nature walk around the Gizo Forest Park and a S$60 trip to Saeraghi.

Places to Stay

Along with the rest of Gizo, some of the accommodation places suffer recurrent water shortages. It's best to check whether there are 24-hour water supplies before booking in.

At the bottom end of the scale is the *Western Council Rest House*, which charges S$3 for a bunk in a four-bed dorm. There's no bedding, mattress or fan provided. It's pretty basic, and not recommended.

The *Western Provincial Government Rest House*, at S$6 a night, is cleaner and has cooking facilities. It's built for visiting government staff, so any newly arrived official takes priority over you, even if you already have a room.

Halfway up the hill above the town is *Phoebe's Rest House* (☎ 60161). There are three double rooms at S$24 a head. As well as cooking and laundry facilities, there are magnificent views from the balcony. It seems as if everyone who stays here likes it.

The very friendly *Paradise Lodge* (☎ 60021, PO Box 60) has a fine ocean view, plentiful water supplies, and accommodation for up to 40 people. A bed is only S$25. Three meals a day cost S$25, or you can cater for yourself.

The *Koburu Tavia Lodge* (☎ 60257, PO Box 50), on the same hilltop as the Paradise Lodge, has three guest rooms which are S$35 a head, or S$65 with meals. The *Divers Lodge* on the waterfront is under the same management and has four self-catering guest rooms, again for S$35 a head. The *Gizo Hotel* (☎ 60199, PO Box 30), beside the harbour, has singles/doubles for S$85/100 a night. The hotel has 15 fully serviced, fan-cooled rooms, a restaurant and bar, and a dive shop on the premises.

Places to Eat

The *Gizo Market* operates beside the harbour seven days a week. There are always plenty of fish, fruit and vegetables for sale. The largest food store in town is the Gizo branch of the *Solomon Islands Consumers Supermarket*, and there's fresh bread at the *Gizo Daily Bread Kitchen*. The *Fast Food Snack Bar* beside Rendova Trading does takeaways only.

The friendly *Trescoll Island Restaurant*, down a side alley beside Gizo Stationery & Sportswear, does pleasantly simple meals for around S$4 to S$9 each.

The *Zipale Blue Restaurant* (Zipale means 'sweet honey' in the Roviana language) is open from 7 am to 2 pm and 7 to 9 pm seven days a week. It's Gizo's resident expats' favourite eating place, with meals averaging between S$6 and S$25.

The *Gizo Hotel's* restaurant serves three meals a day. Breakfasts cost up to S$10, while dinners can range up to S$30 a head.

Entertainment

The bar at the Gizo Hotel is popular with the town's expats. It's also a good place to hear bamboo bands and to dance to disco music.

The Gizo Sports & Social Club (☎ 60163) offers free membership to Honiara's G Club members. It's a good place for a quiet drink or a game of pool. It shuts at 8 pm except for Friday, the weekly film night, when it closes at 11 pm.

Films are screened in the Customs shed at the western end of the town. Programmes are advertised by posters on trees by the market, with screenings usually held on weekday nights at 7pm. Adults pay S$1.50, children S$1.

Things to Buy

Carvers often collect around the Gizo Hotel bar when there's music or a dance on there. The dive shop at Adventure Sports frequently has stone carvings for sale.

Getting Around

Movement around Gizo is on foot. Most destinations in the town are close by, though the walk up Timpala Rd can be a real slog on a hot day.

AROUND GHIZO ISLAND

The main road out of Gizo skirts the shore to Saeraghi at the island's north-western end. However, The first stretch is through rain forest and can be very humid.

All distances are from Gizo's main wharf.

Nusambaruku (1 km by canoe)

This village is clearly visible across the water from Gizo, and has several houses raised on stilts above the sea. About one km further on is the Malaita Fishing Village (named thus because it's populated by Malaitan settlers).

Although a long track connects Nusambaruku and the Malaita Fishing Village, it's much quicker to travel between the two by motor canoe. However, once you get to either place, you should ask the villagers' permission to land, and explain your business.

Gizo Forest Park (1.5 km)

This Forestry project is to identify the best trees for future reafforestation programmes. Arrows direct you along a footpath three-quarters of a km long which skirts the small plantation.

New Manra (3 km)

This small fishing village was the first Gilbertese resettlement site in the Solomons.

Titiana (4 km)

Ghizo's main Gilbertese village is often pronounced 'Sisiana'. In its centre is a large maneaba.

About 500 Micronesian people came to Titiana and New Manra between 1955 and 1962. They were from drought-stricken Manra Island in eastern Kiribati.

Pailongge (6 km)

Pronounced 'Pye-long-y', this neat shore-side Melanesian village's two main features are friendliness and 2.5-metre-high surf. Surfies are welcome as long as they act respectfully. Unfortunately, some have used this village as they pleased, causing villagers embarrassment and uncharacteristic annoyance.

Saeraghi (11 km)

The road runs parallel to golden, sandy beaches, which are completely empty of people. Immediately across the water is Ranongga.

Saeraghi has a protecting reef with plenty of coral and small, colourful fish. It also has one of the Solomons' most beautiful beaches, about half a km before the village begins.

Saeraghi people are very friendly and will greet visitors with interesting displays of seashells for sale. Some of these are excellent value, such as large cowries for S$1.

GHIZO'S ISLAND NEIGHBOURS
Logha Island

There's a sandy beach on this green-canopied island's north-western side. One km from Gizo, its only settlement is Logha Village.

Nusatope Island

Narrow one-km-long Nusatope is two km from Gizo. It has an attractive coral garden on its western side and a sandy beach at its northern tip. Travel over to Nusatope in one of the airlines' motor canoes, and return when the next flight comes in, for S$5 each way.

Kennedy Island

Seven km from Gizo is Kennedy Island. It is surrounded by both sand and coral shoals and is also known as Plum Pudding or Kasolo. This is where John F Kennedy and his 10 shipmates swam ashore after their patrol boat *PT 109* was cut in half by the Japanese destroyer *Amagiri* in August 1943.

Kennedy and his crew clung to their boat's still-floating bow section all night, drifting with it to Sagharughombe Island. As there were no coconuts or water there, they moved over to Kennedy Island. Kennedy then swam via Olasana to Naru Island to rescue some supplies from a wrecked Japanese barge. Four days after their shipwreck, they were found by two islander scouts, who took them to Quomu Island, north of Vonavona, and later on to Patuparao, an islet nearby. Two days later they returned to the US base on Lumbaria Island, Rendova. The whole ordeal had lasted six days.

Mbambanga Island

Only four km from Gizo, Mbambanga is also called Long Island. It has a sandy beach at its north-western end, an offshore reef extending all the way to Olasana, and plenty of lobsters.

Olasana Island

This sand-surrounded island, 1.5 km south of Mbambanga, has marvellous coral, particularly at its north-western tip. Like Kerukeru Island, it's a favourite spot for Gizo picnickers.

Both Dive Wreck & Reef Gizo and Adventure Sports organise picnics and barbecue trips to Olasana on Sundays, costing S$15 a head for food, and about the same for the ride there.

Gizo Lagoon

This shallow coral formation encloses the islands from Epangga southwards to Mbambanga, with another stretch between Kennedy and Mbimbilusi. Clear, blue water with sand or coral bottoms is the norm for both areas.

Several of these islands have long, sandy shores, including Leorava, Epangga, Mbatusimbo, Mbimbilusi and Naru.

Varu & Njimiri Islands

This pair of islands, about 3.5 km north of Saeraghi, both have beaches at their south-eastern ends. They are part of a large reef system which spreads from Ghizo's northern tip.

GHIZO ISLAND DIVE SITES

The Ghizo area's dive choices include drop-offs, wrecks, walls, caves, drift dives, coral gardens, tropical fish, manta rays, eels, turtles, and pelagic fish such as groupers, barracudas and sharks. Top dive sites line Ghizo's eastern edge all the way from Njari to Naru Island.

Njari Island Barracudas usually collect here.
Grand Central Station
Toa Maru Lying between the mainland and Sipi Undu Island is the well-preserved 140-metre-long wrecked Japanese freighter *Toa Maru*. The ship sank after being torpedoed near her bow. There's still crockery, unopened saki bottles, a motorbike and two small two-person tanks aboard. Lying on her starboard side, the vessel is only 100 metres from shore and resting from about 18 metres down at her bow to around 37 metres at her stern.
Lembu Bay This inlet has very beautiful gardens of staghorn, plate and table corals.
Kerukeru Island There's a reef with plenty of staghorn corals on the north-eastern side of the island.
Nusatope Island There are gigantic clams, gorgonia sea fans and black coral nine metres down on the island's western side. This is a popular night-dive site.
Corsair Fighter Lying between Nusatope and Gizo, this US WW II aircraft is on the sandy sea bed accompanied by clown fish and nudibranches.
Panapagha Island There's a beautiful coral garden to the south-east of the island.

1	Njari Island
2	Grand Central Station
3	*Toa Maru* Wreck
4	Lembu Bay
5	Kerukeru Island
6	Nusatope Island
7	Corsair Fighter
8	Panapagha Island
9	Panapagha Gap
10	Kennedy Island Wall
11	Kennedy Island Reef
12	Olasana Reef
13	Joe's Wall
14	Naru Wall
15	Naru Gap
16	Inner Naru
17	Manta Ray Road

Panapagha Gap This is a busy site for moving fish. In addition, there are often sharks sleeping or resting on the sea bed 27 metres down.

Kennedy Island Wall This wall-dive site along the eastern side of the island offers 30-metre visibility and the chance of seeing large pelagic fish.

Kennedy Island Reef The southern side of the island is a shallow dive along a colourful reef. Both Kennedy Island sites are good night-dive spots.

Olasana Reef This shallow, sloping reef is also good for snorkelling. There's a range of corals, large sponges and eels as the reef shelves to a sandy sea bed. It's also another good night-dive venue.

Joe's Wall This wall dive has a 300-metre drop-off, and is to the north-east of Makuti Island. There are also attractive coral gardens in the shallows nearby.

Naru Wall This one-km-long drop-off is to Naru's north and falls to a depth of 60 metres. It's covered with soft and plate corals.

Naru Gap Large pelagic fish, black corals and sea fans abound to the north-west of Naru Island.

Inner Naru This 18-metre dive is among very colourful fish and an immaculate coral garden.

Manta Ray Road The sea bed to the south-east of Naru Island is sandy 30 metres down. You're almost guaranteed to see manta rays here, sometimes as many as 15 at a time.

NEW GEORGIA ISLAND

New Georgia Island, the largest island in the New Georgia group, dominates the central

Ghizo Island Dive Sites

part of the province. It is nearly 85 km long, 41 km wide at its broadest point, and 2145 sq km in area.

The island, given its name by Shortland in 1788, is fringed by the Roviana and Marovo lagoons and their many tiny, coconut-covered sand and coral islets. Marovo Lagoon, on New Georgia's eastern seaboard, is the world's largest island-enclosed lagoon and has been proposed for World Heritage listing.

In contrast, New Georgia's inshore coast is mainly swamp. Inland there are several breached volcanoes (most notably Mt Mase and Mt Mahimba) whose craters radiate outwards in massive, narrow-crested ridges.

Most of the island's 19,000 people live along New Georgia's southern shores. There are four main languages spoken, of which Roviana (the old name for western New Georgia) and Marovo are the commonest.

History

Head-hunting was New Georgia's former claim to fame. The practice developed because people believed the skull contained the life-force of a person. The purpose of head-hunting raids was therefore to acquire the victim's personal power by capturing his skull. Oral traditions from the Roviana Lagoon tell of war canoes covering distances of over 250 km each way in raids on southern Guadalcanal, Santa Isabel and Choiseul.

Raiding parties usually returned with male heads and female captives. These warlike forays were particularly devastating to Santa Isabel, decimating the population along its southern shore.

On returning from a raid, some of the captives were killed and eaten while others were enslaved. Slave women's children however, were given full customary rights to tribal land.

Not surprisingly, these head-hunting expeditions were greatly feared. Consequently, the less warlike among New Georgia's people settled inland on hilltops so they could see their enemies coming. Sentinels were posted day and night.

By the late 19th century, British trading interests in the area could not permit this lawlessness to continue. At the same time, European axes and guns had made killing too easy.

In 1892, New Georgia's head-hunting and slave-raiding reached a peak, so HMS *Royalist* was ordered to suppress it. Every village in the Roviana Lagoon was shelled or burnt, and the fortress at Nusa Roviana destroyed.

The next year the protectorate was proclaimed over much of the Solomons, including New Georgia. One of its principal aims was to suppress head-hunting. Equally as important as British law were Methodist missionaries. The combined effect was an end to head-hunting, cannibalism, slavery and sorcery.

Although it took many years to bring lasting peace, the scourge of head-hunting was mainly laid to rest by WW I. However, there were still isolated incidents up to the 1930s.

New Georgia was the scene of very fierce fighting in WW II. Coastwatcher Donald Kennedy's small group of islanders near Seghe kept the Japanese guessing with many daring guerrilla raids, until they were relieved in June 1943 by US forces. During the following two months, there was violent combat, particularly around Munda and Mbaeroko Bay, until the island was finally cleared of Japanese late that August.

Climate

New Georgia's annual rainfall is recorded at Munda and averages 3552 mm (140 inches). It rains on about seven days in every 10, with morning humidity at 89% or more from January to September. The afternoons, however, are much milder, with humidity usually around 76%. Temperatures vary between 32°C and 22°C.

Arts

Tomokos The traditional war canoe, or *tomoko* (also *tomago*), is only made nowadays for ceremonial purposes. In the past, those produced in the Roviana area could carry 30 to 40 fully armed men on a head-hunting raid. Their sides were heavily

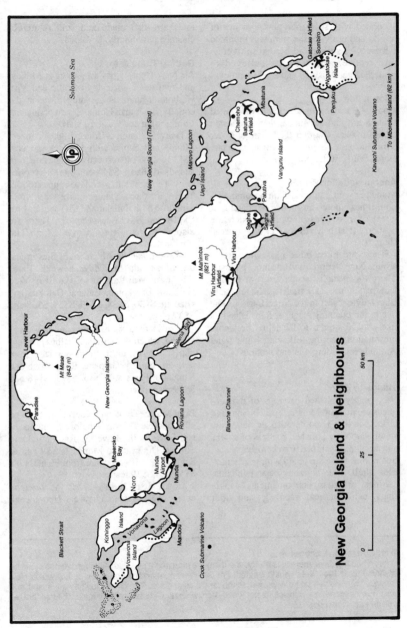

New Georgia Island & Neighbours

decorated with shell inlay and carvings of insects and birds. At the stern was mounted a *kesoko* – a seated bird-headed spirit creature whose presence was believed to guarantee good fishing and a safe journey.

Information

Medical Services In addition to the United Church hospital at Munda, there are seven clinics in New Georgia. These are at Noro, Viru Harbour, Seghe, Paradise, Canaan, Hapai and Keru Island.

Accommodation & Food

Munda is well equipped with accommodation. It has a hotel, an island resort and four guest or rest houses, two of which are onshore. It also has a market and a bread shop.

There are three other places to stay in around New Georgia, and one more planned. There's a specialist scuba resort at Uepi, a leaf rest house at Paradise, and a small, island-style resort in the Nono Lagoon. The one in the planning stage, at Raro Island, is likely to be similar to the latter. For more information, see the following Munda and Around New Georgia Island sections.

Things to Buy

Very highly polished carvings of nguzunguzus are made at Munda, Viru Harbour and in the Marovo Lagoon. Also produced are small, smoothly polished replicas of sharks and dolphins fashioned from kerosene wood. Sometimes these are inlaid with pearly nautilus shell, like nguzunguzus. Pendants, earrings, bracelets, hair ornaments, napkin rings, pandanus-leaf handbags and floor mats are also made and sold relatively cheaply, particularly in Munda.

Getting There & Away

Air New Georgia has an airport at Munda, and two other airfields at Seghe and Viru Harbour. Munda is the only place in the country, other than Honiara, with permanent Immigration and Customs staff.

Daily Solomon Airlines flights connect Munda and Seghe with Honiara and cost S\$173 and S\$140 respectively. The fare from Munda to Gizo is S\$44, and there's a service daily. The fare from Munda to Seghe is S\$56. There are three connections a week from Munda to both Ballalae and Choiseul Bay for S\$118 and S\$115 respectively. There are also flights to Ringi Cove, Mono and Yandina.

Western Pacific Air Services flies in and out of Munda four days a week. Fares between Munda and Kukundu, Viru Harbour, Barakoma, Batuna, Gatokae and Gizo are S\$36, S\$38, S\$48, S\$59, S\$68 and S\$37 respectively.

Viru Harbour is a former logging-camp airstrip, which Western Pacific flies into regularly. Nearby destinations serviced from here are Batuna, Gatokae, Ringi Cove and Kukundu. Fares are S\$36, S\$43, S\$48 and S\$59 respectively.

Boat Marine Division vessels from Gizo go all round New Georgia before going northwards to Vella Lavella, Ranongga and Simbo. The price to Munda is S\$9 and to Seghe S\$21. If you come from Honiara it's S\$53 and S\$39 respectively.

Coral Seas Ltd's vessel the *Iuminao* charges S\$62 1st class between Honiara and

---

Traditional Land Ownership

In head-hunting days, there was always the danger a man might be killed; although women could be enslaved, their lives were usually spared. For this reason inheritance of land is matrilineal in New Georgia, with women being regarded as the land's custodians. The chief allocates tribal land to a woman's descendants subject to her death-bed wishes. Consequently, female children are as welcome as male ones. ■

Munda on its weekly Western Province trip. The *Iuminao* stops about two km offshore from Munda, and is met by a horde of motor canoes. Some travellers have missed it by not knowing which wharf the ship waits at. The fact is it stops at neither. You embark or disembark by motor canoe as it rides at anchor between Munda Point and Hombu-hombu Island.

If you're arriving at Munda, just ask one of the canoe owners who come out to the *Iuminao* for a lift ashore. If you're leaving, ask the people where you're staying to organise a canoe for you. The cost shouldn't be more than S$5. Most other vessels use the Munda Wharf at Lambete.

Olifasia Shipping's *Olifasia II* visits the Marovo ports weekly for S$36 a head en route between Honiara and Gizo. Its fare to Munda and Noro is S$45. KHY's MV *Hiliboe* charges the same between Honiara and Munda on its weekly service.

Yacht Anchorages around New Georgia are of varying holding and comfort. These are at Munda (ie Lambete and Kokenggolo), Canaan, Kalena Bay, Viru Harbour, Seghe, Lever Harbour, Paradise, Valuli Point, Rice Harbour, Mbaeroko Bay, Noro, and Mbuini Tusu, Vakambo and Keru islands.

Getting Around
The only roads in New Georgia are the US-built crushed-coral tracks around Munda, the new road from there to Noro, and the logging route from Viru Harbour to Kalena Bay. Elsewhere transport is by motor canoe, small copra launches or on foot.

MUNDA
New Georgia's largest settlement is a collection of small villages stretching six km along the shore from Ilangana to Kindu. The whole area is called Munda.

Although all is peaceful now, the Munda area was the scene of frenetic WW II activity, as it was an important Japanese base of 4500 troops. Once it had been captured by the Americans, its size was greatly increased by lengthening the airfield, laying an extensive

network of roads, and building many Quonset huts. Plenty of wartime structure's remain.

Munda is also well known for its many pink and blue orchids, and shoreside fresh-water pools. Ask the owners' permission before you photograph their orchids or inspect the pools.

Information
In Munda you'll find a hospital, an NBSI agency, a Solomon Telekom branch, a post office, a Customs and Immigration station and airline ticket counters. Electric power goes off in the town at 10 pm.

Things to See
Distances are from Munda Wharf.

Munda Airport (0.1 km)
The three-km-long runway begun by the

Boy with bamboo panpipes

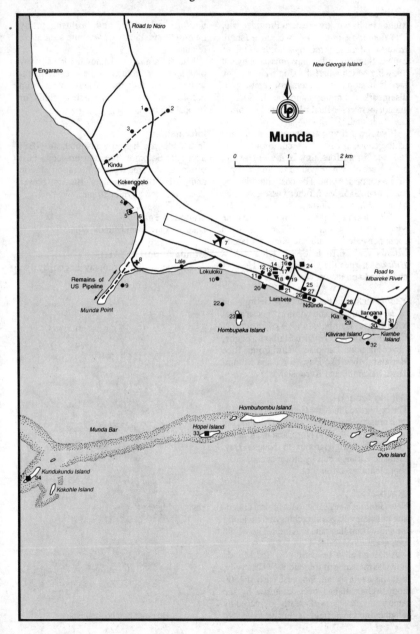

Road to Noro

Engarano

1
2
3

Kindu

Kokenggolo

4
5
6

New Georgia Island

Munda

0   1   2 km

Remains of
US Pipeline

8
Lale
Lokuloku
10
11
12 13 14
15
16
17
18 19
21
20
Lambete
25
27
26
28
Ndunde
Kia
29
Ilangana
30
31
Road to
Mbareke River
24

9
Munda Point

22
23
Hombupeka Island

Kilivirae Island

Kiambe
Island
32

Hombuhombu Island

Munda Bar
Hopei Island
33

Ovio Island

Kundukundu Island
34
Kokohle Island

<table>
<tr><td>■</td><td>PLACES TO STAY</td><td>8</td><td>Hospital</td></tr>
<tr><td></td><td></td><td>9</td><td>Japanese Biplane Wreck</td></tr>
<tr><td>21</td><td>Agnes Lodge</td><td>10</td><td>Wildcat Plane Wreck</td></tr>
<tr><td>23</td><td>Maqarea Resort</td><td>11</td><td>Government Offices</td></tr>
<tr><td>24</td><td>Sogabule's Lodge</td><td>12</td><td>Police Station</td></tr>
<tr><td>26</td><td>Vera's Guest House</td><td>13</td><td>Solomon Airlines/Customs and</td></tr>
<tr><td>33</td><td>Hopei Island Guest House</td><td></td><td>Immigration/Air Terminal</td></tr>
<tr><td>34</td><td>Kundukundu Rest House</td><td>14</td><td>Post Office/Solomon Telekom</td></tr>
<tr><td></td><td></td><td>15</td><td>Japanese War Memorial</td></tr>
<tr><td>▼</td><td>PLACES TO EAT</td><td>16</td><td>NBSI Agency</td></tr>
<tr><td></td><td></td><td>19</td><td>Western Pacific Air Services (Inside</td></tr>
<tr><td>17</td><td>Methodist Cooperative Supermarket</td><td></td><td>Ternottchell Developments)</td></tr>
<tr><td>18</td><td>Hot Bread Kitchen</td><td>20</td><td>Munda Wharf</td></tr>
<tr><td></td><td></td><td>21</td><td>Agnes Lodge & Munda Diving</td></tr>
<tr><td></td><td>OTHER</td><td></td><td>Services</td></tr>
<tr><td></td><td></td><td>22</td><td>Site of Japanese Nelly Bomber</td></tr>
<tr><td>1</td><td>Japanese Cave</td><td>25</td><td>Court House</td></tr>
<tr><td>2</td><td>Japanese Guns</td><td>27</td><td>Woodcarvers House</td></tr>
<tr><td>3</td><td>Well</td><td>28</td><td>American Dump</td></tr>
<tr><td>4</td><td>Kokenggolo Slipway</td><td>29</td><td>Sunken Amtrak</td></tr>
<tr><td>5</td><td>Kokenggolo Wharf</td><td>30</td><td>WW II Bond Store</td></tr>
<tr><td>6</td><td>United Church Western Regional</td><td>31</td><td>Ocean Landing</td></tr>
<tr><td></td><td>Office</td><td>32</td><td>Underwater Dump</td></tr>
<tr><td>7</td><td>Munda Airport</td><td></td><td></td></tr>
</table>

Japanese is behind the straggling line of villages and parallel to the shore. They needed a base to help them capture the US WW II airfield at Henderson on Guadalcanal. The Japanese tried to keep their plans secret, even going so far as connecting the tops of trees in Munda's coconut plantation. Their aim was to cut away most of the trunks, leaving only a few trees to act as supports for the remainder and their overhanging palms fronds. This was discovered within two weeks by islanders who immediately informed the Americans. The US reaction was to bomb the site regularly, effectively depriving the Japanese of the airfield's use.

The majority of government offices are congregated around the airport terminal. There's a very small fruit-and-vegetable market by the nearby wharf.

Ndunde (1.0 km)
There are two freshwater pools here – both containing turtles and fish – and a small crocodile farm. The owners will show you them on request.

Kia (1.6 km)
The huge pile of war materiel rotting in the bush is known locally as the American Dump. In the scrub are rusting aircraft parts, tractor, truck and bulldozer chassis, two small Japanese guns and several broken up US landing craft.

There's a number of corrugated iron huts by the shoreside, each with a rusty open petrol drum protruding from it. These are copra driers which islanders have made from the huge number of empty petrol drums left here after WW II. Just 20 metres out from the small coral jetty in front of the dump is what looks like a sunken US amtrak. It's in two metres of water.

Four large rusting pontoons lie half submerged in the shallows along Kia's waterfront, and many small, colourful fish have made their home inside the badly corroded frames.

Ilangana (2.3 km)
This village is immediately behind a huge concrete pad supported by old 44-gallon

petrol drums, likewise filled with concrete. This pad once supported several Quonset huts used as wartime store sheds, which were collectively known at the time as the Bond Store. To one side is a small, reinforced-concrete hut where the paymaster kept the soldiers' wages until pay day.

Kiambe Island
(2.3 km & 0.1 km by canoe)
This small islet is only 100 metres from the shore at Ilangana. Behind it is another US dump. Landing craft carrying jeeps were scuttled here in water between five and 10 metres deep.

Lokuloku (1.3 km)
Going west from Munda wharf, you come to Lokuloku, where there are two aircraft lying in shallow water. Both can be seen by snorkellers.

Furthest away, about 600 metres from shore and four metres down, is a Japanese Nelly bomber. Local people will canoe you to the spot. Closer in is a US Wildcat. It's only 200 metres out from a fish trap, and is beside a pole sticking out of the water.

Munda Point (3.6 km)
A long, rusting pipeline leads north from the shallows at Munda Point to Kokenggolo. World War II tankers used to unload here at the rate of 3000 tonnes of fuel per day. There's a sunken Japanese biplane about half a km towards the island proper from the point. It's close to the shore and covered by two metres of water.

Kindu (4 km)
Immediately opposite the junction of Kindu's footpath with the Noro road is another, much more overgrown track. Follow this track for about 300 metres through bush to a concrete pad where there are two Japanese anti-aircraft guns. There's a small memorial post between them.

On returning from the guns, turn north-wards (right) up the Noro road. About halfway up on the left of the first hill, there's

a small cave where several Japanese hid. The entrance was sealed up, leaving them entombed inside.

There are several other caves by the airfield where Japanese hid, but these are not so easy to find. When looking for them, ask villagers for *gunny* for the Japanese gun memorial at Kindu and *bye* for the caves.

Hombuhombu Island (2.5 km by canoe)
There's a sunken motorised pontoon in shallow water just beyond the island's small jetty. It's complete with driver's cab, now colourfully encrusted in coral.

Kundukundu Island (6 km by canoe)
This sand-surrounded island has a long, white sandbar at its north-eastern end, and coral gardens only 100 metres from its eastern shore.

Kokohle Island (7 km by canoe)
Pronounced 'Co-coh-high-ly', this islet has a sand beach along half of its eastern side. Turtles come here to lay their eggs.

Activities
Scuba Diving & Snorkelling Munda Diving Services (☎ 61133, PO Box 9) operates from Agnes Lodge and visits numerous wall, wreck and reef dive sites close to Munda. It quotes in Australian dollars and charges A$45 for a fully equipped dive, and A$15 for a snorkel trip. It also does PADI open-water certification courses for A$250, and offers a 10% discount on all dives for anyone who arrives with a Lonely Planet Solomon Islands guidebook!

Organised Tours Agnes Lodge arranges picnics, snorkelling, rainforest walks, crocodile spotting, fishing, lagoon trips, sightseeing and game fishing. Paddle and motor-canoe hire is by the hour.

Tour destinations include Mbaeroko Bay and Enoghae Point in New Georgia, Skull Island off Vonavona, and Lumbaria Island in Rendova. Other trips include visits to the Dog Stone on Roviana Island, the Nusa

Hope crocodile farm, and the Stones of Bau at Mt Bau.

Prices vary from S$60 an hour for motor-canoe hire up to S$600 for an overnight crocodile-spotting expedition.

The Maqarea Resort also organises snorkelling, windsurfing, fishing and lagoon trips. However, if you just want a paddle canoe to yourself, ask local villagers. They are likely to only charge you about S$1 whether you have the craft for a few minutes or all day.

Vera's Guest House will take you on a half-day chartered canoe round trip to Lumbaria Island in north-western Rendova for S$77.

Places to Stay

Guest & Rest Houses *Vera's Guest House* (pronounced 'Vee-ra's') is under the same management as the Kundukundu Rest House. You can make a booking for either at the Woodcarvers House in Ndunde.

Vera's lodge has two rooms, shared washing facilities and kitchen, a shoreside garden, and overflow facilities at the green-painted house opposite. The nightly cost is S$20 a person.

The *Kundukundu Rest House* on Kundukundu Island, six km across the water from Munda, offers the cheapest lodging in the area, at S$6 a night. There are three rooms with three beds each, plus shower unit and kitchen, though it lacks a toilet and running water. You can also camp overnight here if you wish for a nominal fee, or visit during daylight hours for S$3.

Sogabule's Lodge in Lambete, also called Soba's Lodge, has three rooms and shared washing and cooking facilities for S$15 a night, and is popular with visiting volunteers.

The *Hopei Island Guest House*, on the island of the same name and three km from Munda, has one unit, though more are planned. The cost is S$100 a night, and there's room for up to six people. Bookings are through Agnes Lodge (see the following Hotels section), which will organise transport for S$50 to take you to the island

initially, and then to bring you back from it at a later date. As the guesthouse is self-catering, either bring your own food or ask staff at Agnes Lodge to organise everything.

Hotels The *Maqarea Resort* (☎ 61164, PO Box 66) (pronounced 'Mangarea') is on Hombupeka Island and about 700 metres from Munda. There are four bungalows, and a bar and restaurant with regular island dancing. Singles/doubles are S$75/120, while meals vary in price between S$10 and S$30. Transfers to and from Munda are only 40c.

Agnes Lodge (☎ 61133, PO Box 9), opposite the air terminal at Lambete, has rooms in the old wing without private showers for S$50 a night. The two newer wings have singles/doubles with fan and shower for S$100/150. There's also a backpackers' dormitory with beds costing S$20 each. The rooms are fresh and cool at night, as the building is beside the sea.

Breakfasts cost from $10 to S$25 each, lunches can be between S$20 and S$40, while dinners are S$40 or more. However, cheaper sandwich meals can be arranged if you prefer. There's also a bar.

Places to Eat

The large *Methodist Cooperative Supermarket* by the runway is Munda's principal store. There's also a *Hot Bread Kitchen* near the airport terminal.

Entertainment

Film shows are at the court house. They're advertised by posters pinned up on trees around Munda.

AROUND MUNDA

The wartime road around Munda has been extended northwards to Noro. However, it's only accessible to motor vehicles eastwards now as far as the Mbareke River, though you still can walk along it as far as the Piraka River.

All destinations are east of Munda Wharf,

except Noro, which is north-west. Distances are from Munda Wharf.

Nusa Roviana (4.5 km by canoe)
The notorious head-hunter Ingava ruled from this coral-walled fortress on Roviana Island until it was destroyed in 1892. His tribe had a wild dog as its totem and worshipped at a rock carved like a dog before going on head-hunting forays. The Dog Rock is still there, but it's now broken.

The fortified village was built up of layers of coral, with the Dog Rock on top. The path to this stronghold was lined with shells to give warning of any intruder's approach.

The fortress was up to 30 metres wide in some places. Over 500 metres of coral wall still remain, though forest has now covered much of the area. There's also a giant's cave nearby. You should expect custom fees to be charged at both sites.

Holupuru Falls (6 km)
This 10-metre-high waterfall is just to the north of the bridge over the Mburape River. Below the falls is a three-metre swimming hole. There's a S$5 custom fee to swim in it. You'll need a guide to show you to the falls and an interesting bats cave nearby.

Mt Bau (11.3 km)
More than 10 stones and pillars stand on raised platforms deep in the bush on top of Mt Bau, and represent ancestral spirits. Villagers treat these monuments very seriously and will refuse to take anyone whom they suspect will act disrespectfully at the site. Island traditions hold that anyone who doesn't act reverently there will get a custom sickness.

Getting There & Away The site is about nine km inland from the coast at Ilangana on a very overgrown bush trail towards Enoghae Point. You will need a guide, and should expect to pay a custom fee.

Noro (16 km)
Noro, to the north-west of Munda, is where the pole-and-line boats operating in Western Province are based. There's a large cannery employing 400 people here, and a sizeable copra storage shed. Noro is expected to become the Solomons' second-busiest port in the near future, and its population to grow to about 2000.

Information Noro's facilities have been expanding slowly, though it already has an NBSI branch, a Westpac agency, a police station, a Hot Bread Kitchen, electricity and piped water.

Getting There & Away It's a S$2 minibus fare between Munda and Noro. Most of the services are early in the morning or late in the afternoon, carrying people to and from work.

Nusa Hope Island (24 km by canoe)
There's a crocodile farm here; the entry fee is S$10. There are also plenty of wild crocodiles in the waters nearby and in the lagoon's river mouths further east.

AROUND NEW GEORGIA ISLAND
Roviana Lagoon
The lagoon is protected by offshore islands 20 to 40 metres high and extends 52 km eastwards from Munda to Kalena Bay. Within it are many small islets formed from coral shoals.

Swimming comes easily to the people of Roviana Lagoon. In 1920 a young islander called Alex Wickham went to Australia and taught the world to swim the crawl. His forebears had been using this swimming style for centuries in the lagoon.

Araroso Point
Directly below the point are three caves containing shell valuables and skulls.

Viru Harbour
This major WW II Japanese base is now a logging and saw-milling centre. Traditional carvings and fish-hooks are made at Tombe,

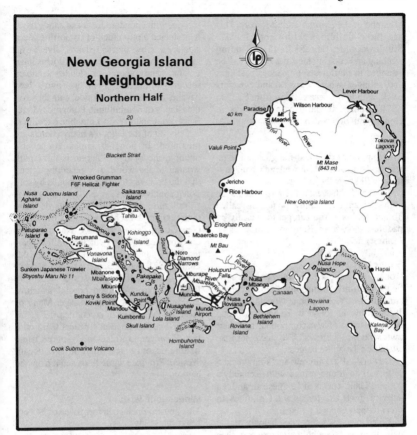

New Georgia Island & Neighbours

Northern Half

the cliff-top village overlooking the eastern side of this inlet.

Ships approach Viru Harbour between tall coral cliffs as small canoes paddle across the one-km-wide port. Houses reach down to the shore, many of them standing on stilts over the water. In the 19th century five coral-stone bastions protected the sea entrance from head-hunters. Three ancient fortresses are close to Tombe, while a fourth is near Tetemara on the harbour's western side. The oldest and most impressive one is inland. There are several stone monoliths or coral-rock platforms on nearby ridge tops, usually enclosed by rings of upright stones or coral walls. There are also some caves which were used in head-hunting days as burial places or hide-outs. Ask local people to show you these sites, if you're interested.

A more modern relic – a large Japanese gun from WW II – keeps a lonely vigil on the cliffs above Tetemara.

Nono Lagoon
This attractive seven-km-wide lagoon is just to the west of Seghe.

Places to Stay There's accommodation near

Mbareho at the *Horena Island Resort*. This has three buildings with room for 12. Singles/doubles are S$25/45, including washing and cooking facilities. Visits can be arranged to rainforests, archaeological sites and villages where carvers and weavers work, with tour prices varying from S$22 to S$70 a head. Island Chain Holidays in Honiara can organise bookings.

Raro Island

There are plans for a leaf-hut guesthouse on this sand-surrounded islet. Island Chain Holidays will know the details.

To the south-west of Raro, there's an eight-km spur of sandy peninsula called Tombo Maloku. You can get to it easily by paddle canoe from Raro, or motor canoe from Seghe.

Seghe

Donald Kennedy's coastwatcher base near Seghe was only 18 km south of the Japanese stronghold at Viru Harbour. Nonetheless, the Japanese never found it. Kennedy's group had a prisoner-of-war compound, and their own schooner with which to make surprise attacks on Japanese barges.

Downed Allied aircrew and shipwrecked sailors often found refuge with Kennedy's people. Their reports of Japanese air and sea activity gave US forces vital minutes to prepare their counter strokes.

Allied successes depended heavily on the help their coastwatching islander friends gave them. A much-prized reward was a bag of rice for every Allied sailor and downed aviator (friend or foe) that the islanders rescued.

Seghe has grown up around the airfield built by US Seabees in 10½ days flat. There's an intact P38 Lightning fighter at the end of the runway in six metres of water. Scuba divers often sit in its cockpit to be photographed.

Marovo Lagoon

Skirting adjacent Vangunu Island, the lagoon extends 110 km up the north-eastern coast of New Georgia to Lever Harbour. This shallow lagoon, with abundant reefs and sandy cays, is protected along much of its north-eastern side by narrow barrier islands, five to 60 metres high. Many of these landforms have golden, sandy shores or slender sandbars reaching out from them. Marovo's best beaches are on the lagoon side, with those on the islands of Sanihulumu, Porepore, Matiu, Sambulo, Landoro and Lumalihe excelling.

Only 20 of the lagoon's many islands are inhabited. In novelist James Michener's opinion, the Marovo Lagoon is the eighth wonder of the world. It's generally agreed that the best way to see the lagoon is by ship going southwards.

Tall mountains radiate outwards from their extinct breached volcanic rims near New Georgia's eastern shore. Narrow crests are separated by deeply incised valleys, particularly in the case of Mt Mahimba and Mt Hungu, 821 and 605 metres high respectively. These tall landmasses descend into large, mangrove-fringed coastal swamps, especially near the Njai Passage. Many of these are the homes of crocodiles.

The Marovo Lagoon's waters teem with fish. However, to protect this resource, game fishing is only permitted in the ocean. Western Province regulations ban it from the lagoon.

Mindeminde Islands

This tiny archipelago is composed of 34 very beautiful, sandy islets.

Uepi Island

With the shallow waters of the Marovo Lagoon to the west and the deep waters of the New Georgia Sound to the east, Uepi (pronounced 'Oo-py') is ideally placed to be a prime scuba-diving centre.

The three-km-long, one-sq-km islet has an extensive reef around it – ideal for snorkelling. You can be lying in complete safety with your body in 30 cm of water at Uepi's jetty, looking into the depths down a 30-metre submarine wall.

There are several notable dive sites. These are at Uepi Point, Charopoana Island – a drift dive through teeming fish – and Landoro

New Georgia Island & Neighbours
Southern Half

Island, with its drop-off and beautiful coral gardens. There's also Monggo Passage's sharks and barracudas, and Embolo Passage's submarine cave. Like many of the islands nearby, Uepi has a small resident coconut-crab population. Much more plentiful are the mangrove crabs regularly served for dinner.

The Uepi Island Resort (☎ 22176) has a fully equipped dive shop, and charges S\$65 for a one-tank dive, and S\$75 at night.

Places to Stay & Eat Daily accommodation at the *Uepi Island Resort* (☎ 22176) in one of five cabins costs S\$150/208 for singles/doubles. There's also a slightly cheaper guest room in the main building for S\$100/146.

There's a compulsory S\$72 daily surcharge for meals that everyone seems to agree are magnificent. Routine motor-canoe excursions take visitors from Uepi to nearby islands to watch custom dancing or to see carvers at work. Otherwise, you can go beachcombing, fishing, windsurfing, bushwalking, paddle canoeing or on river trips.

Getting There & Away It's a 40-minute motor-canoe ride from Seghe Airfield.

There's a transfer fee of S$36/18 for adults/children.

Vakambo Island & Village
There's a S$1.50 custom fee to see this attractive island. It's also a convenient access point for visits to the sand-fringed Tatama and Kotu Kuriana islands.

Mondomondo Island
The small bay on the eastern side of this island is noted for its fishing. Yachts find trolling particularly successful.

Keru Island
Keru is an attractive islet close to Ramata's sandy shore.

Tokovai Lagoon
This eight-km lagoon is the home of many wood carvers.

Paradise
This large village welcomes outsiders. It's in an attractive position behind a string of reefs, on the southern bank of the Maerivi River. Two km upstream from the village are sparkling rapids.

Paradise is the centre of a breakaway religion called Etoism, or the Christian Fellowship Church (CFC). In 1959, followers of Silas Eto, later called the Holy Mama, broke away from the Methodist Church in New Georgia.

The CFC is formed along kinship lines, and believes its members' land should belong to the church, emphasising communal progress through village cooperation. This movement is strongest between Wilson and Rice harbours in north-eastern New Georgia.

The villagers are the custom owners of many archaeological sites in the nearby mountains. They will guide you to these, including 843-metre-high Mt Mase's crater rim, if you wish.

Places to Stay Paradise has a *village rest house*. The CFC can also help arrange accommodation in other nearby villages if necessary.

Enoghae Point
Several large Japanese WW II anti-aircraft guns are still hidden in the scrub, along with a pile of live ammunition.

Mbaeroko Bay
There was a very determined wartime Japanese garrison at Mbaeroko Bay. They held the besieging Americans off for five weeks before finally being overwhelmed in August 1943.

A silent reminder of WW II is the sunken Japanese freighter near the shore. Its masts protrude above the water, with its upper works visible to snorkellers at low tide.

The freighter was bombed as its crane was loading cargo on to a barge alongside. The derrick is still swung out with the rear axle of a truck hanging over its tender, which also sank. The ship is still leaking oil.

Crocodiles commute between Mbaeroko Bay and Hathorn Sound in New Georgia, and Vila River on Kolombangara. They can sometimes be seen on the surface as they glide across the two km of open water between these two large islands before proceeding more furtively under the cover of New Georgia's mangrove shores.

VANGUNU ISLAND
This 520-sq-km volcanic island has a very indented coastline and two distinct centres. Mt Vangunu's 1123-metre-tall crater dominates the south and is often shrouded by clouds. In the north-east is 520-metre-high Mt Reku, whose several isolated rocky pinnacles tower over the Mbareke Peninsula, where most of the island's 4000 people live, including many carvers. The swampy Nggevala River forms a natural division between the island's two parts.

Mendaña may have seen Vangunu in 1568 as he named a largish island in this area Ysla de Arrecifes, meaning 'Island of Reefs' (ie the Marovo Lagoon). Seventh Day Adventists are numerous in Vangunu, so it may be hard to organise anything on Saturdays.

Information
Medical Services There's a clinic at Mbatuna.

Accommodation
There are small resorts on Matikuri and Telina islands, houses for visitors at Mbatuna and Chemoho, rest houses at Kopinae Island, Cheke and Kichombelo Point and empty houses available on Varusu Island. For details, see the following Around Vangunu section.

Getting There & Away
Air Western Pacific Air Services flies regularly into Batuna. Fares from there to Gatokae, Viru Harbour, Munda, Kukundu, Gizo and Honiara are S$23, S$36, S$68, S$82, S$91 and S$114 respectively.

Boat The *Iuminao* stops at Gasini, Chea and Patutiva when travelling on its weekly voyage between Honiara and Gizo. Marine Division vessels charge S$15 between Gizo and Mbatuna.

Yacht Anchorages are at Chemoho, Mbatuna, Mbale and Matikuri Island.

Getting Around
Footpaths are few on Vangunu. Most transport is by motor canoe.

AROUND VANGUNU ISLAND
Patutiva
Thatched houses are built on stilts by the water. There's a fruit-and-vegetable market held here on Tuesdays when the *Iuminao* calls in.

Marovo Island
Sasaghana on the island's western side has many woodcarvers. On its eastern shore is Chumbikopi, where villagers have a war canoe on display, and do custom dances by prior arrangement.

Telina Island
Many stylish modern carving designs have spread from this SDA island, and its woodwork is highly regarded.

The *Lagoon Lodge* has three huts with room for 10 people close to Telina Village. These are complete with cooking facilities, showers and toilets. Singles/doubles are S$20/35 a night, and children under five are free.

Laghemba Falls
This waterfall is about three km inland on the Laghemba River. There's also a river pool to swim in two km downstream, close to the sea. There's an iron-roofed *rest house* nearby at Kichombelo Point, with room for four people.

Cheke
There are two rather basic *rest houses* at Cheke for S$20 each a night.

Chemoho
There are several islands near Chemoho with dazzling, sandy beaches. Matiu and Porepore are the closest. The best plan is to charter a motor canoe for the day and try to see Sanihulumu, Sambulo and Lumalihe.

Chemoho is a subprovincial headquarters. There's an SDA house available for visitors for around S$10 a person.

Mbatuna
There is another SDA house here which visitors may use for about S$10 a head.

Kopinae Island
There's a leaf hut for two people, complete with showers, toilet and cooking equipment, on this tiny island. Singles/doubles are S$20/35 and children are free. Bookings and arrangements to get there can be made at Gasini and Chemoho.

Varusu Island
Only 800 metres from sand-fringed Sanihulumu Island, Varusu has 10 leaf houses for SDA meetings. These are often available for hire.

Mbopo

Clear rivers flow into the sea here and at nearby Chara Point, offering cool and refreshing swimming.

Matikuri Island

Matikuri and the surrounding area have many attractive beaches, good fishing, beautiful sunsets and several custom sites to visit.

The *Matikuri Island Rest House* has four leaf houses costing S$35 an adult and S$17.50 a child, and a communal dining hall. Ask around at Seghe Airport and local people will direct you, though you should send a message in advance warning of your intended arrival to ensure there is room for you at the rest house. Transport to and from Seghe is S$20 a person each way.

NGGATOKAE ISLAND

Also spelt Gatukai and Gatokae (and pronounced 'Gat-oh-kye'), Nggatokae was first seen by foreigners when Captain Manning in the *Pitt* saw the island in 1792. Not realising it was a separate landmass from Vangunu, he named it Cape Traverse.

Nggatokae is formed from a large volcanic cone, reaching its peak 887 metres up on Mt Mariu's narrow crater rim. There's an area of raised reef near Peava in the east. Coastal areas on the Marovo Lagoon's northern side are swampy.

Nggatokae and its nearby islands are 110 sq km in size. Many of its 1200 people are carvers. In the past, war canoes from Nggatokae raided as far as Choiseul, nearly 200 km away.

Information

Medical Services There's a clinic at Penjuku.

Accommodation

Nggatokae has five places where you can stay: at Sombiro on Nggatokae itself, and on four small neighbouring islets. These are at Mbili, Tambapaeva, Tenggomo and Mbaghole. There are also plans for accommodation at Penjuku and Mbiche. For details

see the following Around Nggatokae section.

Getting There & Away

Air The name of the airfield for this island is Gatokae. Western Pacific Air Services flies into Gatokae regularly, and fares between it and Batuna, Viru Harbour, Munda, Gizo and Honiara are S$23, S$43, S$68, S$91 and S$114 respectively.

Boat The *Iuminao* stops at Mbili Passage, (described on its manifest as Billi Passage), arriving around midnight en route from Honiara to Gizo. The return journey is at sunset, which is usually magnificent. The Marine Division charges S$36 between Honiara and Nggatokae.

Yacht The island's anchorages are at Mbili, Penjuku, and Kavolavata.

Getting Around

Boat You can organise a motor-canoe ride from either Mbili Island or Penjuku to make a trip through the lower parts of the Marovo Lagoon. There's also an enjoyable canoe trip from Penjuku along the base of the Marovo Lagoon to Sombiro, with a diversion up the Sombiro River if required.

Walking A coastal footpath connects most places in Nggatokae.

AROUND NGGATOKAE ISLAND

Mbili Island

This long, slender SDA island one km to the north of Nggatokae is the first stop in the Marovo Lagoon for ships from Honiara. It's noted for its carvings and wonderful sunsets. There's the *Tugava I Rest House* in Mbili Village if you need to stay overnight.

Tambapaeva Island

There's a leaf house on this island one km to the west of Mbili called *Tugava II Rest House*.

Tenggomo Island

Jakes Sport and Gamefishing has its base on

Top: Gorgonian fan coral (MMcC)
Bottom: Tropical reef fish from Marovo Lagoon (GC)

Top: Boy warriors from Maramasike Island (SIID)
Left: Sulufou, an artificial island off Malaita Island (SIID)
Right: Two female canoeists, Sikaiana Atoll (SIID)

this island. It can take you fishing for marlin, tuna and sailfish for S$380/640 a half/full day. It also has accommodation for S$15 a night.

Sombiro
Gatokae Airfield is at Sombiro. There's an SDA building here which serves as a *rest house*.

Peava
Mbulo Island's custom owners live beside Peava's sandy beach. You will need their permission to visit it.

Mbulo Island
Unused agriculturally, Mbulo is four km from Peava. Its steep, craggy cliffs are formed from a raised reef which surrounds a 200-metre-high volcanic core. Caves in its cliffs were used in former times as graves. There is also an ancient burial ground near the island's centre.

Mbiche
The people of this village were avid head-hunters until they were shelled prior to WW I by an Australian warship acting for the British government.

Paka, one of the last head-hunting chiefs in the Solomons, is buried at Mbiche. His skull is still visible beside his grave.

This village has plans to provide overnight accommodation for walkers hiking their way around Nggatokae.

Penjuku
This SDA village is very tidy. Many of its people are weavers or stone carvers. Nearly all visitors are met by a local elder who performs a welcoming dance at their arrival. There's a S$2-a-head charge to see it, which is the equivalent of an entry fee. A leaf *rest house* is being built.

Mbaghole
Pronounced 'Bag-oh-ly', this village on Kingguru Island is in a very picturesque setting, with palm fronds overhanging the beach. However, a local woman was taken recently by a saltwater crocodile in a nearby river, so take care.

There's a *rest house* here costing S$25 a night, including food.

Kavachi Submarine Volcano
Kavachi was above the sea's surface from late April to early June 1991. It rose about 15 metres high, spitting volcanic magma out constantly. The volcanic island grew to about a third of a hectare, before subsiding again below the waves. Sunsets all around the area were a spectacular blood red, their brilliant colours caused by volcanic dust.

Kavachi has erupted four times in the past 40 years, each time in a different position. In 1991, it appeared 19.5 km south-west of Nggatokae. In 1952 and 1972 its eruptions were much closer to Tetepare Island. On the latter occasion, it threw plumes of sea water and rock 60 metres into the air, though no island was formed. There was also activity in 1985 when it briefly caused surface water to boil.

MBOROKUA ISLAND
Called Murray's Island by Manning in 1792, Mborokua is 62 km south-east of Peava. It is four sq km in size and uninhabited, an isolated dead volcano, breached on its western side. The sea surges into its half-moon-shaped bay, making a difficult mooring for any vessel attempting a visit.

VONAVONA ISLAND
To the north-west of New Georgia, and separated from neighbouring Kohinggo by the beautiful Vonavona Lagoon, Vonavona is a mainly flat 70-sq-km coral-limestone island. Alternatively called Wana Wana or Parara, Vonavona has about 2000 people. Rarumana and the area around Mbanone and Mandou are the island's two main centres of population.

Local fisherfolk use vines collected from the bush, making them into a net which is then laid in the sea and dragged towards the shore. A juice in the vine stuns the fish, which are easily caught.

Accommodation

You can stay on Lola, Quomu and Pakepake islands. For details, see the following Around Vonavona section.

Getting There & Away

Boat As there's no airfield on Vonavona, your best bet is to charter a motor canoe from Munda. Charters to the lower end of the Vonavona Lagoon cost about S$50 plus fuel.

Yacht The only recognised anchorage in Vonavona is at Bethany. However, although there's a great deal of reef in the area, the Vonavona Lagoon's shallow, sheltered, often sandy-bottomed waters should offer plenty of comfortable moorings.

Getting Around

There's a three-km-long footpath along the coast at Rarumana in the north-west, and another 10-km stretch joining Mbanone to Kumbonitu in the island's south-east. Otherwise, transport is by canoe.

AROUND VONAVONA ISLAND
Vonavona Lagoon

This lagoon extends for 28 km between the tiny islets of Blackett Strait and the long, sandy island of Nusaghele nine km from Munda at the eastern end of the lagoon.

Within this area are many picturesque, sand-surrounded islets and connecting sandbars. Coral-encrusted shallows are interspersed with deeper sections. These combine to present a visual delight of dark greens (tree covered islands), white strips (sandbars and beaches), light blues (coral-bearing shallows) and dark blues (deeper areas). The best way to see all this is from the air.

Most of the inner chain of islets along Blackett Strait are surrounded by white coral-debris beaches. You can walk between some of these at low tide, as there's often only a very narrow passage between them.

Skull Island

The tiny islet at the tip of Kundu Point has two skull houses, or reliquaries, containing the skulls of several chiefs. The most recent ones date from the 1920s, though others go back to early head-hunting days up to 300 years ago. The skull houses are small, triangular-shaped caskets which also contain the chiefs' clamshell-ring valuables.

The custom owners live at Kumbonitu. They charge a S$10 fee to see the skulls, whether there's one of you or a party.

Mandou

Outside each house in this CFC village is an *aroso*. This is a structure composed of two poles connected at the end by a bamboo rod. Below this rod, which is decorated with orchids and hibiscus flowers, are two shorter poles. The aroso is said to vibrate violently at various times throughout the day. These vibrations have religious significance to the CFC.

Mbuni & Mbarasipo

Bukaware baskets, trays and shields are made in Mbuni, while baskets and pandanus handbags are Mbarasipo's products. They can be purchased direct from the weavers themselves.

Nusa Aghana Island

Scuba groups come here regularly from Gizo to enjoy this sand-surrounded island's reef diving. There's an attractive sandbar stretching one km to its east.

Cook Submarine Volcano

This volcano, first reported by HMAS *Cook* about nine km south-west of Mandou, erupted in 1964 and 1983. Another eruption was reported in 1963 about 17 km west of Koviki Point.

Lola Island

The *Zipolo Habu Resort* (☎ 61164, PO Box 66, Munda) on Lola Island has two leaf-house bungalows, with shared washing facilities and kitchen. Singles/doubles are S$40/60 a night, and camping is also possible. Meals are extra, with dinner costing S$16. Motor-canoe trips to Skull Island, about 2.5 km away, are S$20 a group.

Quomu Island

Tiny Quomu, or Q-Island, is the home of the *Q-Island Resort* (☎ 22902 Honiara, PO Box 131, Gizo). Although the island is only 100 metres in diameter, there are plenty of interesting spots nearby to visit by motor canoe.

Quomu has three self-contained bungalows a few metres from the shore. Cheapest rates for singles/doubles are S$22/37 a night. Camping is also possible for S$5 a head. Meal prices are similarly reasonable. Access to Quomu is from either Ringgi or Gizo, and costs S$60 by motor canoe from Ringgi or S$80 from Gizo. Lagoon-tour prices vary between S$20 and S$30 a head. The area is ideal for snorkelling, but you'll need to bring your own gear.

Pakepake Island

There's a leaf-hut *rest house* on this island. There are also white-sand beaches, fishing, snorkelling, and bushwalks to enjoy while you're here.

Vonavona's Dive Sites

These two dive sites are regularly visited by Gizo-based dive operators.

Grumman F6F Hellcat This US WW II naval fighter was ditched in October 1943 in a perfect water landing. It's still intact, complete with guns and ammunition. The plane is 11 metres down and about 200 metres south-east of Quomu.

Shyoshu Maru No II This Japanese trawler lost the transducer from its hull when it chipped a reef. It slowly filled with water without the crew realising until too late. The vessel lies about three km north-west of Rarumana and 35 metres down. It's hard to find because of poor underwater visibility.

KOHINGGO ISLAND

Also called Arundel, Kohinggo has about 850 people. It nestles between Vonavona and New Georgia's north-western tip and is about 110 sq km in area. The reefs around the small chain of islets along Kohinggo's northern shore teem with highly coloured fish.

AROUND KOHINGGO ISLAND
Saikarasa Island

The Japanese mounted several guns at the western end of this island in WW II to close off the Blackett Strait to shipping. Most of them have now been removed.

Tahitu

There's a wrecked US Sherman tank here. It was lost in action when US marines overran a Japanese strongpoint in mid-September 1943.

RENDOVA ISLAND

This 400-sq-km island lies due south of New Georgia's Roviana Lagoon. It's 42 km long and home for 3000 people.

Rendova Peak (1063 metres high) dominates the island. To the south are highland plateaus overshadowed by the 820-metre-tall Mt Herohiru. There's a small network of lagoons along the northern coast.

Rendovans regularly perform war dances

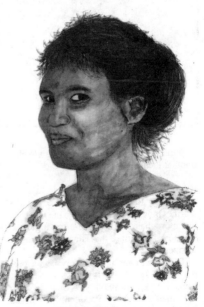
Rendova Island woman

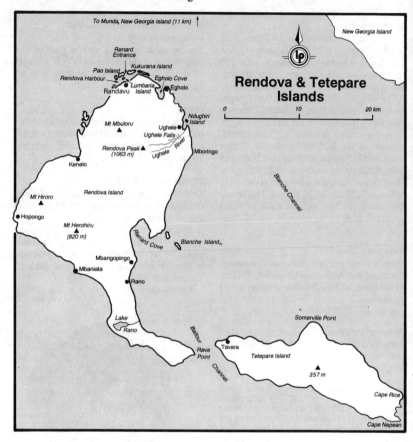

at cultural festivals. Bamboo bands are also popular locally.

History

In WW II, Rendova was liberated by US marines in June 1943. Although the Japanese had more than 20 large anti-aircraft guns at Rendova Harbour, the island was easily recovered.

The Americans immediately began preparing to seize the Japanese airfield at Munda, 11 km away on New Georgia. John F Kennedy, later US President, was based here at the time.

Information

Medical Services Rendova's only clinic is at Ughele.

Activities

Organised Tours Scobie's Walkabout of Newcastle, Australia, stays up to seven days at Lumbaria on its regular visits to Western Province.

Accommodation

There's a small resort at Lumbaria Island. There's also an Agricultural Department hut at Ughele which is sometimes available. For details see the following Around Rendova Island section.

Getting There & Away
Boat The *Iuminao* arrives at Ughele from Honiara early every Monday morning en route to Gizo. It calls in again on Tuesday mornings on its way back to the capital. Marine Division fares from Ughele are S$9 to Munda, S$12 to Gizo, and S$43 to and from Honiara.

Canoe Rides from Lumbaria to Munda cost about S$60 by chartered motor canoe. They leave early in the morning, as the sea gets quite choppy even by midday.

Getting Around
The only way around Rendova is by motor canoe. It costs S$70 for a chartered ride between Ughele and Lumbaria.

AROUND RENDOVA ISLAND
Ughele
Most visitors only spend 15 to 20 minutes here when the *Iuminao* calls in. The market stalls by the jetty operate solely on ship days (Mondays and Tuesdays) but there's always plenty of fruit for sale at the time.

The harbour's clear water is ideal for swimming and snorkelling. There's also a lagoon with an attractive sand beach about two km along the coast to the north.

Rendova Island hut

The small Ughele Falls is about two km up the Ughele River. However, as it provides the village's water supply, it's not for swimming in.

You'll need the chief's help to find somewhere to stay in Ughele. Alternatively, you could ask the local Agricultural Department staff to let you borrow their hut, which is sometimes available for hire.

Rendova Peak
The mountain above Ughele, also called Mt Longguoreke, is often shrouded in clouds. To climb it takes two days return, and requires a guide. Initially the ascent is reasonably easy, but nearer the top the ridges become very steep and the going is tough. Ask at Ughele for both a guide and permission from the custom owners to climb it.

Egholo Cove
Egholo Cove is a large coastal inlet with plenty of spots to explore in a canoe. There's a rusting war wreck on the shore at its southern entrance beside the small settlement of Egholo.

Rendova Harbour
In 1943, this inlet served as a US naval base housing 15 to 20 PT boats at a time, including John F Kennedy's *PT 109*. The Americans hid large guns on Pao and Kukurana islands and used them to bombard the Japanese at Munda across the channel. On the night of 1 August 1943, all the PT boats here set out hastily to intercept four Japanese destroyers which were ferrying 900 men to reinforce their base on southern Kolombangara. One of the destroyers, the *Amagiri*, accidentally ran down *PT 109* on its return journey. Two of the US crew were killed instantly, but 11 others, including John F Kennedy, managed to reach an islet near Gizo. Six days later, Kennedy and his shipmates were rescued by Solomon Islanders. The film *PT 109* was made of this memorable event in 1960.

Lumbaria Island
Lumbaria is a pleasantly quiet islet resort

with plenty of nearby sandy beaches. You can snorkel around looking for sunken war remains, dive for shells, or view large fish, including barracudas swimming around the nearby Renard Entrance.

When tour groups arrive at Lumbaria, they get the full treatment. A lookout blows a conch warning of their arrival and warriors appear. Once it's clear the visitors are friendly, the chief welcomes them with a bamboo band and guitar music.

The John F Kennedy Museum is beside where Kennedy lived in between naval actions. There's a collection of WW II memorabilia, including US and Japanese machine guns and helmets. There's also an idol which was once worshipped, and several weapons from head-hunting days. The entrance fee is S$3.

Places to Stay & Eat The *Lumbaria Island Resort* (PO Box 27, Munda) has two houses with six bedrooms. Singles/doubles are S$30/45 a night. Meals are available at S$35 a day.

Randavu

There's a sunken US two-seater warplane in about 10 metres of water near Randavu. Its snorkellable and in very clear water. Villagers will point out the spot to you.

Mbangopingo

This village's dancers have performed at several international festivals. Their dances include the Heruo, about the seasonal ripening of ngali nuts in October, and a dog-imitation dance.

TETEPARE ISLAND

With an area of 120 sq km, Tetepare is 26 km long, but only seven km wide. Also called Montgomerie Island, Tetepare is rugged, rising to 357 metres at its centre.

Underpopulated and virtually unused, Tetepare has been proposed as a nature reserve, although this has not yet been finalised. Only about 50 people live on the island in Tetepare's only settlement at Tavara on its western tip.

People from Viru Harbour in New Georgia occasionally come over to Tetepare to hunt crocodiles. The island's saltwater croc population mostly lives along Tetepare's north-eastern coast between Somerville Point and Cape Rice.

Getting There & Away

Boat The Marine Division fare from Ughele in Rendova is S$9. It's the same price to Viru Harbour in New Georgia.

Canoe A chartered motor-canoe ride from Tavara to Ughele would be about S$95, to Viru Harbour S$120.

Getting Around

Any movement beyond Tavara is by motor canoe.

KOLOMBANGARA ISLAND

Nduke, as many of its residents call Kolombangara, is an almost-perfect example of a near-circular, cone-shaped volcano. The island is 685 sq km in size and 30 km across. It rises from a one-km-wide coastal plain through flat-topped ridges and increasingly steep escarpments to the rugged crater rim of 1770-metre-high Mt Veve. Inside the crater, this four-km-wide extinct volcano falls abruptly to its deepest point 1000 metres below.

Most of Kolombangara's 4500 people live along its south-western shore, with no village further than 500 metres from the sea. Three-quarters of the island is uninhabited.

Logging has been a major activity for the past 80 years. As much of the original rainforest has now gone, there are considerable efforts to replace it with timber plantations.

History

There are several 500-metre-long stone platforms on Kolombangara's ridges. These were built for defence against 19th-century

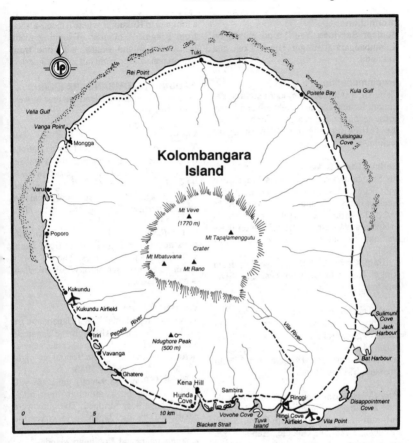

head-hunters. Despite such measures, the population had shrunk by the 1890s to a mere 150 people, with the survivors congregated along the south-western coast, leaving the rest of the island deserted.

Because of this lack of population, the Protectorate government alienated the whole island in 1894. Between 1905 and 1931, agreements were drawn up giving the British company Lever Brothers logging rights to two-thirds of Kolombangara.

The island was an important Japanese base in WW II, particularly around Ringgi and Vila Point, with about 4000 men garri-

soned on it. However, when the Japanese were bypassed when Vella Lavella was liberated by the Allies in October 1943, they rapidly withdrew.

With the return of peace, logging resumed. By 1968, however, 90% of Levers' concession was logged out. Disputes with the custom owners of the remaining land led to the company's withdrawal in 1986.

A new approach is being tried. Kolombangara Forestry Project Ltd (KFPL) has a concession to grow commercially useful timber in plantations, leaving what remains of the rainforest to survive.

Information
Medical Services You'll find clinics on Kolombangara at Ringgi, Hunda Cove and Kukundu.

Accommodation
There are rest houses in modern buildings at Ringgi, Poitete Bay and Kukundu, and leaf-house accommodation at Iriri. For details see the following Around Kolombangara section.

Getting There & Away
Air Solomon Airlines connects Ringi Cove with Seghe, Munda, Gizo and Honiara once weekly. Fares to Munda and Gizo are S$34 and S$35 respectively, while it costs S$185 to Honiara. Western Pacific also covers these destinations, and flies into Kukundu for S$23.

Ringi Cove Airfield is two km from Ringgi. Kukundu Airfield is beside the SDA mission.

Boat The *Iuminao* calls in to Ringgi on Monday afternoons from Honiara, and returns again from Gizo on Tuesday evenings. Marine Division vessels charge S$53 between Ringgi and Honiara. It's S$9 to Gizo and S$12 to Munda.

Yacht There are anchorages of varying qualities at Ringgi, Vila Point, Jack Harbour, Sulimuni Cove, Pulisingau Cove, Tuki, Mongga, Kukundu, Ghatere, Hunda Cove and Sambira.

Canoe Kolombangara to Gizo is 45 minutes by motor canoe, with islanders often going to market there on Mondays and Wednesdays. Fares aboard a shared canoe should be no more than S$11 between Kolombangara's south-western coast and Gizo, and S$18 from Ringgi. Shared rides from the island to Noro in New Georgia are about S$12, and S$22 to Munda.

Getting Around
A tractor trail extends 38 km around the island to Tuki in the north. This continues as a footpath to Kukundu, where it meets a track from Ringgi. A number of logging roads follow the inland ridges, with one from Ringgi penetrating eight km into the interior.

AROUND KOLOMBANGARA ISLAND
Distances around the island are east to west from Ringgi.

Ringgi
This is the main base for KFPL's operations on Kolombangara. Although the township was very quiet once Levers departed in 1986, it has since revived and the Ringgi Club and its bar are again the centre of local social life. Wednesday night is Ringgi Night at the club, and is a good time to visit.

The *Ringgi Club* has a very comfortable guesthouse costing S$20 a night each, including kitchen facilities. There's also a junior rest house, which provides overflow accommodation.

Vila Point (4 km)
This was the principal WW II Japanese base on Kolombangara. Although the Japanese withdrew before a US assault came, several fierce naval actions were fought at night nearby in May and July 1943.

Some 150-mm (5.9-inch) guns are still hidden in the bush, although their brass casings have been stripped. The guns were positioned by the Japanese to cover the eastern end of Blackett Strait between Kolombangara and Kohinggo islands.

Saltwater crocodiles live in the Vila River area.

Disappointment Cove (4.5 km)
Several downed aircraft and abandoned guns from WW II can still be found in the undergrowth, while two Japanese freighters and a submarine lie in the nearby depths. They are shallow enough to be reached by scuba divers.

Sulimuni Cove (12 km)
At Sulimuni Cove, which is also called Bennett Cove, there's a sunken Japanese

destroyer whose stern is partly exposed. You'll need a boat to get aboard it, even at low tide.

Poitete Bay (30 km)
A local *Forestry Department rest house* sometimes has room for visitors. Contact the area manager if you want to use it.

Vanga Point (52 km)
A cache of shell-money rings, now in the Honiara museum, was found here in the 1970s. It was hidden under some small cliffs inside the local mission's land. Traditional valuables were often buried during periods of head-hunting raids, and also when the missions arrived. When the missionaries instructed people to forsake their old cult objects, some islanders hid them instead.

Mongga (53 km)
About three km inland from Mongga there's an array of ancient stone walls extending over nearly 700 metres. Between two and three metres high, they were built as a defence against head-hunters.

Kukundu (65 km)
A narrow golden-sand beach extends for half a km on either side of this large SDA mission village. There's also a *rest house* costing S$10 a person a night.

Iriri (67.5 km)
This friendly village (sometimes called Iririri) gives a warm welcome to visitors. There's a cool swimming spot in the nearby Pepele River, and a large bat's cave to explore. Iriri also has a leaf *rest house* and a small lake.

Ghatere (73.5 km)
Six km inland on 500-metre-high Ndughore Peak is a small hot-spring site. Nearby are the remains of some abandoned 19th-century fortified villages.

Hunda Cove (77.5 km)
There are several archaeological sites locally, including a number of ancient fortifications at nearby Kena Hill.

Vovohe Cove (87.5 km)
The Japanese built several underground tunnels near this inlet in WW II which they used for ammunition storage. Ringgi is five km further on.

Climbing Mt Veve
Most walkers depart from one of five places on Kolombangara's western side. These are Ghatere, Vavanga, Iriri, Kukundu and Vanga Point. All have guides available for hire, but several are SDA, so avoid Saturdays. Expats say that it is best to start at Vanga Point.

If you want to visit the remains of abandoned fortified villages, go via Iriri, as several custom owners live there.

The Moss Forest is near the top of the mountain, or crater, as it is called locally. The mountain's upper reaches are thickly wooded, and rainfall is so heavy that the trees are covered in moss. Although the summit is often clear of clouds in the early morning, it's regularly covered in mist by noon.

It's a 14-km climb to the crater's edge, taking seven or eight hours. To get the 'shrouded in mist' feeling, sleep overnight in the forest. You'll have magnificent views from the top early in the morning before the cloud sets in.

Guides to the crater cost between S$8 and S$12 a day. Bring a tent for your night out on the mountain.

Two-day round-trip mountain climbs via Iriri are organised in Gizo by the Gizo Hotel and Paradise Lodge. Including the price of a guide, canoe rides and a night on the mountain, these tours cost S$150 each for up to three people.

SIMBO ISLAND
Simbo is eight km south of Ranongga and 31.5 km south-west of Ghizo. It's only 12 sq km in size but has 1500 people, giving a population density of 125 per sq km.

Simbo has an active thermal area in its south and is about 7.5 km long. The island is dominated by two young volcanic cones, both over 300 metres high. Its northern half is separated from the south by a fertile isthmus.

Simbo's coastline has coral-sand bays in the north. A submarine volcano about five km south of Cape Satisfaction was active in 1964 but has been dormant since.

History
Simbo people in pre-European times traded with New Georgia for turtle shell and handicrafts, selling megapode eggs and vegetables in exchange. Pottery shards have also been found on the island, though whether they were made on Simbo or traded from elsewhere isn't certain.

Simbo was seen in late 1787 by the Americans Read and Dale, and visited by the Briton Shortland in the following year. He was surprised to find the islanders recognising iron, though it wasn't clear whether this was from driftwood, earlier unrecorded European contacts, or inter-island communications about foreigners and their unusual possessions.

The US whaler *Patterson* was the next vessel to visit. It arrived in 1803 and was well received. Indeed, Simbo was one of the first islands in the Solomons to welcome foreigners, with European traders living permanently there from the 1840s. Known variously as Eddystone, Narovo, Simbo or Mandeghughusu Island, Simbo had become a regular stopping place between eastern Australia and the Chinese coast by the 1860s. Despite this, Simbo, along with Ranongga, became a notorious head-hunting centre in the 19th century. Sorties against Choiseul and Santa Isabel were routine, with one raiding party coming back with 93 heads!

Arts
Tapa in Simbo turns blue-green when it's washed in the island's hot volcanic springs. Rare examples have been stained brown this way.

Information
Medical Services The island's only clinic is at Narovo.

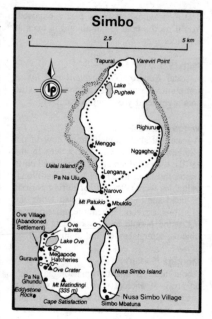

Activities
Organised Tours Paradise Lodge, along with the Western Province Tourist Information Centre and the Gizo Hotel, all at Gizo, organises day trips from Gizo to see the Ove Crater and the megapode hatcheries. This is arranged with the Simbo landowners for about S$150, including custom fees. If there's a group of you, the cost may be as low as S$70 each, including the island's S$20 a head landing fee.

Accommodation
Simbo people are prepared to accept day visitors, but may not be so keen on overnight stayers. There's no organised accommodation, but if you still want to try, send a service message to the Simbo Area Council asking for permission.

Getting There & Away
Boat The Marine Division fare between Gizo and Simbo is S$9. There's also the

Gizo-based vessel the *Vele*, which services Simbo and the Shortlands alternately.

Yacht Narovo has the island's only wharf. Yacht crews should see the Simbo Area Council on arrival regarding staying, washing, drinking water, etc, and follow any instructions closely.

Canoe Seas are very rough between Ranongga and Simbo. Any motor-canoe ride to the island requires wet-weather gear, takes much longer in blustery conditions than the 1¾ hours it takes in calm weather, and can be quite frightening if the seas are at all choppy.

There are usually canoes between Gizo and Simbo on Monday and Friday afternoons. A shared one would be about S$25 each way or S$150 to charter. A shared ride from Simbo to Keara on Ranongga's western coast costs around S$10 a person.

Getting Around
Movement is mostly on foot, though the route to the volcanic area is usually across water.

AROUND SIMBO ISLAND
Archaeological Sites
There are skull houses, petroglyphs, bonito-increase sites (bonito are tuna), abandoned villages, fortress remains and a clamshell collection on Simbo and its diminutive neighbour Nusa Simbo. These sites are sacred to Simbo people, even if they appear neglected. You must get permission, hire a guide and pay any custom fees required before you visit them.

Skull Houses The most important skull site is Pa Na Ghundu, which has 12 coral-stone reliquaries complete with skulls and clam-shell money. It's concealed by trees close to the western base of Mt Matindingi. Another one is Pa Na Ulu, which is on the small headland just to the north of Mt Patukio, while a third site is at Gurava, close to the abandoned settlement of Ove Village. Some of these sites are centuries old and contain the skulls of highly regarded ancestors, while other craniums belong to head-hunting victims.

Petroglyphs There are two petroglyph sites at Righuru, and another one just to the west of Nggagho. The most interesting one is at

Vareviri Point, where there are rocks with canoe and bird symbols on them.

Bonito-Increase Shrines Although these structures are small, bonito (ie tuna) worship was important in Simbo ritual and was intended to guarantee large catches of the fish. There are two sites east of Nusa Simbo Village and another large one at Ove Lavata which is a line of large individual stone piles.

Abandoned Villages The coral-slab house bases on the western side of the path beside Lake Ove are all that remain of Ove Village, abandoned since its inhabitants were driven out by volcanic activity earlier this century. You'll also see other isolated sites around the island, including some beside the harbour, just to the south-west of Narovo.

Fortress The remains of the coral-walled fortress of Simbo Mbatuna and an accompanying dancing circle are at the southern end of Nusa Simbo.

Clamshell Collection There's a clamshell collection at Mengge.

Lake Ove

The lake is deep green because sulphur drains into it from the nearby hillside. There's a hot spring at the lake's south-eastern end, making the waters nearby too hot for swimming. Villagers often bring fresh megapode eggs there to cook them in the naturally heated waters.

Ove Crater

This yellow, sulphur-covered crater is on the western edge of 335-metre-high Mt Matindingi. There are fine views of Lake Ove and Simbo's western coast from its top. There's also a place about 200 metres south-east of the crater where the ground is so hot that food placed on it cooks in a few minutes.

The mildly steaming crater has several outcrops of pure-yellow crystalline sulphur in it which is collected by islanders as a cure for skin infections. There's a fumarole at the shoreside immediately below the crater.

There are two megapode hatcheries on the mountainside. One is above the lake, while the other is very close to the crater. There are also megapode holes at the bases of some nearby trees.

The warm, soft ground around the hatcheries is cleared and raked by villagers, and small thatched roofs are placed over it to entice the birds to use its shelter when laying. There's also a hatching area nearby where eggs are left uncollected to prevent over-farming. A stick with fruit on it outside any one of the hatcheries means you are forbidden to enter.

Getting There & Away The best way to the volcano is by boat, mooring at Ove Lavata beside a small coral garden and wading ashore across very slippery boulders. There's a footpath from there which goes beside Lake Ove and up to the crater. However, you must first get permission to visit the area from the land owners, who live in Narovo.

Cape Satisfaction

The ground is warm here, but a bearable temperature. One km offshore is Eddystone Rock, named by Shortland's crew in 1788 after a similar rock off south-western England.

Nusa Simbo Island

This two-km-long island is joined to its larger neighbour by a small bridge at the base of Mt Patukio. There's a hot spring 100 metres to the south of the bridge on the main island's side. The water's always warm here.

You'll find more megapode hatcheries in Nusa Simbo Village. Ask the custom owner of the site if you want to see them.

Narovo

Simbo's main village is connected by footpaths to Nusa Simbo, Righuru and Tapurai. There's a colourful reef to the north-west of the village, and a small island called Uelai with surrounding coral gardens at the harbour's mouth.

Tapurai
This large village has a half-km beach. There's a dead volcanic crater on the nearby hillside, now occupied by Lake Pughele.

RANONGGA ISLAND
Ranongga is a 28-km-long, rugged, narrow island. Its high western coast falls abruptly into deep water, while the eastern coast is much lower, with terraces and onshore reefs. Its tallest point is the 869-metre-high Mt Kela.

Ranongga is sparsely populated, with 3000 people in its 145 sq km. Most of these live along the sheltered eastern coast. Ranongga and Simbo people often treat each other as wantoks. Consequently, young Ranongga men are keen to find Simbo wives and bring them back to Ranongga to live. However, Simbo women know that, although Ranongga's villages may be by the shore, the food gardens are high up on the island's hillsides. The thought of clambering daily up to these gardens often crushes any romantic feelings Simbo girls have for their Ranonggan suitors.

The only dwellings on Ranongga are leaf houses. What few motors there are power canoes – there are no cars at all. Cooking is usually on wood fires, as gas and kerosene are still uncommon.

History
Ranongga, also known as Rononga, Ghanongga and Vesu Ghoghoto, was first seen by foreigners when the Americans Read and Dale sailed through Western Province in November 1787. Like Simbo people, Ranongga people were keen head-hunters – particularly in the 19th century – and made routine raids on Choiseul and Santa Isabel. The island's last head-hunting party sallied forth in 1936.

Culture
Even now parents tell their children stories based on memories of head-hunting raids. In the past no man was permitted to marry until he had been on one of these expeditions. Once he had done so, he was allowed to sleep with a woman captured from another tribe. The resulting offspring became full members of his clan, with rights to own land on the island.

Accommodation & Food
There are no rest houses on Ranongga, though larger villages, such as Koriovuku and Pienuna, may have an empty house you could borrow. So send a service message to the chief, and come prepared to camp. Also bring food to eat and exchange, as stores are few and far between on Ranongga.

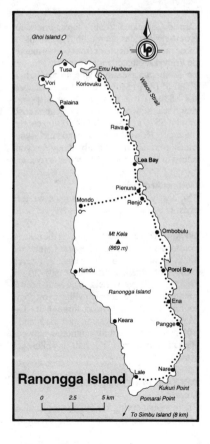

Ranongga Island

Information
Medical Services There are clinics at Emu Harbour, Pienuna and Keara.

Getting There & Away
Boat The Marine Division charges S$9 deck class from Gizo, and the same price to Simbo.

Yacht The only anchorages on Ranongga are at Emu Harbour, Renjo and Keara. The eastern side is usually calm from October to May, while the western coast is rough. From June to September inclusive, it's the other way round.

Canoe Compared to ship fares, prices for motor-canoe rides are prohibitive except for those made for rides to or from Gizo's market on Fridays. A shared motor canoe to Pienuna on Ranongga's eastern side from Gizo is about S$18. To Mondo on the western coast it's S$30. A trip through the usually very rough seas between Simbo and Pienuna costs around S$20 a head, or S$120 if you charter the canoe. However, motor-canoe fuel sometimes runs short, possibly delaying your return to Gizo until new supplies arrive.

Getting Around
The best way around Ranongga's western coast is by motor canoe.

Walking There's a footpath along the eastern coast from Emu Harbour down to Lale on the south-western tip of the island. However, these footpaths are sometimes only 30 cm wide and not very clear. You will need a guide, and should ask each village you come to for permission to pass through it. The same applies to the crossing over the island's 400-metre-high central mountains between Pienuna and Mondo. It's a half-day hike each way.

AROUND RANONGGA ISLAND
Mondo
There's a hot-spring site 500 metres south of Mondo. Villagers bathe in the thermally heated water and use it to cook their food. A custom fee is often charged to see or use it.

VELLA LAVELLA ISLAND
Usually known simply as Vella, and formerly as Mbilua, the island is wooded and mountainous. Together with its small neighbour Mbava, it's 670 sq km in size and has a population of 7000 people who speak a Papuan language and mostly live on its eastern coast.

Mt Tambisala in Vella's north-east is 790 metres high, yet its crater floor is close to sea level. Inside is a swampy flood plain and hot sulphur steam vents. Four km to the south-east, the Ulo River passes through an active thermal area.

Volcanoes in the island's north-west have produced a series of small sister cones, notably the Songga and Sukoe hills. In the south another quiescent volcano, the 520-metre-high Supato Peak, is bounded by coastal swamps.

History
Vella Lavella was first seen by foreigners in November 1787 when the Americans Read and Dale viewed it from their vessel the *Alliance*. More recently, the Japanese occupied the island in WW II, but lost several large warships trying to prevent the Americans wresting it back from them. When the US lost the light cruiser *Helena* off Vella, about 175 of her survivors swam ashore and were hidden by islanders until the Americans rescued them 10 days later. The Japanese were finally driven out in October 1943 by a joint US and New Zealand force after more than a year's occupation.

Fauna
Vella has a wide range of wildlife in its rainforest, while marlin and sailfish can occasionally be seen breaking the surface in Vella Gulf. Bird and insect life is prolific and includes megapode birds in the Ulo River area, and parrots and butterflies everywhere. Snakes are also plentiful, with the main one being the small, nonvenomous burrowing snake.

Crocodiles Villagers report seeing fresh-water crocodiles in the sulphurous Ulo River (pronounced 'Ooh-low') and its adjacent creeks. They hide in the day, but are active at night. Vella people say this crocodile mainly eats fish and is normally only danger-ous to dogs and very small children unless it has grown unusually long.

Villagers say there are no human-eating saltwater crocodiles in the Ulo River, but there are small numbers in the Oula River (pronounce 'Oh-lah') and its tributaries on the island's swampy western side. Vella people call them alligators to distinguish them from the comparatively retiring fresh-water species.

Information
Medical Services There are clinics on Vella Lavella at Vonunu, Kolokolo, Karaka, Mboro and Iringgila.

Accommodation & Food
The island has a guesthouse at the Liapari Plantation and a leaf-style rest hut at Maravari. Villagers will let you camp over-night at Simbilando, Paroana or Karaka if you get delayed around Ulo River. For details see the following Around Vella Lavella Island section.

Getting There & Away
Air Western Pacific flies regularly into Vella Lavella's two airfields of Barakoma and Geva. Fares from Barakoma to Gizo, Kukundu, Munda and Honiara are S$24, S$26, S$48 and S$207 respectively. From Geva they are S$44, S$43, S$66 and S$221. A flight between the island's two airfields costs S$33.

Boat The Marine Division charges S$12 deck class from Gizo or S$17 from Munda. It's S$12 if you want to visit Simbo or Ra-nongga from Vella.

Yacht There are anchorages of varying quality at Liapari Island, Pusisama, Lambu-lambu, Kokolope Bay, Simbilando, Mboro, Liangai and Iringgila.

Canoe The Liapari Plantation canoe charges S$7 to cover the 70-minute, 25-km journey between Liapari and Gizo; other canoe owners are likely to charge S$14 for a shared ride over the same route, and S$85 for a charter.

Getting Around
The WW II US-built road connects Liapari Island with Ruruvai, although many of its bridges have been washed away. A rather worn-out track continues on to Lambulambu,

Japanese Stragglers
When Japan withdrew her troops from Vella, 300 men were left behind. Many of them disappeared into the bush and hills to avoid capture by the Allies.

Since 1959, local people have occasionally reported seeing Japanese-looking men hiding in Vella's rainforest. Elderly Asiatic males with loin cloths and long beards have been reported stealing food from villagers' gardens. For a while Japanese veterans made up to three visits a year to Vella to find them.

In 1965, one Japanese straggler was located after first being seen by a woman in her garden. The ambassador flew over the area distributing leaflets saying, 'The war is over!', so the man gave himself up, returning home to receive full national honours.

There have been more sightings since then, including one in 1989 near Vorambare Bay, close to where the Japanese made their last stand. Consequently, some villagers think there may still be one or two stragglers left. Island cynics instead say the 'last Jap' may be a story put out to lure more Japanese visitors. If the story is true, this man has spent 49 years hiding in Vella's jungles, and would be at least 65 years old by now. He is probably happier where he is and prefers to be left alone. ■

and there's also a track to Supato. Every-where else must be reached by canoe.

AROUND VELLA LAVELLA ISLAND
All distances are from Liapari Plantation.

Liapari Island
This small plantation island has a very rustic atmosphere, with cows chewing the grass outside the settlement's houses and parrots flying through the surrounding coconut trees.

Liapari is protected by reefs which join it to its two small neighbours, Mbarambatu

and Karokoni islands, at low tide. Both have sandy beaches at their north-western ends. There's also a short golden-sand beach beside the plantation buildings.

Things to See & Do You can go beachcombing between Liapari and Mbarambatu at low tide or snorkel, windsurf or water-ski as long as you've brought your equipment. The best snorkel sites are on the western sides of Karokoni and Mbarambatu islands, and near the wooden bridge between Liapari and Vella.

There's a small freshwater swimming hole

Top: Island in Langa Langa Lagoon (MMcC)
Left: Malaitan women performing a traditional dance (DH)
Right: Man with croton leaves at Malaitan ceremony (SIID)

Top: Children at Lilisiana, Malaita Island (DH)
Left: Man waiting to take part in a traditional dance (SIID)
Right: Two men on Pileni Island (SIID)

around two km from Liapari on the road to Vonunu. The water's a greeny-blue due to the high level of copper and sulphur in the ground.

Liapari Plantation organises motor-canoe rides to the Ulo River thermal area. This is a full-day round trip and costs up to S$170.

Places to Stay & Eat The *Liapari Guest House* (☎ 60216) has two bedrooms, complete with cooking facilities. The cost is S$50 a night, regardless of the number of people staying. There's lighting between 7 am and 10 pm when the Liapari Plantation generator is operating.

The plantation has a well-stocked store. Company staff are usually happy to cook for you for a small fee.

Lake Kolokolo
(1.4 km, 1-km side-track & 3-km walk)
The lake is half a km long by 300 metres wide and has some freshwater crocodiles in it. Take the track to the west (left) about 400 metres beyond the Liapari Bridge. It terminates about one km later by the shore on the Rovomburi Passage. The route onwards to the lake is via Esorolando Point along the shore, but you'll certainly need a guide.

Vonunu (3.5 km)
The main village locally is connected by a 100-metre-long sandbar to tiny Kalanga Island.

Serulando Point
(6 km & 13.5-km side-track)
Petroglyphs depicting former chiefs adorn the top of the hill overlooking Serulando Point. There are more on the shore at Supato two km further on. Beyond at Oula is a long, sandy beach.

Maravari (15 km)
There's a leaf *rest house* here costing S$20 a head, with food available.

Kolokolo (22.5 km)
There are attractive coral gardens in the shal-

lows at Kolokolo. At Niarovai, 2.5 km further north, a war memorial commemorates the New Zealand forces who landed here in September 1943 to reinforce the US marines already in action on Vella.

Orete Cove (31 km)
There are several one-metre-high blow holes at Mbeiporo and Kundurumbangara points, one km to the south and 1.5 km to the north respectively of this attractive inlet.

Lambulambu (35 km)
A Japanese freighter sank in the harbour here in WW II. It's 12 metres down but underwater visibility is poor.

Villagers will show you the high walls constructed locally for defence in head-hunting days. Valapata, four km further on, has similar remains.

Simbilando (35 km & 11 km by canoe)
This large village is imposingly positioned on a hillside facing the sea. The reef 2.5 km away at the eastern tip of nearby Tambitambi Island is particularly colourful. There are more coral gardens 2.5 km due north at Paroana.

Ulo River Thermal Area
(35 km & 21.5 km by canoe)
The first thing you'll notice at Paraso Bay is the brown volcanic sand heated by thermal activity. The footpath to the hot springs is about five km long and takes one to 1½ hours. You cross two small creeks immediately beyond the beach and then cross the Ulo River twice before reaching several large trees on its southern side. These have deep holes in their bases and are hatcheries where megapode birds lay their eggs in the thermally heated ground. A few people live in the area and harvest these eggs, but it's a small operation compared to those of Savo and Simbo.

Immediately beyond is a mud pool on the southern (left) side of the path. After this there are two km of hot springs known colloquially by islanders as the Volcano. It's very desolate compared to the thick bush along the Ulo River. The only plants growing in the thermal area are bracken and dozens of small pandanus trees.

You can go further and climb nearby Nonda Hill, Kumba Hill and Mt Tambisala, where there's more thermal activity, but you'll have to camp out if you do. Villagers will let you sleep in Simbilando, Paroana or Karaka if you're late back from the thermal area or rough seas delay your return.

The custom owners of the Ulo River thermal area live at Simbilando, so you'll need to call in there first. The custom fee is S$20 to see the whole two-km-long site, or S$2 just to view the first mud pool. They'll also provide one or two guides, who you should pay S$2 to S$3 each for half-a-day's work.

MBAVA ISLAND

Known also as Baanga, Baga, Bagga or Bag Island, most of the coastal part of this 36-sq-km landform is low lying and marshy, except for the 230-metre-high quiescent volcanic peak on the island's eastern side. The only permanently occupied part of it is tiny Inia Island off Mbava's eastern coast. However, this may change, as Mbava is believed to be gold bearing.

Getting There & Away

Boat There are anchorages at both Somolo and Singgataravana harbours.

The Shortland Islands

Only nine km from Bougainville in Papua New Guinea, the scattered islands of the Shortlands group lie at the Solomons' northwestern tip. The main island is Shortland itself, or Alu as it is often called. Its principal neighbour is Fauro.

About 3500 people live in the group's 340 sq km. Copra production and logging are the main industries.

Shortlands people and their wantoks, the Treasury Islanders, are keen to keep their identity unaffected by outside influences. Many refuse to learn any Melanesian language other than their own. Consequently, they will reply to other islanders in English, even if spoken to in Pijin. This applies particularly to the elderly and traditionalists among Shortlands people, though the young are less inclined to follow this rule.

Visitors to the Shortlands should always ask permission to enter a village, and then see the chief. Otherwise you will be asked to leave. Melanesian chiefs in these islands have a status akin to that enjoyed by chiefs in the Polynesian outliers – considerably more, that is, than their counterparts elsewhere in the Solomons have.

Shortlands people are much more direct in their manner than islanders elsewhere in the Solomons. If you do something wrong, you'll be told so, whereas in other parts of the country villagers will usually tactfully overlook your error.

Visitors to the Shortlands should always ask first before strolling through someone's vegetable patch or coconut plantation. The answer almost invariably will be yes, and once given, that permission is yours for a lifetime. But if you don't ask, villagers may wonder if you are being deliberately secretive and are planning to steal some food.

History

Villages between 800 and 1000 AD were generally built on coastal sites close to a creek.

The modern age began when Captain John Shortland saw the group in 1788 from the *Alexander*. However, outside contact was limited at first, with ancient customs continuing unaffected. On one occasion warriors from Mono captured Fauro and massacred most of its people.

In 1878 a local chief called Gorai began supplying blackbirders with labourers for overseas plantations in exchange for guns. These new weapons enabled him to rule over all the Shortlands.

The Shortlands were the first islands in the Solomons group to be occupied by the Japanese in WW II. However, when the nearby

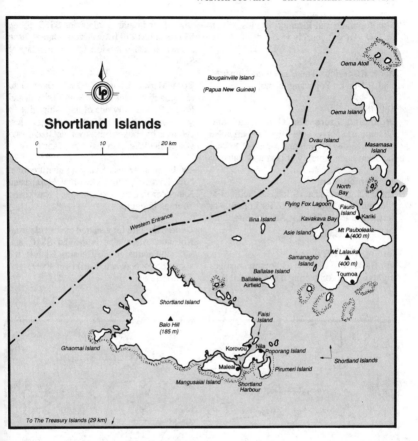

Shortland Islands

0   10   20 km

Bougainville Island
(Papua New Guinea)

Oema Atoll

Oema Island

Ovau Island

Masamasa Island

North Bay

Flying Fox Lagoon

Fauro Island   Kariki

Kavakava Bay

Ilina Island

Asie Island

Mt Pauboleala ▲(400 m)

Samanagho Island

Mt Lalauka ▲(400 m)

Ballalae Island

Ballalae Airfield

Toumoa

Shortland Island

Faisi Island

Balo Hill (185 m)

Ghaomai Island

Korovou   Nila   Poporang Island

Maleai   Pirumeri Island   Shortland Islands

Mangusaiai Island   Shortland Harbour

To The Treasury Islands (29 km)

Treasury Islands were liberated by the Allies in late 1943, the Shortlands were bypassed. They were left as isolated prisons of men and material – until the war ended in 1945 – unable to be resupplied or evacuated, and of little value to their occupiers.

Arts

The Shortlands used to be a major centre for pot making, with the oldest remains so far discovered dating back to between 800 and 1000 AD. About 40 abandoned village sites have so far revealed pieces of broken pottery. However, the industry declined once trading vessels arrived selling metal or enamel utensils. No-one has made any pots in the Shortlands for over 20 years.

SHORTLAND ISLAND

Shortland is about 22 km long by 16 km wide. Only Balo Hill in its centre rises as high as 185 metres.

Shortland's north-western side is dotted with reefs and islets and is good for fishing, swimming and diving, while many of the islands on the north-eastern side have sandy beaches. In the south-east a reef surrounds both Poporang and Pirumeri islands, which are low, flat and densely wooded.

Information
Medical Services There's a church-run hospital at Nila on Poporang Island.

Activities
Organised Tours The Gizo Hotel and Adventure Sports, both of Gizo, organise two to five-day diving/land packages to visit the Shortlands, notably Nila and Ballalae.

Accommodation
There's a guesthouse with basic facilities at Nila and a rest house planned for Lofang. For details see the following Around Shortland Island section.

Getting There & Away
Air Ballalae has three Solomon Airlines flights a week connecting it to Choiseul Bay,

Gizo, Munda and Honiara for S$53, S$99, S$118 and S$270 respectively. One of these connections also services Mono, for a fare of S$50.

Boat Marine Division vessels from Gizo charge a S$29 deck fare to both Korovou and Fauro. Periodically one of their ships does a seven-day medical trip, often causing its few cabins to be booked out. Another Gizo-based vessel, the *Vele*, also visits the Shortlands.

Yacht Anchorages of varying quality are at Nila, Korovou, Nuhu, Ghaomai, Harapa and Kamaleai Two on Shortland, and Kariki and Toumoa in Fauro.

Canoe The fare for a shared canoe ride from Korovou to Ballalae is around S$10, and S$25 to Falamai in the Treasury Islands. It's about S$24 between Kariki on Fauro and Choiseul Bay.

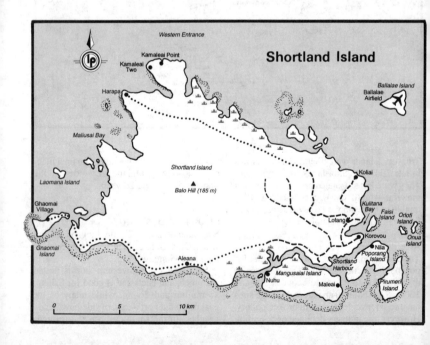

You used to be able to enter and leave the Solomons by taking a motor-canoe ride across the Western Entrance separating the Shortlands from Papua New Guinea's Bougainville Island. This route is closed while Bougainville is trying to secede from Papua New Guinea. The Papua New Guinea government regards any foreigners who visit Bougainville as having entered Papua New Guinea illegally. The Solomons government cooperates with this and refuses permission for anyone to leave the country this way.

Getting Around
There is a network of logging tracks in the eastern part of this low-lying island.

Boat There are plenty of motor canoes at Korovou and Nila to take you around the island, to Ballalae Airfield or across to Fauro. Charter fares between Korovou and Nila are about S$3 each way, while shared canoes from Korovou to Ballalae and Kariki in Fauro should be around S$7 and S$26 each respectively.

AROUND SHORTLAND ISLAND
Korovou
Korovou, the local subprovincial headquarters, is at the end of a narrow spit between Kulitana Bay and Shortland Harbour. There are several Japanese aircraft sunk at their moorings in the bay. Others lie submerged three km from Korovou at Shortland Harbour's western end, which was a WW II Japanese seaplane base.

Faisi Island
Faisi was the first place in the Solomons to be seized by the Japanese, in April 1943, and was used by them as a wartime destroyer base. There are attractive reefs along the island's eastern side and also beside its small neighbours, Orlofi and Onua islands.

Nila
You can stay at the *Nila Guest House* beside Poporang Island's jetty for S$15 a night, with lighting by hurricane lamp. There's a large trade store at the nearby mission.

Several Japanese seaplanes and barges lie in 10 to 15 metres of water, all sunk at their moorings. Hidden in the bush near the guesthouse are more Japanese remains, including three large coastal batteries, parts of four seaplanes, and a command centre.

Lofang
This logging settlement exports timber directly to Japan. There are plans for a rest house here.

Harapa
This was the original Gilbertese settlement in the Shortlands and received its first newly arrived Micronesians in 1962. Since then, the village has grown in size, while other Micronesian settlements have sprung up at nearby Kamaleai Point, Kamaleai Two and Laomana Island. There's plenty of bird life on the small islands in nearby Maliusai Bay.

Maleai
The Shortland's largest village is on Mangusaiai Island, and was the pottery centre for the whole Shortlands until the process died out recently. You can still see some remains, as long as you ask Maleai's chief first.

Ghaomai Island
The island has several fine beaches and an attractive reef.

Ballalae Island
Until recently, this small, unpopulated island, with its tiny grass airstrip, was the unlikely site of an international airport and entry point into the Solomons. It no longer is, for cost reasons.

There are three moderately well-preserved Japanese Betty bombers in the thick bush beside the airfield, as well as other wrecked ones nearby. Unexploded bombs are scattered along the seashore, and some seaplane wrecks lie in the shallow waters surrounding the island.

Ballalae was the scene of great cruelty towards Allied civilian prisoners in WW II. About 470 were brought from Singapore and forced to build the airstrip. Many died in

1943 from dysentery or exhaustion, while others were shot for saying the Japanese wouldn't win. Some deliberately ran into the path of US bombs during air raids and were killed. The remainder were beheaded when the airbase was completed.

The proposed Solomon Islands WW II museum plans to open a branch at Ballalae once its display at Henderson Airport is operational.

FAURO ISLAND
This long, hilly island with steep volcanic ridges rises at two points to 400 metres. Its coastline is surrounded by reefs as are its many small neighbouring islands. Lightly populated Fauro is 19 km from Shortland and 29 km long.

Some of Fauro's adjacent islets are no more than sandbars, while others have a canopy of coconut trees. Fishing, swimming, snorkelling and diving are good all around, but especially along the island's southern coast.

Fauro's northern part is shaped like a long hooked arm, and is the remains of a drowned volcano. All along this narrow isthmus are dazzling, sandy beaches.

Information
Medical Services The only clinic on the island is at Kariki.

AROUND FAURO ISLAND
Kavakava Bay
The sunken Japanese freighter here is hard to see from the surface, and still leaks oil.

Flying Fox Lagoon
There have been no flying foxes here since a cyclone in 1972. However, this small lagoon is a good place to find mud crabs and large oysters. Fishing is good, though there are plenty of stingrays in the area.

Ilina Island
There's a white-sand beach on this small islet. Called Obelisk Island in the 19th century, it is also known as Elina.

Ovau Island
Fauro's largest neighbour, Ovau, used to contain many wild pigs, though their numbers are now greatly reduced. There's also good game fishing in the area. Anyone wishing to visit Ovau should first get permission from the chief of Samanagho Island.

Oema Island & Oema Atoll
Well-stocked with clams, both the island and the atoll are treated as bird sanctuaries by local people.

The Treasury Islands

Mono and Stirling are the only substantial members of the Treasury Islands group. First seen by Dale and Read in 1787, and given their name by Shortland one year later, the Treasuries are 29 km south-west of the Shortlands and have an area of 80 sq km.

MONO ISLAND
Although its people speak Alu, the language spoken in the Shortlands, Mono was

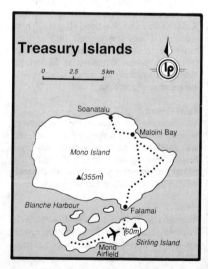

originally settled by people from north-western Vella Lavella, who landed on Mono's northern side at Soanatalu.

Information
Medical Services The only clinic in the Treasuries is at Falamai.

Accommodation
Falamai has a leaf-style rest house.

Getting There & Away
Air The Treasuries' airstrip is on Stirling Island, but it is called Mono Airfield. The one Solomon Airlines flight each week is from Gizo. It continues on to Ballalae and Choiseul Bay. The fares between Mono and Ballalae, Choiseul Bay and Gizo are S$50, S$78 and S$96.

Boat Marine Division deck fares from Gizo and Choiseul Bay to Mono are S$23 each. However, it's only S$9 between Korovou in the Shortlands and Falamai.

Yacht The Treasuries' usual anchorage is at Falamai.

Canoe Traffic is light between Mono and Shortland, though there's often someone going to Korovou on Friday morning and returning Sunday. A shared canoe ride there costs about S$25.

AROUND MONO ISLAND
Falamai
Almost all the Treasury Islands' 1400 people live in this large village. The ancestors of these friendly islanders killed 18 of the crew of the British whaler *Offley* in 1842, and 33 of the crew of the US vessel *Superior* 20

years later. Captain Simpson in HMS *Blanche* brought peace to the area while surveying it shortly afterwards.

Falamai has a community library and a black-sand beach. All visitors should ask the chief's permission to see the area.

STIRLING ISLAND
Unpopulated Stirling is on the opposite side of Blanche Harbour, and 1.5 km from Mono. You'll find an airfield, the remains of a large WW II Allied base, and a network of tracks on this narrow six-km-long raised coral platform. A chartered motor-canoe ride from Falamai costs S$5 each way.

At the end of WW II, a large number of US aircraft were abandoned here. There weren't enough pilots to fly them back home, so they were deliberately bent and then bulldozed into the bush to prevent further use. Although most have now been removed, there are still wrecked planes in the sea at the base of the island's cliffs.

Choiseul Province

The Solomons' newest province, Choiseul (pronounced 'Choy-zul'), was established in late 1991. Lying along a north-west to south-west axis, Choiseul Island and its adjacent islands together are 3294 sq km in size. Two large daughter islands lie close to the eastern tip of 161-km-long Choiseul Island. Only 200 metres across the Nggosele Passage is the largely unoccupied Rob Roy Island, while eight km further east is Wagina, a centre of Gilbertese resettlement since 1962.

Three-quarters of Choiseul Province's 14,000 Melanesian people live in the main island's western half, and there are a further 2000 Gilbertese living in Wagina. Choiseul people are quite distinctive. They are extremely dark – almost ebony in colour – and are usually tall, with fine, lean, straight features.

Wagina's people, in contrast, are all Micronesian.

Choiseul Island

Choiseul Island was traditionally called Lauru. Although its political links are with the Solomon Islands, Choiseul Island's cultural links, like those of the Shortlands, are with Bougainville in Papua New Guinea.

Never more than 36 km wide, Choiseul Island is a long, narrow, densely wooded island whose interior is cut by steep, rugged ridges and deep gorges. Its highest point, near the centre, is Mt Maetambe, a volcanic cone whose rim rises to 1060 metres.

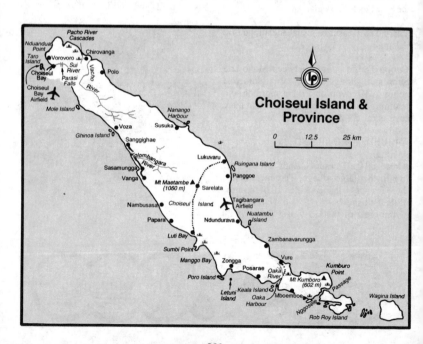

Much of Choiseul Island's shoreline consists of long, narrow beaches, some of them bordered by large, shallow freshwater marshes. Fens, occasionally the homes of saltwater crocodiles, are extensive along the coast and in some isolated inland areas. A swamp along the Oaka River in the island's south-east almost bisects Choiseul Island.

Although the island had a comparatively quiet time in WW II, there are several wrecked barges and aircraft in the shallows along Choiseul Island's western coast. Because of the island's limited facilities, few of these potential scuba sites have been explored yet.

History

Mendaña's 1568 expedition saw a large island north-west of Santa Isabel and called it San Marcos. This was probably Choiseul Island.

Louis de Bougainville, 200 years later in 1768, named the island after Choiseul, the French foreign minister of the time. In the 19th century, head-hunting and slave-raiding parties from the New Georgia group regularly attacked the island. In the 1870s Liliboe, a central Choiseul Island bigman, evened the score by leading raids westwards. He also made forays against neighbouring Wagina until it was totally depopulated.

Joint negotiations between Britain and Germany granted Choiseul Province to Germany in 1886, but then ceded it to Britain in 1899. In 1916, Sir Hubert Murray, the lieutenant governor of New Guinea, reported there were ferocious tribal wars on Choiseul

Island, though these were brought under control by a peace treaty in 1921.

The Japanese landed on Choiseul Island early in 1942, and some remained there till the end of WW II. The island's inhabitants suffered little from the occupation, though there were ever-present fears of ill-treatment and the seizure of their crops by the occupiers. Consequently, chiefs organised constant patrols throughout the island.

Except for brief diversionary landings at Voza, Sanggighae and Choiseul Bay in late 1943, the only permanent Allied force on Choiseul Island was 18 coastwatching islanders. This tiny force killed 93 Japanese for the loss of only one man.

One of their number, who later became a Church of Melanesia archdeacon, would only use one bullet per target. He waited silently near Japanese camps until a soldier went into the bush alone and then killed him with a single round.

Climate

Choiseul Bay in the north-western part of the island receives 3559 mm (140 inches) of rain a year and has 260 days of precipitation annually. Temperatures range between 31°C and 23°C throughout the year. Morning humidity levels hover around 88%, reaching 90% for three months a year, while afternoon humidity averages 79% or less.

Arts

Bukaware, although it originated in Bougainville, is also made in Choiseul Island in small quantities. A few potters are still active

---

Kesa Money

An old form of shell currency used in Choiseul Island is called *kesa* money. It was used in the past for bride price, compensation payments, land settlements, peacemaking and forming alliances.

Nine clamshell cylinders made one kesa. A man's status would depend on how much of this currency he owned. Each unit's history, and all the transactions it had been through, were widely known.

Traditionally, an entirely different people from the modern-day Choiseulese made this money. They were a light-skinned race – possibly Polynesian – who collected huge numbers of clam shells from all over the island before settling on tiny Nuatambu. Some say they then disappeared. Others believe they were at first allowed to settle and trade their kesa currency, but were later killed ∎

at Choiseul Bay and around Chirovanga. These are the last places in the Solomons where this traditional craft survives.

Today, small-sized kesa money is found in most parts of Choiseul Island. Larger examples are only seen in the Nuatambu area, the currency's original source.

Culture

Legendary People Many Choiseul Island people believe in a mythical tribe, the Voromangas. They have never been seen, but are believed to live at the source of the Kolombangara River which flows out of Mt Maetambe. Villagers say Voromangas can occasionally be heard in the mountains blowing their panpipes and conch shells, especially inland from Sasamungga. Like the Kakamoras, they are said to be very strong.

According to another tradition there are also some monkey-like inhabitants in Choiseul Island's interior – the Sinipi. These legendary people are said to resemble cave dwellers, and use shells as knives to cut up mangoes, their favourite food.

Every village is said to have a *basana*. Traditionally, this is a spirit with two long front teeth and lengthy black hair. Basanas can trick people, or help them find food and track enemies. In head-hunting days, war canoes bore the dog-like face of a basana as a figurehead on their prows.

Traditional Burial Methods The distinctive carved stone burial chambers of north-western Choiseul Island are called *ndolos*. They are about one metre high and 50 cm in diameter. In the centre is a hollow for the chief's bones. Pre-Christian Choiseulese believed that once these bones were placed inside it, the Ndolo became the sacred habitat of spirits.

Information
Medical Services

There's a church hospital in Sasamungga, and there are clinics at Mole Island, Papara, Posarae, Nuatambu, Panggoe, Susuka, Polo and Chirovanga.

Activities

Organised Tours Two Gizo dive operators, Adventure Sports and Gizo Hotel, organise diving/land packages which include Choiseul Island.

Accommodation

As well as a leaf rest house in Choiseul Bay, there's a more modern one at the mission at Sasamungga. Most villages should be able to spare a hut for visitors as long as you make it clear you're only staying one night.

It's best to work out your itinerary well in advance when visiting Choiseul Island and Province. Before sending a service message, find out who to contact at each place – whether it's the priest-in-charge of a mission or the village chief. Once you get there, two tobacco sticks and some pages from a small school notebook should be a fair B&B price in a Choiseul Island village! Local missions are usually very welcoming, but prefer donations.

Getting There & Away

Air The province's only operational airfield is on Taro Island in Choiseul Bay. Solomon Airlines flies in three times a week, connecting the island with Ballalae, Gizo, Munda and Honiara for S$53, S$96, S$115 and S$268 respectively. There's also a Solomon Airlines flight connecting Mono with Choiseul Bay for S$78.

Western Pacific Air Services will re-use Tagibangara Airfield, six km north of Ndundurava, once it's operational again.

Boat Marine Division vessels from Gizo travel around Choiseul Province every two weeks, usually leaving on Mondays on an eight to nine-day voyage. Fares are cheapest from Gizo to Posarae (S$45) and most expensive from Gizo to Chirovanga or Choiseul Bay (S$56).

Medical and police teams sometimes accompany the Marine Division's round trip to Choiseul Province's coastal villages as part of their regular duties, providing a unique opportunity for you to see them in action. However, cabin and bunk space is usually pretty limited on such occasions.

The Vasivapada Trading Company of Gizo has a ship called the *Thomas E* serving Choiseul Province. It does an eight-day round trip from Gizo, first to Luti Bay and then around the island's northern coast.

Getting Around

There are only 25 km of road on Choiseul Island, with the longest section being between Vanga and Sanggighae. Narrow footpaths connect most of the villages in the western end of Choiseul Island. Elsewhere travel is by motor canoe.

AROUND CHOISEUL ISLAND
Choiseul Bay

Part of the settlement, especially government buildings, has sprung up beside the airfield on Taro Island. The remainder, including the school, is on the mainland opposite at the Sui River's exit to the sea.

Although it's a small place, Taro Island has the new provincial headquarters, a post office and a leaf-style *rest house* on it. It's best to contact the provincial secretary before you arrive to see if there's any spare room for you, or if there's anywhere else you can stay.

Beyond the mainland part of the settlement and up the Sui River is the attractive Parasi Falls. Go there by canoe, as it's a rather swampy area.

The attractive village of Vorovoro is six km north of Choiseul Bay. Two km beyond, at Nduandua Point, there's a plantation with a large collection of kesa money and ancient carvings. Also in the area are a number of archaeological and tabu sites.

Sasamungga

This is the largest village in Choiseul Island and the United Church mission here has a *rest house*. Contact it in advance by radio to check if it has room for you.

Coconut plantations are almost continuous along this stretch of coast. The largest concentration is at Sasamungga, by the village's sandy beach.

Canoes travel far up the Kolombangara River to the high grasslands at its headwa-

ters. This is a popular area for hunting wild pigs with spears, bows and arrows.

Nambusasa

In 1936, a cargo cult developed here. Its followers believed a large steamship would arrive laden with all kinds of trade goods. Warehouses were erected to receive the expected cargo, while bullyboys terrorised all nonbelievers. The movement collapsed, to general relief, in 1940.

Mt Maetambe

Some alluvial gold has been found on this mountain. There's a path up it from Luti Bay's sandy beach. The trail climbs to over 750 metres at Sarelata – Choiseul Province's only inland village. Then the path descends to Lukuvaru on the island's eastern coast. It's a two-day hike and requires a guide.

Manggo Bay

Here there are a number of caves and rock sites where early people used to live. These are at either end of the bay, at both Sumbi Point and Poro Island. A black-sand beach runs along much of the shore.

Letuni Island

Opposite the village of Zongga (pronounced 'John-ga') are several small offshore islands. One of these, the tiny heart-shaped Letuni, has white, sandy beaches all around it.

Oaka Harbour

A pleasant beach separates the sea from a swamp. Islanders canoe four km up the nearby Oaka River and then take a marshy track across the island to Vure on the other side.

Mboemboe

There are several small, sandy offshore islets opposite this village's beach.

Chirovanga

A few local women still make pots for use as funerary urns or cooking ware. Once a pot is made, it's dried for a month, then decorated in between two firings. One km inland from Chirovanga are the Pacho River Cascades.

Vacho River

This river is the longest Solomons waterway navigable by canoe. On both sides of the Vacho's upper reaches are attractive grass-covered hills interspersed with rocky outcrops and ravine-like valleys.

Lukuvaru

The beaches between Lukuvaru and Nuatambu Island are a dark-olive colour. There's a high proportion of minerals in the local sand.

Nuatambu Island

This is actually two small islands joined by a sandbar. The words *nua tambu* mean sacred island. The large amount of broken clam shell found here indicates that Nuatambu was the principal manufacturing site for kesa currency. Ancient ceramics have also been collected here, suggesting that pots may have been made at Nuatambu as long ago as 1000 AD.

Nuatambu is slowly sinking, and the large amount of broken pottery and clam shell found at very low tides indicates that it may have been larger in the past.

There's an ancient burial site on the hill nearest the mainland. It's surrounded by a tall coral and limestone wall.

Long stretches of white-sand beach extend from Nuatambu to Kumboro Point at Choiseul Island's eastern tip. The few exceptions are at headlands, in the occasional deep black-sand bay, or where there are mangroves.

Mt Kumboro

There are fine views from the summit over southern Choiseul Island, Wagina and northern Isabel Province. Although it's only a three-hour climb from the coast here, you will need a guide to find the path.

Rob Roy Island

Also known as Vealaviru Island, Rob Roy is an unpopulated island mainly given over to coconut trees and rainforest. Its tallest point is only 150 metres high. Because of the small number of people using the area, there are still plenty of fish, dugong and turtles locally.

Wagina Island

Also called Vaghena Island, this 78-sq-km landform was first observed by foreigners in 1769. The French explorer Jean de Surville, in the armed merchant ship *St Jean Baptiste*, called it Île de la Première Vue (the first island seen). In the late 19th century, Wagina's original Melanesian population fled after being decimated by disease and head-hunting Choiseulese and New Georgians who were keen to secure the supply of the island's turtle shell – a valuable commodity at the time.

Between 1963 and 1964, Gilbertese people moved here from the overcrowded Phoenix Islands in the eastern part of what is now Kiribati. Micronesians from all over the Solomons regularly take holidays on Wagina, as most have relatives on this island.

Although Wagina is a slightly raised reef, its highest point is no more than 40 metres above sea level. Just offshore in the Hamilton Channel are several coconut-covered islands with sandy shores. There are also many small islets off its northern side, all with white-sand beaches. This part of Wagina is unpopulated and is partly mangrove swamp.

Large deposits of bauxite have been found on Wagina. These have not yet been mined, as the minerals are in the cultivated part of the island, and there have been custom ownership disputes over who owns the bauxite: the Gilbertese settlers or the original Melanesian landowners.

Wagina's 2000 people live in three beachside villages on its southern side. Turtles swim and breed in local waters, and islanders hunt them for their meat and eggs.

Other Solomons people often call the Gilbertese *Sagabo*. This is because their word for goodbye is *tai kabo*, with the 't' pronounced like an 's'.

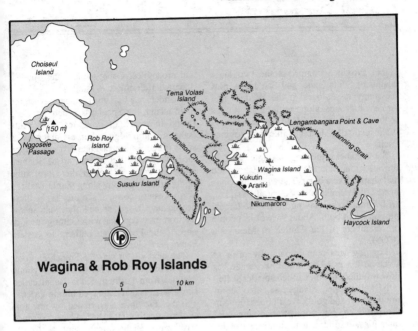

Wagina & Rob Roy Islands

Choiseul Island

(150 m)

Nggosele Passage

Rob Roy Island

Susuku Island

Tema Volasi Island

Hamilton Channel

Lengambangara Point & Cave

Manning Strait

Wagina Island

Kukutin
Arariki

Nikumaroro

Haycock Island

0   5   10 km

Information
Medical Services There's a clinic at Kukutin.

Accommodation
There are no organised lodgings on Wagina, so contact either the chief or village priest/minister to ask if he can arrange accommodation for you. Kukutin is Roman Catholic and has a mission, whilst the other two villages are United Church. Bring plenty of your own food if you want to eat more than just swamp taro and fish!

Getting There & Away
Boat On average, there's a ship or launch from Gizo every week. The Marine Division charges S$29 between Wagina and Choiseul Bay, and S$43 from Gizo.

Getting Around
Transport on Wagina is on foot along the track between Kukutin and Nikumaroro, or by canoe to the nearby reefs.

AROUND WAGINA ISLAND
Lengambangara Cave
This large cave is 35 metres from the sea at Lengambangara Point. It's currently used to house platforms where men rest while on fishing expeditions. Local legends tell of its use over many centuries.

Nikumaroro
There's an ancient burial site on top of a nearby cliff, with a flat coral slab forming a chamber over human bones.

Tema Volasi Island
This tiny islet, housing an ancient Melanesian burial ground, is at the top of Hamilton Channel.

Isabel Province

Isabel Province comprises the two large islands of Santa Isabel and San Jorge, plus the many lesser ones in the Western and Arnarvon groups, along with lonely Ramos to the east. The main island, Santa Isabel, is often just called Isabel – like the province itself.

Santa Isabel is the longest single island in the Solomons. It is 181 km long, 30 km wide and shaped like a cigar. The whole province has 17,500 people in an area of 4014 sq km, with Santa Isabel having by far the largest proportion of both. About 96% of its people are members of the Church of Melanesia (COM).

Logging was a major activity prior to Cyclone Ida in 1972. The timber trade has now resumed, but on a much smaller scale.

Nickel, copper, manganese, zinc, chromium, silver and gold have all been found in the province, but not yet in commercial quantities. In addition to the traditional activities of fishing and farming coconuts for copra, some villagers grow coffee and cocoa and run cattle, while others dive for trocchus shells and bêche-de-mer.

HISTORY

Mendaña sighted Santa Isabel on 7 February 1568 and anchored the following day. He called the inlet Estrella (Star) Bay and the island Santa Isabel after the patron saint of his voyage.

Relationships between Spaniards and islanders were initially friendly. The visitors were impressed by the local chief, Bilebanara, who wanted to learn Spanish and promised to supply food in return. When insufficient supplies came, the explorers began seizing hostages, offering to exchange them for much greater amounts of food. This soon led to violence.

Meanwhile, the Spaniards were horrified by Santa Isabel people's cannibalism. They also disliked the worship of lizards, snakes

and crocodiles. Consequently, the Spanish departed after only two months.

Islanders say that during their stay on the main island, the Spaniards penetrated deep inland in search of gold, reaching Santa Isabel's central ridge. Others claim there was some fraternisation, and that as a result some local people have a smattering of Spanish blood in them. Although there are some light-skinned people along Santa Isabel's north-western coast, it's more likely these people have instead some Polynesian ancestry from past contacts with Ontong Java, or one of the Polynesian outliers in eastern Papua New Guinea.

The next visitor was the French explorer de Surville, in 1769. He captured a young islander from northern Santa Isabel called Lova Saragua and displayed him in Paris.

Isabel Province was visited by few foreigners after this until 1845, when the French missionary Bishop Jean-Baptiste Epalle went ashore unarmed at Midoru in south-eastern Santa Isabel. When he refused to exchange his episcopal ring for two lemons (one partly eaten), he was mortally wounded. Although rescued, he died three days later. His attackers kept his shoes, roasting them for lunch!

In the mid-19th century, Isabel Province's population suffered repeated head-hunting and slave raids, mainly by people from Simbo, New Georgia and Malaita. In addition, epidemics of influenza, dysentery, whooping cough and measles (all brought by European sailors) took a terrible toll.

The head-hunters stripped most of Santa Isabel's southern coast of people. Many fair-haired women were carried off as slaves, while most of those who survived fled to the eastern end of the island. Others sought refuge by building houses in trees. One such dwelling, 18 metres up, was equipped with piles of stones for the inhabitants to hurl down on enemies below.

The Church of Melanesia's predominance

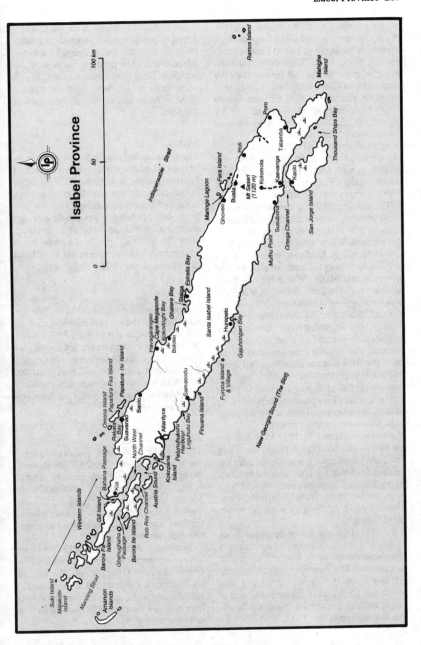

Isabel Province

100 km

50

0

Indispensable Strait

Ramos Island

Mahighe Island

Poro

Tatamba

Thousand Ships Bay

Hofi

Fera Island

Kolomola

Kaevanga

Kaolo

Maringe Lagoon

Ghoveo

Buala

Mt Sasari
(1120 m)

San Jorge Island

Susubona

Muthu Point

Ortega Channel

Havagarangao

Cape Megapode

Kokodoghi Bay

Ghatere Bay

Sisiga

Estrella Bay

Santa Isabel Island

Boloitei

Hurepelo

Gajuhongan Bay

Omona Island

Rakata

Papatura Faa Island

Suavanao

Papatura Ite Island

Baolo

Samasodu

Finuana Island

Furona Island
& Village

Allardyce

Kokopana Island

Patunuhukuru Harbour

Loguhutu Bay

New Georgia Sound (The Slot)

Western Islands

Bahana Passage

North West Channel

Kia

Austria Sound

Rob Roy Channel

Gill Island

Barora Fara Island

Gherughaha Passage

Barora Ite Island

Suki Island

Malakobi Island

Amavon Islands

Manning Strait

in the province's affairs began in 1866. Bishop Patteson healed Chief Soga of Sepi, nephew of Santa Isabel's most famous head-hunting chief, Bera. Soga, who had been dying of malaria, showed his gratitude by converting to Christianity and making sure everyone else did so too! He also helped bring head-hunting raids to an end by organising effective resistance to them in south-eastern Santa Isabel.

In 1886 Britain and Germany both proclaimed spheres of influence over the Solomons, with what is now Isabel Province coming under German control. However, in 1899, this area was transferred to Britain.

The missionaries and their local helpers, the catechists, were much more influential prior to WW II than was the remote British government. When village constables, later known as village headmen, were appointed in 1923, inevitably the question was asked of government officials, 'Who is boss – king or archbishop?'. On Santa Isabel, in practice it was the Anglican archbishop!

In 1929, Richard Fallowes, a British missionary who supported local people's right to autonomy, pressed for a Santa Isabel parliament. This popular message soon spread throughout the area and on to Nggela. Firmly opposed by other missionaries and the authorities, Fallowes was deported in 1934. At the time, any European who supported the idea of indigenous self-rule was considered to be a threat to imperial power.

Fallowes returned in 1939 to reorganise his campaign. Sometimes called the Chair and Rule Movement, it was named after the chair and wooden staff (or rule), the symbols of traditional Solomons authority. Although popular in Santa Isabel, Fallowes was expelled again in 1940, causing the movement to languish.

In 1942, Japanese forces occupied Santa Isabel and its neighbours, establishing a large seaplane and barge base at Suavanao in Rakata Bay. The Americans made frequent air attacks on the harbour, including two accidental bombings of friendly islanders at Baolo and Kia. These raids forced the Japanese to withdraw in late 1943.

Santa Isabel's scouts were particularly active, winning a small skirmish at Mufhu Point in late 1942, and rescuing 28 downed Allied pilots while the Japanese were in the province. Once pilots were rescued, islanders secretly passed them down the coast at night to be picked up by US seaplanes at Tatamba.

FAUNA

The Thinking Rat used to be present also on Malaita Island but now is restricted to Isabel Province, although there is a related species in Guadalcanal. This friendly creature lives at the top of tall trees, eats nuts and fruit, and bears one offspring a year. Adults weigh about one kg and can be up to 75 cm long. How the 'thinking' part of its name arises isn't certain, but this may relate to its habit of using its jaws and feet to open nuts.

PEOPLE

Although the people of Isabel Province are Melanesian, they vary considerably in colour. Three-quarters of them live in Santa Isabel's south-eastern corner and have light-brown skin, with curly or wavy hair ranging in colour from black to blond. In contrast, the people of Kia have jet-black skin and dark, sometimes straight, hair – like the people of Choiseul Island.

ARTS

Tapa is made locally from the bark of paper-mulberry trees and tinted a lightish blue, using a dye made from crushed orchid leaves. Shell money is still purchased from Malaita Island to pay bride price and to settle custom-ownership disputes, while dolphins' teeth are used to make necklaces and sometimes as currency.

Traditional dances from Isabel Province are regular events at Solomons cultural festivals. The most common one, the bao, or stick dance, in the past used to celebrate the launching of war canoes, the birth of a first-born child, or the successful end of a fishing or head-hunting trip.

CULTURE
Local Customs
Inheritance is matrilineal in Isabel Province, with ownership of land passed on through the mother. This developed in head-hunting days. Though men could be killed, women's lives usually were spared. So, to ensure custom ownership survived, matrilineality became the rule.

Legendary People
Many local people insist there used to be a pygmy tribe in the province's mountains called the Mongoes. Described as too stupid to survive, they used to steal even when offered gifts freely. Akin more to fairies or leprechauns than humans, they are said to have died out in WW II.

INFORMATION
Medical Services
Buala, the provincial capital, has a 30-bed hospital. There are also 10 clinics spread around the province at Nodana, Bibili, Tatamba, Vulavu, Kolotubi, Susubona, Samasodu, Allardyce, Kia and Bolotei. Malaria is widespread, especially in Santa Isabel's southern coastal villages.

ACCOMMODATION
People in this province are very hospitable, with many villages having a leaf house strangers can use, though you will need to supply your own food and cooking gear. On arrival in a village, always ask the chief where you can stay. Often accommodation will be free of charge.

Buala has two rest houses, while nine of the larger villages around the province have leaf-style visitors' houses. Those at Kaola on San Jorge, and Kaevanga, Kolomola, Samasodu, Kia and Baolo on Santa Isabel are owned by the local COM parish, while the ones at Buma, Tausese and Poro belong to the village. Tatamba has no specific visitors' house, but local people say there's often space available there should you need it.

WATER
Water supplies are good, with 50% of the area's rural population receiving fresh, drinkable water.

GETTING THERE & AWAY
Air The province's only airfield is at Fera. Solomon Airlines flies in twice a week for S$92 each way. Honiara is Isabel Province's only regular air connection.

Boat
Services between Isabel Province and the national capital are provided by the Isabel Development Corporation (☎ 23337), with offices at the top of Honiara's Lena Cinema. Their largest vessels, the *Ligomo IV* and *Ligomo V*, together provide a weekly service between Honiara and Buala, charging S$23 each way. On alternate weeks these voyages continue on to Kia, visiting all ports around the province and costing S$16 from Buala and S$28 from Honiara.

The *Solomon Princess II*, owned by the Solomon Island Navigation Services (☎ 22404) in Honiara's NPF Plaza, has a twice-monthly service to Buala. The Marine Division also services the province, charging S$29 to Buala and S$41 to Kia.

Yacht There are wharves at Buala, Tatamba, Kaevanga, Allardyce and Kia. Santa Isabel also has 13 anchorages: at Cockatoo Island, Thousand Ships Bay, Susubona, Gajuhongari Bay, Furona, Finuana Island, Samasodu, Loguhutu Bay, Palunuhukuru Harbour, Kokopana Island, Suavanao and Kokodoghi and Estrella bays. In addition, there are anchorages at Astrolabe and Albatross bays on San Jorge.

Two channels in the province require particular care. The Ortega Channel is usually navigable to a minimum depth of 2.4 metres. The North West Channel between the mainland and Barora Ite Island is exceptionally narrow – in places only 7.5 metres wide – and can be extremely turbulent due to frequent tidal races accompanying routine changes of tide. There are also concealed rocks and overhanging branches to contend with, making any passage through the channel hazardous for yachts and canoes.

GETTING AROUND

Transport around the province, except for that in the Buala area, is easiest by motor canoe or ship. However, Isabel's coasts are very exposed to rough weather, especially its south-eastern and western coasts.

When people in Isabel Province talk of roads, they mean anything from single-lane cart or logging tracks down to what are no more than very obscure, windy and slippery footpaths barely half a metre wide. Always ask how broad local roads are before setting out.

To/From the Airport

Fera Airfield is three km from Buala, on Fera Island. The Solomon Airlines agent's canoe crosses the Maringe Lagoon for S$5 each way and takes 10 minutes.

Boat

The Isabel Provincial Assembly (☎ 35029) owns two small vessels, one of which – the MV *Walande* – has one cabin. These travel around the province weekly from Buala, calling at many small villages along the way.

Canoe Local seas are often extremely rough, and motor-canoe journeys are usually wet and expensive. A trip between Buala and Kia takes a full day, consuming between 13 and 15 gallons (about 59 to 68 litres) worth of fuel each way. So a charter there can cost you up to S$400.

Tractor

There are 22 km of genuine tractor routes in the province, 17 km of which connect Kaevanga to Kolomola. In addition to those around Buala, there's a short track between Kamaosi and the sea at Kasera, another between Buma and Visena, and some mostly overgrown logging roads around Allardyce.

Walking

There is an arduous bush trail across the centre of south-eastern Santa Isabel connecting Hofi with Kolomola, where you can often catch a tractor down to Kaevanga. The route is across dense, scrub-covered valleys and steep mountain ridges, and can only be done with guides.

An easier, but still strenuous and often indistinct, route is from Buala along the coast to Putukora, and then on to Tatamba. It begins behind the COM church at Jejevo and is immediately slippery, windy and obscure. It's like this all the way, except when it follows the shore or reaches the tractor route between Buma and Nodana. You'll need guides for this route too. Frankly, ships or canoes are much easier.

Santa Isabel Island

Formerly known as Ysabel, Santa Ysabel, or Bugotu or Mbughotu (the names of a local language), this large, mainly volcanic landmass consists of steep and sheer-sided mountain ranges dissected by narrow river valleys. Mangrove and freshwater swamps are common in the lowlands.

There are several long-established inland villages in south-eastern Santa Isabel. Some are on ridges as high as 500 metres, built there for defence during the violent headhunting days of the mid-19th century.

About 75% of Santa Isabel's people live on 20% of its land in the south-east, leaving most of the central and northern parts of the island uninhabited. Consequently, the average population density is slightly less than 5.2 per sq km.

Fishing is exceptional off Santa Isabel's north-western tip. Fish race each other to take any unbaited, unlured line being trolled behind a yacht or motor canoe.

BUALA

About 2300 people live in Buala (pronounced 'Bwar-luh'). This very quiet little town is spread along 2.2 km of the attractive 10-km-long Maringe Lagoon, between the leaf-style village of Sapitol and the more modern settlement of Jejevo. Buala also includes the original Buala Village, the government centre at Buala Station, and the rather oddly named Jejevo Backway.

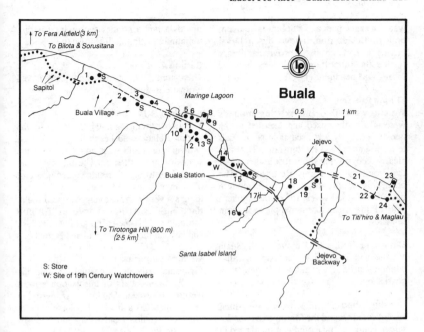

1   Hall
2   COM Church, Buala Village
3   Seaslug Shed
4   Community Centre
5   Police Station
6   Provincial Government Workshop
7   Fuel Store
8   Wharf
9   Canoe Park
10 Hospital
11 Post Office & NBSI Agency
12 Provincial Government Offices
13 Solomon Telekom
14 Provincial Assembly Rest House
15 Solomon Airlines Agency
16 Power House
17 Small Cascades
18 Swamp
19 DBSI
20 Mothers' Union Rest House
21 Sports Ground
22 Library & School
23 Church of Melanesia Jetty
24 Church of Melanesia HQ & Jejevo
    COM Church

Buala Station begins at the bridge over to Buala Village and extends eastwards to another bridge, this time beside some small cascades. Beyond is Jejevo.

Buala hugs a narrow littoral strip between the Maringe Lagoon and Tirotonga Hill's very steep sides. Forests and coconut plantations cling precariously to the rugged escarpment, which climbs to 800 metres over only 2.5 km.

Information & Orientation

Within the Buala Station area are the provincial government offices and workshop, the hospital, the police station, the post office, NBSI and Solomon Airlines agencies, a wharf, a canoe park and a Solomon Telekom branch. In addition, Jejevo has a DBSI branch, a sports ground, a provincial library (inside the school), another jetty and the local COM headquarters.

Things to See

Watchtowers Two pre-existing mounds were artificially raised and fortified in the late 19th century and used as lookout posts to warn against head-hunting raids. The most clearly recognisable site is just to the east of the Provincial Assembly Rest House. The other, smaller one, now built over by modern houses, is just to its west and on the southern side of the road. Local people call them towers.

Churches Both COM churches in Buala Village and Jejevo have sections of altar panelling strikingly inlaid with fragments of pearl shell.

Seaslug Shed Seaslugs, or bêche-de-mer, are collected around the Maringe Lagoon for sale in Honiara, and stored in a small shed in Buala Village. You can often see the bêche-de-mer drying outside in the sun.

Places to Stay

Best is the friendly *Mothers' Union Rest House* in Jejevo, at S$15 a night. It has six double rooms and communal washing and cooking facilities. Also available in Buala Station is the *Provincial Assembly Rest House*. This has fan-cooled double rooms for S$15 a head, including use of kitchen and showers.

Places to Eat

There are six stores in the Buala area. The one opposite the seaslug shed in Buala Village sells fish and kumara chips at lunchtime on weekdays.

Entertainment

Friday night is Buala Night, which alternates between the community centre in Buala Village and the smaller hall about 400 metres further west. The action begins around sundown, and continues on to at least 10 pm, sometimes lasting until sunrise the next day.

Getting Around

There are 2.5 km of roads and neatly paved footpaths in Buala.

AROUND BUALA

The two province-owned tractors use the lagoon's black-sand beach to get to Bilota, two km to the north-west, and Sorusitana, the same distance further on. The only easy way beyond, or to the shoreside settlements east of Jejevo, is by motor canoe. Otherwise, there's a very narrow overgrown and indistinct bush trail from Jejevo to Titi'hiro (pronounced 'Ti-tee-ro') one km to the east, and beyond there to Maglau and Nareabu.

Maringe Lagoon

Five small islands face Buala, giving the usually calm waters of this lagoon a most picturesque aspect. The largest is low-lying Fera, which has a small wild-horse population, and golden sand along much of its northern rim.

Fera is connected by a nine-km-long fringing reef to Vaghena, the attractive island nearby, and to Juakau Island. There's more good underwater viewing between Juakau Island and Nareabu. Vaghena Island has four short stretches of golden sand on its western side, while Juakau has brown beaches on both sides of its north-western tip.

Tirotonga

This village is about two km south-east of Buala and about 600 metres up on Tirotonga Hill, from where there are panoramic views over the whole Maringe Lagoon. You can reach it via Titi'hiro.

Mt Sasari & Mt Kubonitu

Four km inland from Buala is the province's highest mountain, Mt Sasari (1120 metres), with Mt Kubonitu (1065 metres) four km further south. You can see Malaita and the Nggela Islands from both. There are paths up both mountains which guides from Buala Village will know.

Tafala

There are several abandoned villages south of Buala, some only a few km from the sea, others deep in the bush. High in the mountains beside Mt Kubonitu is one called Tafala, where there are some tabu stones. Although it's only seven km south-west of the town, it's 11 km on foot. You will need a guide.

AROUND SANTA ISABEL ISLAND

Poro

There's a long, sandy beach at Poro, with surf sometimes up to two metres high.

Tatamba

This village is a subprovincial headquarters. Nearby is Tanabuli Island, a WW II coast-watcher site, and Lighara, which has a white-sand beach.

Lokiha

The Lumasa Seseo Cave at Lokiha is about one km north-west of Mboko Point. It was used as a women's seclusion place during childbirth and has a face carved beside its entrance.

Sigana

Most of Sigana's houses are on small, sandy Sigana Island. It's half a km from the mainland, where the remainder of the village is. Seven km to the south-east is Vikenara Point – a place of very rough seas.

Mahighe Island

This island, which is covered in coconut palms, has a white-sand beach on its western shore. Although Mahighe is unpopulated, nearby Pilo Island has a small settlement.

Sepi

Both Bera and Soga are buried at Sepi. Bera's grave is a pile of stones, while Soga's is a Christian one. Nearby are several skull houses, tall artificial mounds used as lookouts in head-hunting days, and Sepi's sandy shore.

Vikenara Island

The sunken Japanese destroyer *Asagiri* lies in deep water two km due south of Vikenara Island, which also has sandy beaches.

Tinoa

One km inland is a skull repository and a well-preserved 19th-century *toa*, or fortress, built of limestone rock.

Mboula Point

The remains of Bera's main fortress are only a short distance inland from Mboula Point. Its limestone walls had gun emplacements on them in head-hunting days.

Cockatoo Island

Bishop Patteson used to camp on the island's sandy beach in the 1860s. Patteson often had a pet cockatoo perched on his shoulder, hence the island's name.

Thousand Ships Bay

This sheltered waterway was a popular anchorage for 19th-century traders. It was also used by the Japanese fleet in 1942 to form up prior to its assault on Tulagi. There are several attractive coral gardens on its south-eastern side.

Kaevanga

As this is one of Santa Isabel's more fertile and populated areas, Kaevanga has stores and a market. A track runs up into the hills to Kolomola past an orange plantation at Kolotubi where you can buy oranges direct from the villagers.

Beyond Kaevanga the coast is at first rocky, then mangrove-lined beyond Mufhu Point. Inland the landscape is high and ridged. Occasional small, sandy islets lie between one and two km offshore.

People of Santa Isabel's central area suffered most from head-hunting. Although raids ceased over 80 years ago, the only major settlements between Kaevanga and Allardyce are those at Susubona and Samasodu. This lack of inhabitants extends across the island to the northern coast.

Furona

This small village occupies the whole of tiny

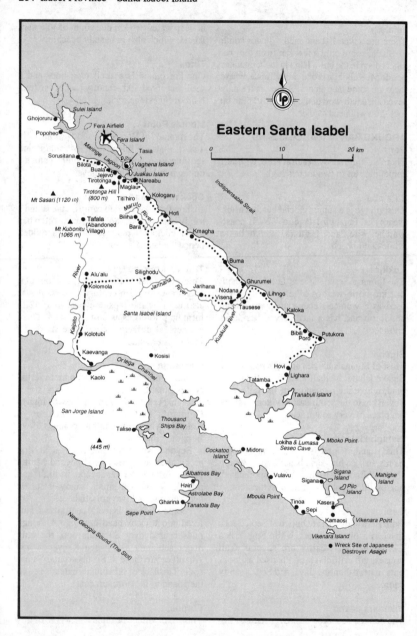

Furona Island, one km from the mainland. About 12 km to their north-west is the shark-shaped and coral-surrounded Finuana Island.

Allardyce

This was the nation's principal logging centre until Cyclone Ida in 1972 destroyed the area's best timber.

Kia

With over 1500 people, Kia is the province's second-largest settlement. It was built in head-hunting days to command all three channels approaching it. These are the Bahana Passage, North West Channel and Ghehughaha Passage.

Many of Kia's houses are built on stilts over the water, while standing imposingly over them is an enormous, iron-clad COM church. There's good swimming off the nearby coral islets.

The oral traditions and language of Kia's people are similar to those practised in New Georgia's Roviana Lagoon. In the past, there was a trade network with Choiseul and other western areas. Because of these links, they were treated as westerners (people of Western Province), which usually protected them from the wrath of the head-hunters. Even now, canoe transport is sometimes available to southern Choiseul.

There's a small crocodile farm in Kia, and there are plenty of trocchus shells and bêche-de-mer in the area.

Suavanao

Although islanders salvaged most of what the Japanese left behind when they hurriedly withdrew in late 1943, there are still several downed US aircraft hidden deep in the bush.

Local people regularly visit Papatura Faa, Papatura Ite and Omona islands to tend their coconut trees, while scuba fans find plenty of fish and colourful coral on the reefs around these low-lying offshore islands.

Cape Megapode

The north-eastern coastline is irregular, with many swampy bays and a few sandy beaches separated by rugged promontories and sheer cliffs. Close to one of these marshy inlets is Cape Megapode, named after the many incubator birds nesting there.

Although Mendaña reported that this area was heavily populated, 19th-century head-hunting has left it with only six settlements north-west of the Maringe Lagoon.

San Jorge Island

The province's second-largest island, named Ysla de Jorge by Mendaña's Spaniards, was subsequently also called St George. Its inhabitants knew it as Moumolu-Naunitu.

Despite its 200 sq km, San Jorge has only 500 people. The largest of its four villages is Kaolo, the subprovincial headquarters.

San Jorge has attractive coral growth and golden, sandy beaches at its eastern end, particularly in both Astrolabe and Tanatola bays. A few hundred metres to the west of Sepe Point in the adjacent inlet is a wrecked Japanese barge. Small amounts of ammunition litter the nearby beach.

Much of north-eastern San Jorge is extremely swampy, with several shallow marshes inhabited by saltwater crocodiles. In the island's centre is a 445-metre high point from where you can see the Nggela and Russells groups.

A local delicacy on San Jorge is mud-shells. They're found in the mangroves and taste like scallops.

The island is popularly considered to be a place where the spirits of dead Santa Isabel people reside. Consequently, you should ask permission wherever you go on San Jorge.

The Western & Arnarvon Islands

With more than 100 islands of varying sizes, the Western Islands, along with the tiny Arnarvon Islands, cover 432 sq km. None of them are permanently inhabited, and although some have hills and ridges, many scarcely protrude above sea level. Though some of these islands are swampy and unused, most have extensive reefs and sandbars. Fishing is unsurpassed, and turtles breed throughout the area, especially in the Arnarvons.

Gardens and coconut trees line the extremely narrow North West Channel which separates Barora Ite Island from the Santa Isabel mainland. Kia families canoe across the channel to tend their crops here.

There are very attractive lagoons throughout the Western Islands, notably Austria Sound and Rob Roy Channel. In addition, Gill Island near Kia has a particularly fine, white-sand beach, while Malakobi Island further to the north has another beautiful one. Suki Island is excellent for scuba diving, with colourful coral gardens, turtles and sharks.

Ramos Island

In 1568, Mendaña gave the name Ramos to Malaita Island. In 1824, however, the Russian hydrographer Krustenstern misread his charts and instead bestowed the name on tiny present-day Ramos.

This slender 1.5-km-long island is accompanied by a smaller companion islet, plus nine low rocks which jut vertically from the sea. Together their area is less than one sq km. Ramos is 39 km due east of Poro, and locally called Onegou Island. There's no population – only the spirits of the dead. It is generally held to be a prime fishing spot, and people say that the ghosts come from other nearby islands to make it their final resting place.

Malaita Province

Of the province's 93,000 people, all but 2000 are Melanesian. The remainder are Polynesian and live on the two isolated atolls of Ontong Java and Sikaiana.

Malaita Island, which is shaped like a begging dog, and its immediate neighbour, Maramasike, occupy about 98% of the 4243 sq km province. Together they are 191 km long and 47 km wide.

While the Polynesian islands have been noted for welcoming sailors, for a long time both Malaita and Maramasike islands were feared by Europeans. Even so, they provided many labourers for the 19th-century sugar-cane plantations in Fiji and Australia.

Transport is limited, making enjoyment of the province's varied attractions difficult and time consuming. Most notable of these are the artificial islands, the vigorously surviving traditional customs – especially shell money and shark worship – and Polynesian atoll life on Ontong Java and Sikaiana.

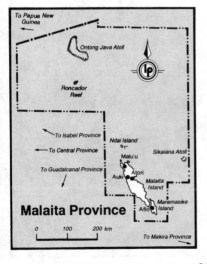

Malaita Province

To Papua New Guinea
Ontong Java Atoll
Roncador Reef
To Isabel Province
To Central Province
Ndai Island
Malu'u
Sikaiana Atoll
To Guadalcanal Province
Auki
Atori
Malaita Island
Maramasike Island
Afio
To Makira Province

0   100   200 km

Malaita Island

Malaita Island's interior is elongated, with narrow coastal plains often merging into small swamps. The inland highlands, eroded by deep valleys and sharp ridges, rise to a 1303-metre peak at Mt Kolovrat.

The island's many fast-flowing rivers act as natural barriers to cross-island movement. The geographical divisions that contributed to the constant intertribal fighting of the past have since ensured the survival of many different dialects and languages.

Malaita is pronounced 'Mal-eye-ta' by northerners and 'Mal-a-ta' by southerners. Over the years, the island has had several other names. Mendaña saw it on Palm Sunday, so called it Ramos, meaning 'palm fronds' in Spanish. In 1767, Cartaret named the island after himself, while at other times it's been called Maiden Land, Maleita, Malayette and Malanta. Malaitans often call it Mala, which is really the name for the island's northern part only.

Malaita Island has a large inland population of about 15,000 people. Many Malaitans from the central and south-eastern parts of the island still worship ancestral spirits and live almost entirely by shifting agriculture and barter.

The artificial islands in the Langa Langa and Lau lagoons are a distinctive feature of Malaitan life. These have been built in the shallows with coral boulders taken from the nearby reef. Some of the inhabitants of these islands worship sharks.

History
The Kwaio (pronounced 'Kwoy-oh' or 'Koy-oh') people, from Malaita Island's east-central mountains, cite genealogies going back 150 generations to about 1400 BC, although there is as yet no scientific

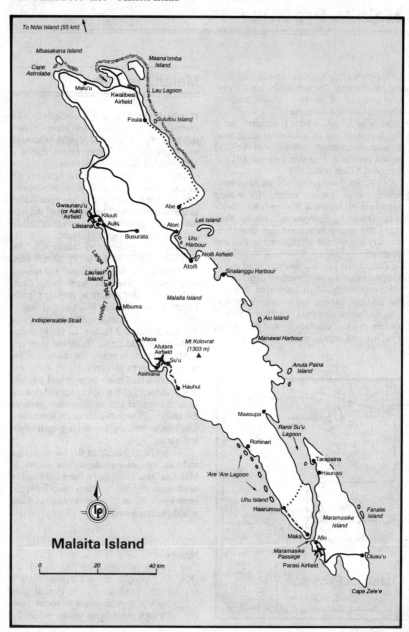

To Ndai Island (55 km)

Mbasakana Island

Cape Astrolabe

Malu'u

Maana'omba Island

Kwalibesi Airfield

Lau Lagoon

Fouia

Sulufou Island

Abe

Leli Island

Gwaunaru'u (or Auki) Airfield

Kilu'ufi

Auki

Lilisiana

Atori

Busurata

Uru Harbour

Atoifi Airfield

Langa Langa Lagoon

Laulasi Island

Atoifi

Sinalanggu Harbour

Malaita Island

Indispensable Strait

Mbuma

Aio Island

Maoa

Manawai Harbour

Afutara Airfield

Su'u

Mt Kolovrat (1303 m)

Anuta Paina Island

Asimana

Hauhui

Maasupa

Raroi Su'u Lagoon

Rohinari

Tarapaina

'Are 'Are Lagoon

Haunasi

Uhu Island

Fanalei Island

Haarumou

Maramasike Island

Maka

Afio

Olusu'u

Maramasike Passage

Parasi Airfield

Cape Zele'e

Malaita Island

0   20   40 km

evidence to support these claims. The oldest archaeological remains found so far come from certain Kwara'ae villages and date back to 440 AD.

Mendaña's expedition in 1568 saw Malaita Island, but did not venture ashore, while Cartaret, who saw it 199 years later, only called in at tiny Ndai Island.

In the early 19th century, a foreigner could count his life expectancy in minutes rather than years if separated from his ship in Malaita Island waters. Life was also dangerous for islanders themselves. Villages were fortified against the head-hunting raids that occurred regularly, both locally and against Santa Isabel.

Despite this warlike reputation, by the 1870s Malaita Island had become a favourite recruiting place for blackbirders. Malaita's population was larger than that of other islands and there were many landless men prepared to volunteer for overseas work.

Labourers were often kidnapped by blackbirders rather than recruited, and frequently islanders were killed. Soon Malaita Islanders learned to distrust all White people, regularly murdering them to avenge earlier atrocities committed by other Europeans. This was particularly so among the Kwaio – the fiercest and most traditional and independent of the islanders.

In 1880, the *Borealis* was looted and its crew killed by Kwaio. In 1882, a similar fate met the *Janet Stewart*, and in 1886, many of the crew of the *Young Dick* were also killed.

The British Protectorate government promised retaliation for such violence. In 1907, a punitive expedition was sent following the plundering of the *Minolta*.

In 1911, HMS *Torch* led another expedition following the murder of a South Seas Evangelical Mission (SSEM) priest – again by Kwaio tribespeople. Uruilangi was burnt down in retribution. This time the islanders were innocent, although they had been guilty of the 1886 incident. Tit-for-tat fighting continued with a Kwaio attack on the *Ruby* three days later.

Perhaps surprisingly, given their fighting spirit, many Malaita Islanders went voluntarily to north-eastern Australia to work on sugar-cane plantations there. Between 1871 and 1903, about 9000 Malaita and Maramasike islanders were recruited. Many had returned by 1906, bringing back with them tempting morsels of the White people's world, such as calico and Snyder rifles.

Malaita Islanders, while they were often said to be the South Pacific's best workers, were also the most volatile, often fighting among themselves or with people from other islands. In 1909, a district office was opened in Auki, a sign that government by punitive raid was over. Despite this, intertribal skirmishing persisted. When asked in 1920 by the League of Nations about Malaita and Maramasike islands, the British government admitted, 'There is incessant warfare'. No Malaita Island man ventured far without his bow and arrows, or rifle. Although men usually went naked, women wore grass skirts.

The Kwaio Rebellion On 4 October 1927, District Officer William Bell and his cadet, Lillies, were at Kwaiambe in Kwaio territory to collect tax. With them were 14 north-Malaita Island special constables. The two officials each sat at a table, waiting to receive the Kwaio bush people's head-taxes of five shillings a person (about S$1.27), and the surrender of their beloved Snyder rifles, the possession of which had recently been made illegal.

Some tribespeople paid, but Basiana – the local *ramo*, or contract assassin – tricked Bell and crashed his rifle down on to the official's skull, splitting it open. In the ensuing melee, Lillies and 13 of the 14 police were also killed.

The reaction in Tulagi, the Solomons' capital at the time, was excessive. A force was raised of European volunteers, later derisively called the Whisky, or Breathless, Army. Meanwhile, the Australian cruiser HMAS *Adelaide* sailed from Sydney.

Although the volunteers were useless, the government's 40 north-Malaita Island police proved totally relentless. Of the 200 Kwaio arrested, six were hanged the following year at Tulagi (including Basiana), while 30 died of dysentery or despair in jail. The authorities acknowledged 60 to 65 were killed by the local police, and about 100 more died of starvation in the bush after their gardens were destroyed. However, the Kwaio claim 1246 were killed, and 59 villages, 538 shrines and 1066 gardens destroyed.

The cruiser shelled all the villages it could find. The European volunteers, more concerned about their whisky than their duties, spitefully sprayed the Kwaio's taro gardens with weedkiller, destroying them almost permanently.

The north-Malaita Island police's main sport, other than hunting people, was to desecrate Kwaio shrines. Consecrated ritual objects, ancestral relics, slit drums and sacrificial stones were defiled or destroyed. This ruthless policy subdued the Kwaio but left a long legacy of ill feeling towards all aspects of government.

There were many reasons for the Kwaio Rebellion. The confiscation of rifles had removed the symbol of early 20th-century Malaita Island manhood. In addition, tribespeople objected to a head-tax which both cost them money and gave them a foreign rule they strongly resented. This head-tax often meant that relatives had to enlist on labour ships so other family members could pay the tax.

The Kwaio felt their ancestral gods would not provide good yam and taro crops if the new religion of Christianity was not firmly resisted. They also disliked the newly created village headmen. Appointed by the Protectorate authorities, these villagers were often accused of misusing power and of making false charges against innocent fellow Malaita Islanders.

Marching Rule By 1939, Malaita Islanders were understandably refusing to work on any plantations where expatriate managers and overseers used whips and dogs. However,

despite the careless bombing by US planes of two Malaita Island settlements, including Laulasi, in August 1942, many Malaita and Maramasike islanders went to Guadalcanal to work at the huge US base there. They found the US forces a complete contrast to their prewar colonial masters, and extremely generous. Furthermore, Black Americans wore the same clothing as Whites, ate the same food and used the same equipment.

When US troops of both races decried British colonialism, they found many eager Malaita and Maramasike islander ears. Although British officials had remained at their posts in northern Malaita Island throughout hostilities, and US forces repeatedly announced they were leaving, many Malaita and Maramasike islanders hoped the Americans would stay to rule the Solomons after the war.

By late 1945, a mass movement called Marching Rule, or *Maasina Rulu*, or *Ruru* (an 'Are'Are expression for Brotherhood Rule), had emerged to unite Malaita and Maramasike islanders. The movement's aim was for Malaitans to manage their island themselves – independently of the churches and the colonial authorities – to receive better pay and work conditions on plantations, and to earn a better return on any taxes they paid.

Malaita and Maramasike islanders resented the way island customs were treated lightly by the government. For example, adultery was punishable by death in traditional Melanesia, but to the British it was a matter of little concern.

So the Marching Rule Movement set up its own courts. These dealt with breaches of customary law and the failure to observe the movement's rules or pay its taxes. Offenders were fined by Marching Rule courts or imprisoned in their own jails. However, serious matters such as murder, rape and assault were handed over to the colonial authorities.

Whole villages moved to the coast. New ones were built like US army camps, complete with three-metre-high stockades and tall watchtowers with sentries to guard the gates at all times. Meeting halls were built and Marching Rule flags displayed.

While some aspects were nationalistic and anti-British, other elements of Marching Rule were cargo-cultist. Huts were erected to house the many gifts expected from the USA. Lookouts were posted daily to spot the ships believed to be bringing this hoped-for bounty, while rumours abounded of mysterious US planes landing in the interior.

For over two years the British warily cooperated with Marching Rule. However, by mid-1947, government on Malaita and Maramasike islands was at a standstill, and action was needed to halt the persecution of those islanders who refused to join the movement.

Mass arrests began, and in 1949 as many as 2000 people were detained for refusing to demolish their stockades. By 1950 relationships with the government had improved, though some die-hard elements resisted until 1955. Not surprisingly, this episode left many Malaita and Maramasike islanders with a deep distrust of Britain.

Since Independence, fears have been expressed (mainly in the western Solomons) of possible Malaita and Maramasike islander domination. Although among the last to benefit from the spread of schools and churches during the colonial period, Malaita and Maramasike islanders, who make up 27% of the country's population, now occupy top positions in all walks of national life.

Climate

Auki has 236 rain days a year, with an average total annual rainfall of 3271 mm (129 inches). The wettest period is from January to March, averaging over 350 mm a month. May and June are the driest months, each receiving less than 200 mm of rain. Morning humidity reaches 90 or 91% six

---

Artificial Islands

A distinctive feature of Malaita Island is the large number of artificial islands, particularly in the Langa Langa and Lau lagoons. These have been built on sandbars or exposed reefs by heaping boulders up until a permanent landmass remains.

Some of the larger artificial islands are surrounded by a coral wall, giving the appearance of a coastal fortress. However, the majority are very small and consist of nothing more formidable than a number of houses on stilts.

Although new human-made islands are being built even now, a few go back many generations to the 1550s. Some islands are more than one sq km in size, though most are much smaller – some only large enough for one or two dwellings.

At first sight the houses may look flimsy, but in fact they are usually sturdily built of bamboo, palm and pandanus leaves. Although the cookhouses are usually on the ground, the sleeping area is raised on stilts to permit air to circulate underneath, and to provide room for tidal surges during cyclones.

Should a young married couple decide to build an island, they will make it initially big enough for one or two houses and then add to it as the family expands. They first scour large, smooth stones from the floor of the lagoon, ferrying them by canoe to the proposed site. Once the mound of rocks has risen to a height of between two and three metres above sea level, the island builders fill in the holes between the stones with sand. Only then are houses built and coconuts palms planted.

Although one small island was built in six months by a husband and wife, the majority take over a year and require regular help from friends and relatives. While a few palm trees may eventually take root, most food comes from mainland gardens, or through fishing. The islands' only supply of fresh water is rain; all other drinking needs have to be met by carrying water over from the mainland.

The islands were originally built as an escape from the endemic warfare plaguing Malaita Island, especially in the 19th century. As all land was already owned, there was none for an expanding population. So island builders maintained gardens onshore by agreement with mainlanders, tending their crops by day and returning home at dusk. Also, by constructing an island only a short distance from shore, a cool, mosquito-free environment could be secured. Finally, some were fisherfolk – such as those from Lau Lagoon – who exchanged their catch with mainlanders for crops. ■

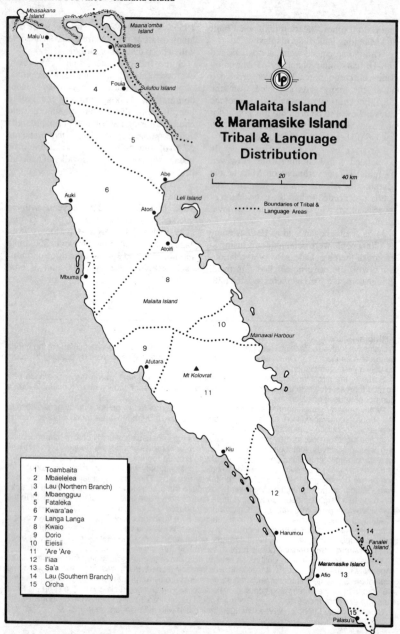

Malaita Island
& Maramasike Island
Tribal & Language
Distribution

0   20   40 km

•••••• Boundaries of Tribal &
         Language Areas

1   Toambaita
2   Mbaelelea
3   Lau (Northern Branch)
4   Mbaengguu
5   Fataleka
6   Kwara'ae
7   Langa Langa
8   Kwaio
9   Dorio
10 Eieisii
11 'Are 'Are
12 I'iaa
13 Sa'a
14 Lau (Southern Branch)
15 Oroha

months a year, while afternoons average 77%. Temperatures range between 23°C and 30°C.

Fauna

Islanders say there are both freshwater and saltwater crocodiles in Malaita and Maramasike islands. The small freshwater species is in some of Malaita Island's northern rivers, while the larger, seawater variant lives in the south's muddy, mangrove-lined estuaries, including the 'Are'Are and Raroi Su'u lagoons and Maramasike Passage.

People

There are 15 tribal language and dialect groups, of which the 21,500 Kwara'ae from north-central Malaita Island are the largest. In addition, there are 12,500 'Are'Are speakers in southern Malaita. Another large tribe is the 11,000-strong ancestor-worshipping Kwaio, who live in the mountains along the east-central coast.

Around 12,000 Lau·people live in artificial islands off north-eastern Malaita Island and along Maramasike's south-eastern seaboard 145 km to the south. Another 10 smaller language groups make up the remainder of the island's population.

Sometimes called the Yorkshiremen of the South Pacific, Malaita and Maramasike islanders are often disliked by people from other islands, who treat them with careful reserve. Malaita and Maramasike islanders cling more tenaciously to their customs than other Solomon Islanders and are said to be dour, withdrawn and aggressive, quick to anger and unlikely to forget an injury. On the other hand, once a Malaita Islander or Maramasike Islander becomes your friend, the friendship usually lasts.

Many of the nation's political leaders are Malaita Islanders, and as a people they are go-getters. The island's young have often deserted the province's restrictive economy, where only copra and cocoa produce any income. Consequently, Malaita and Maramasike islanders now live and work in all parts of the country, where their presence as migrants and workers occasionally inspires resentment.

Arts

Tattoos Although some older Malaita Island men have tattoos by their eye creases, younger men nowadays prefer facial engravings on their cheeks. These are small circular lines or crisscross designs drawn on the face, arms or back – but without colouring. Facial engraving is done with a bone or wooden instrument to mark out the pattern and to cut away the flesh. The operation is repeated several times over a period of days. Coconut water and lime juice is applied to prevent bleeding and to aid the formation of scars.

Shell Money The island's traditional currency, shell money, is used only for bride price, payment of certain ceremonial debts, compensation for insults and injuries, the purchase of land, pigs or canoes, and as personal adornment when worn around the neck at ceremonies.

Shell money is made of small pierced discs, usually taken from the shell of the pink-lipped spondylus, or spiny rock oyster. It can also be made from mussels, pearl shell, the chambered nautilus, or from the lips of a conch – but these have less value. Pink, red, orange and brown are the favoured colours, followed by white and black.

A large piece of shell is smashed up into tiny rounded fragments, each of which has a hole pierced in it. Next, the white pieces of shell are heated on stones to produce orange and brown hues. After this, the pieces are all strung with a length of fibre from the stalk of a bush, or nowadays nylon twine.

In the past, the shell pieces were polished by vigorous rubbing on a grinding stone well lubricated with water and black sand. Nowadays, soapy water is usually preferred. Pink shell money is the most valuable – and worth twice the also highly prized red shell money.

A typical complete length, or string, is called a *tafuliae* and contains many hundreds of discs within its 10 legs, or strands. These are one fathom long (almost two metres), and each is divided by turtle-shell plates. These tafuliaes are worth up to S$300. If need be, lengths may be broken off into shorter amounts to buy smaller items. At one time in northern Malaita Island, the cost of a bride was 50 strings of shell money, whereas in some southern parts of the island only one spear was required to buy a wife.

Although in isolated bush villages people may still pay 30 to 40 fathoms of shell money for bride price, church influences have brought some realism along the coast. Mission villages have set a maximum price of five strings of shell money for each bride (worth S$1500). In the past, however, a young man often put himself and his family into lifelong debt simply to buy a wife. Nowadays, all a young Malaitan has to do is to work in Honiara for a year or two to save the required cash.

Other Traditional Currencies Malaita Islanders also make shell currency armbands, forehead discs, necklaces, pendants and earrings. Some types of shell jewellery, particularly headbands, have porpoises' or dolphins' teeth in them, while flying-foxes' teeth are also used in some parts as bride price.

Noncurrency Items Small bride dolls are made of blackened kerosene wood, reflecting the importance of marriage in Malaita and Maramasike islands' traditions. War clubs recall the island's violent past.

Loya cane and bukaware baskets are decorated with black and brown designs, and red and yellow-painted combs are completed with spokes made of palm wood. Caneware is very strongly woven and includes trays, coasters and table mats. The baskets made by Kwara'ae women are used by them to carry washing or garden produce.

Small, simple figures, representing birds and people as well as traditional subjects, are carved and inlaid with shell. In northern Malaita Island dance sticks are usually painted black, with hornbill designs on top.

Model 25-cm-long bonito canoes are carved, while forehead discs are fashioned out of clam and turtle shell. Locally produced oyster-shell pendants often carry a frigate-bird motif, while some ear decorations are made of flying-foxes' teeth.

Musical Instruments Panpipes of bamboo, played in groups of four, eight, 10 and even 16 or more tubes, are common on the island. The pipes are often arranged in double rows.

Slit drums are made from hollowed-out logs, with a narrow gash cut in the centre of each one. Laid on their side, they are beaten with sticks to emit a deep, resounding boom. Although not as ornate as those in Vanuatu, they are widespread in south-western Malaita and Maramasike islands.

Rattles made from hollow nuts are attached to dance sticks and to the legs or wrists of dancers in many parts of the island. Conch shells are often used to summon people or to send messages, and at times are used for musical accompaniment.

Culture
Malaita's varied cultural life has fascinated anthropologists since W G Ivens wrote about the Lau Lagoon in *Island Builders of the South Pacific* in 1930. Roger Keesing spent much of the 1970s in east-central Malaita, studying the life of a Kwaio chieftain. (He also combined with Peter Corris to write *Lightning Meets the West Wind*, about the 1927 Kwaio uprising.)

Local Customs Descent is patrilineal in Malaita and Maramasike islands, unlike in the western Solomons. In the bush, married men and women still sleep separately in houses confined to one sex only, and in many parts of Malaita and Maramasike islands custom rules over adolescent love affairs.

In the more traditional areas, it is forbidden for a man to make love to an unmarried girl. Such an activity could cause the girl's father first to sue for damages and, if these were not forthcoming, to seek revenge. Shell money and pigs would be expected from the offender – or the equivalent in cash from a foreigner.

Ramos A ramo, or *lamo*, was a Malaitan

warrior-leader who operated as a paid assassin. Such people still exist, but ritual contract killing no longer occurs. To be a ramo, a man had to kill at least one other person and then intimidate or terrorise all who objected to his action. A Malaitan who wanted revenge would pay for a ramo with pigs and shell money. Alternatively, the target might himself bribe the ramo to kill one of his enemy's relatives instead.

Shark Worship Sharks were often worshipped, and some Malaita Islanders still believe human spirits reside in them. A shark-man could summon one, sending it to sink an enemy's canoe. The shark would either kill the person there and then, or bring the victim back to be ritually killed later.

Dolphin Drives These are elaborate affairs, with villagers clashing stones together underwater to create a resonating effect which attracts dolphins into shallow inlets. They are then slaughtered for their meat and teeth, which are used in some places as traditional currency.

Pigs Pigs were another form of traditional currency. Pig exchange ceremonies, in conjunction with shell money or dolphins' teeth, were plentiful in Malaita and Maramasike islands, and still are in the Kwaio area – although not as elaborate as in parts of Papua New Guinea and Vanuatu.

Information

Medical Services Malaita Island has three hospitals: government ones at Kiluufi (near Auki) and Malu'u, and an SDA one at Atoifi. The island's dentist is based at Kiluufi. On the western side of the island, there are medical clinics at Mbita'ama, Fauabu, Aimela, Obafau, Auki, Talakali, Mbuma, Maoa, Hauhui, Rohinari, Wairokai and Maka. Along the eastern side, there are medical clinics at Matakwalao, Kwailibesi (Kwalibesi), Fouia, Sulofoloa, Abe, Atori, Nafinua, Namola'elae, Sinalanggu Harbour, Olomburi and Maasupa.

Accommodation

Auki has two places offering adequate accommodation. There are church rest houses at Mbuma, Su'u, Rohinari, Malu'u and Takwa, and village rest houses in Adakoa and on Kwai and Ngongosila islands. Villagers in Sulufou and Mbasakana may also be able to find you somewhere to stay, and more lodgings are planned for Malu'u.

In addition, most large villages would probably have a visitors' house. Possibilities include Kwari'ekwa, Heo, Hauhui, Hapai, Kiu, Waimarau and Tawairoi on Malaita Island's south-western coast.

Water

Auki only has water pressure at three or four designated times a day, for about 1½ hours on each occasion. Often there's no water after mid-afternoon until early the next morning. Because of this irregularity of supply, it's wise to treat or boil all drinking water in Auki.

Getting There & Away

Air Solomon Airlines flies daily between Honiara and Auki, and once a week direct to Parasi. Air fares from Honiara to Auki are S$69, while those from the capital to Parasi are S$91.

Western Pacific Air Services has frequent flights into Auki, Afutara, Atoifi and Kwalibesi from Honiara. Its fares from the capital to Afutara and Auki are S$62 and S$63 respectively. The fare from Honiara to Atoifi is S$73, while the fare to Kwalibesi is S$81. The fare from Atoifi to Afutara or Kwalibesi is S$32. From Afutara to Kwalibesi it's S$59.

Boat The Marine Division has a regular service between Honiara and Malaita Island. The fare to Auki is S$21, while the fare to Malu'u or Maka is S$29. Fares from Auki to Malu'u and Maka are S$12 and S$21 respectively.

Coral Seas Ltd's vessel the *Iuminao* sails each weekend from Honiara to Auki and back. Fares for deck passengers are S$22, while 1st-class seats are S$36. The company's other ship, *Compass Rose II*, does a similar return service midweek.

The Solomon Islands Navigation Services' deck-class fares to Auki and Malu'u on its vessel *Solomon Princess II* are S$22 and S$34 respectively. Tavuilo Shipping in Honiara's M P Kwan Building has a weekly service to Auki with its MV *Faalia*. The deck-class fare is S$20, while its two cabins cost S$45 each.

Getting Around
To/From the Airport Gwaunaru'u Airfield is 10 km from Auki and an S$8 ride in the Solomon Airlines bus.

Boat If you need to travel around by ship or launch, the Malaita Province Shipping Office in Auki will have the details you require.

Yacht There are wharves at Auki and Fouia. Anchorages include Mbita'ama, Malu'u, Haleta (on Maana'omba Island), Kwalo'ai and Scotland islands, Sulofoloa, Atori, Uru and Sinalanggu harbours, Olomburi, Manawai Harbour, Ai'ura Island, Maasupa, Maka, Wairokai, Rohinari, Waisisi Harbour, Kiu, Mbuma and Laulasi. In addition, yachts often moor beside Aio and Anuta Paina islands' sandy beaches.

Truck There are about 326 km of roads on Malaita Island. These run north from Auki to Fouia, across the island to Atori and Atoifi, and southwards to Asimana. There's also a track from Su'u to Hauhui, and another between Haarumou and Maka. Trucks are scarce. The best times and places to get a ride in Auki are at the wharf or nearby market when a ship calls in, or at 1 to 2 pm on other weekdays. The return from the country to Auki usually requires an early start.

Malaita Island has the longest stretches of road in the Solomons, but they are almost completely unsealed. Road surfaces are regularly eroded, as many routes are prone to flash flooding – especially the road to Atori.

Truck fares from Auki are about S$6 to Asimana, S$7 to Atori, S$8 to Malu'u, S$9 to Atoifi and S$13 to Fouia. There are no car-rental or taxi services on the island, but it's possible to charter trucks at times – at considerable cost.

AUKI
The small township of Auki (pronounced 'Ow-ky'), has been Malaita Island's capital since 1909. Its two main streets are Loboi and Hibiscus Aves.

A town of about 4000 people, Auki has a small shopping centre, some provincial government buildings, churches and a boat-

1 Library	18 Auki Hot Bread Shop
2 Auki Bookshop (Main Branch)	19 Auki Bookshop (Town Branch)
3 SSEC Transit House	20 Shell Oil Depot
4 Fa'asitoro Lookout	21 Malaita Province Shipping Office & Provincial Government Workshop
5 Power House	22 ANZ Bank
6 Jail	23 Solomon Islands Consumers Supermarket
7 DBSI	24 Auki Mini Cinema
8 Primary School	25 Sports Ground
9 Police Station	26 Auki Rest House
10 Clinic	27 House on Stilts
11 Auki Lodge	28 Westpac/JT Enterprises
12 Solomon Airlines	29 Coral Seas Shipping Office
13 NBSI	30 Auki Market
14 Post Office	31 Wharf
15 Provincial Government Offices	
16 Court House	
17 Boatyard	

building yard within its borders, plus a hospital close by.

It's one of the most photogenic of the Solomons' main towns. Its most attractive features are the nearby leaf-house villages of Ambu and Lilisiana on either side of the inlet, and artificial Auki Island across the harbour mouth.

In the 1920s, the town had a perimeter fence. Any Europeans who ventured beyond it always took an armed escort. Elderly Malaitans, when asked how things have changed in their life, say it's good to be able to go to Auki without fear of ambush.

Information

Money Auki has three banks: the ANZ, the NBSI and Westpac. They're open from 8.30 am to noon and from 1 to 3 pm five days a week.

Medical Services Auki's hospital is at Kiluufi, 3.5 km north of town. There's also a clinic in Loboi Ave.

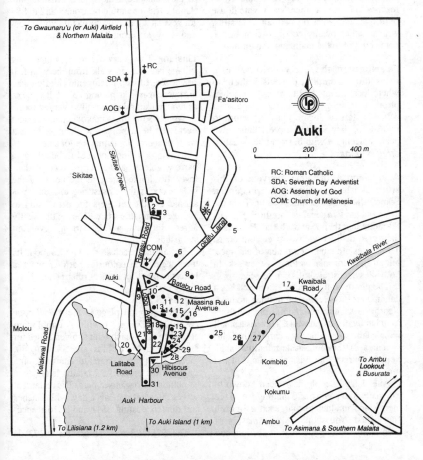

Things to See

Lookouts There are good views over Auki and its harbour from a high point at the southern edge of Fa'asitoro, about 200 metres behind the jail. Even better ones are along the steep hillside road to Busurata, just to the east of Ambu. These offer very fine views over Auki Harbour, Osi Lagoon and towards the Nggela Islands from gaps in the roadside shrubs. This is all the way from around 700 metres along the hillside road as far as its crest half a km further on.

Kombito Just before the Kwaibala River reaches the harbour, there's a private house built over the water on two concrete stilts, with a rather rickety coconut-palm bridge connecting it to the mainland at Kombito.

Fa'asitoro In the early colonial era, Fa'asitoro was the place just outside the town where local people had to dress themselves prior to entering Auki to see the district officer's staff or doctor. On their return to Fa'asitoro, they would strip off their town gear, replacing it with bush clothes – calico or grass skirts.

Auki Island At one time, everyone on this artificial island was a shark worshipper. Some still are. The island is one km from the town and has two separate families within its 80-metre length, one at each end. Both have their own distinct walled-off custom areas. These sites are tabu for women of any race, but all right for men as long as they ask. In both sites ancestral skulls can be seen.

The family at the north-western end has a dancing area where pig ceremonies are held. Nearby is a large ceremonial pig pen surrounded by dry-stone walls. There is a small female tabu spot, which is a childbirth seclusion area, on the south-eastern family's side. Female tourists may visit this site, but not men.

Auki Island people have been known to ask visitors to pay a S$50 landing fee to see their island and then to charge extra for each site visited. You should ask permission of each family before you visit its section, and also inquire about photos. The people may want to impose fines if you take unauthorised pictures of items such as ancestral skulls (or handle the skulls without the relevant family's leave). If the islanders do try to impose a fine, don't argue; just be very apologetic and, with luck, that will suffice.

There's a small islet just to the north of Auki Island. Extending southwards from them both is a five-km-long stretch of colourful coral growth.

Getting There & Away Plenty of canoes go to the island from the wharf, Lilisiana and Ambu. The fee should be around S$2 to S$4 for several small boys to paddle you across and show you around.

Lilisiana This very friendly, welcoming village is a 1.2-km walk from the wharf. It has dozens of very photogenic children who are ever eager to be photographed. It also has several houses raised on stilts over the shore.

Women sometimes make shell money and necklaces here, polishing them on special work benches. Some may be for sale.

Lilisiana's very peaceful beach is a narrow, golden sand spit beside coral shallows. It's immediately to the north of the village and is the closest one to Auki. You should ask the villagers for permission to swim or sunbathe there. They will usually agree, but have a rule barring revealing swimsuits.

Beside the beach is the Osi Lagoon. Its trees teem with colourful parrots, and sea birds are plentiful at its northern end.

Places to Stay

The most central place is the *Auki Lodge* (☎ 40131, PO Box 9), with six double fan-cooled rooms – each with shower. Rates for singles/doubles/trebles are S$50/70/80, inclusive of tax. Tours to Langa Langa Lagoon and northern Malaita Island can sometimes be organised here. The restaurant serves three basic meals a day, with lunches and dinners costing S$11 and S$16 respectively.

The *SSEC Transit House* (☎ 40173) is

very clean and popular with visitors. It has three rooms with a total of eight beds and charges S$20 a person. The kitchen is communal, and there are shared showers and toilets.

The *Auki Rest House*, which has two large dorms with over 10 beds in each for S$5 a night, is not recommended.

Before booking in anywhere, it's worth checking out which establishments have the most water-catchment tanks to supplement the town's inadequate supplies

Places to Eat
The daily *Auki Market* sells fresh fish – mainly bluefin tuna – fruit and vegetables. Its best time is early on Saturday mornings when the *Iuminao* arrives from Honiara. Tuna costs about a quarter of its Honiara price here.

The buns sold at the *Auki Hot Bread Shop* are the only hot food available in the town. There's also a local branch of the *Solomon Islands Consumers Supermarket*.

Entertainment
The Auki Mini Cinema in Hibiscus Ave has three showings daily between 9 am and 3 pm.

AROUND AUKI
All distances are from Auki wharf.

Dukwasi (5 km)
To the north-east of Auki is Dukwasi and the Riba Cave. The custom fee often starts around S$20, but you may be able to reduce this if you protest vigorously. You will need a guide.

The cave is very slippery and covered with the excreta of hundreds of swallows. There are stalagmites, a sink hole, several large subterranean chambers and, finally, an underground river. Come with a powerful torch (flashlight) and in old clothes.

Onebulu Beach (9 km)
The Auki area's best beach is a two-km-long strand terminating at its northern end where the Fiu River reaches the sea.

Gwaunaru'u Airfield (10 km)
A sandy beach fringes the airfield as far as the large village of Koa three km beyond, where there's a good reef for snorkelling.

SOUTH-WESTERN MALAITA ISLAND
All distances are from Auki wharf.

Langa Langa Lagoon
Extending from seven to 32 km south of Auki, this lagoon is famous for its artificial islands, particularly Laulasi and Alite.

Radefasu (7 km)
From the sea, Radefasu resembles a human-made island, as it's built out into the water on a coral platform. Shell money is made locally and most households have some to sell.

Laulasi Island (16 km & 2 km by canoe)
This artificial island was built in the early 1600s. Ancient traditions are zealously preserved by its people, who have an impressive show for tourists at their cultural centre.

Behind a wall and separated from the public area are three ancestral spirit houses where the skulls of ancestors and dead enemies are housed. Only males may enter this part. The female seclusion area is similarly reserved for women.

If you go to Laulasi with a tour group, you will have a brief canoe ride to the island from Talakali. Usually another canoe leaves the island at the same time with several women aboard who sing welcoming songs. As you land, warriors oppose your arrival with various traditional weapons. To bring peace, the chief offers the warriors several lengths of shell money, and begs them to spare the visitors' lives. You may come ashore once the warriors' leader has accepted payment. After some traditional dancing, shell money manufacture is demonstrated and necklaces are offered for sale.

Despite tourism, shell money is still Laulasi's main income. Much of Malaita Island's output is sold to Malaitans who have settled in other parts of the country, and also to people in the Nggela Islands, Guadalcanal and Santa Isabel, who use it as bride price.

Activities Tours of the island can be arranged by JT Enterprises (☎ 40197) of Hibiscus Ave, Auki, or Tour Solomons of Honiara. JT Enterprises will take you by motor canoe from Laulasi to see shell money being made, for S$130. There are extra charges if you want to see tabu places such as the shell repository.

Tour Solomons offers a full-day air and canoe round trip from Honiara for S$550 each for up to four people.

Getting There & Away To visit Laulasi independently means a S$2 truck ride to Talakali, an SDA village 16 km from Auki. As long as you avoid Saturdays, you should be able to arrange a return trip by dugout canoe for about S$4, or by motor canoe for up to S$18, depending on how long you're on the island. The Laulasi villagers will charge a S$30 landing fee to see their island, but don't expect any traditional dances.

Alite Island (20 km & 3 km by canoe)
There are in fact two Alite islands. Halfway along the larger, elongated, unpopulated and natural one's eastern shore, and about 300 metres away, is a much smaller, artificial island. This is where Alite's villagers live, and where there exist similar traditions of shell-money making and shark worship as those practised at Laulasi.

The larger island has a sandy beach on its western side. There's coral to view and sea-shells to collect. You can get a canoe there, or to the artificial island, from Arabala, an attractive village on the Malaita Island mainland which is built on stilts out over the water.

Sililiu Island (26 km & 2 km by canoe)
The island has sand beaches all around it. The closest place to find a canoe to get you there is two km away at Bina.

Mbuma (32 km)
The Roman Catholic mission has a *rest house* at Mbuma (pronounced 'Pooma'). However, you should first inquire at the Roman Catholic church in Auki to see if there'll be room for you at Mbuma.

Asimana (48.5 km)
The road stops at Asimana. You'll have to walk from here, and cross three creeks and two rivers to reach Su'u.

Su'u Harbour (56 km)
The two artificial islands in Su'u Harbour are

Shark Calling on Laulasi

The animists on Laulasi worship sharks as their totem. In dramatic ceremonies, several of which were held as recently as the 1970s, these human-eaters are actually fed by hand. The whole ritual has an incredible culmination when a small boy rides on the largest shark's back after villagers have beaten stones together rhythmically under the water to summon the creatures.

The village priest calls out the name of a particular shark, which then swims by the boy, who stands on a rock in about 30 cm of water and feeds it a piece of pork. The younger, smaller sharks are fed first. Finally, the oldest and largest shark receives the biggest piece from the boy, who then climbs on its back. It then swims around the lagoon with the boy on its back, returning to the submerged rock for him to disembark.

The Laulasi people explain this phenomenon by saying a shark ancestor in the past had promised not to attack the islanders as long as they fed it and its descendants pork. In return, people would be left unharmed and the sharks would ensure that a plentiful supply of tuna remained in the area.

Because of these traditions, clothing which is predominately red or black is absolutely tabu on Laulasi. Black is the colour of local pigs, the usual sacrifice to the sharks, while red could be mistaken for blood, and thereby arouse the sharks and ancestors believed to be residing in them. Consequently, you will not be allowed to wear these colours while visiting Laulasi. ■

probably Malaita Island's oldest ones. There's a *rest house* at the local SSEC mission, and an airfield at Afutara, two km to the north. The coastal road continues as a track to Hauhui.

To carry on further south is only possible by motor canoe or in a ship. These call in at the larger centres in the 'Are'Are Lagoon, and at Maka beside the entrance to the Maramasike Passage.

Kiu

Marching Rule began here in 1944. An old timber-hulled vessel is wrecked near the inlet's mouth, one km to the north-west of Kiu.

'Are'Are Lagoon

The lagoon begins 27 km south of Su'u, and is 29 km long by one km wide, stretching southwards from Rohinari to Uhu. A 15-km track connects Haarumou with Waimarau and Maka.

The lagoon's islands, which are covered with coconut palms, are long, slim and low, with continuous white beaches on their ocean sides (especially Uhu, Maroria and Komusupa islands). Mangroves fringe their inland lagoon side. On the mainland shore, the land rises from swamps to thickly forested highlands.

Western 'Are'Are people make single strands of shell money, each worth about S$40. Up to 100 of these are required for bride price, so a local man may need S$4Roman Catholic mission000 to marry.

Rohinari

The *Roman Catholic mission* has accommodation but a visit requires prior permission from the Roman Catholic authorities in Auki, or the priest-in-charge here.

Haarumou

Shell money is minted and carvers make panpipes at the Haarumou People's Centre. Local pipe bands will perform from dusk to dawn for S$20 for each musician. There's a footpath over the mountains from Haarumou to the Raroi Su'u Lagoon.

Waimarau

Waimarau has a custom house with carvings of men, women and fish where ancestral bones are stored. Women may not enter, but can peer in through the doorway.

NORTHERN MALAITA ISLAND

The northern road from Auki to the Lau Lagoon follows the coast from Sisifiu to Silolo, providing frequent sea views. Long stretches of white-sand beach line the shore. Distances are from Auki wharf.

Dala (24 km)

The Dala Agricultural Research Station does studies into cocoa and coconut farming, fungus control and hybrid propagation. Just call in at reception and ask to have a look around.

A junction inland, 1.5 km beyond Dala, connects Auki with Malaita's eastern coast.

Sisifiu (44 km)

There's a custom house here containing many ancient artefacts. Local carvers make reproductions for sale.

Mbita'ama (65 km)

A marine cave called Mana Ruuakwa at nearby Kwaiorua Point penetrates inland, terminating in a deep hole in the ground, with blue water clearly visible. Whenever the hole has been filled in, the sea has flushed it out.

Sharks come in here to sleep. Some local people feed pork to them, believing the sharks are gods.

Newly made shell money is often available for sale in Mbita'ama. There are also a few relics around from WW II.

Afufu (68 km)

This small fishing village is a centre of traditional dancing. The dances focus on everyday activities such as fishing and ngali-nut collecting. Another dance is about girls collecting seashells to decorate themselves for festivals.

The only major Allied action occurring in WW II on Malaita was the destruction of a

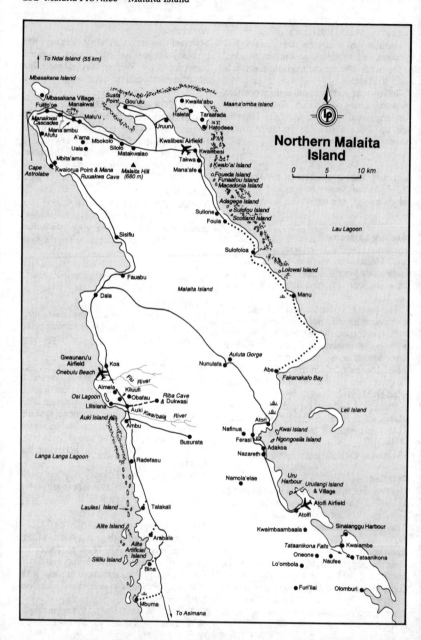

Japanese radio station here by US marines in November 1942. It was the sole Japanese outpost on the island.

Mbasakana Island (75 km)

This beautiful island (pronounced 'Mbatha-kana') is just over two km long by one km wide. Surrounded by a fringing reef and attractive white-sand beaches, this flat land-mass is about 1.5 km across the water from Fulifo'oe on Malaita's northern coast.

People from Mbasakana Village, where half the island's 250 inhabitants live, will point out an interesting cave if asked. Villag-ers here are very welcoming, and may be able to find you somewhere to stay, as long as it's only for one night. You can organise a motor-canoe ride to the island in Malu'u. Otherwise, a paddle-canoe ride from Fulifo'oe should be about S$3 for the round trip.

Manakwai (79 km)

There are some small cascades here and a river to swim in.

Mana'ambu (81 km)

Several young-men's tree houses (called *biu* and pronounced 'bee-you') are in use here. The usual occupants are two boys of 11 or 12 and two other males in their late teens or 20 years of age. Boys who have recently been initiated live in the houses because they are now considered to have matured beyond the need for maternal care.

Malu'u (82 km)

This small subprovincial headquarters, com-plete with hospital, is a good halfway stop between Auki and the Lau Lagoon. Although the beach is rather limited, there's some lively surf to ride, along with some good snorkelling off the reef. The town has some small stores, a market on Wednesday and Saturday mornings, and electricity and piped water supplies.

The Malu'u Roman Catholic church has a two-bedroom *rest house*, which you should contact the Roman Catholic church in Auki

for permission to use. There are plans for a new hotel, to be called Malu'u Lodge.

You can arrange dugout-canoe rides to the reef and to a wrecked Japanese plane, both for S$4. Truck rides to Sulufou cost about S$5.

A'ama (82 km & 4-km walk)

A trail to the hilltop behind Malu'u leads to A'ama, where there's another biu. You will need a guide.

Uala (82 km & 5-km walk)

The hike to Uala's skull house is through thick bush, takes three hours, and requires a guide.

Mbokolo (87 km)

A sandy beach extends to Silolo. The best part is at Mbokolo.

Matakwalao (92 km)

There are several traditional sites near Matakwalao and the 680-metre-high Malaita Hill behind it. You will need a guide, whom you can find at Malu'u on a market day, to explore the area.

Maana'omba Island
(106 km & 3 km by canoe)

This pleasantly flat island, with white-sand beaches on its western side, is only four by two km. Its 700 people live at either end of the island, many of them at Taraafada, Hatodeea or Kwaila'abu. The sea is only 1.5 metres deep for most of the three km sepa-rating Maana'omba from the mainland.

Gou'ulu (107 km)

Beaches stretch east from Suafa Point to Uruuru. There's good snorkelling all through this area, especially at Gou'ulu.

Lau Lagoon

The lagoon is about 35 km long and contains more than 60 human-made islands. It stretches from the shallows between Uruuru and Maana'omba, where there are several such artificial islands, down to Lolowai – the most southerly human-made landform. Over half have been built in the last 60 years. The ever-present fresh sea breezes make these offshore villages much more pleasant and cool than the often-humid mainland.

On some of the Lau islands, Christianity is practised in tandem with old beliefs and traditions. Some people are still animist or pagan, worshipping sharks as in the Langa Langa Lagoon, especially at Funaafou.

A few of the islands have rather unexpected names, such as Macedonia and Scotland. Members of the family that built the latter one had worked for a Scot in Western Province. His name was Scot, so they called it Scotland after him.

If you want to visit an artificial island, ask onshore whether it's all right to do so. Then, on arrival there, ask for the chief and repeat your request.

Takwa (108 km)

Several of the islands are within easy reach by canoe from Takwa's shore. There's a market every Saturday, where shell money and porpoises' teeth, as well as cash, are used as currency.

The Roman Catholic mission has a *rest house*. Ask the priest-in-charge for permission to stay prior to your arrival.

Foueda & Funaafou Islands (116 km)

These two artificial islands are still very traditional, with chiefs being buried in their canoes in the men's club houses. Visitors may not enter these, though you may be allowed to peer in from outside. Both islands also have non-Christian altars and cemeteries, as well as skull houses.

Funaafou is large for an artificial island – about half a km in size – and has about 400 residents. Shark-calling rituals, similar to those in Laulasi, occur on average here every three years – most recently in 1985 and 1988.

Mana'afe (111 km)

The cultural centre at Mana'afe allows foreigners to take part in Lau village life.

Sulione (118 km)

There's a market every Monday and Thursday, where people from the nearby artificial islands come to trade.

Fouia (120 km)

The road finishes at the wharf but a footpath continues southwards to Abe. You may be able to get a motor canoe there to Atori, to connect you up with the cross-island road back to Dala.

Adagege Island (120.5 km)

This large artificial island is especially custom-oriented. Women are restricted from entering those areas of the village where there are animist temples and where skulls are kept. There's another walled-off section which is a women's seclusion zone. You'll recognise the priest by the dolphin-teeth necklace he wears.

Sulufou Island (121 km)

The oldest and largest of the human-made islands in the Lau group, Sulufou is a strikingly picturesque village on stilts. The one-sq-km island is circular, is about half a km from shore and has a most dramatic aspect from the sea.

There are four main families on the island, each with its own traditional anchorage. In addition, a large COM church made of stone and timber dominates the village. In front of this building is a stone where refugees from

---

Lau Childbirth

Traditional childbirth rituals are still followed by the Lau Lagoon's animists. Women cut the umbilical cord themselves, then wrap their babies in pandanus leaves and paddle themselves back on small rafts to their island villages, escorted by other women in canoes. For 30 days they are confined to the *bisi*, or women's seclusion house. ∎

Shark Calling on Funaafou Island

The chief priest begins to suspect sharks will attack people unless they are ritually fed freshly killed pork. As in the ceremony at Laulasi, sharks are called, fed and a young boy rides around the island on a selected one's back. As long as this occurs satisfactorily, the priest can expect that his spirit at his death will enter sharks at will, moving between the smaller reef varieties and the larger pelagic species as required.

However, if the small boy is attacked or killed by the shark, the priest has to compensate the family for their child. He also is barred from repeating the ceremony, so his spirit loses the chance at his demise of entering sharks. ■

northern Malaita Island used to sit, pleading for sanctuary.

Sulufou is very densely populated, with about 1000 permanent residents and up to 2000 at Christmas. The island was the home of the young Scottish castaway John Renton from 1868 to 1875. His name is remembered locally with affection even now.

If you want to stay, ask the No 1 chief, who will try to find you an empty house to use for one or two nights only, for between S$3 and S$5 each person a night. A dugout-canoe ride from the mainland costs around S$1 each way.

CENTRAL & EASTERN MALAITA ISLAND

The road across the mountainous interior to the east coast around Atori and Atoifi is regularly washed out during the midyear wet season. Beginning near Dala, the route's most scenic spot is at Nunulafa, where the road crosses over the Auluta Gorge 20 metres below.

Atori

This village, 61 km from Auki, is a sub-provincial headquarters, and has a cultural centre.

Fakanakafo Bay

There are several surfing beaches and bays north of Atori. This one is the closest. A footpath goes from here along the coast up to Fouia and past another surfing beach at Manu, 14 km to the north.

Kwai Island

Three km to the south of Atori is Kwai and its surrounding beach. Access to this beautiful, but overcrowded, islet is by canoe. The *Kwai Island Rest House* is near the island's spirit house.

Ngongosila Island

Half a km from Kwai is the sand-surrounded island where Bell and Lillies were buried after their murder in 1927 at the hands of Kwaio tribespeople. There's a narrow sandbar you can use at low tide to reach Kwai Island.

Ngongosila is even more crowded than Kwai. There's a small *rest house* here too.

Leli Island

It's six km by boat from Atori to Leli Island. The best beaches in the area are on this sand-surrounded, unoccupied coral atoll. Its only visitors are fisherfolk and snorkellers who have to make a 20-minute motor-canoe trip to reach it. In the 1880s, several ships were looted here.

Adakoa

You'll find the *Adakoa Rest House* in this village, seven km south of Atoifi.

Atoifi

The road stops at Atoifi, the main centre for Kwaio people who have left the bush. There's a small hospital and a Kwaio cultural centre here, and several traditional villages in the nearby bush.

Kwaimbaambaala

Tourists may visit this traditional Kwaio

village as long as prior arrangements have been made with the chief.

Sinalanggu Harbour
Villagers call whales here in the same way certain other Malaita Islanders call sharks. In the bush behind the inlet are many old fortifications (called *labu*) and shrines from earlier generations of Kwaio people. Labu are usually hilltop settlements whose nearby ridges have been used as natural defences and fortified with walls where necessary.

Inside a labu are ancestral shrines and a men's meeting house, while dwelling places are usually outside. Three within 10 km of Sinalanggu Harbour are at Oneone, Lo'ombola and Furi'ilai. You will need a guide and each custom owner's permission to visit them. If this is refused, accept it gracefully.

Kwaiambe
Two British officials and 13 north-Malaita Island police were killed here in 1927 by Kwaio who refused to pay head-tax and surrender their rifles.

Tataanikona
This beautiful spot with a waterfall and pool below it is a three-hour climb up a cliff face from Kwaiambe.

The Kwaio
About 1000 of the 11,000 Kwaio people live in the mountains of east-central Malaita Island. They have rejected the modern world in favour of the religion of their ancestors. Their stronghold is the isolated mountainous interior between Uru Harbour and Olomburi.

These Kwaio believe the ancestral spirits are omnipresent, watching over both the living and the dead. According to the Kwaio, every event is caused by an ancestor. The task of the living is to inquire through magic which spirits are causing any perceived misfortune and what is required to placate them – usually the sacrifice of pigs. At the same time, mortuary and marriage feasts continue, while pigs and shell money are the currency, not cash.

Magic is regularly used, especially for revenge and healing. Among the Kwaio the distinction between sorcery and religion is blurred. While sorcery is sometimes employed for personal gain, it's routinely performed by the whole clan as a ritual.

Traditional dress persists; unmarried girls and women go naked and smoke pipes, while married women wear only minute T-pieces. Traditional staffs demonstrate authority, and bows and arrows, clubs and spears are always present when Kwaio bush people gather for feasts and law making. Sporadic violence still occurs, caused by acts of seduction or adultery, insults against a person or their ancestors, and pig or taro theft.

Villages are built along the traditional pattern – men's houses above, domestic dwellings in the centre and menstrual huts below. These small, scattered bamboo houses, built flush to the ground, are shifted every few years.

In defiance of the national and provincial governments, the Kwaio refuse to pay taxes, pass judgement in serious criminal cases in violation of national law, and deal with offences through the payment of shell money or pigs.

Kwaio bush people have declined to take part in provincial and national activities until they are paid compensation for their people who died during the 1927 rebellion, and for the desecration of ancestral sites at the time. Since the mid-1980s, they have been seeking S$294.6 billion to compensate for all the dead Kwaio, desecrated shrines and destroyed villages. Naturally, the Solomons government is not keen to encourage this claim. In fact, little has been heard of it since the late 1980s, when Christian Kwaios began explaining to their bush wantoks that this sort of money just doesn't exist to be paid.

Visits to the Kwaio East-central Malaita Island's mountainous interior is only very seldom visited by Westerners. As government officials themselves require escorts here, they discourage foreigners from contacting the Kwaio. Nonetheless, trips inland are possible for those who can afford to pay penal rates for guides, and are prepared for a possible angry rejection by the Kwaio once they find them. As recently as 1965, an SSEM medical missionary from New Zealand was murdered by Kwaio people in Atoifi. ■

Naufee

Very traditional Kwaio bush people live in this village three km south-west of Sinalanggu Harbour. Young married women go naked except for a small T-piece, though older women may wear a short grass skirt instead. Ground ovens employing preheated river stones are used for cooking.

Manawai Harbour

The eastern coast between Manawai Harbour and Maramasike Passage offers good hunting for wild pigs. There are also plenty of swordfish to be caught at sea.

Aio, Anuta Paina & Ai'ura Islands

All three islands have attractive sandy beaches. The hill on Anuta Paina, or North Sister, offers a view along Malaita Island's eastern coast as far as the Maramasike Passage. Its neighbour Ai'ura Island is also called South Sister.

Anuta Ni'ia Island

Also called Windmill Island, this sandy islet in Raroi Su'u Lagoon has megapode birds which lay their eggs in the island's warm sand. To see them, you must first get permission from the custom owners at Maro'u in Takataka Bay.

Ndai Island

Ndai is 55 km north of Malaita Island. First called Gower by Cartaret in 1767 and then Inattendue Island (meaning 'unexpected') by the French explorer de Surville two years later, Ndai is a semi-oval-shaped, slightly raised coral structure with a surrounding reef. It's seven km long and 3.25 km across.

Ndai has six small, brackish lakes, is low lying, and covered with forest and scrub. Its highest point is only 20 metres above sea level.

Ndai has just under 100 Melanesian inhabitants, though their language has some Polynesian features. The island's only village is Bethlehem. However, there are remains of an abandoned settlement called Ndai in the south.

Tradition says the spirits of dead Malaita Islanders go to Ndai. In another legend, the maximum number of people living on the island at any one time may only be 100. If anyone extra is born there, or comes to stay from elsewhere, someone will die. Consequently, unless numbers are down, the chief will only allow you a very short visit.

Getting There & Away

Boat Marine Division vessels charge S$21 between Auki and Ndai.

Canoe A chartered canoe ride from Malu'u in northern Malaita Island, with a few hours on the island, would cost about S$170.

Maramasike Island

Small Malaita, as Maramasike is often called, is separated from Malaita Island proper by the 20-km-long Maramasike Passage. It's a narrow, snake-like waterway.

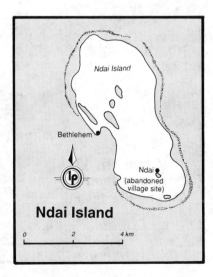

Ndai Island

In places it's less than 400 metres wide and occasionally only four metres deep. Despite this, there is plenty of coastal shipping travelling through it.

This 700-sq-km island has about 7000 people. It's distinguished by low hills separated by long, high limestone ridges, and an indented shoreline.

Information
Medical Services Maramasike has four clinics: at Rokera, Sa'a, Port Adam and Tarapaina.

Accommodation
There's a visitors' house at Haunasi. There is no rest house any more in Afio, or across the Maramasike Passage at Maka, though islanders could probably find you somewhere to stay if need be.

Getting There & Away
Air Solomon Airlines services Parasi once a week from Honiara for S$91.

Boat Marine Division fares from Honiara to Tarapaina and Rokera are S$33. Fares to Port

Southern
Malaita Island &
Maramasike Island

Adam are S$36. Vessels for Afio sometimes anchor instead at Maka at the southern tip of Malaita Island.

Solomon Islands Navigation Services' ship *Solomon Princess II* pays a weekly visit to Maramasike from Honiara for S$40 each way. In addition, Coral Seas Ltd's *Compass Rose II* does a monthly return trip between Honiara and Maramasike.

Yacht There are anchorages at Port Adam, Mapo Harbour and Oau. Temporary havens for passing yachts can be found in a number of small bays around the island, as well as in Raroi Su'u Lagoon and the Maramasike Passage.

Getting Around

There's a road from Afio via Rokera to Olusu'u. There's also a footpath from Rokera via Cape Hartig and Palasu'u to Sa'a and Olusu'u.

Three villages in the north are connected by paths to Haunasi. These are Manuitili, Nitauhi and Taori.

AROUND MARAMASIKE ISLAND
Afio

Although written sometimes as Apio or Atio, local people pronounce this subprovincial headquarters as Afio. A dugout-canoe ride over to Maka on the opposite bank of the Maramasike Passage costs about S$2.

Parasi

There are petroglyphs in the nearby Chiholai River valley of a bigman called O'oburo, who died there. Other designs include a frigate bird, a hand and some as yet undeciphered motifs.

Hugnoli

This large archaeological site has many burial stones and shows some similarities to Polynesian sites further east in the Pacific. You will have to get permission to visit the area from the custom owners at Weihii.

Palasu'u

Dancers from Palasu'u decorate themselves with streaks of white paste made from ashes and then dance while playing bamboo pan-pipes. Six km to the north at Olusu'u are sand beaches.

Fanalei Island

This island is surrounded by sand, as is its small neighbour Malau, or Mary, Island. As Fanalei is only one metre above sea level, some of its houses are built on stilts out over the water.

Walade Island

This picturesque artificial island is inhabited by Lau speakers like those of the Lau Lagoon in northern Malaita Island. It's only 200 metres from the shore and highly populated, with some of its leaf houses built with two storeys. The coast to the north of Walade (pronounced 'Walande') is very rugged and prone to rough seas.

Custom rules, in Walade and nearby Fanalei. Large numbers of fish, turtles and dolphins inhabit the area. The latter are hunted for their teeth for use as bride price. The standard fee is 1000 dolphins' or porpoises' teeth and five fathoms of single-strand shell money from Laulasi.

Raroi Su'u Lagoon

The name of the lagoon means middle passage. Its calm, protected, mangrove-fringed waters are full of clams and shells. At its northern tip is the appropriately named Pyramid Island.

Haunasi

This village has a cultural centre where traditional arts and customs are preserved. Islanders work here making handicrafts and recording genealogies, legends and traditional music.

Tarapaina

Local shells are transported to northern Malaita Island to be made into shell money, as they are considered the province's best. It's a two-km canoe ride from here to O'orou Island, an extinct volcano.

Kau

The remains of a US WW II aircraft wreck are exposed at low tide on the shore. Five km to the north-west is Sail Rock, used for target practice by US aircraft in WW II.

Sikaiana Atoll

The triangular atoll of Sikaiana (pronounced 'Sik-eye-arna') lies 212 km to the north-east of Malaita Island. The lagoon has three small, raised islets on its western side, while Sikaiana Island, built up from an extinct 45-metre-high volcano, is to the east. The atoll's total land area is less than two sq km, and it has a population of about 400.

The whole atoll is just over 10 km from east to west, and over six km at its widest point. In its centre are the deep waters of the Te Moana Lagoon, with a number of sandbars and coral heads close to the main island.

Only Sikaiana Island and two of the three islets are inhabited: there is a village on both Matuiloto and Matuavi. There are also two small artificial islands, although only one – Te Palena, which is a mere 50 by 30 metres in size – is occupied. The other, older one – Hakatai'atata – is currently abandoned.

The surrounding reef descends steeply, with tremendous depths only a few metres out. Lack of anchorages and a heavy swell make access to the island extremely difficult. Small inter-island vessels visit regularly to collect copra and bêche-de-mer. Access is by canoe across the treacherous reef.

Sikaiana's volcanic soil is extremely fertile. Freshwater swamps on the main island have been artificially deepened to sea level to provide taro beds. Fertility is preserved by regular mulching with vegetable matter from beyond the swamp.

History

According to tradition, the discoverer of Sikaiana was Tehuiatahu, who came with a number of companions from an unknown Pacific island called Luahatu. In due course, his followers split into three clans, which were ruled alternately by kings from two of these three groups.

Over time, drifters from other Polynesian islands arrived, creating a fourth tribe. Meanwhile, land ownership remained in the hands of the two original ruling clans. There was constant dissension until the land issue was resolved in a just way by a king called Mono.

This island group was first reported to the outside world in 1606, when Luka, a Sikaianan prisoner of war, was found by Quiros in the Duff Islands. He described his home island to the Spaniards, who recorded it as Chicayana. He told them of several two-way journeys between it and the Duffs, as well as Samoan visits and devastating Tongan raids.

Captain Hunter in the *Waaksamheyd* saw Sikaiana and its neighbours in 1791, naming them the Stewart Islands. In the following years whalers and vessels seeking turtle shells and bêche-de-mer occasionally visited, some using Matuavi as a shore base for melting down whale blubber.

In 1844, Captain Cheyne of the *Naiad* found two English beachcombers here, and in 1859, the crew of the Austrian warship *Novara* made a detailed description of island life.

Most of Sikaiana's migrants arrived before recorded history. However, in 1861 the whaler *Two Brothers* rescued 43 Micronesians from Kiribati who were adrift in two canoes. They were put ashore in Sikaiana, where 36 of them stayed – a number equal to 20% of the island's other population at the time.

Sikaiana suffered heavily in 1986's Cyclone Namu, losing most of its coconut palms. The atoll has found it hard to recover and consequently is still rather economically depressed.

People

The inhabitants of Sikaiana are Polynesian, and probably originate from many sources,

Top: Tikopian people helping load copra at Nembao, Utupua Island (DH)
Bottom: School house, Tikopia Island (GC)

Top: Boys beside what is said to be Mendaña's anchor at Nepa, Nendo Island (DH)
Bottom: Dancing circle, Banua, Nendo Island (DH)

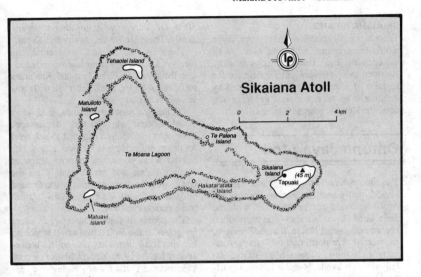

but especially Tuvalu and Tonga. Their very mixed language has a number of Maori features, plus some Tongan expressions. The black-haired, brown-eyed islanders are said to be the most handsome and easy-going of the Solomons' Polynesians. Because of the similarity of their language to that of the people of Ontong Java, they treat the latter as their wantoks.

A Tongan form of filarial mosquito is present in Sikaiana. This is the only place other than Tonga where it can be found, which suggests it was brought by a Tongan migration or raid at some time in the unrecorded past.

Culture
Loincloths are occasionally still woven on hand-looms from banana fibre that has been soaked in the sea to make it slightly shiny. The cloth was then dyed with a checked pattern.

An especially long cloth was traditionally made for pregnant women. Wearing it was believed to guarantee the return of a good figure after pregnancy and childbirth. Some Sikaianan women dress in this material even now.

Information
Medical Services There is a clinic close to Tapuaki.

Drinks
Although the average annual rainfall is about 2500 mm (98 inches), there are no creeks. Drinking water is scarce and comes from shallow wells and rainwater catchment tanks.

An alcoholic beverage of fermented coconut juice is the island's speciality, its manufacture learnt from early 19th-century whalers. It's called palm toddy or white beer because it goes milky once it's ready to drink.

Getting There & Away
Boat The fare from both Honiara and Ontong Java to Sikaiana Atoll is S$44 on the Marine Division's regular three-weekly shipping service. From Auki it's S$41.

Yacht Although crossing the reef is exceedingly hazardous, especially at night, the lagoon is usually calm. Islanders can advise you where to anchor.

SIKAIANA ISLAND

Tapuaki, on Sikaiana's western shore, is the atoll's main centre, with four other small villages on the island's opposite side. Between these villages and Tapuaki are the remains of a stone boundary line placed by Tehuiatahu to restrict a rival group of settlers, the Hetuna, whom he later killed.

Ontong Java Atoll

The country's northernmost point is Ontong Java. Equally well known as Lord Howe Atoll, it should not be confused with the three Lord Howe Islands – one more often known as Nibanga Noi in Temotu Province, another 700 km north-east of Sydney, Australia, and a third in Tonga. Many of its 1600 Polynesian inhabitants call it Luaniua (variously pronounced 'Loo-an-ee-wa' and 'Loo-an-new-wa' and also spelt Luanguia and Leuaneua).

Lying just south of the Equator and 258 km north of Santa Isabel, this attractive atoll is shaped like a boot with its toe pointing to the south-east. It's about 50 km from north to south and 57 km wide.

This immense lagoon has 122 islands within it. It's the largest in the Solomon Sea, and exceeds 1400 sq km. However, the total land area is only a minute 12 sq km. The widest piece of dry ground in both Luaniua and Pelau measures only one km, while the average breadth of many of its islands is only a third of this.

Except for three isolated rocks, no land is higher than 13 metres above sea level, while most islets are barely two to three metres high, making the whole atoll vulnerable to rising sea levels and the greenhouse effect. These small, long, low and narrow landforms are composed entirely of coral debris.

Tiny islands rise from the reef, mainly in the south-east. The only two with sizeable populations, with a lagoon-side village each, are Luaniua with 1200 people and Pelau with 350. A few other islets have temporary shelters where a small number of people – about 50 in all – are now living almost permanently. These are Ke Ila, Avaha and Kapai.

There are fine beaches, good coral, and plenty of fish throughout the lagoon, and excellent fishing along Keku Lau and Kea'auloa reefs, and at Ke Ila. Local fisherfolk will show you where to cast your line.

On the two populated islands, freshwater swamps occur where natural depressions have been artificially deepened to sea level for use as mulching pits for swamp taro. The coastal areas consist of narrow strips of coconut palms and scrub, mainly on the ocean side. In any one year, it's estimated 600,000 coconuts are consumed – almost one a person each day.

The people of Ontong Java pay in copra for goods at the atoll's two small stores on Luaniua and Pelau. They also collect beche-de-mer for the Hong Kong Chinese market, and trocchus shells for processing overseas into 'pearl' buttons and ornaments.

Houses here are still built flush to the ground. A network of poles form the frame, while the roof is a thatch of pandanus leaves. The kitchen is part of the main building, with smoke rising through a hole in the roof. Islanders call this traditionally designed dwelling a custom house.

As coconut palms are too precious to be felled and there are few trees of any other sort, paddle canoes are usually made from driftwood washed ashore after a storm. The makua, or chief, makes the first incision with a chisel to drive off evil spirits, before the log is hollowed out. Seaweed is rubbed over the hull to seal any cracks, booms are attached and an outrigger fitted.

History

Pottery has been found dating back 2000 years. Studies into the atoll's language, Luanuian, suggest it is related to both the Samoan and Tongan tongues. It's believed to have separated from its mother language in about 300 AD, passing first through Tokelau or Tuvalu to the east before reaching the atoll from there.

The present inhabitants trace their ancestry back 36 generations to about 1200 AD.

The legendary first coloniser was one Marou, who floated ashore from the north to be met by two couples already there. According to legend, they had just finished making Luaniua. They accepted his leadership once he built them a *haleiku* – a traditional house of worship. A descendant of Marou's called Akapu made several 1400-km canoe journeys to Tikopia to bring back turmeric, landing on Malaita Island and Nendo en route.

Although linguist's consider Ontong Java's language to be related to Tuvalu's, islanders claim their original homeland to be Tokelau. Oral histories tell of several attacks over the centuries by Tokelauans attempting to impose their authority over refugees from Tokelau who had settled in Ontong Java.

The Dutch adventurers Le Maire and Schouten may have sighted Pelau and its adjacent islets in 1616. Abel Tasman, on 22 March 1643, was the first definitely to see the atoll. He called the group Onthong Java, as he believed this sighting was the precursor of good fortune. *Untung* means 'luck' in Malay, and 'Java Luck' was a 17th-century Dutch expression for 'Good Fortune'.

In 1791, John Hunter was the first European to step on to Ontong Java's soil, renaming it Lord Howe Atoll. Subsequently, whalers and bêche-de-mer traders visited, followed in the 1870s by blackbirders.

Germany annexed the atoll in 1893 but ceded it to Britain in 1899. Meanwhile, in 1895, employees of 'Queen Emma' of Rabaul in Papua New Guinea (a part-American, part-Samoan woman) established a trading post at Luaniua. As happened so often, new contacts brought new diseases – malaria, tuberculosis and the 1919 worldwide flu epidemic.

About 2000 people lived on the atoll in the early 1900's. The area was closed to foreigners in 1939, as numbers had plummeted

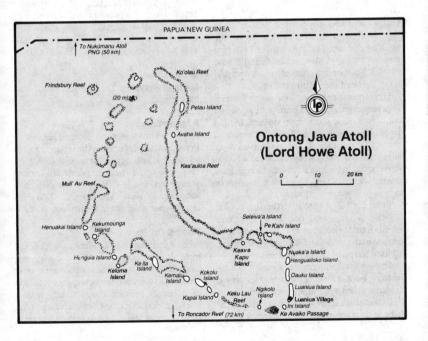

drastically to below 600. Since then, population numbers have climbed back towards their earlier levels.

Fauna

There are sea birds everywhere in Ontong Java. Some islanders, like those on Anuta, keep frigate birds as free-flying pets. Also plentiful is the black-naped tern, which is believed to breed only on this atoll. This medium-sized nearly all-white sea bird has a black line running from its eyes to the nape of its neck. In front of the tern's eyes is a small black patch.

There are plenty of megapode birds, usually in pairs. They lay their eggs in mounds of mulch they've built themselves. Although some people collect megapode eggs, others will eat neither the birds nor their eggs because megapodes are traditionally associated with the atoll's cultural hero, Akapu. Consequently, there's no danger of overconsumption.

Arts

Gaunt, geometrically shaped female deity figures were a distinctive feature of the atoll's statue art. The lower part of the face was portrayed as an inverted triangle with straight lines to represent the eyebrows and nose. Some of these still survive.

Graveposts, called *ke ava* in the Ontong Java language, are made from both wood and coral rock, complete with stylised human faces. These posts are a distinctive feature of the atoll's cemeteries and are carved with adzes and clamshell scrapers. Some wooden graveposts have birds carved in relief on them, while others have fish motifs in memory of people lost at sea.

Pearl shell is shaped to make fish-hooks, necklaces and nasal pendants. On ceremonial occasions, some men wear an ornamental nasal pendant designed in the stylised shape of the human form.

Ontong Java women use a back-loom for weaving banana fibre. Loincloths made on this device are then dyed yellow with turmeric.

Basket-work fans are beaten against the hand as an accompaniment to women's songs.

In the momo'sanga dance, their bodies and clothes are stained yellow with turmeric.

Tattoos In Ontong Java, many men and women are tattooed. The forehead is decorated with marine or geometrical designs in childhood. Later, the tattoos are extended to other parts of the body. Some islanders have tattoos in the shape of the hook islanders use to catch a local delicacy, the oil fish.

Culture

If you marry someone from Ontong Java, you will find the male line owns the coconut groves and does the fishing. In contrast, the female side maintains the taro plots and is prominent domestically. Postmarital residence is in the woman's house.

Makuas & Pohoulus The two main islands each have a chief priest called a *makua*. Above them is the *pohoulu*, who is like a king. In the past, he had the power of life and death over his subjects. If an islander angered him, the pohoulu would pronounce a sentence of death, and within a few days the victim would just waste away and die – as if by magic – having lost the will to live.

Information

Medical Services Luaniua and Pelau both have clinics.

Accommodation

If you want to stay on either Luaniua or Pelau, you should contact the village chief in advance. If he is agreeable to your visit, he'll find you somewhere to sleep. If instead you're on a one-day visit by ship, ask someone to show you around. This will ensure your presence is readily accepted.

Food & Drinks

Although rainfall is moderate, with 2550 mm (100 inches) on average each year, finding fresh water has been a chronic problem in the atoll. However, the multitude of coconuts provide the islanders with a toddy, or alcoholic drink, which is fermented from coconut water. Dried clamshell meat is plentiful and turmeric is always available to flavour food. (The latter is also used to decorate the body and clothes at traditional ceremonies.)

Getting There & Away
Air There's no airfield as yet, though one is planned for Pelau.

Boat The three-weekly Marine Division vessel anchors at both Luaniua and Pelau. Fares from Honiara and Sikaiana to Ontong Java are S$45, and S$42 from Auki. A ship ride between Luaniua and Pelau costs S$9.

Yacht Some yachts have exited the Solomons from Ontong Java. This is acceptable as long as you inform Immigration in Honiara in advance, and also the island police officer or local chief when you depart. Entry protocol is, naturally, the reverse of this process.

Yachts and ships can use 23 passages through the reef. Ke Avaiko Passage to the south of Ini Island brings you to the main anchorage at Luaniua.

Getting Around
Boat A shared motor-canoe ride between Luaniua and Pelau, 66 km apart travelling inside the lagoon, would cost around S$35.

AROUND ONTONG JAVA ATOLL
Luaniua Island
There's plenty to see, including haleikus and *maraes* (Polynesian sacred places) in Luaniua Village. The main haleiku, called Som'aru House, is in the *malae*, or village centre, beside a large stone which was once worshipped as a god. Nearby is a cemetery with traditionally carved headstones. On the reef is the WW II wreck of a US Aircobra aircraft.

Pelau Island
This island's name is derived from the Malay word *pulau*, meaning island.

The Ko'olau cemetery is 100 metres in from the beach on the islands' north-western side. It's the burial place of the Ko'olau people who are believed to have arrived from the north in the distant past and settled in Pelau. Their gravestones are cleanly cut coral monoliths varying from one metre to three metres high.

Roncador Reef
Islanders call the reef Ke Uopua and consider it to be a good fishing ground. However, visits are infrequent as it's over 72 km due south of the atoll across open sea.

On 1 February 1568, one of Mendana's ships narrowly avoided shipwreck on Roncador Reef. Mendaña called the reef Los Bajos (shoals) de la Candelaria because he had found them on the eve of the feast of Candlemass. They were sighted again by Mourelle in 1781 and called El Roncador (the roarer).

Nukumanu Atoll
About 50 km due north of Ontong Java is Nukumanu, or Tasman, Atoll in Papua New Guinea. Despite the colonial-era boundary separating the two island groups, the people of both are pure Polynesians and regard each other as wantoks. Despite the often rough seas, motor canoes ply between Nukumanu and Pelau on a monthly basis. The 350 people of Nukumanu collect bêche-de-mer and sell it to Pelau for resale to Honiara's Chinese.

If you want to visit Nukumanu, you should ask Immigration in Honiara first. An Ontong Java boat driver may be willing to take you there for a day or so. However, the driver won't want to breach official restrictions on the islanders' traditional cross-border trade by helping foreigners make illegal and unrecorded exits or entries from or to the Solomons, especially while Bougainville Island is attempting to secede from Papua New Guinea.

Makira/Ulawa Province

Makira, Ulawa and their seven small neighbours are sometimes called the Eastern Solomons. Together they occupy the country's south-easterly end, with only Temotu Province beyond.

Makira, the main island, has 3043 sq km of the province's 3188 sq km, and is 139 km long by 40 km wide. Seven of the adjacent islands are within 32 km of the main island. Ulawa, however, is 75 km away.

The province has 26,500 people and is well known for its preservation of ancient traditions. Carvers are plentiful in Star Harbour, Santa Ana and Santa Catalina, whilst dancers from the same areas and those from Ulawa are particularly skilled.

HISTORY

Makira/Ulawa Province's first inhabitants, the Lapita, settled at Pono'ohey on Makira Island, where pottery from about 1400 BC has been found.

Although much of Makira/Ulawa Province's past was violent, there were also long periods of peace. During such times, ceramics were made, trade flourished between Makira and Ulawa, and large canoes came annually from Temotu Province.

At other times, there was fighting between coastal and bush people. Men from Santa Ana Island would hire themselves out as mercenaries and attack the Makiran coast. For safety, many people lived deep inland. Professional murderers were active until the early 20th century. One, called Sam, proudly boasted he had 64 killings to his tally!

The first-born child was often buried alive by its father. Captives were either burnt or trampled to death, and their skulls stored as trophies for posterity.

Ancestor worship was practised all over the island. When a chief died, his body was placed on a platform up to 10 metres high and ritually washed daily until only the skeleton remained.

Human flesh was considered to be essential for any feast. Sometimes guests invited to a ceremony were captured and eaten.

Hernando Henriques – one of Mendaña's expedition leaders – sighted Makira Island in May 1568. The Spaniards' policy of seizing hostages to exchange for food provoked many angry responses. Three lines of canoes attacked the expedition members at Ulawa, while another 93 individual canoes attacked them at Waiae Bay. However, a queen treated them well at Old Pawa in Ugi and ransomed a local chief they had captured.

On Mendaña's return in 1595, one of his four vessels (the *Santa Isabel*) was lost during a volcanic eruption on Tinakula in Temotu Province. Remains found at Pamua on Makira Island's northern coast suggest

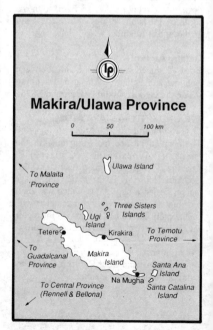

the survivors landed and built a fort there, though what their ultimate fate was may never be known.

Jean de Surville found the province again in 1769, relabelling several islands with French names. Although other explorers followed, including Shortland in 1788 and Ball two years later, it was whalers who made the first lasting contacts. The US vessel *Ann and Hope* sold some trinkets in 1798, but by 1849, nails, metal tools and glassware were being traded regularly at Makira Harbour for turtle shell, pigs and food. By the 1860s, whalers who routinely careening their ships there had given the name Makira to the whole island. Meanwhile, a number of European traders settled on Ugi and Santa Ana.

A small band of Marist missionaries had arrived in 1846, but by the following year, three of them had been killed and eaten, another had died of malaria and the remainder had prudently withdrawn,

Despite the favourable reception whalers were receiving at Makira Harbour, life elsewhere in the province remained dangerous for foreigners until the early 1900s. Indeed, HMS *Curaçao* shelled and burned Ubana in 1893 for refusing to hand over its villagers who had murdered a European trader there.

Makira Island was ravaged by epidemics in the early 20th century. Nearly every year dysentery, whooping cough and chest infections swept through the island. Before one epidemic in 1910, there were five small villages near Pamua with about 200 people. After it, there were none. Again, in 1920, there were three deaths to every birth on Makira Island.

To make conversion easier, the missions encouraged people to move to the coast. This quasi-migration, well underway by WW II, sped up when the Marching Rule Movement from Malaita and Maramasike islands briefly took hold in the mid-1940s. Consequently, the province's population is now almost exclusively coastal.

FAUNA
Birds
The Makiran mountain rail lives only on the main island, in highlands over 650 metres above sea level. It's a fairly large 25-cm-long flightless bird with a bright-scarlet bill and legs, and practically no tail. The body is mostly brownish-black, but dark slaty-blue from head to breast.

There are three other subspecies endemic to the province. The red-throated fruit dove on Ugi and Makira islands has a snow-white head and chin. There's a lowland relative in Ugi and Santa Ana of the pink-spotted fruit dove, and a mini-version of the glossy swiftlet on Makira Island.

Crocodiles
There are more saltwater crocodiles in this province than in any other part of the country, and there are occasional fatalities. Most bays and rivers on the southern coast of Makira Island, from Oneibia to the Weraha River near Mwaniwowo, have sizeable colonies of the reptile – especially Maro'u Bay. There are also large concentrations in the Three Sisters group.

Turtles
The small and very rare olive, or Pacific Ridley, turtle nests occasionally in a few places around Makira Island's coast, the only part of the Solomons it's known to visit.

ARTS
Houseposts of between two and four metres in height are made with designs of naked human figures on them, or with figures that are half human and half fish or bird.

Light-coloured wood is carved, then blackened and decorated with mother-of-pearl inlay. Turtle-shell or pearl-shell ornaments are also made, sometimes incorporating dogs' teeth as currency.

THINGS TO BUY
Carvings of naked human figures up to 1.5 metres tall are made in eastern Makira Island at Star Harbour, and also in Santa Ana and Santa Catalina. They cost between S$100 and S$600 each.

Makira Island

Alternatively known as San Cristobal, the main island was initially called Santiago by the Spaniards, but was renamed San Cristobal by Mendaña. Others have called Makira Island either Arosi, after the language of the island's western end, or Bauro – the vernacular of the Kirakira area.

Two-thirds of Makira Island's 20,000 people live on the northern coast. Much of the southern shore is sparsely populated,

especially between Makira Harbour and Mwaniwowo. The inhabitants are pure Melanesian, except for a number of resettled Tikopians at Nukukasi.

Makira Island's mountains run like a spine down its centre, their highest point reaching 1040 metres, then fall steeply to the sea along its southern shore. At the same time, a large number of rivers penetrate the island in roughly parallel lines every two to five km.

Makira Island has more inland swamps than any other island in the country. Some of them are as much as 80 metres above sea

level, while one, stretching due east from the Northern Wairaha River towards Maro'u Bay on the island's south-western coast, is over 17 km in length.

Climate

Makira Island's weather station at Kirakira records 235 days of rain and an average rainfall of 3601 mm (142 inches) a year. Morning humidity levels reach a very muggy 95% in February, averaging 93.3% for the six months between January and June. The humidity only falls below 90% from September to November, when it averages 86%. However, the second half of the day is much more pleasant, as afternoon humidity levels remain close to an average 76% throughout the year. Temperatures range between 31°C and 20°C, with the coolest month usually being August.

Arts & Culture

Pre-Christian religious and ceremonial life in Makira Island was closely bound up with fishing. As the islanders' gods were mainly associated with the ocean, sharks, bonito and frigate birds appear on many carvings, while a number of traditional dances are based on a shark theme or legend.

In the past, it was widely believed that the spirits of dead people resided in sharks. In certain parts of the province, some males were thought to be closely related to sharks from birth. If the shark was injured, so also would the man be.

It was also believed a child could swim and play with a shark which had the same name as the youngster. Sacrifices were often made to sharks, and at death a man's bones might be put inside a wooden carving of the fish.

Legendary People Kakamora legends abound, including one in which it is claimed that a Kakamora child was caught in 1969 on Makira Island. Apparently, once the Kakamora grew up, it escaped.

Information

Medical Services Kirakira has a 72-bed hospital and there are plans to extend this to over 130 beds. There are eight clinics around the island. These are at Aringana, Tawaraha, Tetere, Maroghu Harbour, Paregho, Na Mugha, Karie and Nasuha. Malaria and water-borne illnesses are the principal health problems. Only a quarter of the people have clean water supplies, and sanitary toilets are the exception rather than the rule outside the provincial capital, Kirakira.

Accommodation

Makira Island lacks the village-level accommodation that has sprung up recently in Western Province. However, there's a rest house operating in Kirakira and another one that was closed but may have reopened again by the time you read this book.

Tetere and Na Mugha are government centres and the two villages most visited by foreigners outside the provincial capital. If you want accommodation at either of these, or elsewhere around the island, inquire in Kirakira at the provincial government offices (☎ 50111) where you can stay. Staff may know of newly built village visitors' houses they use themselves that you can perhaps stay in too.

Getting There & Away

Air There are six flights a week between Honiara and Kirakira's airfield at Ngorangora. The Solomon Airlines fare is S$129 each way. There is a service once a week to Santa Ana, which costs S$57, and another twice a week to Santa Cruz Airfield on Nendo, which costs S$220.

Boat The Isabel Development Corporation (IDC) vessels *Ligomo IV* and *Ligomo V* make weekly trips between Honiara and Makira Island's northern coast for S$38 each way. They also operate a fortnightly service between Kirakira and Santa Ana for S$16.

Marine Division vessels from Honiara call regularly at Waimasi Bay, Kaonasughu and Kirakira, charging S$36 to each destination. Journeys between the provincial capital and Ugi or the Three Sisters are S$15. It's S$9 to Santa Ana or Santa Catalina, and S$12 to Ulawa.

Yacht There are small jetties at Kirakira and Na Mugha, and anchorages at Maoraha Island, Waimasi and Hada bays, Makira and Marunga harbours and Mwaniwowo.

Canoe Motor-canoe rides are quite reasonably priced as long as they're shared. The 23-km journey from Kirakira to Su'uta'ata'a in the Three Sisters group costs S$12, while the 36-km trip to Pawa on Ugi is S$16. The 77-km ride to Santa Ana and the 80-km ride to Santa Catalina cost around S$39 and S$40 respectively.

Getting Around
There's a 48-km-long unsealed road along the northern coast between the Waimakarima and Warihito rivers. A 27-km-long track continues westwards from Nukukasi to the Wainuri River. Travel anywhere else on the island is by motor canoe. Shared rides the 64 km to Na Mugha and the 119 km to Makira Harbour cost S$32 and S$60 respectively.

To/From the Airport The four-km tractor ride from Ngorangora Airfield into Kirakira is free.

KIRAKIRA
A government station was established at Kirakira in 1918. Since then, it has become Makira's provincial centre, and the home of 3200 people. It is pleasantly shaded by a dense, but colourful, canopy of trees.

Information
Kirakira has a hospital, a post office, a police station, a library, Solomon Airlines and NBSI branches and provincial government offices.

Things to See & Do
There's a large, dilapidated old house up the main street. This used to be the district officer's residence in colonial times, and is supposed to be haunted. A girl hung herself from the entrance after an unhappy love affair with a former district officer. Her ghost is said to be very beautiful, and if you meet her she'll be very friendly at first but then turn nasty!

It's rather stoney for swimming at the tiny jetty, but there's a sandy beach about one km to the east of the town. The leaf-house village of Ngorangora is the same distance to the west.

Places to Stay & Eat
The *Provincial Government Rest House* (☎ 50111) has eight double rooms with communal kitchen and washing facilities for S$20 a person.

The *Meda Lodge* is closed pending renovation but may reopen late in 1992. Kirakira's stores are usually well stocked with fresh bread, and there's also a small market by Puepue Creek.

AROUND MAKIRA ISLAND
The north-western coast of Makira Island is rugged and sparsely inhabited. Thickly wooded hills frequently reach right down to the water-line. These timber-clad uplands, and the island's mountainous spine, are often cloud covered.

Elsewhere, northern Makira Island has long black-sand beaches – at Wanione, Maghoha and Waimasi bays and also at Maro'u. Behind them are narrow plains.

Ngorangora Airfield
Aircraft land here only a few metres from the sea. The coral shore at the airfield's eastern end has a number of small blowholes. Kirakira is four km to the east.

Pamua
The passengers and crew of the Spanish galleon *Santa Isabel* are believed to have landed near the headland three-quarters of a km to the east of Pamua in 1595, after becoming separated from Mendaña's second expedition. Remains of a hilltop fortress have been discovered there, and pottery from it positively identified as 16th-century Spanish.

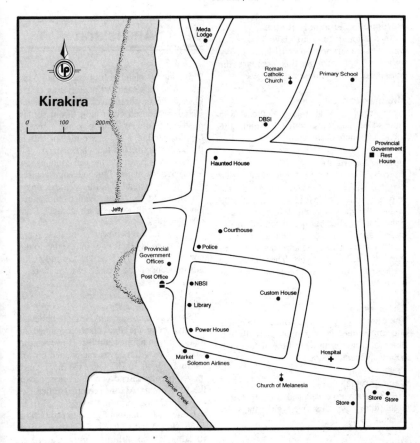

The small sand-surrounded island opposite Pamua is called Maoraha.

Maro'u
A long black-sand beach stretches along the shore to Tawatana. Outrigger canoes are still built here.

Harani'ia Point
At the point is Hauni Araha Rock. Dead people were brought here as it was believed their spirits would then leap from the rock into the sea and swim to paradise – believed to be around 80 km away off Guadalcanal's Marau Sound.

Makira Harbour
The Solomons' most protected anchorage, Makira Harbour was a favourite spot for whalers. It's characterised by a narrow inlet and a wide, sheltered lagoon. Its black-sand beach is interspersed with rocky shores and mangrove swamps. The fishing is excellent, with tuna especially plentiful.

Tetere, the main village locally, is a sub-provincial headquarters.

Maroghu & Marunga Harbours
Both sheltered harbours have black-sand beaches interspersed with mangrove swamps. All through this area are the remains of many abandoned villages.

Mwaniwowo
Heavy rainfalls soak this settlement from June to September. About 6000 mm (236 inches) fall here each year.

Surville Peninsula
There's a custom house with impressive carvings at Wosu. Several villages on the two-km-wide peninsula's southern side contain the grass-covered remains of rectangular, coral-walled burial enclosures, locally called *hera*. The largest concentrations are at Naruka and Panisa, which have two and three of them respectively. There's another on the peninsula's northern coast at Mwareiraro.

Ghoroweni Point
There are two caves at this point, one a burial site containing a large number of skulls, the other a sea cave with white lime pictographs both inside and outside.

Cape Surville
In 1931, a severe earthquake and 10-metre-high tidal wave destroyed the cape's 18 villages.

Na Mugha
There are many woodworkers living around this subprovincial headquarters, which is frequently called Star Harbour after the nearby inlet. They specialise in carving houseposts with large, naked human figures or sharks portrayed on them. These are then painted all over in black and white.

Offshore are two small sand-surrounded islands, each with an extensive and colourful reef.

Tawarogha
Surfies have found some good waves here between May and July.

Santa Ana Island

This friendly island of 1600 people is 7.5 km from Makira's eastern tip. Formerly called Owa Rafa, or alternatively Owa Raha, the island is a raised coral atoll. From certain positions Santa Ana can look like a peaked cap. Mt Faraina, a 143-metre-high plateau in the centre, dominates the whole island.

Santa Ana is very fertile and contains low levels of phosphates. Taro and bananas grow well in the island's north, while kumara flourishes to the west. Walled enclosures have been built to fence off gardens from foraging pigs.

The island has two beaches on its western side. Turtles lay their eggs on the one to the north of Mary Bay. Seas are too rough for this to occur on the island's eastern shore.

History
The sea caves at Rate and Feru are believed to have been the first places occupied in Santa Ana, in about 1280 BC. However, the island's first village was established on Mt Faraina around 30 BC. Once the inhabitants moved permanently down to the seashore in the 14th century AD, the principal settlement moved to Mwaroqorafu.

Gallego, in Mendaña's first expedition in 1568, named and visited both Santa Ana and its smaller neighbour Santa Catalina. However, Spanish hostage-taking at Mary Bay led to a dawn attack by the Santa Ana Islanders. In reprisal the Spaniards burnt the nearby village. Finally, exasperated by islander resistance and their failure to find gold or make mass conversions, the Spanish sailed back to Peru, taking with them three Solomon Islanders as proof of their discoveries.

In 1769, Jean de Surville spied Santa Ana and Santa Catalina and called them the Îles de la Délivrance, or the Deliverance Isles, as they were the first inhabited places he reached after being becalmed. Santa Ana was seen again by Lieutenant Ball in 1790 in

HMS *Supply*, and this time it was called Sirius Island.

Santa Ana's people traded and raided as far as eastern Guadalcanal. They also engaged in regular commerce with the people of Santa Catalina Island and the Star Harbour area of Makira Island, as they all shared a common language. Santa Ana also received occasional trading visits from Nendo and the Polynesian parts of the Reef Islands. From 1877 onwards, it had one or more resident European traders.

Until WW II, young men's initiations on the island required participation in a huge tuna hunt. Though these only occurred every few years, young males were barred from marrying until they had taken part in one.

Traditionally, Santa Ana's leaf houses were built flush to the ground. Until the 1970s, slightly more than half were still constructed this way. Nowadays, only a few remain, mostly at Nataghera. The remainder are almost entirely built on stilts, though the kitchen sections remain on the ground.

Arts

Santa Ana is renowned for its small, ornately crafted ceremonial food bowls, dance sticks and fishing floats. These are carved from a light-coloured softish wood which is then blackened with charcoal and inlaid. The floats are weighted with a stone and their tops decorated with frigate bird, shark and dolphin designs.

Wooden food bowls are usually shaped like sharks or large fish, with a bowl part carved in the centre. Shark-like caskets are made to hold the bones of dead heroes. Bowls with a half-human, half-shark figure called Okro on them are particular favourites. Others have birds, pigs or dogs incorporated into their designs. Modern food and salad bowls are hollowed out of soft wood, and are sometimes inlaid.

In the now-rare *mako mako* dance, members of one party of villagers decorate themselves with red mud, face paint and masks, and shuffle around apparently aimlessly. Then a conch shell sounds, heralding the arrival in canoes of another, darker-skinned group. Those in the latter first inspect the less-sophisticated tree dwellers, then capture some and drive the rest off. This dance portrays saltwater people from the

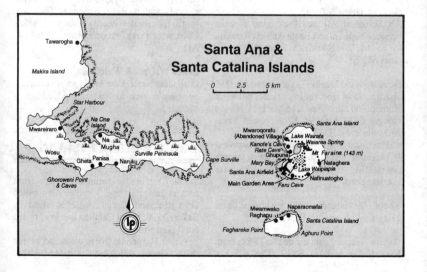

western Solomons overwhelming local bush people, probably in some long-ago head-hunting raid made against this area.

Culture
Santa Ana has a mixture of Melanesian and Polynesian traditions. Although the islanders physically resemble Melanesians, their property-ownership customs are similar to those of the Polynesians, whose ancestral lands belong to families rather than clans.

Information
Medical Services There's a clinic at Ghupuna.

Activities
Organised Tours Tour Solomons of Honiara offers a two-night stay in Santa Ana for S$600 each for up to five people. Though this doesn't include the airfare, it involves being met by spear-carrying warriors and seeing ceremonial dance displays, traditional cooking demonstrations, carvers at work and Nataghera's custom houses.

Accommodation
Ghupuna has a leaf-style rest house.

Getting There & Away
Air Solomon Airlines flies once a week between Honiara and Santa Ana via Kirakira for S$165. The Kirakira to Santa Ana sector costs S$57.

Boat Both the Marine Division and the IDC charge S$44 for their service between Honiara and Santa Ana. The Marine Division charges S$12 between Kirakira and Santa Ana, while the IDC's fare is S$16.

The Coral Seas Ltd vessel *Compass Rose II* makes a return journey once a month connecting Honiara with all Makiran/Ulawan ports.

Yacht The island's only anchorage is at Mary Bay, also called Port Mary.

Canoe A shared canoe ride the 77 km from Kirakira is around S$39. The 6.5 km

between Mary Bay and Santa Catalina would be about S$3, or S$10 if you charter.

Getting Around
Footpaths connect the island's three villages, and there are trails up Mt Faraina from both Ghupuna and Nataghera.

AROUND SANTA ANA ISLAND
Nataghera
There are two traditionally designed custom houses where ancestral skulls, bones and war canoes are kept. Females may not enter, nor may photographs be taken without permission.

The custom houses' most striking exhibits are houseposts with human designs. These dramatic sculptures represent spirits who were believed to combine human abilities with those of birds, fish or other animals.

Many small caskets and bowls with spirit figures carved on them are also stored inside. Several are shark-shaped and hold ancestors' bones.

Mwaroqorafu
This village was permanently abandoned after a devastating epidemic in the 19th century. Nowadays, only ruined walls, mounds and well sites remain. There's a small rockshelter nearby called Kanofe's Cave, which was first occupied in about 140 AD.

Lakes Wairafa & Waipiapia
Both lakes' waters are too brackish to drink, but they're fine for swimming, fishing or canoeing.

Santa Catalina Island

Santa Catalina is about eight km from Makira Island's Cape Surville. Also called Owa Riki, and named Massey's Island by Ball in 1790, Santa Catalina is a low, raised coral platform.

About 300 people live in the island's three main villages, which are concealed by trees and spread along Santa Catalina's sandy northern shore. Subsistence gardening and copra production are the main activities. There is very little surface water, even though Santa Catalina is in a high-rainfall area.

Arts
Santa Catalina's ceremonial food bowls are ornately carved, as are dance sticks, houseposts and model fish.

Culture
The island's major annual event is a festival called Wogasia (pronounced 'Woe-R-zia') which lasts for a week in May or June. Its main event is a spear fight in which people occasionally get hurt, followed by a marriage partnership ritual.

Annual yam-increase ceremonies occur over two or three days in March, soon after the crop has been harvested.

Accommodation
There are no rest houses on the island, but if you ask the chief well before your visit, he may be able to find you somewhere to stay.

Getting There & Away
Boat The Marine Division charges S$44 between Honiara and Santa Catalina, and S$12 from Kirakira.

Canoe A shared canoe ride across the water from Santa Ana is S$3, and about S$40 for the 80 km from Kirakira.

Getting Around
Low-lying Santa Catalina is only 3.5 km long and two km at its widest point, so all movement around it is on foot.

Ugi Island

Alternatively known as Uki Ni Masi, and also in the past called San Juan and Golfe Island, Ugi is 11 km due north of Makira Island. The island, about 10.5 km by 6.5 km,

has about 2000 people, most of whom live along Selwyn Bay's golden, sandy shore.

Ugi is a raised coral reef reaching up to 160 metres at its highest point. Much of this land is covered with scrub, though coconut groves and food gardens flourish near Pawa. Ugi has a pleasant climate and receives about 3000 mm (118 inches) of rain a year.

Ugi has an onshore reef reaching from the island's south-western tip to the middle of Selwyn Bay. The best beaches are at the island's north-western and south-western points, where there are also coral gardens.

Ugi has its own language. Although the small number of people who live in the Three Sisters group use the same words, their pronunciation is slightly different.

Arts
Black wooden bowls inlaid with pearl shell are made in Ugi.

Information
Medical Services There's a clinic at Kerepei.

Accommodation
There's no organised accommodation in Ugi despite the island's attractive beaches. Officials often stay at Pawa's large mission school, though you'll need to radio the priest-in-charge first to make sure he has enough room for you also.

Getting There & Away
Boat Marine Division services from Honiara to Ugi cost S$36, while the IDC charges S$38. Kirakira to Ugi is S$5.

Yacht There's an anchorage at Pa'epa'esa-huhu.

Canoe A shared motor-canoe ride between Kirakira and Selwyn Bay would be about S$16.

Getting Around
A network of footpaths connects Selwyn Bay with most villages on the island's northern and eastern sides.

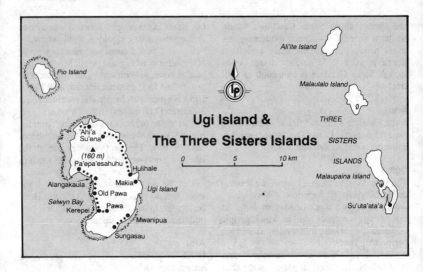

Ugi Island & The Three Sisters Islands

AROUND UGI ISLAND

'Ahi'a

Northern Ugi was strongly influenced in the mid-1940s by the Marching Rule Movement on both Malaita and Maramasike islands. Consequently, this village is built to the layout of a US Army camp, with a large central square and houses in straight lines.

Su'ena

An archaeological site here has revealed continuous occupation of the island since about 1470 AD. Many ornaments were found, including trocchus-shell arm rings.

Makia

The remains of two ancient forts are about two km inland from here, and about one km apart. There's also a traditional shrine at Sungasau.

Pio Island

This small, unoccupied island is sometimes called Bio. About 5.5 km north-west of Ugi, it has an extensive beach on its western side. There's also a long sand spit to its east.

The Three Sisters Islands

Also known as the Olu Malau group, and in the past called Las Tres Marias or Les Trois Soeurs, the Three Sisters lie between 20 and 32 km from Kirakira. All are low-lying raised coral atolls. Because of their lack of fresh water, there's only one village in the group, at Su'uta'ata'a on Malaupaina Island. About 100 people live there, plus a number of now-wild cattle left behind when a plantation closed down. Ali'ite, largely unused by humans, is the home of large crocodiles, monitor lizards and flying foxes.

There are several good swimming, diving and fishing spots, but beware of the many hungry crocodiles throughout the area. They're the main reason for the lack of people!

Getting There & Away

Boat The Marine Division's fare from Honiara is S$36; from Kirakira it's S$9.

Canoe A shared motor-canoe ride from

Top: Canoeing near Mbonembwe Village, Nendo Island (GC)
Bottom: Crustaceans caught off Nendo Island (GC)

Top: No 2 Chief's house, Tikopia Island (DH)
Bottom: Lake Te Roto, Tikopia Island (DH)

Kirakira would be S$11, though, as so few people make this journey, a S$65 chartered trip is more likely. A shared ride between Su'uta'ata'a and Selwyn Bay in Ugi would be about S$17, while a charter would be S$100.

Ulawa Island

Although both physically, linguistically and culturally closer to southern Malaita and Maramasike islands, Ulawa is administered jointly with Makira Island. It's a 17-km by 5.5-km elongated island of about 65 sq km, with around 2500 inhabitants.

The island's thickly forested interior is cut by ravines. The western coast is mainly lined by low coral-limestone cliffs, while the eastern seaboard is generally coral sand. There are some beaches along Ulawa's southern shores.

History
Ulawa was first settled in about 750 AD. Prior to the 20th century, Ulawans traded throughout the Makira/Ulawa Province area, and with Maramasike and south-eastern Guadalcanal. Internal conflict revolved around clan feuds, interrupted by the occasional inter-island raid.

Mendaña's first expedition named Ulawa La Trequeda, or Truce, Island, in 1568, though the islanders made a surprise attack soon afterwards. De Surville in 1769 called it Contrariété, meaning 'annoyance', because his ship was becalmed. Ball renamed it Smith's Island in 1790, though it was known as Ulawa by the late 19th century.

Arts
The *weto* dance originated in Ulawa, although it's now performed throughout the province. It is danced by women on special occasions only, such as mortuary feasts, the instalment of chiefs, and sometimes weddings. As much as four fathoms of Malaitan

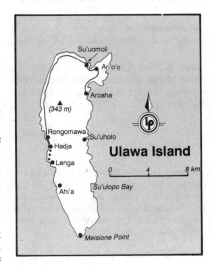

shell money (up to S$1200) is paid to the dancers for their performance.

Men occasionally dance the weto also. When they do, they use dance sticks curved like birds, fish and snakes instead of the hand movements used by women.

In Ulawa many roof decorations are of snakes representing a winged serpent deity. Canoe houses are often ornamented with carvings of a local sea spirit called Tararamanu.

Island craftspeople make dance sticks and ceremonial bowls. Their fishing floats are very similar to those of Santa Ana, and have frigate birds, sharks and dolphins carved on them. The oldest ones are stored as part of the village's collection of traditional objects. Newer carvings may be sold.

Culture
Each group of Ulawan villages has a custom house where important traditional objects are kept. Every clan in the area contributes houseposts for it, including some with a dog's head each.

Information
Medical Services There's a clinic at Hadja.

Accommodation
Hadja has a visitors' house.

Getting There & Away
Boat Marine Division vessels charge S$36 between Honiara and Ulawa. The fare from Kirakira is S$12.

Yacht There are anchorages at Su'uomoli and Su'ulopo Bay.

Canoe A shared motor-canoe ride the 84 km between Hadja and Kirakira costs S$43 and would only be safe in the calmest weather.

The same applies to Walade, 59 km away in Maramasike. The shared fare to or from there would be about S$30.

Getting Around
A 15-km road connects the main settlement of Hadja with Aroaha in the north-east.

AROUND ULAWA ISLAND
Hadja
Ulawa's local administration is at Hadja. Most of the island's people live in a belt of coastal villages around Hadja, especially between Lenga and Rongomawa.

Su'uomoli
This village's design was strongly influenced by the Marching Rule Movement and is built around a large central square.

Temotu Province

Formerly called the Eastern Outer Islands, Temotu Province lies at the Solomons most easterly point. This widely dispersed archipelago is separated from the main mass of the country by the 6000-metre-deep Torres Trench.

The province is made up of three island groups. Firstly there are the four volcanically derived Santa Cruz Islands: Nendo, Tinakula, Utupua and Vanikolo. Contrasting with these are the low coral terraces and sandy atolls of the nearby Reef Islands. Finally, there are the isolated extinct volcanoes of the Duff Islands, Tikopia, Anuta and uninhabited Fatutaka – lonely rocks in an otherwise empty sea.

The islands of Temotu have a total land surface of only 926 sq km, yet they are scattered over a huge 150,000 sq km of ocean. Their nearest neighbours are the Torres and Banks groups at the northern tip of Vanuatu, 173 km to the south-west, while Makira and the main bulk of the Solomons are instead almost 400 km due west.

Temotu's population of 17,500 is predominantly Melanesian, and occupies the larger islands. Polynesians are mainly found on small coral cays or the shores of isolated volcanic rocks.

FAUNA

On the smaller outlying islands of the province, such as the Reefs, the Duffs, Tikopia and Anuta, villagers eat the Polynesian Rat as well as fish, turtles, pigs and chickens. Where rats are, so are there snakes. The docile Pacific tree boa, whose habitat spreads eastwards from Temotu to the Samoas, is very common in the Reefs.

CULTURE

The people of the Santa Cruz Islands and the majority of the Reef Islands are non-Austronesian Papuan-speaking Melanesians like most of the people of Papua New Guinea. Linguistically, they differ from most other Solomon Islanders except for those in the Russells, Savo, Vella Lavella and much of Rendova.

Temotu's culture is quite distinct from that of the bulk of the Solomons. Traditionally there were extensive trade networks throughout the Santa Cruz, Reefs and Duffs areas, and, to a lesser degree, Tikopia and Anuta. Nendo exported food, pigs and crafts in all directions, and red-feather money to the Reefs and Duffs. Both Nendo and the Reefs exported shell discs and fabric to Utupua and Vanikolo. In return, Nendo received wives, sailing canoes and crews from the Reefs and Duffs, and food and weapons from Utupua and Vanikolo. Tikopia exported sennit, tapa, turmeric and mats to Anuta and Vanikolo, receiving birds' eggs from Anuta and food from Vanikolo in return.

INFORMATION
Medical Services

Ringworm is widespread among young children, tuberculosis is prevalent in outlying areas, and there's the local insect-borne malady, Santa Cruz fever, to contend with. In addition, malaria has been a serious health problem, with 600 cases a year in Temotu since the mid-1980s. So bring sufficient medical supplies with you in case the local clinic has run dry.

ACCOMMODATION

Accommodation is very limited in Temotu. Lata, the provincial capital in Nendo, has three places to stay. There's also a small resort in the Reefs. For lodgings elsewhere, you should send a service message to local churches or chiefs, giving them enough time to see if there's a family who will accommodate you. It's best to do this from Lata or Honiara.

Islanders may find it hard to say no to a hungry foreigner, despite their own poverty. So bring food for yourself and to share with

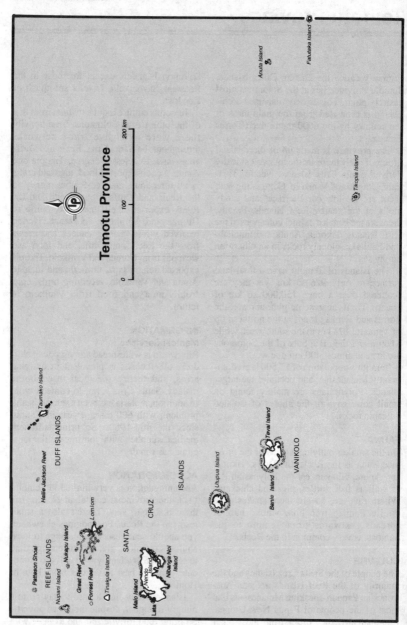

Temotu Province

REEF ISLANDS
Patteson Shoal
Nupani Island
Nukapu Island
Halie Jackson Reef
Taumako Island
DUFF ISLANDS

SANTA
Great Reef
Forrest Reef
Lomlom
CRUZ
Malo Island
Nendö Island
Tinakula Island
Lata
Nibaanga Noi Island
ISLANDS

Ubupua Island

Teval Island
Banie Island
VANIKOLO

Anuta Island

Fatutaka Island

Tikopia Island

0   100   200 km

the families you stay with, as well as betel nut and tobacco to use as gifts or to trade.

GETTING THERE & AWAY

Before setting out for Temotu Province, make sure Immigration in Honiara has stamped your passport with sufficient time. Delays getting back to Lata from the outer islands are commonplace. As Lata has the province's sole airfield, called Santa Cruz, the only way around this far-flung province is by boat.

GETTING AROUND

Boat

Marine Division and private vessels offer monthly services from Lata to the Santa Cruz Islands and the Reef Islands, though the more distant destinations, such as the Duffs, Tikopia and Anuta, are only visited by the Marine Division monthly at best. Indeed, adverse weather conditions sometimes result

in gaps of two or three months between services. Fortunately, considering the rough seas, Marine Division vessels, unlike private ones, usually have up to six cabins each.

Yacht As Immigration officials only visit Temotu occasionally, yacht crews should report to the police station at Lata on arrival in the Solomons before sailing on to Honiara.

Nendo Island

Nendo wins the prize for the island with the most names. Previously known as Santa Cruz, Ndeni, Nitendi, Indemi, Nambakena, Ndende, and even New Guernsey or Lord Egmont's Island, Nendo is the largest landform in the province. Including its small neighbours, Nendo is about 660 sq km in size, 31 km long and 21 km wide.

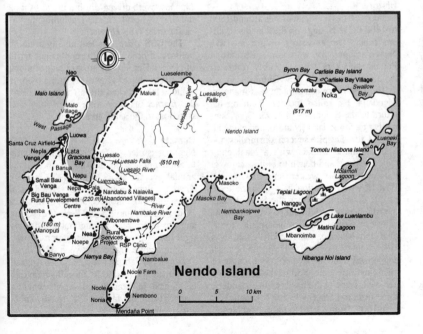

Nendo Island

Nendo's western end is composed of a fertile 180-metre-tall coral plateau. The remainder is volcanic, reaching up to a 517-metre high point in the east, from where villagers can see the Torres Islands of Vanuatu. The northern coast is mainly rocky, but it does have some narrow, attractive beaches similar to those on the western shore. Mangroves are plentiful in the lagoons of the southern and eastern coasts. Inland the island is densely wooded; there are even a few isolated remnant stands of kauri near Nanggu and Luesalo.

Nendo has two small neighbours. Malo lies just north of Lata, while Nibanga Noi is separated from south-eastern Nendo by a one-km-wide channel.

At the island's western end, there are large garden areas and coconut groves, with many betel-nut, breadfruit and cut-nut trees. The same applies on nearby Malo Island. However, the rest of Nendo has few people and is largely undeveloped.

History

Nendo's earliest settlement was around 1500 to 1400 BC at Nanggu on the island's southern coast. The ancestors of present- day Nendo's population were non-Austronesian Papuan speakers who probably migrated from mainland Papua New Guinea.

The first European contact was made by Mendaña. He sailed too far south on his return to the Solomons in 1595. On 7 September he found land (Nendo), and named it Santa Cruz. Despite several skirmishes, the Spanish made friends with a local chief called Malope and began to build a camp at Pala at the south-western end of Graciosa Bay. However, relationships with the local people deteriorated when the Spanish took the islanders' pigs without paying for them.

After a month, some of the Spanish mutinied and Malope, the friendly chief, was killed. On 18 November 1595, the Spanish abandoned their ill-fated colony because of local hostility. Nearly 50 of the settlers had perished, some at the hands of the islanders, some from malaria (including Mendaña).

In 1606, Quiros tried to rediscover Nendo but found the Duff Islands instead. It was left to Philip Cartaret in HMS *Swallow* to chance upon the fabled Santa Cruz in August 1767. He called the area, including the Reef Islands, the Queen Charlotte Islands, as he at first thought it was a new territory. However, violent resistance from the islanders drove him away after only a few days.

In between sporadic European visits, the islanders routinely fought among themselves. For their defence, villages were fortified with coral walls, some of which can still be seen.

While the islanders' could deter most outsiders, they could not keep away foreign diseases. In 1827, Nendo was as heavily populated inland as along the coast. By 1897, the interior was deserted. Then, in fifteen devastating years from 1906, malaria and tuberculosis took a terrible toll, reducing the population from 3000 to only 500.

A major sea action, the Battle of Santa Cruz, was fought offshore in October 1942. The battle was considered to be a draw; the Japanese were driven off, but the USA took the slightly heavier losses (including the aircraft carrier USS *Hornet*).

The USS *Wasp* was lost nearby a month before and now lies in the depths just north of Nendo. Her aircraft are still ranged along her flight deck. However, some people contend this wrecked aircraft carrier is in fact the *Hornet*, as they were sister ships and were lost in the same area.

Climate

Nendo gets plenty of rain – occasionally up to 5800 mm (228 inches) a year, though the annual average is 4325 mm (170 inches). There's a light shower at least three days in every four most months, and eight in every 10 in February and March! Periods of strong sun are interrupted throughout the day by light falls. Consequently vegetation is lush.

Temperatures range between 32°C from December to February and 22.5°C in August. Despite frequent rainfalls, morning humidity is highest in March and April, when it reaches 90%, but falls to 78% in November afternoons.

Fauna

Bird life is plentiful, as are the many large and attractive butterflies. Two bird species are endemic to Nendo only. One, the Santa Cruz white-eye, is a small olive-coloured bird which is fairly common on the island. Also, there's Sanford's white-eye, a medium-sized brown species with a slightly curved yellow bill.

Feral pigs roam the bush around Graciosa Bay. They are the only living reminder of the abortive Mendaña expedition of 1595.

People

Nendo's mainly Melanesian population of 8000 includes people living on Malo and Nibanga Noi. Along with the Reef Islands, Nendo has the reputation for the heaviest beer consumption per head in the Solomons, with Foster's Lager – locally known as Blue can or Fosta – the clear favourite. Some local wags value everything in beer terms. For example, when the price of something is S$3 they will say, 'You mean one Blue can'!

Arts

A few Nendo women still use back-looms to produce very finely woven bags made of hard-wearing, fawn-coloured banana fibre. This material is also used to produce loincloths, baskets and table mats.

Nelo Dance Some islanders wear an elaborate nose pendant called a *nelo* when performing a dance of the same name. These ornaments, made of turtle or clam shell, are treated as family heirlooms.

Nelo dances occur near a full moon and continue from the afternoon until dawn. The eight to 20 performers lead their fellow villagers around a crowded dancing circle

accompanied by much feet stamping and chanting, followed by lavish feasting. Ask around Lata if any of these traditional dances are planned.

Information

Medical Services Lata has a 46-bed hospital. There are also clinics around Nendo at Nanggu and Lueselembe, while one km south of the Rural Services Project (usually called RSP) is the RSP clinic.

Accommodation & Food

Lata has three rather basic rest houses. In addition, you may be able to stay in villages,

Mbonembwe village couple, Nendo Island

but ask the chief first, preferably well before your arrival.

Lata has four stores – including one selling hot food – and a market twice a week. Noole Farm has a weekly market.

Water

Despite heavy regular rainfall, there are sometimes water shortages in Nendo, including in Lata. Some villagers have droughts lasting several weeks, when coconut water is the only potable fluid readily available.

Things to Buy

Red-feather sticks are worn as hair decoration during traditional dances. These 35-cm-long sticks are decorated with an exterior of mainly red feathers, and banded with five white and black stripes. They are sometimes for sale.

Shoulder bags with decorative patterns are woven from the bark of trees, and bows and arrows are used for catching wild pig, birds and fish. You can sometimes buy them at the Lata market or in nearby villages.

Getting There & Away

Air Solomon Airlines has two flights a week between Honiara and Santa Cruz Airfield at Lata, both via Kirakira. The fares from Honiara and Kirakira are S$327 and S$220 respectively. Buy your return ticket in Honiara to avoid paying with travellers' cheques in Lata, which can be tortuous indeed.

Boat The Marine Division vessel takes two days to travel between Honiara and Lata including a brief visit to Kirakira, before it begins its tour of the province, which takes between nine and 11 days. The fare between Honiara and both Lata and Nanggu is S$49, while from Kirakira the fare is S$44. The ship is always crowded at Honiara, so bookings need to be made well in advance.

Deck fares around the province from Lata are S$12 to the Reef Islands, S$14 to the Duffs, S$21 to Utupua, S$32 to Vanikolo, S$42 to Tikopia and S$44 to Anuta.

Yacht There's a wharf at Lata, and small jetties at Luesalo, (also called Shaw Point), Nanggu and Carlisle Bay. Anchorages are at Big Bau'Venga, Nea, Mbonembwe, Lueneki Bay, Byron Bay, Lueselembe, Nepa and the Luembalele River mouth.

Canoe You can take a shared motor canoe the 78 km to Lomlom in the Reefs for S$40,

Red-Feather Money

Nendo is the home of one of the world's most unusual currencies – Santa Cruz Red-Feather Money, or *Touau*. Although none has been made for several years, existing coils of this currency are still widely used for bride price.

Brown pigeon feathers were bound together in plaits to form the basis of a long coil, whose outer visible covering was the red head and breast feathers of the scarlet, or cardinal, honeyeater, a bird of between 10 and 13 cm found only in Temotu. About 600 of these birds with long curved bills were trapped, plucked of a few feathers and then released alive, for each red-feather coil.

When it's still used, bride price normally costs between 10 and 24 rolls, plus some modern bank notes. Despite the large amount of money involved, the girl has the right to veto applicants. Once a decision is reached, the father of the newlywed daughter announces he has red-feather coils for sale, usually for about S$300 each, to any young men with marriage on their mind.

This custom enables Melanesians from Nendo to acquire brides from the small Polynesian-speaking Outer Reefs and Duff Islands. In this way, these islands are able to control their overpopulation. In addition, they export canoes and ocean-going crews, and in return acquire agricultural produce.

Although modern currency and commodities are replacing this form of bride price, if you have a chance to see red-feather money being used, don't miss it. Simply ask the family's permission to watch and then be as unobtrusive as possible. ∎

but the four-hour trip there is often dangerous due to frequently rough seas. If no-one will share a ride with you, you can charter for around S$120.

Getting Around
There are 70 km of motorable roads and tracks on Nendo, all to the west of Lueselembe. These radiate from Lata, except for two Forestry roads that travel inland from Luesalo and RSP respectively.

Movement on land around Nendo is usually on foot. Occasionally, tractors and 4WD vehicles come by, so flag down any you see. Ask them how much it will cost before you get aboard.

Boat The first leg of the Marine Division's round-the-province service usually involves calling in at Carlisle Bay and Nanggu. The fare to each is S$9.

Canoe Shared motor-canoe rides to Carlisle Bay and Nanggu cost S$17 and S$29 respectively.

LATA
About 1500 people live in Lata, while another 3000 live along Graciosa Bay's western shore. In the distance you can see volcanic Tinakula.

Up the hill and about 200 metres from the wharf is a large, grassy park surrounded by modern buildings. Local people call the whole area Lata Station. In 1970, the Protectorate opened a district substation here. Soon a hospital, government offices and modern houses had sprung up.

There's no bank in Lata. Instead, the post office and Moffat Brock's Store near Freshpoint will accept US and Australian dollars, but not necessarily at the official rate. They are unlikely to take any other currency.

Sport is a major community activity in the early evenings and at weekends in the park. Soccer, volleyball and basketball are all popular.

The Provincial Assembly sits one week in every six in the open-sided courthouse beside the library. Debates are always lively and you can stand outside and watch.

Islanders have come from all over the province and beyond to work in Lata. You may see Polynesian students from Anuta and Tikopia, and occasionally Gilbertese settlers, as well as Nendo Islanders themselves. Regrettably, heavy drinking whenever ships call in has resulted in a few local hooligans marring the peace of this beautiful place.

Places to Stay
The *Provincial Government Rest House* (☎ 53026) is behind the SIBC Radio Temotu Building, and has three double rooms plus communal kitchen and washing facilities. It costs S$20 a night, but it's always full during the Provincial Assembly sessions held every six weeks.

Just beyond the jetty at Freshpoint is *Paul Brown's Rest House*, costing S$15 a night. The *Tikopian Rest House* in the area called Tikopian Settlement is the same price, but it's usually fully occupied.

Places To Eat
Moffat Brock's Store near Freshpoint has a small fast- food outlet. The small Lata Market in front of the jetty opens at dawn on Wednesday and Saturday mornings, usually selling out by 8 am. Its specialities are hot taro or cassava pudding with a range of fillings including pigeon, all wrapped up in banana leaves.

GRACIOSA BAY
The road southwards from Freshpoint along Graciosa Bay's shore passes first through what amounts to a cultivated rainforest. A coconut plantation grows among many other trees, including cut-nuts, pawpaws, betel nuts, breadfruit and sumai trees. There are also plenty of bananas and cassava. About 300 metres along the shore is a fish trap made out of coral rock.

About two km further on, the road reaches the first dwellings within a four-km sequence of uninterrupted leaf-house villages. Some are on stilts and have an open verandah, others sit on a low pad of coral rocks, while

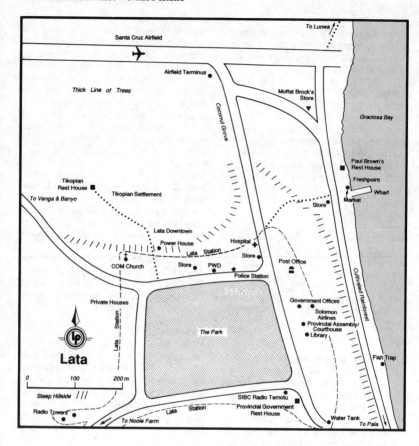

a third group have a small, hut-like annexe which is the cook house. Occasionally there are copra driers made of leaf, instead of the metal ones you'd see elsewhere in the country.

Some of the huts on stilts are young men's houses. Once a young boy has reached adolescence, he leaves his parents' house to live in one of these until he marries.

You can occasionally see small sailing canoes crossing the bay in the distance, tacking back and forth to catch the eddying breeze. Most come from Luesalo on the opposite shore, from where Nendo's kauri

logs are exported. Stiff breezes throughout the area make Graciosa Bay ideal for windsurfing.

All distances are from Lata's wharf at Freshpoint.

Luowa (1.5 km)

This village, to the north of Lata and just beyond Santa Cruz Airfield, has a dancing circle surrounded by smooth coral slabs. Beyond is a pleasant beach with a colourful coral garden and a good view of Malo Island. The water is extremely clear for snorkelling, but the tide through the West Passage can be strong.

Banua (2 km)
The road southwards passes a frequently used dancing circle at Banua. Leaf-house villages continue without interruption to Pala.

Nepu (4 km)
The chief's house is raised on coral stones up on the hillside, indicating his high status. By the shore is another dancing circle.

Nepa (5 km)
What is locally believed to be Mendaña's 16th-century anchor stands by the road. It's very large and in surprisingly good condition considering its apparent age.

Pala (6 km)
Just inland from a long, sandy beach is the pumping station, or water supply, as it is often called, for the whole area. Fresh water

bubbles out from the porous coral rock into a clear, blue pool. You may swim in the creek below, but not in the pool itself.

Mendaña's Graciosa Bay settlement was about 10 metres west of the track to the pumping station. About 50 metres before the building the track crosses a ditch, believed to have been dug by Mendaña's settlers in 1595 for their defence.

Luembalele River (7 km)
This is only easy to cross at low tide. The coastal road continues as a track another 17 km to Lueselembe on Nendo's northern coast. There's a waterfall close to Luesalo.

THE NEMYA BAY TRAIL
The path begins at Pala's pumping station, and immediately leads up the hillside on to the western coastal plateau. The route to Nemya Bay is very indistinct, windy and undulating, so you will need a guide. If instead your destination is the Rural Development Centre, locally called RDC, turn westwards (right) along the trail about 100 metres beyond a cattle fence, itself 500 metres south of Pala. Then continue for a further four muddy km through a beautiful rainforest to RDC.

Nandabu & Naiavila
A short-lived cargo cult emerged at Nandabu in the early 1930s, with followers praying to wooden images for European goods, including guns. A Melanesian police officer drove the cultists out.

Nandabu and Naiavila are abandoned villages on a large 220-metre-high knoll about 1.5 km south-east of Pala. They are surrounded by bush and separated by a 70-

Boys in Mbonembwe village, Nendo Island

metre stretch of undergrowth, bordered in some parts by a wall which surrounds six sq km of remains. These include ovens, houses, a temple, three men's houses, fireplaces, walls and a dancing circle. Ask around Pala for guides if you want to see these sites.

WESTERN COASTAL TRACK TO BANYO

The cart track along Nendo's western coast passes many coral walls and several friendly villages. All distances are from Lata's wharf.

Nepla (0.8 km)

There are wonderful sunset views from the nearby beach at the western end of Santa Cruz Airfield.

Venga (2 km)

This large, neat village (pronounced 'Vengay') has two dancing circles. At low tide villagers beachcomb in the shallows.

Small Bau'Venga (6 km)

The delightfully sheltered white, sandy cove is protected from the sea by two reefs. Its name means 'Venga's smaller beach'. The water here is clear and blue. Less than one km further on is its twin, Big Bau'Venga.

Both beaches are popular picnic spots for Lata weekenders. The coral outcrops and the clear, white sand make for good, safe snorkelling. Some villagers fish here with bows and arrows.

The track continues for another 12 km past Nemba and Manoputi, ending at Banyo. Along this stretch are several freshwater springs close by the high-tide line.

Banyo (18 km)

A footpath climbs up the plateau and joins a track after a further 1.5 km. It's another two km to Noepe and a further three km to meet the road connecting Lata with Noole Farm.

NOOLE FARM ROUTE

This track leaves Lata beside the twin radio towers. It leads southwards across Nendo's western plateau before turning east for New Nea, RSP and Noole Farm. All distances are from Lata's wharf.

New Nea (10.5 km)

A footpath leaves the track and heads southwards to one of the island's prettiest shoreside settings at Nea.

Rural Services Project (RSP) (13.5 km)

The Nemya Bay footpath from Pala meets the track about one km before the Rural Services Project, locally known as RSP. About one km to the south along the route is the RSP clinic, and a footpath eastwards to Nanggu which requires a guide.

Noole Farm (16 km)

There's a market here every Wednesday afternoon. Two footpaths go southwards to Mendaña Point, passing through the three small villages near the end of the peninsula.

MALO ISLAND

This three km by 5.5-km island, also called Tomotu Neo or Trevanion, and La Huerta, or Garden, by Mendaña, has several stretches of sandy beach on its western side. It's 2.25 km from Lata and has an interior of high raised coral with thick bush, including some kauri. Malo Village and Neo, which has good views of Tinakula, are the island's only two large settlements.

Getting There & Away

A shared motor-canoe ride between Lata and Malo Village shouldn't cost more than S$2 each way or S$7 for a chartered round trip, plus your boat driver's time. Otherwise ask someone to take you over and act as your guide for the day.

EASTERN NENDO ISLAND

Along Nendo's northern shore are plenty of long, thin, sandy beaches. These average only 100 metres wide, often merging with alluvial flood plains. Access to the eastern part of the island is only by canoe or ship.

There are several Kakamora legends, including one about a Nendo boy who was taken at the age of 12 and was kept as a servant until he escaped when he was about 40 – sometime since WW II. Apparently he would not tell of his experiences other than to confirm the usual reports about Kakamoras.

Luesalopo Falls

This cool, fast-flowing waterfall is three km from Lueselembe (pronounced 'Loose-a-lem-ba') at the junction of the Luesalopo River. It's ideal for swimming, but you must get permission to visit it, as some nearby spots are tabu.

Byron Bay

This inlet and its village of Mbomalu have a surf beach, and coral gardens for snorkelling. Towering 517 metres above, and three km behind, is Nendo's highest point. From here you can see Vanuatu's most northerly isles.

Carlisle Bay

The protected inlet, which has consistent surf at its entrance, houses two settlements – one on a small island in the bay. At low tide, lava-lava clad islanders walk the 100 metres through the shallows to the mainland village.

There's a decrepit memorial at the harbour entrance to Commodore Goodenough and his two crew, who were killed here in 1875. Carlisle Bay was also the scene in 1932 of the murder of the New Zealand-born manager of a logging company. Already married to a local girl, he returned one day with a beautiful Rennellese maiden – so his jealous Nendo wife poisoned him!

Nanggu

South-eastern Nendo's main village, Nanggu, is at the entrance to the five-km-long Tepiai Lagoon. There's a dancing circle onshore beside this settlement.

The lagoon's mangrove swamps have saltwater crocodiles in them. The Mblamoli Lagoon is seven km away and similar. Inland from Nanggu are kauri forests.

NIBANGA NOI ISLAND

Often simple called 'Noi', Nibanga Noi is also known as Tomotu Noi, Lord Howe, or even New Jersey Island. Despite its similar name, this Lord Howe Island should not be mistaken for Lord Howe Atoll – Ontong Java's other name.

Nibanga Noi is a long, thin sand-fringed island one km due south of Nanggu. Mbanoimba, the only village, is beside the access to the Matimi Lagoon.

Separated from the Matimi Lagoon by a coral bridge a quarter of a km wide is the 21-metre-deep Lake Luenlambu. Although its water is fresh, no streams flow in or out. The lake and the lagoon may originally have been one, but upthrusting earth movements in the past have probably divided them.

Tinakula Island & Volcano

This active volcano, also called Temami, Mami, Tenakula, Volcan and Volcano Island, is 42 km north of Nendo. The eight-sq-km Tinakula rises 850 metres in a near-perfect cone. Its almost completely circular shape

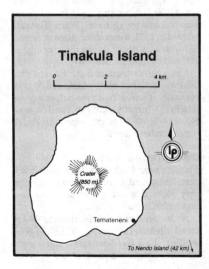

Tinakula Island

0   2   4 km

Crater
(850 m)

Temateneni

To Nendo Island (42 km)

was marred in the 1950s by a massive land-slide on its western side, which a 50-metre-wide lava river occasionally flows down.

Despite the active crater's proximity, Tinakula's forest-covered lower slopes are the home of the extremely rare Santa Cruz ground pigeon. This 25-cm-long brownish-black pigeon has a reddish-purple gloss, and is only found on Tinakula, Utupua and Espiritu Santo, Vanuatu's largest island.

History

Tinakula throws out pumice and ash in periodic bursts every one to two hours. The first record of this was in 1595, when the *Santa Isabel*, one of the ships of the second Mendaña expedition, was engulfed in Tinakula's smoke. Mendaña assumed that the boat had been sunk, but the ship appears to have escaped, probably taking refuge at Pamua in Makira.

In 1767, Cartaret reported eruptions of ash and rock. Later visitors told how the volcano would spew huge red-hot boulders down its side into the sea, producing deep, resounding hisses.

In the 1950s, during a period of apparent quiet, a small village called Temateneni grew up on the volcano's south-eastern shore, with about 100 Polynesian people from Nupani and Nukapu living there. When Tinakula erupted in 1971, a mass evacuation occurred. Eyewitnesses told of flames rising as high as 300 metres from the summit.

Many minor tremors occurred, and five tidal waves lashed nearby Malo and Nendo. Naturally it was a long time before anyone returned. Currently only two families from Nupani – barely 10 people – brave Tinakula's unpredictable temper.

Getting There & Away

Tinakula's one landing spot is a small beach near Temateneni. Getting ashore across slippery rocks is dangerous in calm seas and impossible in bad weather.

A chartered motor-canoe ride the 84-km round trip from Lata is about S$130. In good weather, it's a five-hour round trip – eight when it's rough. If a storm comes up when you are ashore, your boat driver may have to leave you there for several days until the seas are calm again.

Utupua Island

Utupua lies about 70 km south-east of Nendo, and 43 km north-west of Vanikolo. The island is about 12 km across, with an area of 69 sq km. There's a fringing reef two km offshore that completely surrounds the island. Utupua has a deeply indented circular coastline of mainly mangrove inlets with small, narrow black-sand beaches at their mouths.

Utupua's highest peak, the 365-metre-high Mt Rautahnimba, towers above the island. Utupua is densely wooded, with agricultural land and coconut trees limited to its coastal fringes. The island's thickly shrouded interior is one of the only three homes worldwide of the very rare Santa Cruz ground pigeon.

History

Cartaret discovered Utupua in 1767, calling it Lord Edgecombe's Island or New Sark. D'Entrecasteaux sighted Utupua in 1791 while searching for his missing compatriot La Pérouse. He renamed the island Recherche, after one of his expedition's two vessels.

People

Utupua's 1000 mainly Melanesian people are very dark, with short hair. Like Nendo and Vanikolo, this island's three languages are Papuan, in spite of its Polynesian sounding name.

Information

Medical Services The island's only clinic is at Nembao.

Getting There & Away

Boat Marine Division fares from Honiara and Lata are S$54 and S$21 respectively. It's S$12 between Utupua and Vanikolo.

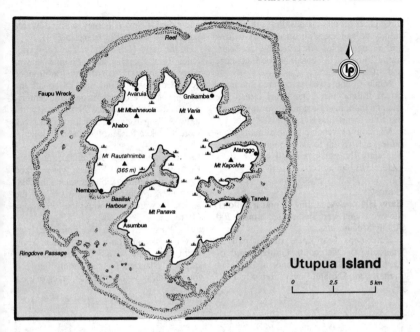

Utupua Island

0   2.5   5 km

Yacht There's a wharf at Nembao, and anchorages at the eastern end of Basilisk Harbour.

Canoe As seas can often be stormy and outboard-motor fuel scarce, journeys to Vanikolo are infrequent.

GETTING AROUND
The sea inside the encircling reef is quite safe for motor canoes and they are the normal means of transport around Utupua.

AROUND UTUPUA ISLAND
Basilisk Harbour
This inlet, named after a 19th-century British exploration vessel, is bordered on three sides by kauri-clad mountains, giving the harbour a fjord-like aspect.

Nembao
Utupua's largest village has a small number of ellipse-shaped leaf dwellings, locally called custom houses because of their traditional design.

Ahabo
People from this Tikopian settlement regularly scour the onshore reef at low tide for seafood. The nearby offshore reef claimed the mission boat *Faupu* in 1971.

Vanikolo

Banie Island and its small neighbour Tevai (also called Te Anu and Lord Amherst's Island) are known jointly as Vanikolo. The two islands, 43 km south-east of Utupua, together are 190 sq km in area and were formerly called Vanikoro. Rainfall is heavy, with an annual average of over 5100 mm (201 inches).

A crater rim forms the main island's tallest peak, the 923-metre-high Mt Banie. The three other mountains beside it are all subsidiary volcanoes, with traces of lava flow still recognisable. An extensive reef surrounds most of the coastline, both onshore and offshore.

Much of the coast is covered by mangrove. Inland are huge kauri trees. The island's thick bush, according to some, conceals the dwarf-like Kakamoras.

Vanikolo's rivers are home to many crocodiles, and flying foxes populate the trees. The slaty flycatcher, a small grey bird, is endemic to Vanikolo.

History

Early History According to oral traditions, the two island were first settled around 200 AD by Melanesians.

Europeans first knew of the pair as Vanicollo or Manicollo. Quiros heard of them while in the Duff Islands in 1606, but did not visit. Cartaret saw Vanikolo in 1767 and called it New Alderney, while Edwards named it Vanikolo Pitt Island in 1791.

In the early 18th century, Tive (a warrior chief from Tikopia) led a Polynesian war party to Vanikolo. According to tradition, he occupied Tevai Island and killed all the Melanesians there. Later in the same century, Banie Islanders forced the Tikopians to withdraw. A Tongan canoe party arrived in 1788, were mistaken for Tikopians and all killed.

La Pérouse & Dillon A French expedition, led by Le Comte de La Pérouse, was wrecked at Vanikolo during a violent cyclone in 1788. Both French frigates, the *Boussole* and the *Astrolabe*, were lost on the island's treacherous reefs.

La Pérouse's ship, the *Boussole*, was driven backwards on to the reef near Vono Point. She sank so quickly that very few escaped. Islanders later said only between four and six survived either the wreck or their

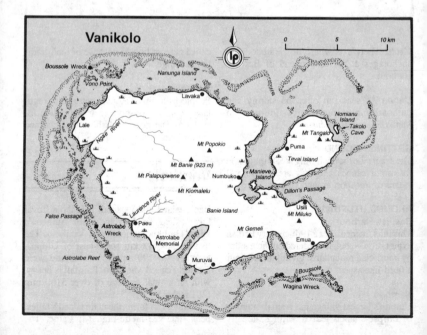

reception on land. Any who got ashore were killed, their skulls being preserved in the local spirit house.

Most of the *Astrolabe's* crew got ashore safely at Paeu. Having constructed a palisade, they then built a two-masted vessel from material salvaged from their wreck. Eventually all but two, presumably unprepared to risk their lives again at sea, sailed away into blue oblivion. Tantalisingly, both Edwards in 1791 and D'Entrecasteaux in 1793 sailed past Vanikolo but didn't land. If they had, they could have rescued these two surviving French sailors, and heard their tale of the disaster.

A Lascar (or Indian) sailor called Joe, left behind on Tikopia in 1813 at his own request, visited Vanikolo in 1820. While there, he spoke to two elderly Europeans, survivors of the La Pérouse wrecks.

Peter Dillon, an Irish trader-explorer, was told of this by Joe in 1826 while at Tikopia. He reached Vanikolo in September 1827 and searched for the two French sailors. However, one had died in 1824, and the other had since left Vanikolo with an islander friend. Having renamed Vanikolo La Pérouse Island, Dillon sailed on to Utupua and Nendo searching for the missing French explorer, but to no avail.

Once Dillon had reported this, the French government dispatched Dumont D'Urville the following year, who built a memorial to La Pérouse at Ramboe Bay. He also searched neighbouring islands for the last French survivor, but without success.

The 20th Century When Dillon visited, he estimated Vanikolo's population to be about 1000 – all Melanesians. By 1932, because of devastating ship-borne epidemics, this number had fallen to 62, though it has now risen to around 550.

In 1923, the Protectorate government established a 'station', or centre, at Paeu, as Vanikolo was more peaceful than Nendo, mainly because of its depopulation. In WW II, Dillon's Passage was used by US and New Zealand forces as a seaplane base.

Vanikolo once had the largest quantity of kauri in the Solomons, but by 1964, when logging ceased, only a few trees remained. Since then, copra has been the main product.

Arts
Vanikolo is renowned for its Temate devil dances. The performers are completely covered in leaves, their outfits representing gods or goddesses and their children. Hollow masks with V-shaped eyes complete the disguise. These are tilted in various directions for comic effect.

Temate are believed to have come from Veluko, a mythical – or since vanished – island between Vanikolo and Tikopia. There are also *tamates* in the Banks Islands of Vanuatu, though these are small figurines carved to represent spirits or mythical beings.

Information
Medical Services There's a clinic at Puma, Vanikolo's largest village.

Getting There & Away
Boat The Marine Division fare from Honiara is S$54, while from Lata it's S$32. Connections to Utupua and Tikopia are S$12 and S$35 respectively.

Yacht There's a jetty at Emua and anchorages at Numbuko and Paeu.

Canoe Motor-canoe journeys to Utupua are infrequent, but when there is one, a shared ride costs around S$22.

Getting Around
All transport around the island is by motor canoe. A shared journey the 16 km between Puma and Emua costs about S$8.

BANIE ISLAND
Emua
This village is Banie Island's main centre. It has traditionally designed, ellipse-shaped houses, a sandy beach and coral gardens.

Muruvai
Outrigger canoes are plentiful at this new

Tikopian settlement. Six km away on the Boussole Reef is the spot where the *Wagina* was wrecked in a cyclone in 1985.

Paeu

Close by the Laurence River is the spot where La Pérouse's survivors built their abortive getaway vessel.

Ramboe Bay

The Astrolabe Memorial to La Pérouse and his crew is on this inlet's northern side. A museum to house the relics recovered from the two sunken French vessels is planned for the site.

TEVAI ISLAND

Tevai means 'water' in Polynesian. However, the only non-Melanesian people currently living in Vanikolo are the 20 or so Polynesians on the tiny island of Nanunga, opposite Lavaka in Banie Island, and the 100 Tikopians who recently settled at Muruvai.

Nomianu Island

This tiny islet was separated from Tevai by a tidal wave in the 1930s. However, it's slowly rejoining its much larger neighbour as silt accumulates in the narrow channel between the two. At the top of Nomianu is Takolo Cave, where the Temate first hid on their arrival in Vanikolo.

Dillon's Passage

This very narrow channel separating Vanikolo's two main islands has been the grave of several ships. Dugong, shark and barracuda can all be found here.

The Reef Islands

The Reefs, also known as the Swallow, Keppel or Matema Islands, lie 78 km north of Nendo. These 16 small landforms total only 78 sq km, yet they are spread over 4000 sq km of ocean.

The Reef Islands can be split into two groups – the Outer Reefs and the Main Reefs.

The Outer Reefs consists of five very small, low-lying, sandy islets only a few metres above sea level. Their principal features are coral-debris beaches, scrub and coconut vegetation, surrounding reefs and a Polynesian population.

The most distant are Nupani and Nalongo, about 71 km north-west of the main group. Closer, but still 28 km away, is Nukapu. Makalom and Pileni are much nearer – only 10 and five km respectively from the northern edge of the Main Reefs.

The principal islands are in the Main Reefs group. These are Nifiloli, Fenualoa, Ngalo, Ngawa, Nanianimbuli, Gnimbanga Temoa, Gnimbanga Nende, Nola, Ngatendo, Pigeon and Matema. The largest islands are only 15 to 31 metres above sea level.

True to their name, the Reef Islands have considerable onshore, and in some cases offshore, shoals. A line of four reefs stretches westwards for 21 km from Lomlom, while the Great Reef extends 25 km in the same direction from Nifiloli.

The Reefs lie in a medium rainfall area, averaging about 4200 mm (165 inches) a year, with October the wettest month. Tidal surges occur during some cyclones, occasionally inundating low-lying villages.

History

Fragments of Lapita pottery and obsidian dating back to 985 BC have been found at Nenumbo on Ngawa Island. One piece has a cruciform design, while another bears a narrow-nosed, slim-faced, round-eyed, moustachioed, surprisingly European-looking face.

Mendaña in 1595 called the Reefs the Yslas Ilena de Muchas Palmas, meaning 'islands covered with many palms'. Cartaret in 1767 thought the Main Reefs were one low-lying island, while Wilson in 1797 only saw Nukapu, Nalongo and Nupani. However, the French explorer De Tromelin, aboard the *Baionaise* in 1828, identified nine of the 11 islands in the Main Reefs group.

Bishop Patteson visited Nukapu in the mission ship *Southern Cross* in 1871. While sleeping ashore, he and two of his shipmates were battered to death.

An Australian blackbirding ship had shortly before kidnapped five young islanders, and the father of the man who killed Patteson had been shot from this vessel. Apparently, the blackbirders had dressed themselves up as missionaries to deceive the islanders.

The bishop's violent death produced an outcry in Britain and Australia, including demands for effective controls over the blackbirders. However, as punishment for its part in Patteson's death, Nukapu was shelled by a British warship.

People

The people of the Main Reefs are Melanesian except for those of Nifiloli, who are Polynesian. Fenualoa is very mixed, while Matema's people, though physically akin to Melanesians, are not pure Melanesians and speak the same Polynesian dialect as the Pileni Islanders. The other Melanesians speak 'Reefs' or Gnivo – the dialect of Lomlom. There is also a noticeably large number of albinos in the area.

The Reefs are home to about 6000, of whom 1000 are Polynesian. A further 500, mainly Melanesians, have moved to Nendo and Makira because of overcrowding.

Arts & Culture

A few female Reef Islanders produce the same finely woven banana-fibre shoulder bags as Nendo woman do. Some female Reef Islanders have cruciform-shaped tattoos on the back of their thighs.

Trading Canoes

Reef Islanders have the reputation of being daring navigators. In addition to visiting Nendo, routine annual voyages were made from Pileni to Santa Ana, 460 km away, and

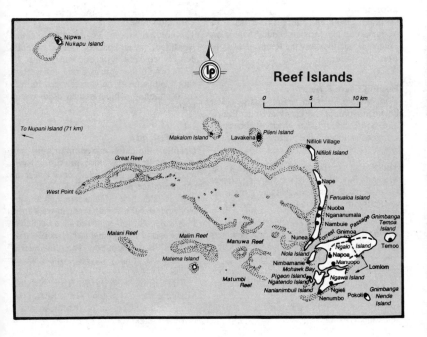

very occasionally even to Rennell, 775 km distant. These journeys were in outrigger trading canoes called *te puke*.

Although trading canoes were mainly made at Taumako in the Duffs, some were also built at Pileni. Unlike Duff Islands canoes, Reef Islands ones had no deckhouse. These nine-metre-long craft had a central crosspiece supported by an outrigger, which carried a raised platform where the sailor could rest. The canoe was powered by a large, claw-shaped sail, and was sturdy enough to cross open seas.

In the 1960s, a Pileni man called Tevake sailed 600 km to the Banks Islands in Vanuatu. He had aimed for Tikopia, 420 km away, but a storm swept him past, so he just kept right on to the next islands – the Banks.

In contrast, two-person dugout canoes are common around Lomlom. These craft use palm leaves as sails, which canoeists discard when paddling against the wind.

Information
Medical Services There are clinics at Manuopo on Ngalo Island and at Nuoba on Fenualoa. Islanders say the Reefs are usually free of malaria.

Getting There & Away
Boat Marine Division vessels charge S$49 between Honiara and Lomlom in the Reefs, and S$12 from Lata. Normal access to Lomlom is through the Forrest Passage.

Yacht The Reefs' main anchorage is at Mohawk Bay. Several of the outlying islands have sandy shores, though there's often an encircling reef to cross first.

Canoe Chartered motor canoes between Lata and Lomlom cost about S$120 for the four-hour-long 78-km journey. However, the resort at Pigeon Island organises transfers for their guests for S$100 a trip. As the sea can be very rough around the Reefs, with occa-sional fatalities, don't tie yourself to a tight schedule.

Getting Around
There is a four-km tractor route on Lomlom, but it is only usable in dry weather.

Canoe A shared motor canoe the 15 km from Mohawk Bay to Nifiloli Village costs about S$8, while the 20-km trip to Pileni costs about S$10. Shared rides to Nukapu and Nupani are S$22 and S$36 respectively.

THE MAIN REEFS
Lomlom
Lomlom is the collective name for Ngalo (or Ngambelipa), Ngawa and Nanianimbuli islands. Lomlom (pronounced 'Lum-Lum') is the main centre for the Reefs, with 3800 people. Its principal village is Manuopo.

There are coral cliffs with several small marine caves, which are only accessible by canoe, at Ngalo's northern tip. Nearby Nola Island is similar, although it lacks Ngalo's beaches because of its raised coral structure.

Fenualoa Island
The northern side of Fenualoa (also called Ngasinue) has no beaches, only coral cliffs densely covered with coconut palms. Its 1200 people are spread along its western shore. Fenualoan food is exchanged for red-feather money, which is then used to buy brides.

Nifiloli Island
Despite ethnically mixed marriages and many centuries of close proximity, only recently has regular social contact become commonplace between Nifiloli's 200 Poly-nesians and their Melanesian neighbours. Nonetheless, at low tide you can walk from Polynesian Nifiloli to mixed-race Fenualoa.

The island has several stretches of sandy beach at its northern end. The remainder is raised coral, thickly covered with coconut palms.

Stretching westwards from Nifiloli Village is the 25-km-long Great Reef. Daz-zling coral and colourful fish make this a favourite scuba site.

Matema Island

Matema, or Nodua, is a beautiful, golden-sand-surrounded island inhabited by 150 friendly Polynesian-speaking people who, while not pure Melanesian, resemble the Melanesians physically. Both scuba diving and fishing are ideal here.

Gnimbanga Temoa & Gnimbanga Nende Islands

These two small islands, sometimes respectively called Pangini and Pokoli, both lie to the east of Lomlom and have only 200 people between them. Temoa has a number of caverns with pools fed by freshwater springs.

Pigeon Island

This tiny raised-coral islet is opposite Ngatendo in Mohawk Bay and the site of the *Ngarando Rest House*. In addition to a small store, the island has two self-contained houses. Prices are S$25 for a dormitory bed and S$50/80 for singles/doubles. To make a booking, radio the resort in advance from Honiara or Lata.

A scuba instructor is sometimes resident to take you to the many dive spots and beaches nearby. Single dive prices are around S$50 to S$60. Underwater visibility is usually at least 30 metres.

Pigeon Island is far enough from Ngatendo to be free of mosquitoes, but close enough that you can walk over to it at low tide.

THE OUTER REEFS
Nupani Island

Isolated Nupani, also called Nimba, is entirely given over to subsistence crops and coconuts. Both it and its smaller, uninhabited sister, Nalongo, or Naloko, Island, occupy a large lagoon five km by six km wide. Some of Nupani's 100 people tend gardens on volcanic Tinakula.

Nukapu Island

Another large lagoon surrounds Nukapu, also called Nipwa and Tromelin Island. About 150 people live here, cultivating edible fruits and nuts in Nukapu's centre, with gardens on the perimeter. There's a memorial to Bishop Patteson's violent death in 1871 in Nipwa.

Pileni Island

200 people live on Pileni, also known as Nimibile. This sandy, palm-covered island, with several good swimming places, is the main centre of Polynesian language and culture in the Reefs. In the past, it was the starting point for many epic sea voyages.

Pileni people probably came from Tuvalu. They have the same deities as islanders on Sikaiana and Ontong Java, and are culturally closer to them than to Temotu's Polynesians.

Historically, Pileni's people were allies of the Sikaianans. On one occasion, a Tongan war party, returning from a battle with the Sikaianans, came ashore at Pileni. Unaware that a hot reception had been prepared for them, they were wiped out by continuous volleys of Pileni arrows.

Makalom Island

Alternatively known as Makolobu, or Booby, Island, uninhabited Makalom is a

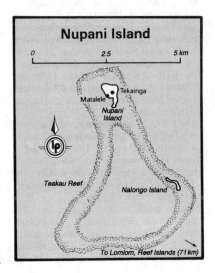

Nupani Island

bird sanctuary for hundreds of boobies. There's also excellent swimming and diving off its reef.

The Duff Islands

The Duffs are a scattered line of eleven small rocks and islands. This 28-km-long group, sometimes known as the Wilson Islands, occupies an area of only 14 sq km. Taumako is the largest of the islands, with a high point of 280 metres, yet it's only six km long.

History
Lapita settlement occurred in the Duffs in about 900 BC. This was followed in the first millennium AD by Melanesian occupation. The Melanesians, in turn, were superseded, probably in the mid-15th century, by newly arrived Polynesians – the forebears of the present-day islanders.

European discovery was made on 7 April 1606 by Quiros, the leader of the third Spanish expedition. He was searching both for Santa Cruz (Nendo), where he had been with Mendaña in 1595, and for the fabled Terra Australis, believed to be close by.

Quiros stayed at Taumako 11 days, asking the local chief, Tumai, many questions about the nearby Pacific. He also received reports from Luka, a Sikaianan prisoner of war he found there, who told of journeys between Taumako and Sikaiana – a distance of around 570 km. Luka, who was renamed Pedro, later reached Mexico with Quiros, where he died soon afterwards.

In 1797, Captain Wilson in the missionary ship *Duff* found these islands again, naming them after his vessel. The missionaries hoped to convert the local chief. Instead, they found a very stratified society. The chief's double canoe ran down any commoner's craft which got in its way in its haste to reach the mission ship first. The churchpeople called Taumako Disappointment Island because no-one there listened to their teachings. Other than these visitors, only the occasional sailing ship came by until the regular shipping services of this century.

People
About 500 Polynesian-speaking people live in the Duffs, maintaining close links with their Reef Islands neighbours. Despite their language's origin – the word *taumako* means 'potato yam' in Polynesian – physically and culturally they resemble Melanesians, the result of intermingling over many generations.

Arts & Culture
The Duff Islands are still ruled by hereditary chiefs. Although keen followers of the Church of Melanesia, they also believe in ancestral spirits – and witch doctors are still consulted.

The Duffs are an active part of the Santa Cruz red-feather-money circle. Some island girls marry for up to 16 to 24 rolls of red-feather coils, between S$4800 and S$7200.

A good time to see these transactions is when the monthly ship calls by. A Nendo or Reef Islander man will come with a stack of red-feather coils, hoping to complete his purchase before the ship sails again four to eight hours later.

Duff Islanders used to trade around Temotu on ocean-going canoes. In Quiros' time, these outrigger craft were large enough to carry up to 50 people, but by the early 1800s, they could only carry 10. Each one had a wooden deckhouse covered with palm leaves so the sailors could rest out of the sun. Although small souvenirs are now made, full-sized trading canoes are only built these days for major international cultural events – and consequently are very rare.

These craft used to sail regularly to the Reefs and Nendo, 109 km and 153 km southwestwards respectively. They even travelled the 580 km to Santa Ana and the 840 km to Rennell, though only very occasionally.

Information
Medical Services There is a clinic at Ngaura.

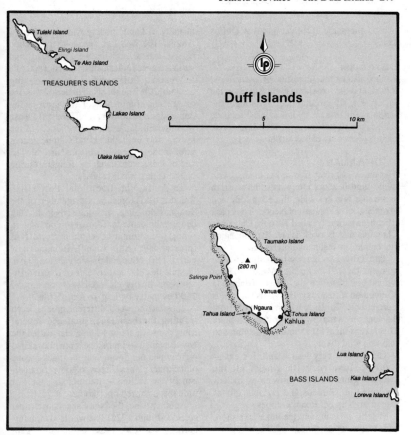

Duff Islands

Getting There & Away

Boat The Marine Division services cost S$54 from Honiara, S$29 from Lata, and S$21 from the Reefs. Vessels anchor along the coast near Salinga Point. Outrigger canoes paddle or punt their way through the reeds and reef between there and Tahua.

Yacht There's another anchorage at Ngaura.

AROUND DUFF ISLANDS
Taumako Island
The island is tall, wooded and craggy, with many sheer drops to the sea. The 250 inhab-itants mainly live opposite the tiny artificial island of Tahua, or beside a beautiful sandy beach at Ngaura. You can walk across to Tahua at low tide.

Tahua Island
In contrast to the ample space on Taumako, 250 people are packed tightly together on this minute, human-made and mosquito-free island, which Quiros called Venecia. Well before his arrival, coral stones had been placed on a sandbar until the resulting land-form was large enough to house a village. There are now more than 30 leaf houses

behind the same fortifications that Quiros saw.

Lakao Island

Lakao, also called Temelfua, or Treasurer's, Island, and the remaining eight islands in the group are all uninhabited. Although the fertile northern side of Lakao used to have settlers, people only go there nowadays to visit their gardens or to collect sea-birds' eggs.

TIKOPIA ISLAND

Tikopia is just over five sq km in size, with white-sand beaches along its south-western shore. It's two km wide, three km long and about 380 km south-east of Nendo. In the past, it has been variously called Tucopia, Chucupia, Chiquipia and Barwell Island. Its population and culture are distinctly Polynesian.

The island is an extinct single-cone volcano, the 380-metre-high Mt Reani, from which you can see the Banks Islands in Vanuatu on a clear day. Below its summit is a crater lake, Te Roto, which is cut off from the ocean by a narrow sand spit, or tombolo. This lake is ideal for swimming, fishing and trapping wild duck.

Tikopia is a very lush island. It's extensively cultivated, with almost all the available ground used to grow crops, including turmeric. Gardens and coconut groves extend high up Mt Reani's slopes.

Marshy areas around the inner lake shore and on the western edge of the island are given over to swamp taro. Plenty of fish are caught off the reef, and turtles are caught in the open seas.

Tikopia has a moderate rainfall, averaging 4000 mm (157 inches) a year; rain is heaviest from October to March. Occasionally cyclones strike with savage ferocity, as occurred in 1952 and 1953. Year-round temperatures average from 25°C to 29°C.

History

Early History Tikopia erupted from the sea about 80,000 years ago, though temporary human occupation did not occur until around 1800 to 1600 BC. Permanent settlement followed in about 1000 BC, when a great quantity of Lapita pottery was made locally. Around 100 BC, local ceramics production ceased. Instead, supplies were imported from various sources in Vanuatu up to about 800 AD.

Western Polynesians began arriving around 1200. The subsequent period was one of gradual elimination of the pre-existing population. According to Tikopians, these were the Fiti-kai-kere, or Fire Eaters of the Earth, who built the island's stone fences prior to the current inhabitants' arrival. The last of these were eaten by Tongans during one of their periodic raids.

Te Atafu, the traditional Polynesian founder of Tikopia, was a member of the Tongan ruling line. Arriving early in the 16th century, he came to Tikopia to dominate it, ruling over similar adventurers from Uvea (present-day Wallis Island), Rotuma (now part of Fiji), Niue and possibly Ontong Java. Despite this, the descendants of Uvean drift-voyagers finally emerged supreme around 1600 by marrying into Te Atafu's line.

Tensions between different groups, each wanting the best land, produced several tribal wars. In about 1700, a clan called the Nga Ravenga (with pale, even white, skins) were wiped out during a night attack by one of the other clans. There was some cannibalism of the victims – traditionally, the last time this occurred on Tikopia.

Another tribe, the Nga Faea, chose ritual suicide around 1725. The whole clan, numbering over 100, took to the sea, again because of land shortage, knowing they faced certain death. As a silent tribute to these two lost tribes, the north-western side of Tikopia is called Faea and the south-west is known as Ravenga.

In the early 18th century, a Tikopian chief called Tive (pronounced 'Tea-vy') took his forces to Vanikolo, 240 km to the north-west. They slaughtered all the Melanesians on Tevai Island. Later in the same century, a Melanesian resurgence drove these Tikopian colonists out.

European Contacts Meanwhile, the Europeans had made their first sighting of Tikopia. Quiros spent a night in 1606

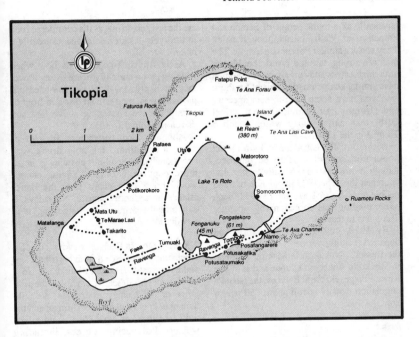

moored offshore, but did not land. Other than Captain Cameron's brief sighting in the *Barwell* in 1798, there were no other visits until 1813, when the Irish explorer Peter Dillon stopped by in his ship the *Hunter*. He landed three passengers at their request – a Prussian doctor called Buckhardt, his Fijian wife and a Lascar sailor called Joe. He returned in 1826 to pick them up.

The Lascar showed Dillon a sword scabbard and other European articles he had found when he had visited Vanikolo in 1820 – apparently remnants of the lost La Pérouse expedition. Buckhardt confirmed that French-made glass and pottery were being used on Tikopia when he arrived in 1813.

When the French explorer Dumont D'Urville visited in 1828 to check this out, he estimated Tikopia's population to be between 400 and 500. Following this visit, 115 people died, probably of influenza or gastroenteritis.

In 1852, a small group of Roman Catholic missionaries came ashore. When the relief ship called by the next year, they had all disappeared. No-one on the island could say where! Most likely, the priests had been killed for challenging the islanders' ancient traditions too directly.

Very few Tikopians were blackbirded because of their initial high mortality when exposed to foreign foods and sicknesses. Although the prohibition came 60 years after blackbirding began, the British authorities banned labour recruitment from Tikopia in 1923, much to the island's older generation's relief.

In July 1928, Professor Raymond Firth began his year-long anthropological studies on the island, which led to the publication of his famous book *We, the Tikopia* in 1936. Even today, it is a great source of pride to the inhabitants.

People

The 1250 Tikopians are light brown and

physically akin to the people of Samoa and French-ruled Wallis Island, though paler. They speak a similar Polynesian tongue. The men are strong, tall and broad shouldered, with thick calves and curly hair. The women have similar characteristics, except for those few who have some Micronesian ancestry and straight hair, acquired from a lost Gilbertese canoe party which reached Tikopia in the 1780s.

Because of the island's small size, strict population control used to be imposed, though recent missionary activity has discouraged this. The 1929 population of 1285 people grew by 36% to 1750 in 1952. Such overcrowding has forced many younger Tikopians to leave.

By 1970, 40% of the population had departed, settling variously in Nukufero in the Russells, Nukukasi in Makira, Muruvai in Vanikolo, Ahabo on Utupua and at White River Village, Honiara. Even so, the island's population density is still about 250 per sq km.

Arts

Tikopia lies outside Temotu's red-feather-money exchange network. Instead the islanders produce mats which are avidly sought by the inhabitants of several other islands in the area, particularly those of Vanikolo.

Some old men wear only a wrapping of plain, undyed tapa made from paper-mulberry trees. In contrast, many young men wear lava-lavas, either like a sarong or as a loincloth. In Tikopia, lava-lavas are also used as a night sheet and sunshade.

Young boys make their own four-string guitars. Sometimes youthful singing groups with handmade stringed instruments follow the occasional foreign visitors around, serenading them with Polynesian songs.

Culture

Tikopian houses, which are ellipse-shaped, flush to the ground and made of leaves, are entered by crawling through a small one-metre-high opening. To exit you must crawl out backwards, facing inwards unless you are the last person out, as it's considered rude to turn your back on someone, especially a chief.

As in Anuta, Tikopian girls bow when walking past a man. If you are sitting down, they are likely to walk by on their knees. In the same way, men will sit down in front of a chief to avoid standing above him and therefore being disrespectful.

Although kava ceremonies are part of Tikopia's tradition, it's only drunk very occasionally, as betel-nut chewing is much more popular. Formerly, trading canoes would bring kava plants from the Banks Islands in northern Vanuatu. Nowadays, it can only be acquired by importing it in powder form.

Tikopian Chiefs Each of the four Tikopian chiefs traces his descent from his tribe's legendary ancestor. The ariki kafika, or No 1 chief, traces his descent from Uvea; the ariki tafua, or No 2 chief, from Niue; the ariki taumako, or No 3 chief, from Tonga; and the ariki fangarere, or No 4 chief, from mixed western Polynesian sources, including Anuta, Ontong Java, the Duffs and Mota Lava in Vanuatu's Banks Islands. However, only 5% of Tikopia's people are members of the latter tribe. These four chiefs represent the island's main divisions and in the past were often political rivals.

The authority of the chief is felt throughout his clan. Everyone knows who the chiefs are and to which group they belong. This system of authority has been left undisturbed, both by the former colonial regime and the post-Independence government. Both have correctly felt that while the chiefs were loyal, so would their people be.

Inter-Island Voyaging In the past, there was frequent trade between Tikopia and the Banks Islands. The ariki kafika has an ancestral claim to a small islet there, called Ravenga. It's just off Vanua Lava, 204 km to Tikopia's south-west. In 1891, a missionary called Coddrington reported that as many as 11 large Tikopian trading canoes used to visit Vanua Lava at a time. However, there have been few successful Tikopian voyages to the Banks since WW II, and none since Independence. Out of about 30 voyages between 1945 and the mid-1970s, 80 of the 100 or so who put to sea were lost.

Anuta is Tikopia's closest neighbour, 150 km distant. The two islands are close enough for the people of both to regard each other as wantoks, each family having a parallel family on the other island to which they belong. Regular canoe visits used to be made to Anuta, with Tikopian canoeists sometimes diverting to desolate Fatutaka for sea-birds' eggs. Another classic trade route was to Vanikolo, where Tikopian mats were traded for Vanikolan arrows. On very rare occasions, voyagers went as far as Rennell, over 1000 km away.

The omnipresent ocean permeates every aspect of the islanders' lives. Wild seas and shipwreck seldom deter them. Such a death is called sweet burial. Tikopians do not say left or right – only inland or seawards.

Information
Medical Services This island's clinic is at Mata Utu. Until 1955, although the anopheles mosquito was known to be on Tikopia, there was said to be no malaria locally. However, an epidemic in that year, described as influenza accompanied by malaria, killed over 200 people. Massage was the island's principal treatment for sickness prior to the arrival of modern medicine.

Accommodation
Getting permission to stay is definitely not easy. And getting away is possible only when the monthly ship visits. You should send a radio message asking the chiefs' permission first, and accept their decision – even if it's no.

Things to Buy
Scale-model souvenir canoes are made, complete with outriggers. Shark-hooks, made from pearl shells, and headrest souvenirs are also produced.

Getting There & Away
Boat The monthly Marine Division service from Honiara to Tikopia costs S$56, while from Lata it's S$42. It's S$23 from Anuta and S$35 from Vanikolo. Ships wait at the island's anchorage for between four and eight hours. The vessel's dinghy brings you ashore at Potikorokoro, where everyone wades past the three fish traps on to the white-sand beach.

Tikopia's few visiting yachts usually anchor off Potikorokoro.

Getting Around
Many small paths wind between gardens and villages, with few places in the island's densely inhabited western half more than

Woman from Temotu Province

five minutes apart. To get the best of your short visit, ask to see one of the chiefs, who will appoint someone to be your guide. Inquire whether you may take photographs as a chiefly edict in 1991 barred cameras from the island.

AROUND TIKOPIA ISLAND
Mata Utu

Close to the No 2 chief's house is the Te Marae Lasi. This was the 200-metre-long tika-dart pitch where interdistrict contests used to be held several times each year. Upright stone slabs at one end indicate past record throws. There's also a dancing circle nearby.

About 200 metres further south is Takarito, where there's the sacred burial place of the Nga Faea tribe and a sacred fish-produce stone. In pre-Christian times, it was believed the island would have plenty of fish as long as the stone was ritually washed and worshipped.

Tumuaki

There are very good views from this raised ledge over the southern part of the island, including of Lake Te Roto.

Potusataumako

A temple in this small village on the southern side of the island is the property of the No 3 chief. This pole-and-thatch structure contains relics of the Taumako clan and is now used as the chief's dwelling. Nearby, at Potusakafika, is a stone fish trap.

Fonganuku & Fongatekoro

The two massive volcanic pinnacles of Fonganuku and Fongatekoro rise steeply from Lake Te Roto's southern shore. On Fongatekoro's summit is the burial place of Pu Lasi, one of the principal ancestors of the Tikopian No 1 chief's line, and traditional founder of Anuta. The tomb is marked by a small rectangular platform and can only be approached by a precipitous trail.

All members of this chief's tribe must, at least once in their lifetime, clamber up here and pay homage to the clan's dead ancestor by placing a basketful of clean sand on the grave. Fongatekoro, meaning 'Fortress Hill', served as a natural strong point during several 17th-century Tongan raids.

Ravenga Tombolo

Less than 100 metres wide in some places, this narrow artificial sand spit protects the lake from the sea. Its low stone sea walls are regularly reinforced.

Lake Te Roto

This beautiful, but brackish, freshwater lake occupies much of Tikopia's eastern half. The lake is about one sq km in size, and is surrounded by swampy land. Te Roto is no more than one or two metres deep along the narrow Ravenga shore, but in its drowned crater centre it drops to 80 metres. Islanders fish with seine nets for the indigenous pink salmon-like kiokio fish, grey mullet and the recently introduced tilapia.

The lake was not always closed to the sea. In 1606, the Spanish recorded it as an open bay. By 1828, Dumont D'Urville noted the tombolo was in place along three-quarters of its present length.

Namo

This village is the site of Te Ava, a channel intermittently opened to allow excess lake water to flow to the sea. It's usually opened after January rains have filled the lake. As the waters flow out to the sea, islanders trap fish with long-handled nets.

Somosomo

Traditional festivals were held here in pre-Christian times. There are also some ancient stone slabs at Matorotoro, one km northwards along the lake's shore, where similar ceremonies occurred.

Uta

Across Te Roto is the sacred district of Uta. In pre-Christian times, annual religious rites were held in the dancing circle and ancient burial grounds here.

Fatapu Point

Just beyond Fatapu Point are some blow-holes. About one km eastwards along the rocky northern shore is the small natural arch of Te Ana Forau.

Te Ana Lasi Cave

The name of this large rockshelter means 'Great Cave'. Food scraps left by Tikopia's first visitors date back to between 1800 and 1600 BC. Immediately below is another natural arch.

ANUTA ISLAND

Diminutive Anuta, also called Anudha or Cherry, lies 450 km due east of Nendo. Its nearest populated neighbour is Tikopia, with which it retains close traditional ties. In addition, 55 km south-eastwards is lonely, uninhabited Fatutaka.

Anuta is only 0.4 sq km in area. It's a small volcanic island with a fringing onshore reef. Anuta's tallest point is the 65- metre-high hill Te Maunga, which is used for intensive dryland agriculture. There's a relatively large, flat coastal plain below it on the island's southern side, as well as two cliff promontories. Additionally, two large rocks rise up out of the sea to the east – Te Fatu'oveu and Fatu'omango. The beaches are of sparkling white sand.

Although seas are often very rough between Anuta and its distant neighbours the Duffs and Tikopia, there's a 23 to 36-metre-deep submarine plateau extending 6.5 km north-west which provides the island with excellent fishing.

High winds occur locally, particularly in December. Annual rainfall averages 3000 to 3500 mm (118 to 138 inches). Storms and droughts alternately devastate the island; particularly bad cyclones occurred in 1916, 1970 and 1972.

Anuta's few visitors comment on the neatness of its gardens. Hillsides are terraced to the summit and plants are mulched and carefully tended. Although the spring at Te Vai is the island's only source of fresh water, Anuta is extremely fertile because of the soil's high phosphate level. There are two fish traps.

One's beside Rotoapi, while the other is on the island's north-eastern shore below Te Maunga.

History

A small group of Lapita people first occupied the island from around 965 to 650 BC. They were followed in about 350 BC by an unknown people, probably Austronesians, who used plain pottery and appear to have remained until between 500 and 700 AD. Anuta was probably then deserted for a long period, perhaps because of cyclones and droughts.

The next settlement was around 1100 AD and possibly Melanesian, although its numbers were probably small. Anutans refer to these people as the Afukere, or Earth-Sprung.

In about 1580, the ancestor of the modern Anuta, Pu Lasi, arrived from Tonga, and found the Afukere in residence. It was a time of alternate droughts and cyclones, so after a short stay he withdrew to Tikopia, during which time it seems that all the Afukere died. On his return, Pu Lasi found instead a motley crew of Uveans, Samoans and other Tongans, and became their overlord. This supremacy is the probable reason for certain Tongan expressions being used by present-day Anutans.

Anuta's subsequent history was characterised by raids by outsiders – particularly Tongans – and internecine strife. One of these civil wars, in about 1790, left only four male survivors – three of them brothers. Once peace returned, Tikopian influence predominated, producing considerable inter-marriage between the people of the two islands.

In 1791, Captain Edwards of HMS *Pandora* passed close to Anuta while searching for the mutineers of HMS *Bounty*, and also saw Fatutaka. The Russian Kroutcheff sighted both islands in 1822.

The next recorded visit was by Captain Markham in HMS *Rosario* in 1871. He noticed the Anutans were Polynesians, chewed betel nut, had large holes in their ears and resembled Samoans. The islanders knew

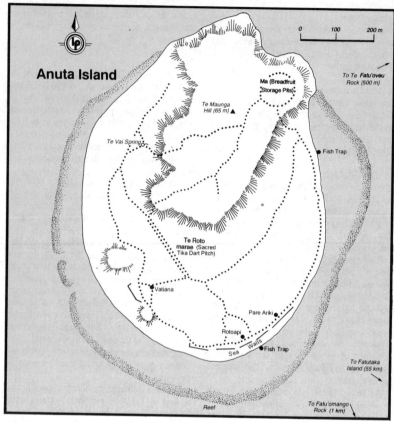

some simple European words and had a taste for tobacco, which suggested that there had been some unrecorded visits by European sailors previously.

The proclamation of the British Protectorate in 1893 left the Anutan chiefs' authority undisturbed. However, at Independence Anuta at first refused to join the rest of Temotu in the new Provincial Assembly, fearing it would lose its traditional autonomy.

Although Anutans now vote in both national and provincial elections, they still look on Solomon Islanders as Melanesian by definition, seeing themselves as inhabitants of an autonomous microstate, independent in mind if not in fact. To emphasise this, Anutans charge all outsiders other than their wantoks, the Tikopians, and including police and officials, S$2 to land.

Anthropologists & Archaeologists Dr D E Yen and Janet Gordon of the Bernice Bishop Museum, Honolulu, pushed the island's history back to 965 BC following their studies on Anuta in 1971. Several other specialists have also visited the island, including the US anthropologist Richard Feinberg, who was there from 1972 to 1973.

People

Anuta's population has hovered around 190 to 200 people for over 100 years. Because of its small size, it's the most densely populated island in the Solomons group. Some of its teenagers look like southern Europeans and have wavy gingerish hair.

Arts

Tapa is made locally from breadfruit trees. It's still worn by many people, especially the two chiefs and their wives.

Anutan girls weave mats to pay their own bride price, and ceremonial clubs and fishing spears are also produced. Clamshell adzes are made for carving, and digging sticks are produced for gardening.

Culture

Tattoos indicate status; consequently, the island's two chiefs are strikingly decorated. As in Tikopia, women bow from the waist when passing a man. Another tradition, like in Ontong Java, is the keeping of frigate birds as free-flying pets.

Anutan Chiefs The No 1 chief is the tui Anuta, or king of Anuta, and what he says is law. He rules in consultation with his *Maru*, or Weekly Council of Elders, and the No 2 chief. The day after the Maru, the *Pono* – a general assembly of all the island's adults – is held at which the Maru's decisions are passed on to the people.

The two chiefs hold their positions as direct descendants of the settlers of the 1580s. The tui Anuta is descended from Pu Lasi, while the No 2 chief's ancestors were Uveans who arrived slightly later.

Information

Medical Services There's only a small medical-aid post on the island, as Anutans have traditionally considered that major illnesses come from breaches of communally acceptable behaviour rather than from germs and the lack of hygiene. Islanders

believe disrespect towards others, particularly chiefs and priests, will lead to sickness. Recovery only comes when offenders acknowledge their guilt and are forgiven by the injured parties.

Officially, there's no malaria on Anuta. However, the local aid post's regular treatment for headaches has often been aspirin and choloquine, suggesting it's present after all.

Accommodation

If you want to stay on Anuta, you must first get permission from the two chiefs by radio. No prior permission – no stay!

Getting There & Away

The Marine Division fare from Honiara to Anuta is S$56, while from Lata and Tikopia it's S$44 and S$23 respectively. Its monthly vessel occasionally abandons its attempts to call at the island if seas are too rough, even though Anutan passengers are aboard. Access for ships' dinghies is difficult, with surf constantly breaking directly on to the reef along its entire length. Dinghies occasionally capsize while crossing the two breaks in the coral near Vatiana, so take dry clothing and cameras in a plastic bag if you want to visit the island.

As long as sea conditions permit, ships anchor for between four and eight hours. That's ample time to see around once you've paid your S$2 landing fee.

Any stopover will be for at least four weeks. If the weather is bad, it could be two or three times longer. So once the chiefs have given you permission to stay, inform the tourist office and the Immigration Department in Honiara. Ask the latter to give you a visa long enough to cover possible delays, and bring plenty of gifts and food.

Getting Around

There are footpaths to every destination on the island, including the breadfruit pits in Anuta's north-east.

AROUND ANUTA ISLAND

Rotoapi

The island's main village, on Anuta's south-eastern shore, is protected by a line of five coral sea walls. Rotoapi's houses are low, ellipse-shaped and thatched with sago or coconut-palm leaves. The island's principal marae, Pare Ariki, is 100 metres to the north-east, and contains four god stones and 19 graves of pre-Christian chiefs.

Vatiana

This second, smaller village is about 200 metres to the west. In front of it is another sea wall. Behind is the Te Roto marae, also called Te Marae Tika. This 180-metre-long pitch was formerly used for competitive tika-dart throwing.

Te Maunga

Anuta has always had adequate food supplies, despite its high population density, because of the many *ma*, or breadfruit storage pits, at Te Maunga's north-eastern end. *Masi*, or preserved breadfruit paste, is stored underground for several years and remains perfectly edible, protected by regular replacement of its covering leaves. After a devastating cyclone in 1970, Anuta declined outside help because there was ample breadfruit in store.

FATUTAKA ISLAND

Uninhabited Fatutaka – also known as Mitre, Fataka or Fatu, the Polynesian word for 'rock' – lies in the domain of Anuta. It's a 1.6-sq-km seasonal hunting ground to which islanders come for sea birds and eggs. Medium-sized sailing canoes are still built in Anuta for the journey to Fatutaka. Although Anutans tended gardens on the island in the distant past, Tikopians periodically felled its coconut palms to prevent marauding Tongans from using it as a base. Consequently, nothing grows there now. Although it's larger than Anuta, Fatutaka is rocky and infertile.

Glossary

Amtrak – An amphibious, tank-sized, tracked vehicle which is used to carry assault troops ashore or across marshes.

AOG – Assembly of God Church.

Atoll – A thin, low-lying island built up from successive deposits of coral and surrounding a central, often-circular, shallow lagoon. Atolls perch on extinct submarine volcano peaks, surrounded by deep ocean. Because they are low lying, they lack soil depth and fresh water, usually offering only a marginal base for human habitation.

Back-Loom – A loom consisting of a few loose sticks and a hand-tied string needle. Tensio
n is provided by tying one stick to a tree or a wall and another to a loop around the weaver's waist. Loincloths and bags are back-looms' most common products.

Bêche-De-Mer – Also known as trepang, seaslug or sea cucumber. Some species of this lethargic, bottom-dwelling sea creature can completely merge into the sand, taking the shape of a rock, yet out of the water they look like burnt black bricks. Others are sausage-shaped and mainly black, brown, green or orange in colour.

When disturbed, some types of bêche-de-mer discharge white spaghetti-like tentacles which are highly toxic, causing inflammation if they touch the skin. Although forms of bêche-de-mer contain stomach toxins, proper processing leaches the poison out. The processing involves gutting, boiling for 1½ hours, washing and drying. As long as they've been thoroughly processed, bêche-de-mer are highly prized by Chinese cooks because they add texture to oriental cuisine.

Bonito – An alternative name in the Solomons for bluefin tuna.

Booby – A gull-sized sea bird with a brown or blackish body and white head. It usually lives in large colonies on tall, sea-girthed rocks.

Breadfruit – A large, starchy fruit with a coarse green skin. It can be boiled, mashed, or fried like potato chips and is a popular food among Polynesians. The tree's sap can be used as a traditional medicine. When wrapped as an emollient over a sprain or bruise, it causes the swelling to subside quickly.

Bush Knife – The Pacific version of a machete or panga. It's used for a range of tasks, including house building, cutting grass and opening coconuts.

Calico – A 19th-century expression, still frequently used by Pacific Islanders, meaning cotton cloth.

Cargo Cult – A religious movement whose followers hope for the imminent and magical delivery of vast quantities of modern wealth and goods (ie cargo) through the generosity of supernatural forces or the inhabitants of faraway countries.

Careen – The process of scraping the barnacles off the hull of a ship after it has been heaved up on to the shore.

Cassava – The edible, starch-yielding root of the tapioca plant. Its young foliage can be consumed as a green vegetable, though poison in the root, indicated by a bitter taste, has first to be leached out by cooking.

Cay – A tiny coral island, or large sandbar, on which vegetation has begun to sprout.

CFC – Christian Fellowship Church.

COM – Church of Melanesia, formerly known as the DOM, or Diocese of Melanesia. It's part of the worldwide Anglican Church.

Copra – Dried coconut kernels which are processed to make oil for margarine and soap.

Coral – A rock-like structure composed of the dead remains of many generations of tiny sea creatures called coral polyps, which live in huge colonies on top of existing submarine formations. By producing a calcified skeleton, they lay a base for the next generation to live on, in the process creating a reef.

They cannot survive in cold or fresh water, or in murky or dark conditions.

Custom House – A building where sacred art objects are stored. This term is also used to describe traditionally designed leaf houses built flush to the ground, as opposed to the more modern ones that are raised on stilts.

Custom Ownership – Traditionally acknowledged ownership of land, objects or even a stretch of reef, whether owned by individuals, families, clans or tribes. Custom owners can refuse access to their property if they wish, and expect to be asked permission before anyone crosses their land or uses anything considered by tradition to be theirs.

Cut-Nut – The common Solomons name for the Tahiti Chestnut. This large relative of the ngali nut has a hard, brown outer shell. It takes a firm stroke from a bush knife to open this shell, hence the name. Inside is a firm, crisp-tasting, greyish-brown chestnut which is often eaten raw.

DBSI – Development Bank of the Solomon Islands.

District Officer – This title was held by those British Protectorate officials who were in charge of a part of the Solomons equivalent to a present-day province.

Edible Fern – Also called *kasume* or fern cabbage, this fern-shaped vegetable tastes like a mild spinach and is often flavoured with coconut cream.

Expats – Short for 'expatriates'. Often used as an alternative to 'European' to describe usually White foreigners who are resident in the Solomons.

Fumarole – A small volcanic or thermal fissure in the ground from which columns of steam, smoke or gas arise, or where naturally heated water bubbles up. Some gases emitted by fumaroles can be sulphurous and may cause choking.

GTS – Guadalcanal Travel Service.

HMAS – His (or Her) Majesty's Australian Ship – the term identifying a ship as an Australian warship.

HMS – His (or Her) Majesty's Ship – the term identifying a ship as a British warship.

IDC – The Isabel Development Corporation.

Kava – The mud-coloured, mildly intoxicating drink made from the roots of the *Piper methysticum*, or intoxicating pepper, plant. Although grown and drunk frequently throughout nearby Vanuatu, it's only imbibed in the Solomons in Tikopia and Anuta, and then solely on rare ceremonial occasions.

Kumara – Pronounced 'Koo-muh-ra' and also known as sweet potato, this plant's tuberous roots have become a staple food in the Solomons. Although it filtered across the Pacific from South America to New Zealand and New Guinea prior to European settlement, it was not grown in the Solomons until it was introduced by New Zealand missionaries in the 1860s.

Lagoon – An area of water sealed off from the open ocean by a network of reefs or sandbars.

Lava-Lava – A length of material similar to a sarong that is cool to wear and wrapped around the waist. It's often worn by men in the outlying islands, especially where Polynesian contacts have been strongest.

Leaf Houses – These standard village dwellings are built of bamboo frames and thatched with sago palm. Most nowadays are raised up to a metre above ground, though traditional ones were most often flush to the ground. Inside are usually a number of raised platforms to sit and sleep on. Otherwise, the occupants use the floor, which is made of betel-nut wood if the house is built on stilts, or hardened earth if it's at ground level.

Mangou – A thin, dark-reddish-green vegetable shaped like a long pen and peeled before cooking.

Manioc – Another name for cassava.

Marae – A place sacred to Polynesians,

including temples, graveyards and ceremonial pitches for tika-dart throwing.

Matrilineal – The line of descent and/or inheritance through the mother's side.

MV – Motor vessel.

NBSI – National Bank of the Solomon Islands.

Ngali Nut – Pronounced 'narly-nut', they are known as bush, or *canarium*, almonds, and are eaten raw as a snack or cooked in puddings throughout the Solomons.

NPF – National Provident Fund.

Pana – A prickly form of yam.

Pandanus – Often called the screw-tree because of the coiled shape of its slender stems, it grows mainly in marshy ground. Its dried leaves are woven into very strong floor mats, while its orange, waxy fruit contains high levels of protein in its edible, but dull-tasting, outer skin.

Patrilineal – The line of descent and/or inheritance through the father's side.

Pawpaw – Also known in parts of Oceania by its Spanish name of papaya, this fruit is orange when ripe and grows on a slender three to four-metre-high tree. It's a staple food throughout the Pacific.

Pelagic – A term used to describe fish living in the upper waters of the open sea.

Polynesian Outliers – The small Polynesian-inhabited atolls and islands on the extreme fringes of the Solomons, as well as the two largish, but isolated, uplifted coral landforms of Rennell and Bellona.

Pole-and-Line – The method of fishing where large numbers of tuna are caught by feathered, hookless lures hanging by a short line from a pole held over the side of a trawler. The tuna are driven into a frenzy when livebait is thrown among them, and will strike at anything, including the 15 to 20 pole-and-line lures dangling in the water.

Pontoon – A temporary floating jetty or bridge.

PT Boat – WW II patrol torpedo boat, usually American.

Purse-Seining – Fishing with a large net which is draped around a school of fish, and then closed like a purse around them.

Quonset Hut – a large WW II prefabricated steel storage shed. Some are still in use today.

Reef – A ridge of coral, rock or sand whose top lies just below the seas's surface. It's called an onshore, or fringing, reef when it adjoins the shore and an offshore reef when there is a stretch of open water between it and the land.

Roti – A soft, pitta-type bread, usually with a curried fish, meat or vegetable filling.

Sago Palm – A three to four-metre-high palm-like tree which is topped with stiff, glossy green fronds. Its slender trunk and leaves are often used as house-building material, while sago (a starchy cereal) is extracted from its roots. During droughts, villagers drain starch from the stem of the tree and eat it as a survival food.

SDA – Seventh Day Adventist Church. Its worship day is Saturday, so its members seldom do any work or business then – even for tourists.

Seabees – The members of the US WW II Construction Brigade – ie CBs.

Sennit – Rope made from the fibrous husks, or outer casings, of mature coconuts.

SIBC – Solomon Islands Broadcasting Corporation.

SIPL – Solomon Islands Plantations Limited.

Slippery Cabbage – A spinach-like green vegetable with reddish streaks through it.

SSEC – South Seas Evangelical Church.

SSEM – South Seas Evangelical Mission, the SSEC's predecessor.

Stamping Drums – From one to 1.5 metres tall, but only about 15 cm in diameter, these drums are made of bamboo and have a hollow centre. They are held in a vertical position while they are rhythmically and repeatedly beaten on the ground to make a tune.

Tapa – The cloth made from the bark of ebony, paper-mulberry trees or breadfruit trees. Though mainly worn by Polynesians, it's also used by the people of a few Melanesian islands on ceremonial occasions. The bark is peeled off, then beaten with wooden or stone mallets until white. Once it's been dried in the sun, it's often decorated with various traditional designs.

Taro – Called dalo in Fiji and Papua New Guinea, this food is eaten as a staple food all over the Pacific. It can be boiled, crushed, roasted, baked, steamed, or fried like chips. There are two main species: swamp taro, which has dark-green, glossy leaves and is only successful in a wet, mulchy soil; and dry taro, which has a matt, mid-green leaf and prefers hillsides irrigated by rainfall. Both plants' large green leaves are often called elephant's ears.

Young taro leaves are edible after cooking and taste like spinach. However, old leaves, or any from a purple-stemmed plant, should not be eaten, as they can give you a very sore mouth. The edible root of the swamp taro is grey and rather dull tasting, while the dry version is purplish and more pleasant, especially with coconut cream.

Tika Dart – A three-quarter-metre-long javelin-like dart with a heavy, narrow, elipse-shaped, stone front end which could be thrown almost 100 metres by a skilled warrior. Tika-dart throwing was a frequent part of traditional Polynesian ceremonies throughout the Pacific.

T-Piece – A small piece of cloth which covers the groin only, leaving the abdomen exposed.

Trocchus – Sometimes called turban shell because of its 'wound-around' shape, the shell of this snail-like tropical sea creature can be polished to make elegant ivory-coloured ornaments. Until the emergence of plastic, most so-called pearl buttons were instead made of the much more plentiful trocchus.

USP – University of the South Pacific. Its main campus is in Suva, Fiji, though there are annexes elsewhere, including one in the Kukum area of Honiara.

USS – United States Ship – the term identifying a ship as a US warship.

Yam – A starchy tuber which is a staple Melanesian food. Yams can range in length from 20 cm to over a metre, be pole-shaped and regarded as male by islanders, or have twin legs (ie female), and weigh up to 45 kg. Their texture can vary from tender to crisp, depending on the species. Yam plants have deep roots, and often the only proof of their subterranean presence is a mass of long, unruly, greenish vines growing freely over a thin, triangular structure of two-metre-high garden stakes.

4WD – A four-wheel-drive vehicle.

Index

Guides to the Pacific

Australia – a travel survival kit
The complete low-down on Down Under – home of Ayers Rock, the Great Barrier Reef, extraordinary animals, cosmopolitan cities, rainforests, beaches ... and Lonely Planet!

Bushwalking in Australia
Two experienced and respected walkers give details of the best walks in every state, covering many different terrains and climates.

Islands of Australia's Great Barrier Reef – a travel survival kit
The Great Barrier Reef is one of the wonders of the world – and one of the great travel destinations! Whether you're looking for a tropical island resort or a secluded island hideaway, this guide has all the facts you'll need.

Sydney city guide
A wealth of information on Australia's most exciting city; all in a handy pocket-sized format.

Hawaii – a travel survival kit
Share in the delights of this island paradise – and avoid some of its high prices – with this practical guide. Covers all of Hawaii's well-known attractions, plus plenty of uncrowded sights and activities.

New Zealand – a travel survival kit
This practical guide will help you discover the very best New Zealand has to offer – Maori dances and feasts; some of the most spectacular scenery in the world; and every outdoor activity imaginable.

Tramping in New Zealand
Call it tramping, hiking, walking, bushwalking, or trekking – travelling by foot is the best way to explore New Zealand's natural beauty. Detailed descriptions of 20 walks of varying length and difficulty.

Fiji – a travel survival kit
Whether you prefer to stay in camping grounds, international hotels, or something in-between, this comprehensive guide will help you to enjoy the beautiful Fijian archipelago.

New Caledonia – a travel survival kit
This guide shows how to discover all that he idyllic islands of New Caledonia have to offer – from French colonial culture to traditional Melanesian life.

Rarotonga & the Cook Islands – a travel survival kit
Rarotonga and the Cook Islands have history, beauty and magic to rival the better-known islands of Hawaii and Tahiti, but the world has virtually passed them by.

Micronesia – a travel survival kit
The glorious beaches, lagoons and reefs of these 2100 islands would dazzle even the most jaded traveller. This guide has all the details on island-hopping across the north Pacific.

Papua New Guinea – a travel survival kit
With its coastal cities, villages perched beside mighty rivers, palm-fringed beaches and rushing mountain streams, Papua New Guinea promises memorable travel.

Tahiti & French Polynesia – a travel survival kit
Tahiti's idyllic beauty has seduced sailors, artists and traveller for generations. The latest edition provides full details on the main island of Tahiti, the Tuamotos, Marquesas and other island groups. Invaluable information for independent travellers and package tourists alike.

Tonga – a travel survival kit
The only South Pacific country never to be colonised by Europeans, Tonga has also been ignored by tourists. The people of this far-flung island group offer some of the most sincere and unconditional hospitality in the world.

Samoa – a travel survival kit
Two remarkably different countries, Western Samoa and American Samoa offer some wonderful island escapes, and Polynesian culture at its best..

Also available:
Papua New Guinea phrasebook.

Keep in touch!

We love hearing from you and think you'd like to hear from us.

The Lonely Planet Newsletter covers the when, where, how and what of travel. (AND it's free!)

When...is the right time to see reindeer in Finland?
Where...can you hear the best palm-wine music in Ghana?
How...do you get from Asunción to Areguá by steam train?
What...should you leave behind to avoid hassles with customs in Iran?

To join our mailing list just contact us at any of our offices. (details below)

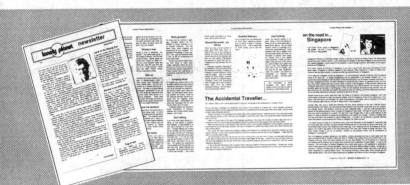

Every issue includes:

* a letter from Lonely Planet founders Tony and Maureen Wheeler
* travel diary from a Lonely Planet author - find out what it's really like out on the road
* feature article on an important and topical travel issue
* a selection of recent letters from our readers
* the latest travel news from all over the world
* details on Lonely Planet's new and forthcoming releases

Also available Lonely Planet T-shirts. 100% heavy weight cotton (S, M, L, XL)

LONELY PLANET PUBLICATIONS
Australia: PO Box 617, Hawthorn, 3122, Victoria (tel: 03-819 1877)
USA: Embarcadero West, 155 Filbert Street, Suite 251, Oakland, CA 94607 (tel: 510-893 8555)
UK: Devonshire House, 12 Barley Mow Passage, Chiswick, London W4 4PH (tel: 081-742 3161)

Lonely Planet Guidebooks

Lonely Planet guidebooks cover every accessible part of Asia as well as Australia, the Pacific, South America, Africa, the Middle East, Europe and parts of North America. There are five series: *travel survival kits*, covering a country for a range of budgets; *shoestring guides* with compact information for low-budget travel in a major region; *walking guides*; *city guides* and *phrasebooks*.

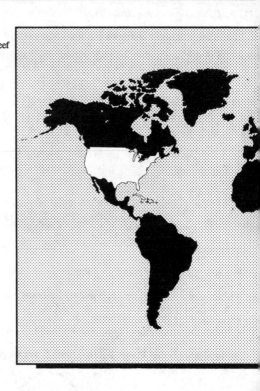

Australia & the Pacific
Australia
Bushwalking in Australia
Islands of Australia's Great Barrier Reef
Fiji
Micronesia
New Caledonia
New Zealand
Tramping in New Zealand
Papua New Guinea
Papua New Guinea phrasebook
Rarotonga & the Cook Islands
Samoa
Solomon Islands
Sydney
Tahiti & French Polynesia
Tonga
Vanuatu

South-East Asia
Bali & Lombok
Bangkok
Burma
Burmese phrasebook
Cambodia
Indonesia
Indonesia phrasebook
Malaysia, Singapore & Brunei
Philippines
Pilipino phrasebook
Singapore
South-East Asia on a shoestring
Thailand
Thai phrasebook
Vietnam, Laos & Cambodia

North-East Asia
China
Mandarin Chinese phrasebook
Hong Kong, Macau & Canton
Japan
Japanese phrasebook
Korea
Korean phrasebook
North-East Asia on a shoestring
Taiwan
Tibet
Tibet phrasebook

West Asia
Trekking in Turkey
Turkey
Turkish phrasebook
West Asia on a shoestring

Middle East
Egypt & the Sudan
Egyptian Arabic phrasebook
Iran
Israel
Jordan & Syria
Yemen

Indian Ocean
Madagascar & Comoros
Maldives & Islands of the East Indian Ocean
Mauritius, Réunion & Seychelles

Mail Order

Lonely Planet guidebooks are distributed worldwide. They are also available by mail order from Lonely Planet, so if you have difficulty finding a title please write to us. US and Canadian residents should write to Embarcadero West, 155 Filbert St, Suite 251, Oakland CA 94607, USA ; European residents should write to Devonshire House, 12 Barley Mow Passage, Chiswick, London W4 4PH; and residents of other countries to PO Box 617, Hawthorn, Victoria 3122, Australia.

Indian Subcontinent
Bangladesh
India
Hindi/Urdu phrasebook
Trekking in the Indian Himalaya
Karakoram Highway
Kashmir, Ladakh & Zanskar
Nepal
Trekking in the Nepal Himalaya
Nepal phrasebook
Pakistan
Sri Lanka
Sri Lanka phrasebook

Africa
Africa on a shoestring
Central Africa
East Africa
Kenya
Swahili phrasebook
Morocco, Algeria & Tunisia
Moroccan Arabic phrasebook
South Africa, Lesotho & Swaziland
Zimbabwe, Botswana & Namibia
West Africa

Mexico
Baja California
Mexico

Central America
Central America on a shoestring
Costa Rica
La Ruta Maya

North America
Alaska
Canada
Hawaii

Europe
Eastern Europe on a shoestring
Eastern Europe phrasebook
Finland
Iceland, Greenland & the Faroe Islands
Mediterranean Europe on a shoestring
Mediterranean Europe phrasebook
Scandinavian & Baltic Europe on a shoestring
Scandinavian Europe phrasebook
Trekking in Spain
USSR
Russian phrasebook
Western Europe on a shoestring
Western Europe phrasebook

South America
Argentina, Uruguay & Paraguay
Bolivia
Brazil
Brazilian phrasebook
Chile & Easter Island
Colombia
Ecuador & the Galápagos Islands
Latin American Spanish phrasebook
Peru
Quechua phrasebook
South America on a shoestring
Trekking in the Patagonian Andes

The Lonely Planet Story

Lonely Planet published its first book in 1973 in response to the numerous 'How did you do it?' questions Maureen and Tony Wheeler were asked after driving, bussing, hitching, sailing and railing their way from England to Australia.

Written at a kitchen table and hand collated, trimmed and stapled, *Across Asia on the Cheap* became an instant local bestseller, inspiring thoughts of another book.

Eighteen months in South-East Asia resulted in their second guide, *South-East Asia on a shoestring*, which they put together in a backstreet Chinese hotel in Singapore in 1975. The 'yellow bible' as it quickly became known to backpackers around the world, soon became *the* guide to the region. It has sold well over half a million copies and is now in its 7th edition, still retaining its familiar yellow cover.

Today there are over 100 Lonely Planet titles – books that have that same adventurous approach to travel as those early guides; books that 'assume you know how to get your luggage off the carousel' as one reviewer put it.

Although Lonely Planet initially specialised in guides to Asia, they now cover most regions of the world, including the Pacific, South America, Africa, the Middle East and Europe. The list of *walking guides* and *phrasebooks* (for 'unusual' languages such as Quechua, Swahili, Nepalese and Egyptian Arabic) is also growing rapidly.

The emphasis continues to be on travel for independent travellers. Tony and Maureen still travel for several months of each year and play an active part in the writing, updating and quality control of Lonely Planet's guides.

They have been joined by over 50 authors, 48 staff – mainly editors, cartographers, & designers – at our office in Melbourne, Australia and another 10 at our US office in Oakland, California. In 1991 Lonely Planet opened a London office to handle sales for Britain, Europe and Africa. Travellers themselves also make a valuable contribution to the guides through the feedback we receive in thousands of letters each year.

The people at Lonely Planet strongly believe that travellers can make a positive contribution to the countries they visit, both through their appreciation of the countries' culture, wildlife and natural features, and through the money they spend. In addition, the company makes a direct contribution to the countries and regions it covers. Since 1986 a percentage of the income from each book has been donated to ventures such as famine relief in Africa; aid projects in India; agricultural projects in Central America; Greenpeace's efforts to halt French nuclear testing in the Pacific and Amnesty International. In 1991 $68,000 was donated to these causes.

Lonely Planet's basic travel philosophy is summed up in Tony Wheeler's comment, 'Don't worry about whether your trip will work out. Just go!'